REMNANTS OF NATION
ON POVERTY NARRATIVES BY WOMEN

Remnants of Nation is a ground-breaking book that introduces a new category of analysis, 'poverty narratives,' through which literature and popular culture are studied in the larger context of economic and literary disenfranchisement. Although issues of race, gender, and sexuality are now circulating in literary studies, and their 'constructedness' is being debated, the relations of class, poverty, and narrative have not been thoroughly examined until now. Here, poverty is treated not simply as a theme in literature but as a force that shapes the texts themselves.

Rimstead adopts the notion of a common culture to include more ordinary voices in national culture, in this case the national culture of Canada. Short stories, novels, autobiographies, and oral histories by Canadian women, including canonized writers such as Gabrielle Roy, Margaret Laurence, and Alice Munro, are considered in addition to lesser-known writers and ordinary women. Drawing on theoretical work from a wide range of disciplines, this book is a deeply radical reflection on how literature, popular culture, and academic discourse construct knowledge about the poor in wealthy countries like Canada and how the poor, in turn, can inform the way we think about nation, community, and national culture itself.

Given the scope of the study, Rimstead's work will appeal not only to literary scholars and Canadian social historians, but also to students and instructors of women's studies, cultural studies, and sociology.

ROXANNE RIMSTEAD is an assistant professor in the Département des lettres et communications at the Université de Sherbrooke.

HQ1453 .R55 2001
0134111516032
Rimstead, Roxanne,

Remnants of nation : on
  poverty narratives by
      c2001.

2009 01 16

Remnants of Nation

On Poverty Narratives by Women

Roxanne Rimstead

UNIVERSITY OF TORONTO PRESS
Toronto Buffalo London

© University of Toronto Press Incorporated 2001
Toronto Buffalo London
Printed in Canada

ISBN 0-8020-4494-8 (cloth)
ISBN 0-8020-8270-X (paper)

∞

Printed on acid-free paper

Canadian Cataloguing in Publication Data

Rimstead, Roxanne, 1953–
    Remnants of nation : on poverty narratives by women

    Includes bibliographical references and index.
    ISBN 0-8020-4494-8 (bound)   ISBN 0-8020-8270-X (pbk.)

    1. Poor women – Canada.   2. Poverty – Canada.   3. Women in literature.
    4. Poverty literature – Canada.   5. Canadian prose literature – Women
    authors – History and criticism.   6. Canadian prose literature –
    20th century – History and criticism.   I. Title.

    HQ1453.R55 2001   305.5′69′0971   C00-932066-0

University of Toronto Press acknowledges the financial assistance to its publishing program of the Canada Council for the Arts and the Ontario Arts Council.

This book has been published with the help of a grant from the Humanities and Social Sciences Federation of Canada, using funds provided by the Social Sciences and Humanities Research Council of Canada.

University of Toronto Press acknowledges the financial support for its publishing activities of the Government of Canada through the Book Publishing Industry Development Program (BPIDP).

For Bobby and Dena, two of my closest friends, whom I lost to fatal illnesses during the years I was writing this book. I want to thank them each for supporting me in their own way. My late sister, Bobby (Barbara Anne Rimstead), was a strong advocate for mentally and emotionally challenged adults. A great confidante and free thinker, she was creative and courageous in her community work and one of the funniest people ever. Dena Goldberg, a much loved professor of drama and literature at the Université de Montréal and a Marxist Jew from New York, was a fine, astute critic of my writing, my politics, and of the smoke and mirrors of academia in general. These were good friends who marched to their own drummers and did so with a flourish.

Contents

Acknowledgments ix

Introduction: Disturbing Images 3
    i The Poor in the National Imaginary 7
    ii The Power of Images 16
    iii Poverty Narratives: A New Category of Analysis 22
    iv The Gender of Poverty 31

1 'Fictioning' a Literature 39
    1.1 Beyond Literature: Ordinary Voices 40
    1.2 Populist Motives 48
    1.3 Cultural Critique as Social Therapy 53
    1.4 Testimony and Radical Knowledge 57

2 Visits and Homecomings 65
    2.1 Susanna Moodie: Poverty and Vice 67
    2.2 Nellie McClung: Social Gospel Rescue 72
    2.3 Gabrielle Roy: Everyday Struggle as Resistance 77

3 'We Live in a Rickety House': Social Boundaries and Poor Housing 86
    3.1 A Genealogy of Poor Houses 93
    3.2 Alice Munro's Gaze – from a Distance 104
    3.3 Homeplace and 'Bugs' 111

4 Theories and Anti-Theory: On Knowing Poor Women   122
4.1 Anti-Theory, Anti-What?   123
4.2 Subjectivities   126
4.3 Theories of the Classed and Gendered Subject   130
4.4 Understanding as Opposed to Mapping Subjectivities   137

5 Subverting 'Poor Me': Negative Constructions of Identity   143
5.1 Cy-Thea Sand's Cultural Smuggling   145
5.2 Maria Campbell's *Halfbreed* and Alternative Status-Honour Groups   153
5.3 The Poor as Colonized Subjects   160
5.4 Decolonizing Poor Subjects through Autobiography   169

6 'Organized Forgetting'   174
6.1 On Autobiographical Memories of Poverty, Class, Gender, and Nation   175
6.2 Poverty as Distant Landscape: Edna Jaques   183
6.3 Class Travelling with Fredelle Bruser Maynard   192

7 'Remnants of Nation'   200
7.1 Poverty and Nation as Reciprocal Constructions   201
7.2 Saving the Nation: *The Diviners*   205
7.3 Strategies of Containment and Exclusion   226
7.4 Counter-national Testimonies   239

8 The Long View: Contexts of Oppositional Criticism   253
8.1 Cultural Studies as a Site of Resistance   254
8.2 A Toolkit of Theory   260
8.3 Representing the Poor within Academic Discourse   267

Conclusion: Taking a Position   275

Appendix: Outlawing Boundaries   287
i Useful Distinctions: Poor versus Working-Class Women   292
ii Setting Up a Cross-Class Dialectic   293
iii Transgressing the National Canon   298
iv Poverty Narratives by Canadian Women (1919–1990s)   305

Bibliography   309
Index   329

Acknowledgments

Many people helped me to complete this book against great odds. My partner, Fernando Guerrero, has been there to offer emotional support and friendship during the rough ride of graduate studies, the dissertation, editing, heavy teaching loads, moves, and transfers. I would not have been able to look poverty in the face without him.

Professionally, I owe much gratitude to Amaryll Chanady, directrice de littérature comparée at the Université de Montréal. Friend and mentor, she saved this research from obscurity by bolstering my sense of worth and by speaking up for the academic value of this exploratory work. Special thanks to Patricia Smart, who read an early draft of this manuscript as my dissertation and not only encouraged publication but also took the time to help the manuscript see the light of day. I am also grateful for a community of materialist feminists, Michele Valiquette, Cy-Thea Sand, Janet Zandy, and many others, whose knowledge of class and gender inspired this research in its fledgling stage. Over the years many colleagues too numerous to mention at the Université de Montréal and McGill University offered encouragement. Thank you all.

The generous funding of agencies and employers helped me to buy books, go to conferences, and have access to computer equipment. I am grateful to the SSHRC for a New Scholar Grant, and to the McGill Faculty of Research and Graduate Studies, the McGill Institute for the Study of Canada, the Syndicat de chargées de cours at the Université de Montréal, and the Faculté des lettres et sciences humaines at the Université de Sherbrooke. I also wish to thank student research assistants Lynn Finnel, Proma Tagore, Martin Behr, and Allison Alcorn for their theoretical research during the latter years of this project. In particular, I wish to thank Robert Rembold for his valiant struggle with our detailed index.

'The Last Feminist Poem,' by Sharon Stevenson, was published in her collection *Gold Earrings* (Vancouver: Pulp Press, 1984). Reprinted with permission of Arsenal Pulp Press. Chapter 2, 'Visits and Homecomings,' is a slightly revised version of 'Visits and Homecomings: Notes toward Discovering the Psycho-Social Place(s) of Poverty,' *Textual Studies of Canada* 5 (Autumn 1994): 46–63. Copyright © Roxanne Rimstead 1994. Chapter 4, 'Theories and Anti-Theory,' is a slightly revised version of 'Between Theories and Anti-Theory: Moving toward Marginal Women's Subjectivities,' which was first published in *Working-Class Studies*, ed. Janet Zandy, special issue of *Women's Studies Quarterly* 23, nos 1 and 2 (spring/summer 1995): 199–218. Copyright © Roxanne Rimstead 1995. Reprinted by permission of The Feminist Press at The City University of New York. Chapter 5, 'Subverting Poor Me,' is a slightly revised version of 'Subverting Poor Me: Negative Constructions of Identity in Poor and Working-class Women's Autobiographies,' which was first published in *The Language and Politics of Exclusion: Others in Discourse*, ed. Stephen Harold Riggins (London: Sage Publications, 1997), 249–80. Copyright © Sage Publications 1997. Reprinted by permission.

To the editorial staff at the University of Toronto Press and the anonymous readers of the manuscript at Aid to Scholarly Publishing and the Press I am also grateful. The manuscript has benefited from the patience and diligence of editors Emily Andrew, Jill McConkey, and Frances Mundy and the careful and rigorous copy-editing of Margaret Allen.

I am indebted to the feminist friends with whom I discussed women's culture over the years: Cheryl, Kate, Dory, Joan, Debra, Nathalie, Sue, Hope, Judy, Joanne, Diane, and many others. You were my community of women outside the text.

REMNANTS OF NATION:
ON POVERTY NARRATIVES BY WOMEN

Introduction: Disturbing Images

There is a struggle over meaning between the poor and the non-poor that actually costs lives. The poor live shorter lives, are victims of more violence, die more frequently in childbirth and from disease, and are more likely to freeze to death on air vents in our cities or die in mine tragedies and other work-related accidents than the non-poor. As David Adams Richards has said in his book by this title, the poor live 'lives of short duration.' Less dramatically, however, the poor are also subject to cultural exclusion in a variety of everyday situations, ranging from not being able to afford access to the technological revolution, bank credit, and housing to not being able to thrive in school because of hunger, stigma, or lack of trust in the system. In Paulo Freire's words, the poor are subject to 'cultural invasion' by the meaning systems of the non-poor and must thus find a way to value their own thoughts about the world. In *Knowing the Poor*, Bryan Green has argued that sociologists must become better readers of poverty by learning to resist the covert way government reports construct the reality of the poor in the interests of the non-poor, the way these reports captivate readers in a content that appears innocent while actually achieving closure over lived reality, and the way these accounts of poverty impose documented reality upon situated reality. Green urges that we develop more emancipatory ways of reading poverty in order to resist setting up the official inquiry and the government document as the ultimate way of knowing the poor.

As readers and teachers of literature, we are part of this struggle over meaning that marginalizes the poor in concrete as well as symbolic ways or liberates them to think oppositionally about their place in society. Since literature has traditionally been the field where individual and collective subjectivities are valorized, we help define the poor when we read or fail to read their voices. Likewise, when we fail to question stereotypes, dominant discourse, and textual conventions of portraying the poor, we may be complicit in the symbolic violence that normalizes the exclusion of the poor in market society. Reading oppositionally means prying open both dominant and subversive representations of poverty in literary works and in everyday, popular discourses. It means recovering previously silenced voices. In this book, I propose to do so by creating a new category of analysis called 'poverty narratives,' a category which includes stories both by and about the poor. In a postreferential age, however, poverty narratives cannot be read as transparent windows onto the experiences and the feelings of the poor. Instead, they should be read as cultural sites where identities are constructed and negotiated rather than merely reflected, cultural sites of struggle between hegemonic and counter-cultural discourses, yet sites where more than discourse is at stake.

This book is as much about the 'poverty of theory' to explain the complexity of everyday experiences, especially among muted subjects, as it is about theories of poverty and representation. Although I draw on numerous theories of poverty the better to understand poor subjects and how they appear in narrative forms and discourses, I am very much aware that no one overarching theory of poverty can make all poverty narratives coherent – not Marxist, Weberian, psychological, discursive, or cultural theory. Consequently, this book does not offer or adhere to one governing theory of exploitation or resistance or one methodology of decoding the ideology behind the images. Instead, these readings theorize the need to hold back from generalizing and to draw on many sources of knowledge, both academic and non-academic, to avoid imposing yet another top-down analytical structure on the poor.

We can disturb the taken-for-granted notion that poor subjects are constituted of despair and silence and an impossible site for radical knowledge by making room for more detailed testimonies and more resistant ideologies, by considering the identities of poor subjects in relation to nation, gender, and class, and by making poverty central rather than a backdrop to our interpretation of textual culture. Instead of throwing up our hands and concluding that the subaltern cannot speak, cultural critics should allow the possibility that poor subjects have special knowledge and can and do speak as cultural subjects in ways that academic criticism has somehow been overlooking or devaluing. Stuart Hall has depicted the possibility that radical knowledge circulates actively but beyond academic grasp as the keeping of a secret: 'It is as if the masses have kept a secret to themselves while the intellectuals keep running around in circles trying to make out what it is, what is going on' (140). I do not propose to uncover *the* secret to resistance against poverty; but, in detailed, textured readings that refuse to overgeneralize about poor subjects or to naturalize oppression, I believe we can uncover many small secrets about subjectivity and everyday struggle as adaptive and resilient steps towards resistance or as self-defeating steps towards consent and domination. If there is one main secret to be uncovered in this process, it is surely not a monolithic identity for the poor or one theory of resistance, but the relational, social logic, the web of meanings that bind the poor and the non-poor.

Poverty exists in relation to affluence. When a society and its national dream admire the rich because they acquire wealth and power that allows them to stand outside the community by virtue of élite schools, restaurants, and estates, the same community must denounce the other polarity, those who do not succeed in the national dream and are therefore denied access to education, nourishment, and housing by the same logic of meritocracy. As John Kenneth Galbraith wrote in *The Affluent Society*: 'People are poverty stricken when their income, even if adequate for survival, falls radically behind that of the community. Then they cannot have what the larger community regards as the minimum necessary for decency; and they cannot wholly escape, therefore, the judgment of the larger community that they are indecent. They are degraded for, in the literal sense, they live outside the grades or categories which the community regards as acceptable' (245). Perceptions and self-perceptions are shaped by the social need to cloak these polarities, this rift within a wealthy nation like Canada, and make differences in access to goods and to culture appear natural, or not at all. Although affluent societies have transformed the poor from a majority to a minority of the population (245), hence reducing their visibility and worth even further in respect to the larger community, Galbraith notes that '[w]e ignore it [poverty] because we share with all societies at all times the capacity for not seeing what we do not wish to see. Anciently this has enabled the nobleman to enjoy his dinner while remaining oblivious to the beggars around his door. In our own day, it enables us to travel in comfort by Harlem and into the lush precincts of midtown Manhattan' (252). The social practice of discursive marginalization and symbolic violence, blaming, naming, or erasing the poor, constructs them as inherently inferior and thus naturally outside of community, the state, the nation, and even cultural representation itself. An oppositional role in this struggle over meaning is to bring more poverty narratives into view and to ask questions which will reveal what is at stake when dominant images fix the subject in this way. What is at stake when poor subjects tell their own stories?

To disturb naturalized images of the poor as outsiders or inherently inferior, I recommend we begin interrogating those images from a politically engaged perspective, but also in a detailed and exploratory way that takes gender, ethnicity, and nation as well as poverty and class into account. The specific cultural and textual readings here are rooted in the geopolitical context and local cultures of Canadian poverty narratives. When the poor speak out as the remnants of nation, national unity itself seems frayed or non-existent, and the relational logic between the poor and the wealthy nation is more apparent. Further limiting the national category to poverty narratives by women highlights gendered experiences. Since class analysis has traditionally assumed a male subject as the focus of labour, class conflict, and even class identity, these readings of poverty narratives focus on women from the outset to redress this potential blind spot and to critique the historical marriage between women and poverty that has led in the 1980s and 1990s to the growing trend of the 'feminization of poverty.' When race and poverty are read together, we discover that there is no formula for untangling these strains of identity. At times, minority racial or ethnic status exacerbates poverty and leads to multiply marginalized individuals; at other times racial and ethnic identity offers an alternative status-honour group (Waxman), alternative communities, and memories from which to construct a self and survive stigma and shame.

The main goals of recovering or rereading selected works as poverty narratives are the following: (a) to bring a number of previously excluded or devalued narratives (for example, oral histories, reportage, and popular autobiography) into the range of critical perception beside better known canonical literature on poverty; (b) to know more about how we construct poor subjects textually and socially by juxtaposing selected works on specific issues – such as disorder, cultural memory, poor homes, shame, the feminization of poverty, and the marginalization of the poor within wealthy nations; (c) to ask why certain images of the poor are invested with greater or lesser cultural power and how they acquire meaning and power over time; and (d) to find methods of understanding poor people as more than mere objects of study entrapped in other people's images – but also as speaking *subjects*, *agents* of cultural change, and concrete beings who live and feel social boundaries and material constraints. Poor people often know about possibilities for social change even when they lack the social power or resistant community to effect those changes. Reading poverty narratives oppositionally means allowing that poor people shape and are shaped by textual realities and that they have valuable knowledge about this process and about national culture as a whole.

i The Poor in the National Imaginary

My concern with nation in this study is not to trace the representation or neglect of poverty in the national literary history. Such a strategy risks simply giving more attention to the centre, the dominant versions of nation, rather than exploring what has been pushed to the outside as the remnants of national culture. This book discusses the way the poor emerge in selected stories and discourses about poverty in relation to a national imaginary, or, in other words, in relation to a shared image of community and a shared national project. Poverty narratives in wealthy countries such as Canada often unfold a national imaginary which locates the poor outside the imagined community on the fringes as fragments of nation. Sustained analysis of the discourse of nation in poverty narratives reveals significant tension between the poor and the 'developed' nation and a struggle over the notion of national community in the face of growing economic inequality. I am also interested in how competing national imaginaries from the left and the right within one nation position the poor differently. For example, dominant concepts of nation, such as the Canadian and American Dream of social mobility or the notion of nation building itself as an inevitable, evolutionary step towards 'development' and wealth, subtly exclude the poor from the national imaginary by virtue of narratives of prosperity and progress. But as Noam Chomsky relates in *Class Warfare*, suppression of the history of the poor, the working class, Native people, and blacks has been the means of driving class warfare underground, beneath cleansing myths of nationhood whereby wealth sprouted from the wise control of natural resources and class became an 'unmentionble five-letter word' divorced from history (59–75).

By projecting 'real poverty' as existing elsewhere, wealthy Western nations such as Canada and the United States often identify the poor as external Others (for example, in the Third World or in the 'Old Country,' the more class-stratified Britain). By containing the poor in ghettoized or stigmatized spaces, we safely manage them as internal Others (for example, marginalized members who are fixed by insults, degrading paradigms, stereotypes, or euphemisms such as 'welfare bums,' the 'underclass,' 'trailer trash,' or 'child poverty'). This troubled relation between the poor and the wealthy nation is so covert that it often seems non-existent. Many poverty narratives show people who feel nationless and alone. Such narratives often dramatize how the care and survival of the poor fall back on families and individuals, especially women, in the absence of a larger caring community. Also, in the absence of a more inclusive national imaginary, the poor often see themselves defined in relation to other forms of community, whether a family, a neighbourhood, a small town, a city slum, a street, a region, or even the poor or homeless as a group – groups which many times prove more humanitarian than nation.

Conversely, current critiques of postnationalism and globalism sometimes posit the nation-state as a possible site for resistance against the exploitative flow of unregulated global capital and corporate monoculture. In *Postmodern Welfare*, for example, Peter Leonard examines the potential of national projects to maintain social safety nets in the form of the welfare state. Without nostalgically resurrecting national welfare systems or the nation-state itself as a modernist project, Leonard proposes that the rebuilding of social programs may be more feasible on the national level once we rethink shared national projects from the left and within the context of altered global relations. Beyond the academic front, lobbying by Maude Barlow and Mel Hurtig against the Canada–U.S. Free Trade Agreement produced a strong, populist citizen movement against unregulated global capitalism in the form of the Council of Canadians (1988). The discourses and practices of nationalism are many and shifting. Hence the positioning of the poor within the nation is always complex but always within our power to change. Warning us against victimology, which entrenches positions and breeds feelings of impotence, cultural critics like John Ralston Saul and Linda McQuaig have urged us to rethink the role of nation and the complexity of Canadian nationalism in a time of global conformity, corporate hegemony, and the 'cult of impotence.'

Critics, among them William DiFazio, in an essay called, 'Why There Is No Movement of the Poor,' have warned that the diminishing role of nations in global capitalism has resulted in the phenomenon of the 'hollow state ... concerned with balancing budgets and eliminating taxes' (151) as a means of defining public good. DiFazio claims that the poor have increasingly given over their voices to advocates and intellectuals who battle in their name against an uncaring nation-state. According to DiFazio, the first target of the hollow state has been the poor. Thus advocates have spent their energy fighting on the level of micro politics, demanding that the modernist function of social programs and care of the poor be restored to the nation-state. DiFazio critiques poverty advocates for their failure to envisage an end to poverty or to mobilize the poor, while fighting these micro-political 'budget battles.' But his description of the silencing of the poor by the 'hollow state' is the point I wish to emphasize here as an axis for radical cultural critique. Even before unregulated global capitalism created a wealthy élite whose interests eclipsed those of the nation-state (hence the emergence of the hollow state), the poor have long been at odds with a bourgeois or middle-class sense of nationhood, according to which the nation is cleansed of disease and sloth when the poor are erased from public view or controlled in terms of their movement and their labour power. The genealogy of bourgeois nationalist discourse used against the poor within the West and the North goes back to the very emergence of nation-states and nationalist discourse, as I will discuss in relation to theories by Partha Chatterjee, Etienne Balibar and Immanuel Wallerstein, and Ernst Gellner (see chapter 7). For example, the two-nation paradigm (nation-within-a-nation) can be traced to its eighteenth-century origins where it was used to describe the poor as strangers within the nation who represented a backward country unto themselves, a 'race apart' within the progressive, industrialized nation of Britain. I study the deployment and adaptation of the two-nation paradigm in modern and contemporary narratives and in social theory with reference to Gertrude Himmelfarb's history of the notion in her voluminous *The Idea of Poverty*.

As many critics of globalization and postmodernism have pointed out, while the powers of the nation-state to control its own economic policy, enforce labour and environmental controls, and support social safety nets have diminished under globalization, conversely, the need for these powers has increased as nation-states are left to deal with greater poverty and unemployment within their own gates and whole new populations of poverty as the middle class erodes. We saw in the 1990s, as in the 1930s with the massive On-to-Ottawa Trek by the unemployed, the emergence of an activist discourse which refuses to allow the wealthy nation to deny its relation to the poor. Marches on Ottawa by the homeless in 1998 and 1999 and anti-poverty marches on Quebec City by women bore the slogan that homelessness counts as a 'national disaster,' especially in northern countries with life-threatening winters such as Canada's. Very recently, municipal and provincial politicians have deployed the image of poverty as national disaster to compete for more federal support for poverty as a social problem. Similarly, local activists have gone to the international front, the United Nations, to demand that child poverty in a wealthy country such as Canada be called a 'national disgrace.' Canada's standard of living rating was recently lowered internationally because of the growing failure of the nation to care about the poor. These are local, national, and international initiatives against the 'hollow' nation, which need not be assumed a natural evolution of global economy. They are living evidence that we need not merely accept the erosion of the concept of a caring nation as historically inevitable, as our lot, but may imagine it anew.

Turning briefly now to the analysis of two specific passages, I would like to demonstrate how intimately the notions of nation and poverty are linked in the popular imagination. The following is a discussion of two train scenes featuring the poor. In the first scene, taken from Mavis Gallant's short story 'Varieties of Exile' in *Home Truths*, a British immigrant to Canada shows pictures of the British poor to a Canadian woman as they ride into the city together on a suburban train. In the second scene, from Hugh Garner's Depression novel *Cabbagetown*, the subjectivities of the poor are more directly rendered in an action scene where police violently deter hoboes from hitching a ride on boxcars. Reading poverty narratives oppositionally brings larger social issues into greater visibility. In the case of these two train scenes, it shows vividly that the perception of the order and disorder of poverty may depend on the distance from poverty the observer can afford. But reading the two scenes together also shows how these positions are connected relationally within a larger, implicit notion of shared culture and national order. Our reading strategies can oppose the invisibility and silencing of the poor by peering more closely, along with Gallant's protagonist, into the images of poverty and asking what they may mean in a struggle over meaning and power.

> Wherever his opinions came from, Frank Cairns was the first person ever to talk to me about the English poor. They seemed to be a race, different in

kind from other English. He showed me old copies of *Picture Post* he must have saved up from the Depression. In our hot summer train, where everyone was starched and ironed and washed and fed, we considered slum doorways and the faces of women at the breaking point. They looked like Lenin's 'remnants of nations' except that there were too many of them for a remnant. (Gallant, 272–3)

For a scary second or two he thought he had been hit by a train on the track behind him, but when he swung around he found himself face to face with a young Royal Canadian Mounted Policeman who was swinging a riding crop ... As he ran he saw that the yards seemed full of Mounties, some in red tunics and others in brown uniforms ... The young Mountie's face was red and he was sweating from the chase. He grabbed Ken's windbreaker and twisted one sleeve of it into a snaffling grip. Then, both of them winded and hardly able to walk, they went down the yards to where other policemen had rounded up a large mob of hoboes who stood like a herd of reluctant cattle surrounded by police. (Garner, 180–1)

The logic of different social attitudes to poverty springs to the foreground when these scenes are read side by side. The first scene underscores the comfort and cleanliness, the orderliness of a suburban train whose passengers possess the leisure and the material security to contemplate the poor intellectually from a distance. As self-styled socialists, the two suburbanites mull over the nuances of Lenin's political discourse but none the less contemplate the poor in Britain from a distance as a separate 'race' in the Old Country. The second scene dramatizes the chaos and disorder of lived poverty by showing transients being dragged from the sides of the boxcars and rounded up by police. Submitted in this way to a master narrative of order and coercion by the national police, the RCMP, the poor are silenced, hidden, controlled as the shameful remnants of nation, tell-tale evidence of disorder and rifts within the nation. Neither image of poverty is truer than the other, but together they appear relational and more coherent.

Although the characters of Gallant's story contemplate the poor in this one scene, poverty is peripheral to their story as suburbanites – the picture of the poor in Britain merely a way for young adults to reflect on the larger world and themselves as expatriates and cosmopolitan intellects who initially flirt with social involvement as they flirt with each other on a train, but who remain strangely alienated from the world around them as one of the many consequences of privilege and exile in their lives. Yet it is precisely the strategy of distancing poverty, concern, and involvement to the periphery of middle-class lives that Gallant discreetly underlines here.[1] In order to maintain that distance, her characters play out a popular strategy that is familiar in Canadian culture: the strategy is to project extreme poverty elsewhere in time or geographic space in order to distance it from the here and now and to make it appear anomalous to the wealthy nation rather than systemic. In this case, the narrator projects poverty back onto the Depression in the Old World – as remnants of the British nation, or rather its very fabric. But this fabric is of *old* nations, not the new with safely divided cities, suburbs separated from slums, and commuter trains allowing rapid transit through the slums to the business section. Both Barbara Ehrenreich and Michael Harrington credit the commuter train and urban sprawl in North America as pivotal to the escape of the middle class from knowledge of poverty in the inner city. The home truth of this North American strategy for concealing poverty is that the middle classes can live in their separate space with separate schools and banks and restaurants in order to preserve the illusion of prosperity and market stability in consumer culture.

In contrast, Garner's hoboes and slum youth cannot afford distance from poverty and the inner city, let alone the existential alienation that comes from such detachment. These men have no time to think before the riding crop comes down across their legs and backs. In this counter-national narrative it is impossible for the reader to dissociate their poverty from the new nation because *Cabbagetown* locates the poor unmistakably in Canada. For example, it takes its title from the name of a once-notorious Toronto slum, and the quoted scene portrays the Royal Canadian Mounted Police as an antagonistic, national police force whose job it is to catch the transient unemployed as they stray out of their proper, ghettoized place in the nation. The strategy of containment here is literal rather than symbolic, physically coercive rather than merely ideological. But physical force and symbolic violence work together. Significantly, Garner's transients do not see themselves collectively as a class of people who could organize and overpower the

---

[1] Gallant does not consistently distance poverty this way, but shows her characters doing so. The aptness of her realism focused on middle-class lives and suburban living in 'Varieties of Exile' exposes these strategies of projection. Two other stories in *Home Truths*, 'Jorinda and Jorindel' and 'Orphans' Progress,' focus on poverty, class difference, and social boundaries more directly and at a closer range.

police, but rather behave as they are perceived, as an unruly 'mob' or 'herd.' Only when they have been forcibly gathered and a police officer is lecturing them on their idleness, will one lone voice from the crowd protest their being called 'bums.' All of them are looking for work, the voice explains, and that is why they are riding the boxcars in the first place. When told to keep silent, the voice retorts: 'Nobody asked me to speak ... If I waited to be asked I'd have to wait forever' (182). (The police promptly sentence some to a month of forced labour in the remote work camps devised to cleanse Canadian cities of the threat of large numbers of unemployed men in the Depression.)[2] Although Garner's scene of men 'riding the rails' and being sent to labour camps lacks the subtlety and eloquence of Gallant's reflective scene about the 'remnants of nations,' Garner's hard-boiled social realism issues from a psychosocial space where characters live and feel poverty rather than gaze at it from a distance. The novel echoes other works of protest (both literary and popular) against the cultural muting of poor and working-class subjects in Canada. For example, Barry Broadfoot's oral testimonies by Depression survivors in *Ten Lost Years* testify to a 'conspiracy of silence' around the collapse of the market system in the thirties and the criminalization of poverty at that time. These oral histories testify to women being sold into marriage or sexual service and men being arrested for 'riding the rails' (15–21, 93–100, 274–88). Like Garner's social-realist scene of violence in the train yards, Broadfoot's oral histories testify to the deportation of the transient poor to forced labour camps, the 'stick to [the] backside,' the criminal record and the labels, the role of the police, and the shame felt by poor subjects (18–19). Both *Cabbagetown* and Broadfoot's oral testimonies construct

---

2 The power of this novel to oppose, if not offend, the dominant national imaginary by dramatizing the underside of the 'developed' nation is reflected in its publishing history as much as its plot. It testified so credibly and bitterly to the lack of choices and life chances for poor youth in a well-known Toronto slum that Garner had to censor it by half before it was finally accepted for publication in 1950 (appearing in its more complete version only eighteen years later, at which time it was a popular success). Although much more contemporary in its concerns about class identity than other proletarian and social-realist novels of the thirties in Canada, *Cabbagetown* is still rarely included in courses on Canadian literature. For example, in the Calgary Conference, held in 1978 to survey the one hundred most important Canadian novels being taught at that time, *Cabbagetown* did not even appear on the ballot of two hundred titles initially sent to teachers and critics, although much more obscure and less popular works did appear.

knowledge of what class oppression and poverty feel like from the inside, rather than of how these subjects appear from a distance.

Since we cannot assume, however, that the truest or most powerful images of poverty are necessarily produced by insiders, we need to study images from both distanced and involved standpoints to understand how these different versions of poverty circulate in relation to each other and how they compete for cultural power. Whose versions of poverty are we most predisposed to believe and why? Whose representations do we aestheticize and to what ends? Whose images are the most and the least disturbing? Why are we disturbed?

Poverty and nation as social constructs act reciprocally on each other through representations of the poor subject. This means that poor people's lives and stories are sufficiently complex that we cannot fix their meaning in a merely abstract or theoretical way. Instead, the meaning of the relation between nation and poverty needs to be teased out of the specifics of each story and out of memories of lived reality as well as decoded with reference to theories of nation, poverty, and representation. In chapter 7, 'Remnants of Nation,' I trace in a news-magazine report about poverty among Native people in Davis Inlet and an advertisement appealing for charity to fight poverty in the Third World how Canada is constructed discursively as a benevolent and progressive nation, a land of opportunity, a model of development – constructions that exploit the discourse of First World nationalism and simultaneously contain or exclude the poor by projecting them onto other places and other times. Conversely, liberatory, nationalist discourses, such as the subtext in Margaret Laurence's *The Diviners*, can appear to 'save the nation' from the rupture implied by the ghettoization of the poor. This novel saves the nation from the rifts caused by poverty and racism through the critical and novelistic re-imaginings of a liberal, humane heroine/artist, thereby fulfilling artistically, in Timothy Brennan's words, 'a longing for national form.' Although Laurence's longing for form has been critiqued as too idealist and humanist by Frank Davey in *Post-national Arguments*, I take into account the class subtext in Laurence's novel by reading it as a poverty narrative, and thus valorize its opposition to bourgeois nationalism. Included in this discussion of how poverty and nation are intertwined are a number of samples of openly counter-national reportage, oral histories, and autobiographies. In these counter-cultural works, the locus of discussion about nation switches to the subjectivities of the poor and reveals alternative imaginings of community that share past and future projects different from those in official versions of nation.

There is a counter-national aspect to the politics of these engaged readings which I would like to clarify. As someone who grew up poor in Canada, I hope to expose the exclusionary social logic that allows a wealthy nation to marginalize and silence the voices of the poor and naturalize that rift within the nation by blaming the poor for their difference. However, I do so on the level of analysis of the images and discourses in selected texts, not by positing a full-scale critique of the national literary establishment, the government, or corporate and class élites for their hegemonic roles. The focus here is on the remnants of nation, not on the centre and its institutions with their complex, shifting, and often heterogeneous ideological functions.

Future studies of poverty narratives in Canada might well choose to look back and map the history of Canadian criticism to show where and why poverty and class were overlooked in literary studies or taken up as important issues, and by whom, and to discuss why a link between poverty, literature, and politics has been relatively fashionable in some periods, such as the 1930s and 1960s, and obscure at others.[3] Such tasks, however, are beyond the scope of the present study. This book does not in and of itself claim to re-vision the whole of national culture or the national canon, but it does hope to contribute one small step in that direction by encouraging people to consider the validity of oppositional subjectivities and of seeing nation differently. The conclusion, entitled 'Taking a Position,' proposes that we adopt a more inclusive paradigm of national culture, such as the one posited by Raymond Williams and Terry Eagleton, that of a common culture which includes the voices of all subjects, instead of one in which national culture is produced by an élite group of artists and held, jewel-like, within a canon; or one in which the national institutions and icons serve the interests of an élite group by silencing the poor.

It is time for both an ethical and an aesthetic reassessment of what it means to keep looking away from the poor in literature and what it might mean for intellectuals to join with 'ordinary people' and focus more critically on the place of poverty in literary and popular culture. It *is* time. The CBC airwaves announce weekly that welfare consensus has

---

3 See, for example, *The Suburb of Dissent: Cultural Politics in the United States and Canada during the 1930s* by Caren Irr (Durham, NC, and London: Duke University Press, 1998).

crumbled in Canada and we can no longer provide a social safety net for those who fall into poverty. The Ontario provincial government has recently adopted regressive policies that criminalize the poor by fingerprinting welfare recipients to combat welfare fraud (even though we know full well that this crime is much rarer and less costly than income-tax evasion by the well-to-do). The popular imagination in Canada can no longer be moved to awareness and responsibility by realistic images of poverty, but must be appealed to through misleading euphemisms such as 'child poverty.' Since we have come to this, the 'hollow nation,' we define the public good as deficit reduction and make the poorest among us finance deficit reduction through medical user fees and reduced access to unemployment insurance. Now that the social programs of our nation are in tatters, it really is time to look more closely at these 'remnants of nation' who are part of the fabric of our communities and our own lives. It is also time for us to look long and hard at how literary culture may be complicit in the symbolic violence against the poor in our everyday lives, a symbolic violence that is unspeakable.

ii The Power of Images

As a label itself, 'the poor' can function as a fiction of separateness and homogenization because, besides signifying objective difference from 'the non-poor,' it simultaneously invokes a long genealogy of discourses on subjective difference and distance. In reality, however, people often pass in and out of poverty in wealthy nations so that lumping 'the poor' together in this fixed category is deceptively monolithic. Contemporary sociological studies often begin by insisting on heterogeneity and shifting membership among the poor and the homeless. As the authors of a recent government study on women and labour market poverty in Canada have emphasized, membership among the poor and the non-poor shifts constantly, and the people moving through each category are fundamentally the same at the outset despite profound differences in material circumstances and social status which poverty brings:

> the poor are not substantially different from the non-poor. Many of the poor have full-time employment and levels of educational attainment similar to the non-poor. The poor are a diverse group made up of the elderly, children, single mothers, husband-wife families, disabled people, and young men and women who find themselves poor from time to time

as a result of a variety of circumstances – separation, divorce, unemployment, a disabling accident, or sickness. (Gunderson et al., 41)

Similarly, in 'Homelessness,' Alex Murray emphasized that the category of 'the homeless' in Canada consists of people who move in and out of the state of homelessness and that their profile shifts according to region, period, and individual circumstances. According to Murray, recent research contests the romanticized notion of the homeless as hoboes who choose Skid Row over work and indicates, instead, that women, children, and families are increasingly present in the numbers of the homeless, though less visible on the street. Furthermore, the majority of homeless single men are not romantic wanderers given to idleness but have been found 'to regard work favourably ... usually they moved to find work and would move elsewhere if work were available' (37). Murray also notes that many are trapped in poverty because the only work they have access to is the exploitative day-labour system into which government employment and welfare agencies in Canada regularly stream them (37). Consequently, Murray calls for two radical correctives to the distorting popular images that separate and homogenize the homeless: first, the recognition of their connectedness to mainstream society and to each other (through alternative notions of community), and second, the recognition of the diversity of people who lose their homes due to variations in regional, historical, and individual circumstances.

So powerful are the hegemonic images of the poor in North America as inherently different and inferior that contemporary sociological studies must continually break down these monolithic, negative images that colonize the popular imaginary in order to pave the way for more factual studies or more sophisticated social theories. Given the power of social myths to shape perceptions of the poor even against scientific knowledge, it is all the more surprising that the humanities have not paid more attention to how these taken-for-granted images are deployed as cultural values in literature.

Behind the homogenization of the poor and the homeless into a race apart lies the buried story of their true connectedness to dominant groups. One learns from reading many stories of the poor and theories of poverty that most of us are at risk of poverty because it is more situational and systemic to social relations in market society than inherent to a separate 'race' of people. Social myths that the poor are idle and inherently predisposed to poverty reassure the middle classes that only those who deserve to or let themselves will fall from economic security. Suppressed narratives of middle- and upper-class social guilt and social fear about poverty comprise the reverse side of the Canadian/American Dream of 'making it' and are thus defining forces in the national imaginary of a wealthy nation.

Looking closely at the pervasive 'fear of falling' in her book by that title, Barbara Ehrenreich probes the fear of poverty in middle-class America and the resulting erasure of the poor from mass consciousness. She concludes that the fear of poverty is rooted in widespread discontent with consumer capitalism itself and the emptiness of its achievements. Despite the moral tenor of the national dream and the persuasive promises of hidden persuaders, she maintains, middle-class Americans sense the void in consumer culture. Furthermore, she writes, the middle class successfully denied 'the jagged edges of inequality' within the nation by moving out of the inner city into homogeneous suburban neighbourhoods where they looked 'out through their picture windows,' and saw 'only an endless suburb, with no horizon, no frontier, in sight.' In fact, she claims, 'they believed that this *was* America' (17–18), hence media announcements in the 1960s that the country had 'discovered' the poor. As I argue later, the recurrent narrative of 'discovering' the poor has been used since the nineteenth century and the 'discovery' of the street people by Charles Booth and Henry Mayhew. This discursive tactic portrays the poor as lost within the dark edges of the nation in order to cleanse the nation of responsibility and to dramatize the poor as exotically different and thus naturally excluded. It goes hand-in-hand with the two-nation paradigm discussed earlier which distances the poor by positioning them discursively in a strange country, the nation-within-the-nation. Ehrenreich notes that the discourse of discovering the poor deployed in the 1990s took place despite a University of Michigan study showing that in the previous ten-year period one out of four Americans had experienced poverty severe enough to qualify them for welfare (48–9). Ehrenreich reminds us that the poor in America comprise 'people who come from many different starting points' but have experienced illness, marital breakup, or job layoff. Although members of the working class are more vulnerable to poverty since they begin with less capital and fewer social benefits, it is the very nature of market, capitalist society that some will experience 'the jagged edges of inequality' while others try to deny that inequalities exist in order to emulate middle-class nationalist dreams of classlessness.

The effect of negative social myths on the subjectivities of the poor in advanced industrialized countries has been, according to many contemporary social and political theorists, that the poor have tended to acquiesce in and thus consent to cultural exclusion. Negative constructions of identity function as powerful, dominant images so that the poor will not revolt, but will instead internalize isolating and blameworthy identities scripted for them through meritocracy, liberal democracy, and the American/Canadian Dream of upward mobility. Studies of class identity and the poor as a group in North America, such as *The Hidden Injuries of Class* (Sennett and Cobb), *The Other America: Poverty in United States* (Harrington), *The Stigma of Poverty* (Waxman), *Worlds of Pain* (Rubin), *The Real Poverty Report* (Adams et al.), and *The Poverty Wall* (Adams), identify the lack of affirmative class identification among the poor as the basis of subordination and self-blame which turn outward-directed anger to inward-directed shame. Although these sources agree that the popular image of the poor as a separate class of people is fundamentally distorting, they emphasize, none the less, that it is a powerful symbolic means of positioning the poor on the outside, especially in their own eyes. Frequent stigmatization imprints itself on poor subjects as a dominant narrative they must resist, internalize, or otherwise negotiate – but rarely ignore. Stigma is the psychosocial space they inherit and inhabit by virtue of falling to the side of the have-nots in a meritocracy, that dark, regressive nation-within-a-nation which the wealthy nation must keep rediscovering, innocently, coyly, and with impunity.

By drawing on cultural theories of identity formation (for example, with reference to Stanley Aronowitz's *The Politics of Identity: Class, Culture, and Social Movements* and Chaim Waxman's *The Stigma of Poverty*), chapter 5, called 'Subverting "Poor Me,"' analyses the internalization of negative constructions of identity by poor subjects in autobiographical works by Cy-Thea Sand and Maria Campbell. I read this internalization as evidence of discursive and symbolic violence against the poor and trace how poor people can be colonized by negative images. With reference to Sidonie Smith and Julia Watson's expanded definition of colonization in *De/Colonizing the Subject: The Politics of Gender in Women's Autobiography*, chapter 5 also examines how discourses of class solidarity and of racial and ethnic pride can mediate negative constructions of 'poor me' and assist in the formation of an oppositional sense of self and community. This oppositional sense of identity is rarely built upon class politics in Canada, but often on 'alternative status-honour groups' (Waxman): for example, the sense of belonging to less marginalized groups than the poor, such as those defined by ethnicity or gender.

As someone who grew up in poverty and saw that poor people are more diverse and complex than the non-poor often realize, I know that no single theory, especially not one generated exclusively by the non-poor, can explain the voices of the poor. Out of respect for the poor and their struggles to maintain 'dignity and daily bread,'[4] we need to acknowledge from the outset that academic theory has too often in the past tended to overgeneralize about the poor, to represent the poor as an object of study to be measured and analysed as a problem, rather than listened to. This is why we need to take the time to consider how academic discourse itself is an important context shaping the study of poverty, a task I take on in the final chapter on contexts of oppositional criticism. In particular, the tendency for theories to make abstractions of identity and subjecthood has meant that characters and speakers bound by poverty are either extracted from their social and material contexts to have their situations falsely universalized or, conversely, are completely reduced to materiality and thus flattened into icons that remain silenced subjects. This is nowhere more evident than in the discussion of living space and poor houses in literature, both of which are often reduced to the aesthetics of personal taste or the background role of setting. Instead, I suggest we read living spaces by probing the connection between materiality and subjectivity – in other words, how it feels to live in poor houses, how poor housing conditions shape sensibilities, how they limit life chances, complicate everyday lives, and impede well-being.

Ironically for a wealthy, democratic society, boundaries around the living space of the poor in Canada are often inscribed as symbolically rigid though materially fragile. Ways of reading about poor houses can be informed by a long social history of control over the movement and living quarters of the poor in Britain, France, Canada, and elsewhere. Discursively, this results in various ways of devaluing poor houses and naturalizing the material need that defines them. They are

---

4 Sheila Rowbotham and Swasti Mitter gave this title to their recent book on the links in economic organizing among poor women in the Third and First World. They drew the title from the chants of poor women workers in India demonstrating against unfair social, political, and economic practices that kept them poor by denying them equal access to and equal power in the market-place.

then seen as the product of poor taste, sloth, or the filth of poor subjects – who are seen to deserve or produce these poor living quarters out of abjectness. Chapter 3, '"We Live in a Rickety House": Social Boundaries and Poor Housing,' interrogates the connection between identity strategies and the politics of living space. This chapter discusses a nineteenth-century poem by Alexander McLachlan, a short story by Alice Munro, and a little-known story by Nancy Holmes called 'Bugs,' by examining the way in which attitudes towards poor houses demonstrate the internalization of exterior class relations, especially in terms of Pierre Bourdieu's theory of the sociology of taste and 'class habitus.' Whether the poor home is represented as metaphoric or literal, the object of poor taste or personal attachment, we need to acknowledge that material reality, material interests, and material history are often at the basis of the symbolic power of poor houses and homelessness in the lives of the poor.

The discourses of poverty may be plural and contradictory, but the roots and consequences of these struggles over meaning are lived out by concrete subjects and, therefore, should not be restricted to a study of textual images alone. If we as a society grant more power to certain images of poverty, it is surely because these images perform a function. Dominant images of poverty tend to rationalize or naturalize the exclusion of the poor, cloak the existence of unequal distribution of wealth and life chances in market society – and also mask what Raymond Williams has called the spirit of 'uncommunity' at the heart of certain divisive practices of culture. I am suggesting that exclusionary cultural practices that keep the poor on the outside of market society and subservient are reproduced in literary studies not only through the dominant images of the poor but also in the way we naturalize these images by reading literary texts without interrogating the ideology behind poverty. Conversely, the field of literary studies needs to recognize resistant images of poverty and how they offer alternative visions of community and the lives of the poor, such as those featured in Sheila Baxter's *No Way to Live: Poor Women Speak Out* and Gabrielle Roy's *Bonheur d'occasion (The Tin Flute)*. Images resist hegemony in a self-proclaimed 'classless' society when they expose the relational aspect of poverty, how the poor exist in relation to the non-poor, how the poor are defined as much by the way the non-poor police and dominate property, economic resources, and culture itself as they are by their own actions and choices. Besides testifying to the 'uncommunity' of a society divided into extreme positions over material interests and the damage that uncommunity visits on individual subjectivity as a practice of violence, resistant poverty narratives may also offer different utopic imaginaries of a society and nation, visions of a more inclusive nation where the public good is defined not by deficit reduction but by sharing and investing in all members of the collective. Such narratives unfold alternative world views where poverty is not simply taken for granted as part of a natural social landscape but rather is resisted in courageous ways through acts of sharing, civil disobedience, and political activism – see, for example, 'A Question of Identity' (Sand), *Cabbagetown* (Garner), and *Waste Heritage* (Baird). We need reading practices that will allow poverty narratives to emerge as sites of radical possibility, where damaged subjectivities may be reconstituted through testimony and speaking out, where resistant poverty narratives may emerge in full relief against the backdrop of a wealthy nation, where alternative values may emerge as people opt out of one national dream based on acquisitiveness and posit another based on community.

iii Poverty Narratives: A New Category of Analysis

Even though we live in times when it is fashionable to speak of marginality and resistance in literature, the way we teach literary texts in North America demonstrates an enduring blind spot about poverty and how it shapes the identities and subjectivities of the poor. Literary criticism has tended to comment on the textual construction of poverty in secondary ways – for example, in the course of studying social realism and urban settings – as though poverty forms the background, but not the subjects themselves. The issue of poverty is rarely centre stage even in inquiries about class conflict in proletarian fiction and working-class writing, or in new radical fields of inquiry such as feminism, postcolonialism, and multiculturalism, all of which are concerned with social justice. Why has poverty largely eluded radicalism in contemporary literary and cultural studies in North America? Clearly, the blind spot is not in the literature itself, which has for centuries dramatized the lives of the poor – from *Les Misérables* and *Oliver Twist* to *Bonheur d'occasion (The Tin Flute)*, *Angela's Ashes*, and *The Beans of Egypt Maine* – but rather in the way we construct literary and cultural categories, such as canons, curricula, and national literatures, and the way we ask questions of texts and character. I do not mean to suggest that poverty narratives have been rigidly excluded from national canons, but rather that we tend to read such works deracinated from important contexts that would help us make sense of the ideology behind the images: for instance, social theories and the social history of poverty; a vast store of images of poverty that circulate within literature and within culture and discourse as a whole; the 'ordinary' voices of the poor themselves, which might reveal something of their subjectivities; and, perhaps most important of all, oppositional politics.

To explore more resistant ways of reading poverty, I propose a new category of analysis called 'poverty narratives' and oppositional reading practices which ask broad theoretical and social questions such as what it might mean politically, ethically, and epistemologically to critique poverty in literature more rigorously. For example, what does it mean in terms of social change for academics to claim to know more about poor people's stories? How do gender and poverty work together to form poor women's subjectivities and life stories? Are the poor, and poor women especially, relegated to the fringes of wealthy nations as mere 'remnants of nation?' How can community and nation be imagined otherwise to address these exclusions?

Previous image-of-poverty studies in literature have rarely been politically oppositional or concerned with the poor as subjects of their own stories. Whereas studies of class in literature have read inscriptions of working-class identity, class conflict, dissent, communism, and labour, they have not examined poverty in a sustained or oppositional way. Furthermore, a recent trend in North American cultural studies has been to devalue class itself as a category of identity and resistance – although authors such as Aronowitz, DiFazio, Fox, Foley, Zandy, Ehrenreich, Irr, and others discussed here are notable exceptions to this dominant trend. Poverty may have escaped radical cultural criticism in the past, but the means are easily within reach to address that blind spot now. By reading oppositionally, we can expose the ideology behind images of poverty and trace how textual constructions not only are rooted in lived power relations but also may reproduce these power relations or challenge them significantly.

Traditional studies of the image of poverty in literature, albeit few and far between, have been thematic, rarely politically oppositional, and generally focused on depictions of the poor by 'great' writers – for instance, Charles Dickens, Victor Hugo, William Faulkner, and Carson McCullers – and on genres or themes related to poverty such as the grotesque, social realism, Depression writing, and the urban landscape. More recently, a few semiotic studies of poverty have appeared, broadening the range of vision beyond the canon to draw on a larger pool of images from the sphere of popular culture and social discourse, but still with little sense that such analyses may constitute important cultural opposition by addressing misrecognition and prejudice. Unlike the study of class in literature, which has been politicized by Marxist and populist methods of recovery and interpretation of working-class voices, studies of the image of poverty have been descriptive rather than oppositional, rarely inclusive of the voices of the poor or concerned about recovery of silenced people, and of only minor importance to literary and cultural studies as a whole. For example, discussions of poverty in literature have rarely reflected back on the construction and ideology of the non-poor in the way Marxist criticism has reflected back on bourgeois and middle-class aesthetics. This book differs significantly from previous approaches because of the politics of the knowledge it constructs. It does not unfold a disinterested, analytical stance, but asks how reading strategies may be informed by an engaged position, by many theories of representation and poverty as opposed to one governing theory, and by selected voices of the poor themselves. It expands the inquiry about poverty in literature by asking how we might read poverty as oppositionally as we now read gender, race, and class in respect to resistant communities and notions of collective identity, or the lack thereof.

A top-down view of poverty is not unique to literary studies. Studies in other fields as well have tended to decode poverty in the field of intellectual history of 'great' ideas and 'great' thinkers or in official discourses of control and regulation, rather than to explore the words, life stories, or disorderly, complex, lived realities of the poor themselves (except, of course, as case studies or social history from below). For example, Himmelfarb's influential history, *The Idea of Poverty*, analyses political, literary, and journalistic texts from nineteenth-century England, rather than the messiness of lived reality among the poor. Bryan Green's *Knowing the Poor: A Case Study in Textual Reality Construction* takes a more socially critical angle, but focuses on the social documents of the Poor Laws and Canadian government documents on welfare to trace the positioning of the poor in official documents. Both are excellent studies of the construction of poverty from the top down, with the former historicizing dominant ideas and the latter analysing the controlling mechanisms of dominant discourses. But neither includes a study of the poor as agents or knowers with the power to rebel against misrepresentation and discursive domination. Having grown up poor myself, I feel a strong alliance with the poor and refuse to consent to top-down academic models of thought that risk reinscribing exclusion or oversimplifying difference.

At the other extreme, documentarism and studies of culture-from-below have reached out to make audible the 'authentic' voices of the poor. As I explain through examples of contemporary reportage and oral histories (Mettrick, Tracey, Broadfoot), even these gestures to include the voices of the poor often subtly reinscribe cultural erasure by presenting the poor as objects of study within somewhat rigid conventions that stress obscurity and rescue.[5] In this book, rather than the traditional 'culture-of-poverty' vantage point that locates the poor in a separate group apart from society, perpetuating the cycle of poverty and consenting to exclusion (see O. Lewis [1961; 1969] and Harvey and Reed [1992]), I also consider the poor as a subculture with the power of agency and resistance, and a subculture that is sometimes negatively defined by dominant cultural groups who cling to material comfort and fear losing it. The fact that many poor people are ashamed of their poverty and do not wish to be identified with the poor as a group means that few choose to see the counter-cultural aspects of poverty, accepting instead its wholly negative designation as 'underclass' or culture of poverty. Importantly, poor subjects themselves often have conflicting views of their power of agency and of the power of the non-poor to determine their life chances. Our vision of the poor should be complex enough to allow for these differences of self-perception

Of all the questions about poverty narratives as a category of analysis, the most crucial to oppositional aims is the question about a focus on poverty rather than one on class. Some colleagues have expressed concerns that the expression 'poverty narrative' may cut these texts off from the positive heritage of a working-class tradition or that it may be linguistically entrapping because of the negative naming. For example it has been suggested that 'resistance' narratives would be a more politically affirmative term to use. However, as not all the narratives do in fact articulate resistance, and as many women in Canada live in

---

5 The construction of the poor within the genre of oral histories is the subject of an article I published in *Essays on Canadian Writing* (1996) called 'Mediated Lives: Oral Histories and Cultural Memory.' A forthcoming article entitled 'Counter-national Imaginings through Documentary and Reportage: In Search of the Poor and the Working Class' is based on a paper presented at the Image of Class conference in Colorado Springs in 1998.

poverty without being working class, it seems wise to retain 'poverty narratives' as a more accurate and inclusive term when studying cross-class utterances about poverty. The positive heritage of working-class consciousness and of a history of class struggle can inform oppositional reading practices even when the texts themselves do not reflect these political values or shared class origins. (See the appendix of this book where these issues are discussed in more detail with reference to Canadian narratives under the subheadings 'Useful Distinctions: Poor and Working-Class Women' and 'Setting up a Cross-Class Dialectic.')

It is possible to expose and learn from the negative aspects of the name 'poverty narratives' by confronting the tension between various connotations of the word itself. As defined in *The Oxford English Dictionary*, the meaning of 'poor' ranges from a statement of circumstance on the one hand – the poor collectively, 'a class of people,' or the 'condition of having little or no material wealth' – to a judgmental evaluation on the other – 'deficiency in the proper or desired quality' (1971 ed., 1208–9). The invisibility, if not the devaluation, of many poverty narratives may result from such judgmental attitudes towards the lives and language of the poor operating in critical standards, methods of reading, and prejudices about knowledge production and taste. The negative impact of being labelled 'poor' in a prosperous, Western nation where few have knowledge of a positive heritage of class politics to depersonalize this stigmatization is a cultural reality for many Canadians. This is part of the very real struggle over meaning between the poor and the non-poor. As I will show in respect to autobiographical accounts of poverty in chapter 5, 'Subverting "Poor Me,"' the experiences of shame and resistance are often complexly intertwined, if not inseparable. Resistance often grows out of shame. Both emerge as powerful elements in subversions of negative constructions of identity.

Recent studies of working-class writing have defined their object of knowledge differently from the present study. Although also concentrating on national contexts for class strife, these studies focus on a more homogeneous category of narratives based on resistant genres, shared themes and ideologies, or the class origins of the authors: for example, Pamela Fox's study of working-class novels in *Class Fictions: Shame and Resistance in the British Working-class Novel, 1890–1945* (1994), Barbara Foley's study of proletarian writing in *Radical Representations: Politics and Form in U.S. Proletarian Fiction 1929–1940* (1993), and Caren Irr's in *The Suburb of Dissent: Cultural Politics in the United States and Canada during the 1930s* (1998) focus on categories of oppositional, working-class narratives and then theorize subjectivities from these categories. They also identify common textual strategies such as dissent, propaganda, resistance, and identity construction. These works mark an important resurgence of interest in class identity and in the theoretical sophistication of class analysis of literature in the context of national cultures. In the case of Fox's analysis, the definition of resistance itself is expanded to embrace narratives which are not generally perceived as resistant, for example, by describing testimonies of shame and isolation as potentially resistant for survivors. Expanded definitions of class resistance in the context of women's lives by both Fox and Steedman have informed my own conception of the politics of resistance. As I have said, however, the present study does not take as its object of knowledge such a homogeneous category of resistant texts, voices from a shared class position, or such an authoritative or fully theorized politics as class resistance. It shows, instead, the need for politicizing poverty when faced with voices that are so often depoliticized or politicized in obscure ways. This is a politics in the making, one which attempts to use class theory along with other theories of social justice to challenge the silencing and marginalization of the poor.

The category of analysis called poverty narratives is a means rather than an end in itself, a means to create a more informed field within which to read oppositionally. For this reason, I do not focus on a taxonomy of the narratives or survey them merely to trace common themes and patterns. Nor are poverty narratives an idealist category of resistant or survivor voices or of oppositional texts. They include the voices of the poor, the once-poor, the non-poor, and a wide range of complex ideological positions, from resistance to domination. This means that the category is cross-class in order to study a dialectic between the poor and the non-poor and to probe the ideological differences among members of each group. Chapter 1, '"Fictioning" a Literature,' discusses the theoretical choices and problems behind constructing this analytical category. These choices are examined and weighed in terms of the goals of creating a literature for political purposes. For example, I discuss why it is valuable to create a category of narratives with a cross-class dialectic, how populist motives can inform the selection of texts and knowledge about poverty, how and why ordinary voices might be brought into view beside literature, how cultural criticism of such a literature can function as a form of social therapy, and how testimony and empathy generated from poverty narratives can comprise radical forms of knowledge about the poor. Since this analytical category is a means rather than an end, however, the entire grouping is fluid, functional, and tentative. The concern for keeping the category broad and fluid is reflected in the title of the appendix, 'Outlawing Boundaries.' We need to keep in mind that poverty narratives as a category of analysis is a constructed field of knowledge which serves a different purpose, a different claim to coherence, from survey or thematic study and which should, therefore, not limit knowledge for the sake of neatness or consistency.

For pragmatic reasons, the present search was restricted within limits – albeit fluid limits of genre, gender, nation, and period – to non-dramatic prose by women in Canada from 1919 to the present, taking in novels, short stories, autobiographies, oral histories, essays, reportage, and letters by women. The list of poverty narratives is, thus, in addition to being cross-class as previously discussed, cross-genre and gender-specific. It crosses levels of culture (literary, popular, ordinary) and, hence, transgresses the canon and notions of literary value as detailed under the heading 'Transgressing the National Canon' in the appendix.[6] To include ordinary voices transcribed as oral histories or reportage, the category of analysis juxtaposes works that are non-literary with those from the national canon. The texts I selected for close analysis are not my favourites, the most oppositional, or the most beautiful, but rather ones which struck me as particularly meaningful when read in juxtaposition with others. A spirit of exploration and inclusiveness guided the collection of narratives. The broad, fluid category allows one to assemble as many utterances about women's poverty as possible in the belief that cultural resistance is best achieved not by focusing discussion on explicitly oppositional narratives but by applying to heterogeneous utterances an oppositional reading practice which interrogates the texts as a site of struggle for power and meaning. Accordingly, the category of poverty narratives, as I envisage it, does not tolerate a selec-

---

6 Much of the detailed discussion about features of the category of analysis as I constructed it are developed in the appendix, not as an afterthought but because the category of analysis is a means, not an end in itself. I can see at least several other ways of constructing poverty narratives besides the way I chose. The end I had in mind was, first, to develop oppositional reading strategies and, second, to open the door to further debate on ideology, recovery, and aesthetics – including other ways of constructing a category of analysis. This involves some reflections on themes and patterns, but only in a secondary way. The focus should not be the category itself but what each narrative says about poverty and how that contributes to the struggle over meaning between the poor and the non-poor.

tiveness based on a prescribed version of reality; instead, it seeks a fuller sense of lived realities and cultural representations of those realities. This fuller sense of poverty would not be the product of a sensual reading experience which strives to know the texture of poverty for voyeuristic purposes; it is one derived from the praxis of collecting, recovering, and juxtaposing diverse utterances about women's poverty in order to examine culturally mediated perceptions and representations and to discover how such cultural production may be related to the exercise of power over concrete lives.

In order to study how narratives deploy images of poverty, we need to alter *the way* we read poverty, not simply *what* we read. That is why I propose that reading strategies, rather than the category itself, be oppositional. While the minority of poverty narratives in my working list are openly resistant, the reading strategies I propose are oppositional in that they aim at decoding the ideology behind the images and doing so from a consciously engaged position. Because these interdisciplinary and eclectic readings consistently step beyond literature to construct knowledge oppositionally, they stem more from cultural studies practices than from literary studies. Ideological meaning cannot merely be exposed; it must be interpreted and teased out of the intertextuality among literary, popular, and marginalized discourses about the poor, circulating in and beyond the text and within culture as a whole. We also need to consider our own motives for reading poverty. Are we seeing what we want to see, uncovering what we want to uncover? Oppositional reading strategies should also take into account the subjectivities of the poor and how they themselves experience dominant images. Whenever possible, I consider, as an alternative to academic theories of poverty, the texts as sources of knowledge about the subjectivities of the poor: for example, as testified to in oral histories, autobiographies, or by characters poised to speak for the poor.

Of course, the experiences of the poor are not reducible to the paper site of textual culture or to language itself. We must constantly remind ourselves that the lives of the poor exceed all textual representation and language. Changes in discursive representations alone will not free the poor from material poverty. Still, the various discourses of poverty are not transcendent or free-floating; they are complexly rooted in lived experience, personal and collective subjectivities, local reality, historical contingency, and lived relations between the poor and the non-poor. Reading oppositionally, then, entails acknowledging that our encounter with poverty, as readers, is bound by a textual plane of culture that is limited but none the less complexly moored in a broader sea of lived relations. Texts about poverty are acted upon by material and political realities and act in turn to uphold or resist those lived power relations, though not mechanistically so. In wealthy nations especially, the poor are defined as remnants of nation because they compromise the stability and morality of the imagined community of nation and expose the 'ragged edges of inequality' to which Ehrenreich referred. The ties between texts and lived experience are formed within specific geopolitical contexts. Geopolitical realities help determine the experiences and subjectivities of the poor and colour relations between the poor and the non-poor. When the study of poverty narratives is located within a national corpus of texts, the sense of community and exclusion represented can be decoded within the context of local and national history with an identifiable state power and national ethos.

Though consistent in spirit and in logic as an exploratory effort, this book is also tentative and reaching, reflecting its origins as essays written over the course of five years. The chapters are self-contained and may be read out of the order in which they appear here; they are joined by a strong interior logic rather than a strict chronology, a logic which unfolds a series of problems to face in order to posit poverty narratives as a new field of study and to defend the right to do so – given the present climate in literary studies in North America that class is 'old hat' and poverty for 'bleeding hearts.' The chapters of this book comprise two types of reflections on poverty and representation: theoretical considerations and specific readings. The theoretical chapters about poverty narratives (chapters 1, 4, and 8) discuss how they can be made to appear without being idealized as resistant or representative of the true voices of the poor. In addition to considering how to 'fiction' a literature for political purposes (Belsey 1985, 1988), these chapters also discuss how the academic and institutional contexts of inquiry determine in part the way we construct radical knowledge about poverty, how subjects are classed and gendered, and how feminist criticism and Marxist criticism of literary texts have neglected to make poor women the subject of study in the past. In an attempt to avoid top-down constructions of poverty, I return again and again to the issue of the limits of theory in providing access to poor people's subjectivities and the value of populist motives in collecting a wide variety of voices.

The chapters which offer sustained readings (chapters 2, 3, 5, 6, and 7) also offer ample theoretical reflections, but on specific issues and selected clusters of narratives, as a means of preventing over-generalization about textual strategies and subjectivities. After arguing that we 'fiction' a new fluid literature for political and analytical purposes, I recommend turning away from the category as a whole to a study of clusters of narratives selected to illuminate lived issues relating to poverty: for instance, poor homes, shame, the psychosocial spaces of poverty, the place of the poor in the national imaginary, isolation, the poor at school, shattered dreams of mobility, gendered experiences of poverty, misrepresentation of the poor, and so on. Readings of popular discourse help pry open and disturb larger, taken-for-granted notions of the poor for closer analysis, for instance, images which iconize or otherwise homogenize the poor.

To understand the power of images of poverty to shape subjectivities and social practice, I have tried to decode textual images in terms of an eclectic and broad range of theories about poverty, representation, and political agency. Resisting the idea that there is any one overarching theory or reading practice that will explain all the diverse inscriptions of poverty, however, this discussion promotes a healthy scepticism about theory in chapter 4, 'Theories and Anti-Theory,' in order to avoid a top-down perspective of poverty that would reinscribe silencing over the voices and experiences of the poor. Ironically, however, this results in more rather than less theory.

The origins of this engaged study are not merely academic, of course. They go back much farther into my personal past where I grew up with deep feelings of rage and indignation at the silencing and deprivation of the poor. To a very great extent, these thoughts and reading practices show how I have educated myself about the power of images exercised against my family and friends while we lived in poverty. I educated myself against all odds because I was angry. My goal was radical knowledge, not refinement or acceptance. Though the theory and readings of poverty narratives are tentative, cautious, and exploratory, the politics of the knowledge created here is unapologetically counter-cultural.

iv The Gender of Poverty

Despite important efforts to recover and anthologize women's voices around the shared experiences of gender, race, and ethnicity in Canadian literature, little has been published on the significance of poverty and class in women's writing. Yet because feminist scholars in the social sciences have openly grappled with the role of class in employment ghettos, labour conditions, the impoverishment of single mothers, the social history of the working class, and the welfare family (Armstrong and Armstrong, Torjman, Gunderson), their studies can cross-fertilize readings of poverty narratives. In order to bring gender, class, and poverty into view in literary and cultural studies, we need to take a step back and examine what it means to reach out to poor women as marginalized 'subjects' through these existing fields of study. We need to assess how different strains of feminist criticism, for example, have both erased and enabled access to marginal women's subjectivities. There are three broad theoretical issues in particular that arise when we look at how feminist criticism can enable access and understanding: first, the process of collecting voices in respect to gendered categories and the way in which poor women's voices tend to destabilize unified gendered categories; second, the process of constructing radical knowledge from reading and collecting these voices; and third, the process of reconsidering assumptions about the individual female subject based on class knowledge. These are theoretical issues about collection and interpretation discussed in chapter 4.

Very briefly, what we find in terms of sociological research when we ask if and how women in Canada experience poverty differently from men are three important areas of overlap between poverty and gender: women face greater risk than men of becoming poor largely because of our unpaid care-giving roles and inequitable pay scales; our experience of being poor is different because women, on the whole, take more responsibility for the most vulnerable members of society – children, the mentally and physically disabled, and aging family members; and our bodies are implicated in our financial insecurity through sexual aggression and sexual exploitation. That is not to say that poor women experience more violence or sexual harassment than non-poor women, but that poverty in capitalist patriarchy makes women more vulnerable to the effects of sexual violence which occur in all classes. For women of all classes who may fall into poverty, gender may close many escape routes and open other traps – namely, prostitution. Indeed, one standard way of writing poor women out of male-centred novels about the poor and the working class is to have them descend through low-wage jobs (waitress, domestic, dance-hall girl) to fall eventually into prostitution and out of the story (consider, for example, the fate of female characters in *Cabbagetown* and *Waste Heritage*). Male characters seem to have more options for escape or resistance (such as strikes, crime, riding the rails, joining the army, and so on).

Focusing on a cross-class group of narratives by and about poor women rather than writing by poor women alone prevents ghettoization of marginal women's voices in a category apart from privileged women's voices. I also wish to concentrate not on women's class status in relation to the market means of production or the occupations of their husbands or fathers but on their own lived relation to poverty in a consumer society that is still fundamentally patriarchal in its distribution of goods and power. The cross-class nature of poverty narratives also aims to make available for cultural study a wider range of dominant and marginalized versions of poverty and to take into account the increasing cross-class phenomenon known as 'the feminization of poverty' whereby more and more women of all classes are vulnerable to poverty through wage-labour ghettos and the dissolution of the family.

The concept of the 'feminization of poverty' was formed only in the late 1970s and first named by the sociologist Diana Pearce (*Urban & Social Change Review*, 1978), and that is one reason why cultural critics have not yet grappled with its implications for the interpretation of class, poverty, and gender in terms of cultural production. The term was originally coined to refer to the startling growth in that decade of the number of poor women, despite increased entry into the labour market. Because of the rapid increase in the dissolution of the family, which left more and more middle-class and bourgeois women vulnerable to poverty, as well as working-class women, and their children, the feminization of poverty became the subject of much discussion in sociology.[7] Critiques of this relatively new concept are discussed later in chapter 4 along with other theories of the classed and gendered subject.

The category of poverty narratives assembles women's writing based on the relation to levels of consumption, the characters' limited access to goods and services and to participation in society, and the importance of poverty in their self-identification or representational modes. Working-class women have traditionally been defined, on the other hand, according to their relation to production; in other words, as

---

[7] See discussions of the feminization of poverty and other ways of understanding women's gendered experience of poverty in Gertrude Goldberg et al.'s *The Feminization of Poverty: Only in America?*, Ruth Sidel's *Women and Children Last*, Mary Daly's *Women and Poverty*, Barbara Gelpi and Nancy Hartsock et al.'s *Women and Poverty*, and Pat Armstrong and Hugh Armstrong's *The Double Ghetto* and *Theorizing Women's Work*.

women who share common class identification based on wage labour and their relation to the capitalist mode of production, which, in the past, was usually gauged through their fathers' and husbands' class status more than their own self-identification with a classed community or with class politics (Abbott and Sapsford). As stated earlier, poverty narratives are not always about 'working-class' women because not all the poor are working class, nor are all the working class poor. Examples of working-class women who are not poor are those who draw an adequate wage from traditional working-class labour (such as factory work and skilled manual labour) to keep them above a certain level of consumption. In the past, anthologies of working-class writing generally highlighted narratives which made little or no reference to poverty but which depicted strong class identification through manual labour, class conflict, alienation of labour, and exploitation. In the present study, such working-class writings are not included unless the level of exploitation plummets the worker's experience below the consumption level which she consciously recognizes as poverty or which restricts her full participation in society.[8]

The two categories do overlap, however. Many of the narratives about working-class women's lives are also about poor women on the wage-labour market. For example, workers who are exploited to the point where they are poor are the domestic workers interviewed in Makeda Silvera's *Silenced*, the maid fictionally represented in Maxine Tynes's 'Borrowed Beauty,' the factory workers interviewed in Prahba Khosla's 'Profiles of Working-class East Indian Women,' the women in the sweat shops recalled in Laura Goodman Salverson's autobiography, *Confessions of an Immigrant's Daughter*, and the seamstresses, clerks, cleaning ladies, and munitions factory workers in J.G. Sime's *Sister Woman*. For the sake of clarity, explicit differences and overlaps between the categories of poverty narratives by women and working-class women's writing should be acknowledged. I return to the subject of useful distinctions between working-class and poor women in detail in the appendix, along with further theorization of the category of poverty narratives as a cross-class construction.

---

8 I wish to thank June Howard from Michigan State University for her encouraging comments on my first conference paper and publication on poverty narratives. She was the first to draw my attention to the fact that this is a category of analysis based on consumption versus production. I am also grateful for theoretical comments made by Chinmoy Bannerjee from Simon Fraser University in the very early stages of this research.

Implicit in the gender-specificity of poverty narratives by women is the feminist critical assumption that women readers, writers, and characters are significantly united by the experience of gender and that this shared experience has an impact on reading and writing practices as well as on the lived experience of poverty. Recently, the assumptions behind such gender categories have themselves been called into question, especially for their essentializing and homogenizing implications (see Costello, Butler). However, Joan Wallach Scott and Rita Felski both argue convincingly for the self-reflexive and strategic maintenance of gender categories for historical and theoretically oppositional purposes. I would also argue pragmatically for the foregrounding of women's narratives because studies of working-class narratives which do not focus on gender-specific categories are bound to give more time to narratives by men simply because such studies usually exist in greater number (for example, see Regenia Gagnier's *Subjectivities*). Importantly, many of the most respected cultural studies of the working class, such as Richard Hoggart's *The Uses of Literacy* and David Hebdige's *Subcultures*, did not theorize their focus on masculine subjectivity, but often used 'working class' synonymously with male experiences and were called to task for this (see McRobbie, Stuart Hall). However, this gender-consciousness came just when attention to class was diminishing and attention to race, ethnicity, consumerism, and discourse was climbing. Thus, backgrounding male culture and foregrounding female narratives in a study of poverty and class still seems strategic at this time as long as we avoid essentialist assumptions about the way men and women inscribe poverty or unfold subjectivities.

Any careful discussion of the themes of working-class solidarity and coalition among the poor requires that the foregrounding of women's narratives ultimately be only that, a foregrounding, and not a limited field of perspective. The gender-specificity of the category should be fluid to avoid rather absurd limits on studying cross-gender narration. For example, in addition to narratives about women by women, one would want to include in the long run women writers' depiction of poverty through a male protagonist's eyes: for example Patricia Blondall's *A Candle to Light the Sun*, Irene Baird's *Waste Heritage*, and Margaret Laurence's 'Horses of the Night.' Similarly, in order to discuss the cultural inscription of gender and poverty in a more comprehensive survey of Canadian literature than the present, one would need to include male authors' depictions of poverty through the eyes of a female protagonist (for example, Sinclair Ross's *As for Me and My House*) and a male transcriber's oral history of his mother's autobiography (for instance, Rolf Knight's *A Very Ordinary Life*); and also male authors' poverty narratives in which women are represented in various roles, from special victims of poverty to sexual objects: for example, Roger Lemelin's *Les Plouffe*, Morley Callaghan's *Such Is My Beloved*, Hugh Garner's *Cabbagetown*, Juan Butler's *Cabbagetown Diary*, David Fennario's *Blue Mondays*, and David Adams Richards's *Road to the Stilt House*.

By exploring how three authors position their female narrators or characters differently in respect to poverty as a psychosocial space, I show in chapter 2, 'Visits and Homecomings,' that the relation of gender to poverty is not fixed but is complexly inscribed in subjective relations. Works by Susanna Moodie, Nellie McClung, and Gabrielle Roy depict poverty as, respectively, a place to descend into, a place to rise above, and a place of everyday struggle. Despite significant variations in describing gender and poverty, however, there are also dominant, discursive patterns that reflect a particular ideology. Ruth L. Smith's theory that an inside/outside paradigm in liberal humanist discourse positions women and the poor on the outside of civil society helps to illuminate the logic of the discursive positioning of poor women in these texts in terms of their ideological implications. Smith argues that this inside/outside paradigm naturalizes symbolic exclusion based on poverty and gender. This paradigm helps explain how and why the extreme outsider position of poor women is reproduced simultaneously by both patriarchal and class hegemony and how the two elide in popular and literary discourse.

Roger Bromley has noted that the discourses of class, nation, and gender elide in women's autobiographies about poverty from between the wars in Britain. Many, Bromley claims, can be read as a form of selective memory that chooses to forget the class implications of personal stories for the sake of preferred memories of personal distinction and a national dream rooted in meritocracy. It is ironic, of course, that poor women are often the site for this national dream of 'true grit' and self-help in both British and Canadian narratives, when in actuality poor women are often more marginalized than men in terms of nationalist discourse. Likewise, more often than men, women are the caregivers in poverty rather than the lone survivors, as we tend to assume the care of children, the elderly, and the sick, a fact which accounts in large part for the growing phenomenon of the feminization of poverty in wealthy countries where social programs have broken down. The irony that poor women should stand in as popular icons for nationhood and self-help merits further exploration of the relation between the discourses and practices of poverty, gender, nation, and class. Bromley has encouraged us to look for collective cultural amnesia on the subject of class history in popular autobiography. In 'Organized Forgetting' (chapter 6), I probe the way collective memories are frequently displaced in autobiographical works which narrate poverty as a distant landscape in an individual's life, particularly in women's lives. The distancing strategies in life stories by Edna Jaques and Fredelle Bruser Maynard seem to produce what Bromley identified as 'organized forgetting.' In keeping with Bromley's theory about popular memory, these autobiographies foreground the poor woman as one who suffers alone and moves beyond her class through the triumph of individual spirit and social mobility.

With its traditionally tacit emphasis on individual subjectivity and 'refined' culture and good taste, the field of literary studies in Canada has often looked away from class divisions among people and their texts, even as other marginal viewpoints such as feminism, multiculturalism, regionalism, and postcolonialism have emerged to challenge the canon epistemologically, aesthetically, and politically. Class criticism in Canada has not yet produced an influential school or movement in literary studies, as outlined under the heading 'Transgressing the National Canon' in the appendix. Whereas class analysis has been quite thoroughly marginalized in Canadian literary criticism, however, narratives about class and poverty are not so marginalized. Poverty narratives as a cross-canon category cannot be sorted neatly into groups of the culturally included and excluded because the closer we look the more nuances, overlaps, and transitions we see in the canonical status of the works. At one extreme in the range of narratives are collections of oral testimonies gathered in streets and factories and usually consigned to sociology rather than literary culture. Sheila Baxter's *No Way to Live: Poor Women Speak Out* and Makeda Silvera's *Silenced: Talks with Working-class Caribbean Women about Their Lives and Struggles as Domestic Workers in Canada* are examples of oral utterances of street women, welfare recipients, and immigrants that have been wholly excluded by the category of literature. At the other extreme, however, are fully canonized poverty narratives – Gabriel Roy's *Bonheur d'occasion*, Marie-Claire Blais's *Une Saison dans la vie d'Emmanuel*, and Alice Munro's *Who Do You Think You Are?* However, few canonized works have been read on the subversive level of identity and meaning where class and gender intersect or poverty and nation shape each other reciprocally. Major works that do treat class issues and poverty in a sustained way have tended to be read otherwise, according to their less threatening humanist or individualist themes or in isolation as token and isolated moments of humanitarian insight or eccentric rebelliousness (for example, one rarely sees sustained class analysis comparing works by Gabrielle Roy, Margaret Laurence, David Adams Richards, Alice Munro, and Hugh Garner, though critics discuss poverty in their individual works in secondary ways). Canadian criticism in French or of French works has been much more enlightened in this respect than English-Canadian criticism, as testified to by class analyses by Ben-Zion Shek, Max Dorsinville, Antoine Sirois, Pierre Popovic, and others. The failure to interpret subversive class themes in canonized works operates as a hegemonic method of incorporating them into the mainstream by addressing only sifted elements of the works in public discourse.

Rereading canonical works as poverty narratives is not meant to fix the status of a work or an author's reputation differently in Canadian literary history or to wrench the work from previous categories of analysis because the primary focus here is elsewhere than on posterity, literary value, or authorial *oeuvres* and reputations; the focus is, rather, on the way literary and popular works in Canada reinscribe or challenge dominant social fictions about the poor. I want to show that canonical works on poverty can be read differently when placed in juxtaposition with non-canonical narratives (for example in reportage, oral histories, or popular autobiography). I also want to disturb the notion of national culture by challenging the popular assumption that Canadian literature and the nation itself are somehow 'classless.' This revisioning of national culture can come about by focusing on the margins, the remnants of nation which embarrass or otherwise compromise the wealthy nation. What is at stake here is much more than toying with the national literature. It is a radical revisioning similar to Barbara Murphy's in *The Ugly Canadian: The Rise and Fall of a Caring Society,* whereby the ugliness is not poverty and homelessness on the margins but the coldness of a wealthy society that will not see poverty and homelessness. If we put the study of our national literature on trial for its complicity in this ugliness, we may succeed only in oversimplifying the role of the canon in the marginalization of the poor. Instead, we need to focus on the remnants of nation in the literature itself to understand how lives and subjectivities become severed from the whole and what we, as a nation, are losing in the process.

Chapter 1

'Fictioning' a Literature

According to Catherine Belsey, it is possible to 'fiction' a literature, in Foucault's sense of the verb, by interrogating old works in new ways, especially by interrogating the dominant subjectivities reflected in the texts and implicit in the category of literature itself. Belsey has described critical discourse as a way of bringing literature, history, and politics together in order to 'fiction' a literature for political purposes: 'the literary institution has "fictioned" a criticism which uncritically protests its own truth; we must instead "fiction" a literature which renders up our true history in the interests of a politics of change' (1988, 410). A *truer* version of history can be called up, according to Belsey's theory, not by gaining access more accurately to real or more authentic history as a single referent represented in transparent documents, but, rather, by reading texts as locations of power and resistance to power. Literature that is read radically as a site of discursive struggle can be used to critique the history of the present as well as the history of the past and to reach into discourses beyond itself: 'And so the autonomy of literature begins to dissolve, its boundaries to waver as the enterprise unfolds. The text does not disappear though the canon does; and fiction is put to work for substantial political ends which replace the mysterious objectives of aesthetic satisfaction and moral enrichment' (1988, 409). My intention here is not to dissolve the canon, but to transgress it. In other words, although I share Belsey's project of fictioning a literature for political purposes, I do not wish to relinquish concerns for literary value while reading poverty narratives. Literary status may determine the impact of certain images, for example, in terms of circulation and discursive authority. Furthermore the aesthetic judgments we make upon reception of poverty narratives may reveal ideological differences among both texts and readers. Since recovering unknown or devalued poverty narratives and rereading canonized texts are goals of reading oppositionally in order to construct new knowledge, neither their aesthetic status nor their anti-aesthetic stance can be overlooked. These are important frames of meaning through which discourses about poverty enter and leave the text and through which they struggle to articulate meaning through the texts.

1.1 Beyond Literature: Ordinary Voices

Instead of attempting a thorough survey of poverty in Canadian literature and popular culture, I propose the category of poverty narratives here in order to collect and juxtapose enough utterances to problematize voices from the centre and from the periphery or, in other words, to open questions about if and how poverty is narrated from different and shared social locations. The category of poverty narratives is also constructed in order to understand how images of poverty become currency, trading across cultural barriers from one social location to another. Since this mixed array of utterances from the broadened field of cultural studies does not conform to literary genres, it includes narratives which are usually read apart from literature as ethnographic accounts, deeply personal testimonials, or popular fiction. Many poverty narratives take the form of life-writing such as writers' autobiographies or popular autobiographies, or the more discontinuous genres of life-writing like journals, letters, public speeches, collective works, oral histories, and testimonial accounts such as Phyllis Knight and Rolf Knight's *A Very Ordinary Life* and Janet Silman's *Enough Is Enough: Aboriginal Women Speak Out*. On the other hand, among those narratives which attempt to construct poverty as a literary object in the context of traditional genres, many may be seen to fall short in terms of literary value – such as Diana Collier's *The Invisible Women of Washington* and Irene Baird's *Waste Heritage* – because they fall outside of canons of literature into the field of popular culture or merely into obscurity as forgotten works awaiting some form of meaningful recovery. Still other very powerful images of poverty may not appear to be narratives at all because they are reproduced and circulated so frequently and insidiously through commonsensical notions, stereotypes, icons, or popular literary conventions.

Although my working category of poverty narratives emphasizes specific types of oral and written narratives, it is important to note that visual representations have great cultural power to fix poverty in icons which re-emerge in our collective consciousness through the practice of writing and reading. For example, as I sit here, a strikingly familiar visual image stares down at me from my bulletin board: it appears on a pamphlet appealing for funds for the inner-city poor in Montreal and shows a child in rags, crouching beneath a stairwell. She is in modern clothing but has the same pathetic face of a Victorian waif as that on posters advertising theatrical performances of *Les Misérables* – oversize, saucer eyes, tousled hair, and a fragile but set jaw line. There is a social logic to such oft-reproduced images which I hope to expose: such as the vagabond perceived romantically as an idle wanderer; the socially mobile individual as a self-sufficient 'class-traveller' moving up 'from rags to riches'; soup lines and bugs as icons of Depression-era poverty; the two-nations concept of a country which naturalizes the gap between the rich and the poor within one nation; the 'undeserving' poor as licentious, drunk, and disorderly; and the 'deserving' poor as children and the working poor, the latter two fused in the pathetic little-match-girl face, an icon weary of hunger and labour yet innocent of sloth or vice.

From where I sit, I can also see visual markers of poverty outside my window: the way passersby wear their poverty or conceal it, and how this gentrified street in Montreal, sandwiched between a wealthy neighbourhood and a decaying one, aspires to ascend and thus erases any connection with the severe poverty that is lived just a few blocks away. None the less, the alley tells another story by coughing up the garbage of the non-poor to those who scavenge there. Last night, I saw a mother and her child rummaging there, and the child pushed a doll carriage full of their takings. On my way to lecture one night, I passed an elderly woman in a wheelchair slowly moving around cars and mud to reach the garbage cans along our alley. Although my partner and I have retrieved old furniture and refurbished it, this foraging is chic because it does not come from necessity. These differences raise questions germane to the types of poverty depicted in literature: for example, forced or bohemian, temporary or generational, isolated or collective, of the working poor or the unemployed. Further, differences in attitude and the 'performance' of poverty (if one can use that word sensitively) are also relevant to decoding images of poverty in literature – for some wear poverty like a badge of nonconformity which they knowingly choose, while others go to great lengths to hide it as shameful.

Besides public displays of need in the alley of my street, each flat must have its private version, the story each family tells itself to explain its relation to poverty, to conceal it, or deny it – and the stories we all tell ourselves, individually, to make sense of our own detachment from poverty, our fear of it, or our entrapment by it. Such seemingly private stories have a tendency to shift as our personal lives change according to lifelines, market shifts, and social discourses of specific places and eras, and we encounter the possibilities of poverty or its remoteness in new ways and different places as shifting subjects: as students, as bohemians, as lovers, as mothers, as the elderly, as activists, as the 'working' poor, as tourists, as homeowners, as the unemployed, as poor or rich relations, and so on. We all spin fictions to position ourselves in relation to the material needs of the poor and our society's symbolic violence against them. As Barbara Murphy claims in *The Ugly Canadian: The Rise and Fall of a Caring Society*, many of these fictions are collective and intimately linked to our sense of peoplehood, but they are not fixed or even steadily progressive:

> If we could measure in some way how we feel about our fellow Canadians, especially those less fortunate than ourselves, we would find we care as little today as we did a hundred years ago. It's true we took a run at compassion, even generosity, during the twentieth century. Following the shock of the Great Depression we spent over 40 years caring about each other. It became acceptable to be concerned, to contribute part of our incomes to looking after those with none. We pointed proudly to our social policies vis-à-vis those of the United States and guarded them fiercely even as late as the 1980s when free trade was negotiated. Where did all that caring go? We take pride in our toughness now, not our generous social policies. We warn the poor and the sick to keep their heads up; they've had their innings. The years of compassion are over. Today we're playing hardball. (11)

Murphy's strategy in titling her work 'The Ugly Canadian,' inscribed over a photo of what seems like a homeless man 'down on his luck,' seems to point to the raggedness of the poor as a referent, but actually turns back against the mainstream sense of peoplehood and national identity to interrogate the dominant on their treatment of the poor. It is we who are the ugly Canadians in that we have lost sight of the goals of a caring society. The title of the present study has something in common with this strategy of ironic reversal, for the true 'remnants of nation' are not merely the poor on the fringe of the bourgeois state (as the quoted phrase from Lenin implies) but the state itself, which has lost sight of its poorer members and thus become frayed in its collective project. Private and personal stories of poverty are brought to bear on the collective narratives of nation which fuel the state and rationalize the horribly uneven distribution of goods in wealthy nations as part of an oppositional reading strategy.

One initial reaction to assess disparate public and personal versions of poverty is to decide which accounts are true and which are merely fictions, but even a cursory familiarity with these narratives should quickly dispel the notion that what is at stake here is a simple notion of truth or falsehood. For as soon as we inquire which seem the most true, we must inquire why some are believed while others are muted or forgotten and why different communities of readers or listeners might respond differently to the same narratives. Thus, we need to jump from the impossible question of the difference between true and fictional accounts of poverty to the more pressing question of power. Which fictions of poverty are most powerfully inscribed in our culture and why? How can we bring into view more of those versions which are the least powerful? What, if anything, does bringing these versions into view have to do with empowering the poor? What do various inscriptions of poverty mean in the context of the culturally muted experience of lived poverty? How can literary versions of poverty, which are usually valorized as aesthetic objects in high culture, be read side by side with testimonials by the poor – or, more to the point, why should they be? These are not, however, questions to order the diverse fictions in any rigid or scientific way from the outset. But they are, I am convinced, more relevant and harder questions about the struggle over meaning between the poor and the non-poor than the question of truth or fiction.

One such study of the power of discourse to fix meaning over the lives of the poor is Bryan Green's *Knowing the Poor: A Case Study in Textual Reality Construction*, in which the power of government to name the reality of the poor in the form of documents is scrutinized as a means of controlling the poor through textuality. Since government documents reproduce selected images of the poor in great number and with great authority, presenting these accounts as valid representations of lived reality, they outweigh the power of more subjective accounts of the lived experiences of poverty by the poor themselves. In other words, the documented reality of official inquiries which are used to diagnose social problems is imposed upon the situated or lived reality of poverty. Moreover, government documents often present this form of reality construction as innocent rather than a form of control, and this is how they use their documented version of reality, as the first step towards rationalizing government intervention into the lives of the poor. Green maintains that we need a more emancipatory form of reading government documents, one which would expose them as constructed rather than transparent windows onto the lives of the poor.

It is crucial to remember when claiming that all narrative versions are somehow true or merely representations, however, that among the concrete subjects who actually live these conditions, many have little notion and little means of constructing their lives otherwise, materially or imaginatively. This is nowhere more evident than in testimonials of the poor to feelings of entrapment and powerlessness in the face of received stereotypes, official labels, and other negative constructions of the poor (Baxter, Green, Sand, Campbell, Holmes). Academic study can be complicit in the muting of these lives and their political possibilities if it concludes abstractly that the subaltern cannot speak or that the truth of representations can be assessed only through absolute relativism. For some of us, poverty is not experienced from a distance or from the position of an audience member or critic, but as the most pressing truth of our existence, past or present, and our core sense of identity. Out of a desire for coalition with the concrete subjects who live poverty daily and are entrapped in its material grip and its symbolic stigma, we need to understand the real limitations of academic exercises which assume that all versions are equally fictional or which deny the many possibilities for political agency among the poor. Academic studies of poverty that claim oppositional goals should train their attention on the recovery of muted voices: the memories, stories, and meanings which might otherwise remain obscured or forgotten after having lost the struggle over meaning. To return to Green's hypothesis about the overpowering discourse of poverty contained in government documents, most notably the Poor Laws of Britain and Canadian official inquiries into poverty, we might note that, just as these discourses comprise an official and dominant way of knowing the poor, so might diverse poverty narratives and oppositional acts of reading these narratives comprise a counter-cultural way of knowing the poor. This is largely because the former set out to make an object of knowledge of the poor for the purpose of controlling a social problem, whereas the latter set out to make a more complex object of knowledge of the poor for analysis, with no goal to contain or control these subjects based on the knowledge produced. Instead, the engaged aspects of the counter-cultural construction of the poor are the desire to advocate for a more caring society by reimagining nation, to recognize more diverseness and dignity among poor subjects, and to lay bare the struggle(s) and commonalities between the poor and the non-poor.

Although poverty narratives testify to widely varying degrees of submission and resistance, many include a textured story of the lived experience of being forcibly poor. They offer testimonies to the situated realities of deprivation, exclusion, symbolic violence, internalized negative constructions of identity, or various forms of social coercion. In the following instance, for example, Leah represents the imaginative and emotional consequences of poverty: 'To me, being poor meant a great deal of rage and frustration, a constant gnawing at my psyche. It meant having no choices, suffering from a loss of control, and ultimately I felt like a victim of circumstances. I lived with a block on my shoulder which spelled "This is not fair" in neon lights' ('Leah' quoted by Baxter in *No Way to Live: Poor Women Speak Out*, 144). In this account, the subject's anger and frustration marked her identity more strongly than the material signs of poverty. The metaphor of flashing lights indicates that signalling anger at poverty was somehow out of control for her, overshadowing other aspects of her identity, gratuitous and brash, rather than purposeful. The testimonial function of her account is emphasized by the use of the past tense, which signals to us that a present 'I' has lived through a process of empowerment or revisioning which allows her to reflect more thoughtfully on poverty as a past identity. The uncontained anger of the past 'I' is transformed into a purposeful, understated anger of testimony.

Novelist Sylvia Fraser has also depicted a testimonial 'I' reflecting back on a self who experienced poverty in a more complex way than she is able to tell. Fraser strikes a tension between the commonsensical notions of the poor that generate extreme, iconic representations and her own remembered, more concrete, but somehow lesser degree of poverty which she calls the poverty of 'just enough.' Her testimonial 'I' weaves its way in and out of icons to show how its own truth is mediated by received popular images:

I've never been bitten by a rat.
   I've never gone to school hungry.

I've never been thrown onto the street by a bailiff.

I almost wish I had. Then I might feel spurred on to rash deeds: the child with an empty belly who vows to conquer the world. Instead: just enough is the poverty of maximum bearable indignities. The blows of the master's whip are steady, dull and dulling – just enough to keep your head down but not enough to make you rear back and snatch the whip. You turn into a plodder with a blistered heel. You have just enough energy to keep up so you don't give up. Just enough is the feel of gritty pavement through the hole in your shoe and chafing of a frayed but starched collar on your stiff neck. It's a mouthful of canker sores you never die of. (*My Father's House*, 133)

In a melancholic but rhetorically subversive way, Fraser inscribes and defies her own entrapment in material circumstances by constructing her autobiographical 'I' out of these two modes of expression: the realistically rendered concrete experiences – 'a blistered heel,' 'a mouthful of canker sores' – which somehow both supersede and reactivate the iconic force of the list of extreme negatives. The motif of the master driving the beast of burden on with his whip frames the realistic testimony of 'just enough' melodramatically, once again setting the psychic extremes in contrast with the everyday, mundane knowledge of experience and also echoing the violent frame of patriarchal domination in Fraser's autobiographical incest narrative. Her testimony of poverty and incest subverts the discursive dominance of melodrama and the sexual power of patriarchy by mimicking the frame of mastery and breaking through. Interestingly, Fraser's speaker, much like the one in Marie-Claire Blais's *Les Manuscrits de Pauline Archange*, identifies herself as poor partly out of contempt for her parents and her home, although many readers would classify her as lower middle class. Furthermore, as in many other narratives about domineering patriarchs, the children and wife are impoverished because the father withholds material goods from them (for example, consider the refusal of patriarchs to share goods with their wives and children in novels and autobiographies such as Gail Anderson-Dargatz's *The Cure for Death by Lightning*, Martha Ostenso's *Wild Geese*, and Claire Martin's *Dans un gant du fer* [*In an Iron Glove*]). The private aspect of Fraser's self-proclaimed poverty raises questions about the objective and subjective measure of poverty. How can we rely on the author/character's self-definition when a number of middle-class speakers see themselves as poor while many of the poor fail to recognize themselves as such?

'Fictioning' a Literature   47

Since there is no infallible objective yardstick of poverty, and many social studies become bogged down in trying to establish one, this study relies instead on subjective criteria. When speakers name themselves as poor, we may read their stories as poverty narratives to analyse how they are constructing poverty. Furthermore, since private households have traditionally fallen outside systems of studying class, women's claims to be poor need to be analysed in terms of a 'domestic sphere of production' and distribution (Delphy) rather than simply in terms of the market sphere.

In a third testimony to poverty, a woman can be heard testifying directly, seemingly transparently, to how she had been silenced on the subject of her lived experience – once again in a confessional mode, but this time without a metaphoric level. Despite the off-hand, informal language, the speaker is signalling knowledge of many larger issues in the construction of her own identity: for example, the pervasive isolation and muting of the poor, how the shame and stigma of poverty enforce silence, the possibility of renaming poverty in terms of class and coalition, the possibility of renaming victims as survivors, the therapeutic value of dialogue for the oppressed, and the idea that countless powerful stories exist outside of high culture, waiting for recovery.

> Now, I work in a milieu where people talk about poverty; people talk about what it's like, and basically where I work everybody is poor, and the people I know are poor, and there is a commonality and there's a solidarity around it. When I grew up poor, I grew up isolated. No one talked about their poverty. There was such a stigma attached to it ... I had never talked about the incredible things that had happened to me, and incredible things had happened to me. You know, my mother had died, I had been a sexual abuse survivor and I had had a horrendous, really tragic life. Like something out of Charles Dickens. Even when I think about it now, it really blows me away. I lived in virtual isolation, I didn't talk to people, I didn't trust people, I was very sick. Very emotionally sick. ('Diana,' quoted by Baxter, 216–18)

Once again, it is interesting how concrete experience is brought into tension with powerful, melodramatic forms of representation when this speaker, like many poor subjects, cites the power of Dickens's fictional versions of poverty to authenticate her own experiences or to speak for her. These confessional or testimonial excerpts communicate an insider's knowledge of poverty and also bring to light some of the subjective concerns of the poor, some of the 'private woes' which may be strategically transformed into 'public issues' through the socially therapeutic process of dialogue (Freire 1970; Torjman).

1.2 Populist Motives

At this point, it is important to situate the literature I am fictioning and my own motives for doing so among the various populist traditions of recovery and oppositional reading strategies which inform it: feminist criticism, cultural studies, Marxist criticism, the sociology of literature, and postcolonial criticism. Although I have borrowed Belsey's notion of 'fictioning' a literature for political purposes, there are significant differences between the present study because of its populist goals and Belsey's project, which is highly theoretical in nature. These differences are not idiosyncratic but indicative of different schools of critics reading for political purposes. For instance, Belsey's notion of ideology is Althusserian and thus presupposes the 'misrepresentation' of subjects by ideology and the task of the intellectual to expose or somehow stand outside the mechanism of misrepresentation through analysis (in Belsey's case, a combination of deconstruction, new historicism, and discourse analysis). My own positioned reading is quite different in respect to the concept of 'misrepresentation' in that I do not see the academic as standing outside or above ideology through analysis but rather as participating in it by the very act of using academic discourse to explicate texts and voices as objects of study and subjects of marginalized accounts. Furthermore, like many critics reading for political purposes, I do not use 'ideology' exclusively in a negative sense, meaning only misrepresentation. It is possible to see ourselves, as academics and teachers, accepting that we cannot somehow stand outside the phenomenon of 'misrepresentation.' If we accept our implication in ideology making and the subjective construction of a discourse on poverty, we can call on our own positions of coalition with marginalized groups to inform theoretical practice. We can valorize the subjectivities of marginalized Others and our own classed subjectivities as important (though not privileged) forms of knowledge which can inform critical choices and help to decode cultural meanings. Instead of attempting to abstract ourselves from our own social realities in order to pursue an unattainable objectivity or scientism, we can examine our standpoints and become conscious of how they contribute to our own constructions of poverty.

Another major difference between Belsey's notion of fictioning a literature and the fictioning of poverty narratives here is the emphasis on inclusiveness and common culture. This creates an initial lack of order in the category, a lack which is, I realize, a disturbing aspect for some. For example, a reader of an early draft was sympathetic with the Marxist goals of reading inscriptions of poverty, class, and gender in terms of ideology and power, but the thought of opening the category to ordinary and popular as well as literary utterances made no sense at all to him and, furthermore, he asked if we should not all be 'deafened by the noise.' I think that his comment showed, besides a Leavisite conservatism about literary value, a wariness of being without the skills and reading practices to make sense of such disparate versions and styles, and this is a wariness often heard in response to canonical challenges. But anxiety about inundation by non-literary voices from outside our field of expertise is not one I share; on the contrary, a wider source of narratives beyond high culture seems immediately more intellectually, politically, and aesthetically stimulating to me than the usual, relatively restricted academic fare, perhaps because of my strong identification with many of the excluded voices. As a woman and as someone who grew up on welfare and much later learned that this meant being among the 'lumpenproletariat,' I share the 'outsider' perspective often articulated in these narratives. And I recognize many of the everyday details and struggles that form the texture of these stories. Moreover, when these voices are politically and culturally oppositional, I often find beauty and hope in that opposition. Ultimately, I think, anxiety about inundation or contamination depends upon one's position as a reader in terms of assumptions about high and low culture and one's need as an academic to control the chaos of information outside traditional fields of expertise. Some of us anticipate new meaning outside the walls of high culture, and we do not fear the loss of control that that implies.

Populist motives in the context of this study mean that ordinary people's thoughts are valued as much as those of artists and academics, but I do attempt to make every effort to distinguish between individual responses to poverty and 'the people's' response. As Jim McGuigan has explored in *Cultural Populism* (1992), the populist approach to culture usually implies a struggle against dominant culture, and one in which 'the people' are interpellated: 'Whoever gets to speak on behalf of "the people" against the current construction of "the power bloc" is winning the game' (16).[1] With reference to theories of populism by Brecht, Laclau and Mouffe, Bakhtin, Hall, Fiske, and many others, McGuigan examines numerous critiques and credos of populism within cultural studies, only to conclude that its time has not simply passed. Instead, new, more complex paradigms need to be sought, according to McGuigan, to revive the oppositional, the economic, and the material in present-day cultural critique, especially in the context of the hegemony of the postmodern. Although populism is one motive for constructing a cross-class, cross-genre category of poverty narratives, its articulation here is not as highly theorized as it could be. None the less, a reluctance to use 'the people' or 'the poor' in an unproblematized way does save this genre of populism from nostalgia or naïve idealism. It is not until the conclusion, 'Taking a Position,' however, that I examine specific populist paradigms of a 'common culture' by Williams and Eagleton in order to lay bare certain cultural values behind the present recovery project and to propose imaginative alternatives to cultural élitism in literary studies. Up until that point, I rely largely on the narratives themselves to posit paradigms of culture which position the poor as outside of or included in the national culture.

Many poverty narratives testify to the texture and feeling of cultural exclusion. Granted, it is possible to understand exclusion through cultural theories such as that of Pierre Bourdieu on the exclusion of the working class in higher education through the institutional reproduction of class stratification and that of Jacques Dubois on the literary institution's exclusion of minority literatures as a means of legitimating itself. But poor women's own utterances and the fictional representations of their experiences also produce valuable knowledge about the impact of social boundaries on cultural access. Poverty narratives often express frustration that the means of cultural production are somehow out of reach for poor and working-class women and in the hands of others. For example, *The Invisible Women of Washington*, a recent but little-known realistic novel on poor women in the United States by Canadian writer Diana Collier, thematizes cultural exclusion by showing how the

---

1 In chapter 8, 'The Long View: Contexts of Oppositional Criticism,' I discuss cultural studies as a site of opposition and the limits of academic discourse to invoke 'the people' in an unmediated way. I also discuss in chapter 4, 'Theories and Anti-Theory,' how populism has contributed to feminist criticism by fuelling our interest in ordinary voices as a site of radical knowledge.

experience of poverty may be distorted by cultural representations which issue primarily from the dominant class. A camera crew barges into an inner-city women's rooming-house, wishing to film typical scenes of poverty. They falsely and uncaringly manipulate those women who fit a popular image of the poor – an old black woman lying with her Bible against her chest – and reject those who do not – the protagonist, Abby-Jean, a robust young woman from the ranks of the rural poor. Abby-Jean scrutinizes the crew at work behind the scenes and the falseness not only of the face which they are trying to construct for the poor, but also of the face which they themselves show in relating insincerely to the poor (151–9). This exposure of falsified cultural production is doubly ironic in the context of an earlier dialogue in which the rooming-house tenants chat and dream about escaping poverty by becoming artists. Trying to imagine plots based on their lives, however, they realize how unlikely it would be to publish stories about women like themselves – a temporary office worker, a janitor, a security guard, a mother – due to exclusionary practices in the market: 'if it didn't have money or sex, it wouldn't be interesting to Them, and They were the ones who decided' (72). A similar dialogue appears in Irene Baird's *Waste Heritage*, where unemployed men in the Depression, including a writer recording the story of their protest marches, reflect on the problem of marketing stories about the disenfranchised. Ironically, both novels have been somewhat buried in obscurity, as the market and perhaps the national literature itself suppress stories of need and resistance within wealthy nations, as though these subjects and subjectivities are simply not worth cultural reflection.[2]

When we do manage to read beyond exclusion and retrieve lesser-known poverty narratives, the power of these multi-voiced narratives to humanize statistics and to broaden public awareness about poverty may be seen variously as a threat, a deliverance, an inconsequential matter, or an object of beauty – depending on both our angle of vision

---

2 How do we account, then, for the popularity and marketability of some poverty narratives, say by Frank McCourt (*Angela's Ashes*, *'Tis*) and Carolyn Chute (*The Beans of Egypt Maine* and *Letourneau's Used Auto Parts*)? Indeed, we should interrogate the relation between popular success and the ideology of the works. Works that reinscribe dominant notions of 'trailer trash' and the 'undeserving poor' tend to gain more power in the marketplace than stories about poor subjects who are angry or indignant. In Canada, for example, note that David Adams Richards's work fails to achieve popular success despite critical acclaim, perhaps largely because his poor subjects indict the system.

and the narrative point of view. For example, Sheila Baxter's intention to collect oral histories and avoid tokenism in *No Way to Live: Poor Women Speak Out* entails the following challenge to the reader's aesthetics: 'This material is not entertaining. It's not meant to be. Some of it is repetitive, but poverty is boring and repetitive. You may find yourself getting bored as you read this book, bored with the sameness of the women's problems and the solutions they suggest. Take that bored feeling, multiply it a million times, and you will begin to get a sense of how boring it is to be forcibly poor' (13). If we take up Baxter's challenge, we enter the book in good faith by releasing the aesthetic expectations normally applied to 'literature' and by concentrating, instead, on the socially therapeutic possibilities of these testimonies. However, there is also the possibility of radical or oppositional aesthetics which finds resistance and anger a relief, if not a pleasure, to read.

A similar aesthetic challenge is indirectly posited by Makeda Silvera in the introduction to her oral history *Silenced: Talks with Working-class Caribbean Women about Their Lives and Struggles as Domestic Workers in Canada*. Silvera attempts to draw fresh perspectives from the reader by insisting on the importance of the women's free-flowing language with all its 'cultural nuances and innuendoes': 'This is an act of empowerment, particularly for these women who work as live-in domestics and for the most part have not been able to speak in their own language on a daily basis but have had to speak in another "language" to communicate with their employer.' Silvera sees her mandate as one of empowerment rather than merely research – 'My task is not merely to observe and record but to facilitate the entry into public scrutiny of those who must be the makers of their own history rather than merely the subjects of the recorders of history' (vii–ix). If we grant these voices their own aesthetic power, intertextual meaning, and cultural memory, then we can valorize them in juxtaposition with more elaborately polished, literary works. Radical aesthetics may valorize testimonies of identity, history, and community as much as or even more than stylistic excellence. Recovering marginal stories is an act of cultural intervention in which aesthetic, epistemological, and political judgments are complexly intertwined.

Conversely, the exclusion of testimonies and standpoints based on ordinary lived experiences of poverty leaves us with a partial, top-down, largely negative view of the poor, grounded in popular beliefs rather than heterogeneous subjectivities. In *Women and Poverty*, Mary Daly identifies as popular social fictions such widely held beliefs as the following: that 'there is no real poverty ... today compared with the 1930s and 40s, [that] no one needs to be poor now with social welfare, and [that] people are poor through some fault or failing of their own' (6–7). One of the most challenging aspects of reading poverty narratives is identifying how they navigate beyond or through these social fictions. For example, British cultural critic Roger Bromley has identified how social fictions and popular tastes shape the narrative strategies of working-class autobiographies. In *Lost Narratives: Popular Fictions, Politics and Recent History,* Bromley discusses how popular autobiographies about working-class women especially tend to dehistoricize and iconize poverty, resulting in cultural amnesia and life stories that are emptied of class-consciousness. It is not that ordinary poor people can know the truth about their experiences while literature, bourgeois culture, and popular fictions cannot, but rather that all of these representations interact in complex ways which often reflect lived power relations. It seems logical, then, to take into account the voices and subjectivities of those who live poverty as well as those who merely etch it.

1.3 Cultural Critique as Social Therapy

As critics and teachers, we can help empower the lesser-known versions of poverty by drawing them into public view and out of obscurity, by locating them culturally among the 'noisy' polyphony of diverse representations, by formulating and teaching oppositional reading strategies which will illuminate or at least help us to reflect on the meaning of these disempowered versions, and by interrogating canonical works, popular works, and recovered voices on the issue of power and cultural reproduction.

There is a significant difference in strategy and methodology between those critics who make their object of study the idea, the image, the discourse, or the material causes of poverty in the text and those who resist making poverty a pure, abstract, or fixed object of study and try, instead, to understand the voices of the poor as subjects of their own stories, producers of knowledge, and agents of political change. I recently sat through two days of an international academic conference on the subject of writing poverty and was stunned by the intellectuals' unwitting complicity in the politics of erasure.[3] Analysts

---

3 This conference produced a volume titled *Ecrire la pauvreté,* edited by Michel Biron and Pierre Popovic.

dissected sentence fragments to locate the genealogy and chains of reference which constructed the place of poverty discursively but confined their views to canonized literary works and social documents such as newspapers. With the exception of a very few, the papers I heard over two days unanimously agreed with the point that poverty could not be represented, or at least not narrated (this without considering any autobiographies or oral histories by the poor), and that the clothing of the poor could be read as transparent, meaning transparent markers of their status (this without considering what clothing meant to the people in it rather than the distanced observer – for example, as protection from the cold, as a commodity with a price, or as a symbolic means of signalling or masking poverty). The speakers also agreed that utterances on poverty were tied to the seventeenth-century liberal construction of the good and bad poor (this without considering oppositional accounts or protests by the poor which contest these liberal or literary discourses and construct themselves otherwise). Few challenges were made to these academics' use of 'the poor' as an oversimplified, monolithic term unrelated to geopolitical realities, to their lack of research on the historically and socially specific lived experiences of poverty in local contexts, or to their exclusion of the voices of the poor – in short, to the type of micro-research from the top down that produces a form of myopia towards the poor. I do not mean to suggest that the exchange of research was without value; to the contrary, it produced a rare and provocative volume on the textual inscription of poverty that is a welcome addition to the small body of scholarship on poverty and literature. My argument is with the politics, not the scholarship, of research whose very frame is complicit in a politics of erasure which keeps the poor outside the field of academic perception except as an object of study and abstraction. When we reverse this exclusionary policy, it becomes clear that the voices which have escaped academic attention are often voices quite capable of challenging academic views of the world epistemologically and certainly ideologically, and voices which are also capable of generating their own oppositional forms of discourse and radical knowledge. I return to the discussion of the limits and radical potential of academic discourse in the construction of the poor in the final chapter of this book, but at this point I would like to probe further how social critique, academic or otherwise, may perform a socially therapeutic function.

When poverty is minutely constructed as an object of study in the sphere of academic discourse across various fields such as anthropology, history, literary studies, and the social and political sciences, there are significant choices to make with respect to challenging existing paradigms of power or remaining complicit with them. David L. Harvey and Michael Reed's highly informative systematic method of assessing academic paradigms of poverty reveals how their formal properties reflect an implicit ideological content. Their goal is to 'construct a theoretical space that maps the metatheoretical contours which structure current poverty debates' (270). One of their observations is that academic debate is usually limited to 'hegemonically approved paradigms' which define poverty as a 'distributive problem' whose solution lies with improving the life chances for the 'deserving' poor, but that radical paradigms which question the system of market distribution are rarely employed as frames of analysis (293). In other words, radical paradigms are consigned to the periphery of debate where they are 'mined' for information about class relations and causes of poverty. I think this explains why reading much of the positivist, sociological, and anthropological material on poverty is such a frustrating experience for a culturally oppositional critic, because it is often fundamentally hegemonic. Another source of frustration, of course, is that traditional class theory and modern applications of it tend to exclude or devalue the special type of oppression lived by the poor. Ruth L. Smith remarked on this aspect of the academic erasure of poverty when she wrote that, along with other disciplines such as social history and philosophy, Marxist theory itself tends to marginalize the poor as a result of its inner logic: 'The association of poverty with nature persists even in critiques of liberal society. As Marx and Engels developed their insight, they increasingly distinguished the industrial working class from the lumpenproletariat who were outside production relations and so outside even the possibility of class conflict and consciousness, false or true' (218).

For a populist critic, assembling voices as a project of cultural recovery is an engaged form of retrieval and of exploration which 'fictions' not only a literature but also an oppositional community. For example, Janet Zandy stresses the role of the reader/listener in helping to create a sense of political possibility which is intimately tied to the concept of a community of concrete subjects who are oppressed in symbolic as well as material ways:

> The process of retrieval and remembrance is crucial for this sense of possibility. Writers who have access to a public audience serve as witnesses or

mediators for those who have been silenced or denied opportunities for self-expression. Oral history as political activity and as literary expression is an important element of this writing. Whether the teller is a hillbilly woman or a meat-packer or a senior citizen, the final literary 'product' is not just one of individual achievement but of a collaborative effort where the literary skills of the listener are joined with the memories of the teller. (Zandy 1990, 11)

In Zandy's moving introduction to a collection of poor and working-class voices, she has not suggested the most appropriate methodology of reading these voices, but has described a position from which to read, a position which never obscures the fact that the 'literary antecedents' of working-class writing, especially working-class women's writing, 'come from material existence rather than canonized literature' (ibid.). To combat a politics of erasure, then, Zandy is not theorizing a methodology which analyses the problematic relation between the text and lived experience but is working from a critical position which refuses to diminish the value of these voices as cultural capital, a position which recognizes and remembers the social context of these voices as muted cultures. The focus on stories, memories, and subjectivities specific to this community of women is a collaborative rather than an individual method of reading and, as Zandy and others have stressed, it is as much about imagining a future, a politics of possibility, as it is about remembering a past – hence our claim for its socially therapeutic power.

The inclusion of marginalized voices as one way to fiction a literature legitimates itself through expanded epistemic claims which bolster coalition politics. Very briefly, I will discuss two of these emergent epistemic challenges to traditionally academic ways of knowing: (1) oppositional theories of literary testimony, and (2) feminist theories of marginal standpoint. These days, the practice of recovering and reading narratives by muted groups as a form of testimony rarely entails positing these testimonies as the ultimate truthful account of a historical situation. Rather, contemporary views of testimony claim to recover suppressed truths or fragments which are now able to surface and challenge the dominant versions of one totalizing truth, usually by representing alternative versions of history, especially from the standpoint of the oppressed. These theories of recovering narratives as testimony are informed by more innovative methods and more complex ideas about meaning and representation than such practices implied under early forms of documentarism, oral histories, and authentic realism. As Gustav Klaus attests in *The Literature of Labour*, early practices of documentarism in Britain sought, rather naïvely, but with good radical intentions, to transcribe as many details as possible from everyday culture in order to mirror reality and thus capture it. For some, this meant sitting for weeks in a local pub and transcribing (in the days before the tape-recorder) as much dialogue as possible. In the current postrepresentational age, however, we are more conscious of producing knowledge as we recover voices. Hence the following reflections on knowledge claims behind the project of social therapy.

1.4 Testimony and Radical Knowledge

Recently, the use of the term 'testimonial literature' has been applied mainly to narratives about extreme situations of violence, oppression, and silencing, such as those lived by Latin American activists, Holocaust survivors, incest survivors, and war victims. It is the extreme invisibility/inaudibility/incomprehensibility of the historical or political events which seem to invite the metaphor of testimony, and it is the context of silence and injustice which gives power to these versions to bring into question assumptions about truth. Furthermore, versions of events, especially of unjust and violent events, which articulate the subjectivities of the disempowered place dominant versions on trial, denying them exclusive credibility. As John Beverly has observed in 'The Margin at the Center: On Testimonio': 'Each individual testimonio evokes an absent polyphony of other voices, other possible lives and experiences' (16). Beverly is referring to his own carefully defined category of life testimonies, but similar concepts of the power of testimonial language to articulate the subject position of the disempowered have been applied to literary testimony by Shoshana Felman, who has argued that the project of illuminating testimony in literature does not necessarily require that one believe in an unmediated referentiality connecting narratives to life experiences.

In *Testimony: Crises of Witnessing in Literature, Psychoanalysis, and History*, Shoshana Felman and Dori Laub have explored possible relations between oral testimonies about life experiences and literature about the Holocaust. Felman, a literary critic and teacher, has taught literature and oral interviews side by side in literature courses at Yale, and Laub, a psychoanalyst who witnesses testimony of Holocaust victims for the Yale Archive, has contemplated the therapeutic function of narration/testimony in the lives of individual victims and in the lives of cultures and communities. Both women conclude that the horror of testimony and the extreme responsibility to bear witness mitigate against historically objective accounts. Laub observes that 'the horror of the historical experience is maintained in the testimony only as an elusive memory that feels as if it no longer resembles any reality. The horror is, indeed, compelling not only in its reality, but even more so, in its flagrant distortion and subversion of reality' (76).

I do not mean to suggest that the horror of testimonials to poverty would be as intense as the horror of accounts of genocide or torture in other forms of testimonial literature, although sometimes this would certainly be the case. What seems relevant to a reading of poverty narratives is that the testimony is not necessarily objectively, realistically, or historically rendered precisely because there is such a difficulty of testifying, beyond silence, sometimes to unspeakable and incomprehensible acts of violence. Thus Felman observes that testimony of trauma as a form of literary utterance will sometimes not even attempt to represent reality transparently but instead will often claim to seek reality and discover in its place a crisis of language surrounding the inexpressible nature of its own substance. She writes: 'To seek reality through language "with one's very being," to seek in language what the language had precisely to pass through, is thus to make of one's own "shelterlessness" – of the openness and the accessibility of one's own wounds – an unexpected and unprecedented means of accessing reality, the radical condition for a wrenching exploration of the testimonial function, and the testimonial power, of the language ...' (28–9). The testimonial power of language, as identified in its literary, psychoanalytical, and historical application, is too complex to explore adequately here; but I would like to focus on one central concept because it might illuminate the present study. Felman and Laub explain that the therapeutic power of testimonial utterance exists largely in its capacity to externalize a story, to 'undo its entrapment' and 'articulate and transmit the story, literally transfer it to another outside oneself and take it back again, inside' (69), thus making it known more profoundly to its own teller. Not only does testimonial language demand a listener, it also derives its power from the fact that it reaches other witnesses who form an alliance around its perceived truths. In a literary sense, textual testimony discovers this alignment of witnesses in a reading community; it accordingly 'adds yet another witness' and becomes linked to other texts, to readers, and to history itself. Thus, Felman explains, 'life-testimony is not simply a testimony to a private life, but a point of conflation between text and life, a textual testimony which can penetrate us like an actual life' (2). For those who can align themselves, politically and empathically, with the truths, the subjectivities, and even the crises of language in testimonies, the impression created is that experience and history itself become more accessible. On the other hand, the mark of a truly oppressive power, as Dori Laub asserts about the Nazi system, is to convince its victims, 'the potential witnesses from the inside,' that what was said about 'their otherness and their inhumanity was correct and that their experiences were no longer communicable even to themselves ...' (82). The reverse of historical access is the result: 'This loss of capacity to be a witness to oneself and thus to witness from the inside is perhaps the true meaning of annihilation, for when one's history is abolished, one's identity ceases to exist as well' (82).

Felman and Laub's explanation of the therapeutic power of testimony extends beyond the individual to the community, not only of the oppressed, but to the community as a whole in the sense that speaking beyond silence means speaking for a fuller sense of history and against systems of oppression. Thus the question of how representative one speaker can be among many becomes another self-reflexive issue which theories of testimony must consider. The issue of representativeness leads to re-examinations of knowledge claims based on insiders' knowledge and of one voice speaking for many – in other words, of the way we authorize speakers from the margin. Also, in this new concern for literary testimony, we can see the blurring of the boundary which once divided anthropology, history, psychoanalysis, and popular culture from literature, evidenced not only in the expanded object of study but also in the observer's attitude to that object, her epistemological claims to 'know' the object, and her concern for adapting ways of reading to political strategy. It is likely, therefore, that the practices of reading testimonies as literature and vice versa need to be shaped by developments in the theory of witnessing across other academic fields (for example, Clifford Geertz's and James Clifford's critiques of participant-observer traditions) and by the changing exigencies of political strategy.

For populist critics, then, the shaping of new categories and the exploration of new reading practices are greatly influenced by the invocation of the knowledge, identities, and subjectivities of marginalized subjects as members of a 'community' of readers and writers/

speakers. There is a constant danger of essentializing, totalizing, or idealizing this oppositional community in the process of invoking it – hence the necessity of bringing the goals of collaboration and opposition to view as a public critical task rather than one situated only in a privileged, private reading of the texts. The 'fictioning' of a community for political purposes, as well as that of a literature, is really a public gesture towards engaging in socially therapeutic action with that community, either by helping to build a sense of reading community, by revisioning history through literature, by expanding the curriculum and questions asked about texts as an exercise in radical pedagogy, or simply by making public what has previously been confined to the private or the muted. However, for poor and once-poor and working-class women, as for many marginal subjects, such projects are difficult because they are ground breaking: they lack authoritative critical precedents, an identifiable audience with shared beliefs within the academy, and established research about poor and working-class women and their own reading practices.

A second type of epistemic challenge, one which expands not only the object of study but also the way we relate to it, is the feminist formulation of standpoint theory. Currently, standpoint theorists in feminist philosophy and sociology are building the epistemological justification for feminist researchers to step outside of a restrictive institutional discourse to assert, indeed to begin to perceive, the everyday complexity of women's lives. Theorists such as Dorothy E. Smith, Alison Jaggar and Susan Bordo, and Sandra Harding, for example, are arguing for, among other reforms, the inclusion of empirical knowledge and subjective and personal knowledge in the conceptualization and methods of academic analysis. Such epistemological adjustments are necessary across the disciplines, they argue, in order to make visible the lived realities of women which have been previously eclipsed by male-biased academic modes of perception. For example, Alison Jaggar has noted that the 'myth of the dispassionate investigator' 'functions to bolster the epistemic authority of the currently dominant groups' and to discredit the observations and claims of subordinate groups – 'The more forcefully and vehemently the latter groups express their observations and claims, the more emotional they appear and so the more easily they are discredited. The alleged epistemic authority of the dominant groups then justifies their political authority' (158).

Thus the exclusion of emotions from self-professed objective study has traditionally meant the exclusion and undermining of marginal or 'outlaw' emotions and the cloaking of dominant emotions in objective garb. In isolation, Jaggar suggests, the validity of outlaw emotions is doubted: 'When certain emotions are shared or valued by others, however, the basis exists for a subculture defined by perceptions, norms, and values that systematically oppose the prevailing perceptions, norms, and values. By constituting the basis for such a subculture, outlaw emotions may be politically because epistemologically subversive' (160). To counter the historic devaluation of 'outlaw' emotions, Jaggar encourages us to make them public, to privilege perspectives from the standpoint of the oppressed (of course, not without question), to make these emotions themselves the subject of critical inquiry, and to establish a continuous 'feedback loop between our emotional constitution and our theorizing' (163). Jaggar is careful to caution that critical reflection on emotion is not a substitute for political analysis and political action but is itself a sort of political theory and action which is 'indispensable for social theory and social transformation' (164).

By making the category of poverty narratives an object of critical inquiry, we would include in academic discourse as 'outlaw emotions' the subjectivities of poor and once-poor women as both readers and writers of cultural inscriptions of poverty. As part of the theory of oppositional reading practice and an alternative mode of critical discourse, we also need to understand the subjectivities of poor and once-poor women as readers as well as tellers of narratives, because readers as well as writers have been part of the culturally excluded community of the poor. In a number of poverty narratives, working-class women are portrayed reading and reacting to a literature which excludes or includes them, but we also need self-reflexively positioned readings to become a part of public and academic discourse. This is not to suggest that academic distortion will be righted through subjectivity alone – for, as Jaggar has stated, 'Emotions are neither more basic than observation, reason, or action in building theory, nor are they secondary to them. Each of these human faculties reflects an aspect of human knowing inseparable from the other aspects' (165). But in order to create the 'feedback loop' between theory and emotion, as described by Jaggar, feminist scholars should be prepared to describe the therapeutic potential of women's poverty narratives by implicating themselves emotionally. Thus it is especially important to hear of the reading experiences of academic women who are poor or once-poor, just as we hear from black women and Native women, for example, on the subject of texts written by their own communities or on the subject of being a racial

'Other' in white society. We need to authorize ourselves and others to speak emotionally about poverty and to claim a sense of solidarity with the poor. Although the poor are rarely seen as a 'people' ripe for revolutionary consciousness or even as a group proud to lay claim to collective identity, we can, nevertheless, valorize the testimonies of poor and once-poor women as alternative forms of knowledge and significant ways of knowing the women and the society that marginalizes them.

Experiential and subjective knowledge of poverty will mean most when complemented by political analyses, social history, positivist research, and critical skills. The project of fictioning a literature of poverty narratives, like many other recovery and revisioning projects, is a reaction to the phenomenon of cultural exclusion of marginal subjects and what that implies about the construction of cultural knowledge. In Canadian cultural criticism in English there have been no surveys of working-class writing or writing by the poor, few surveys of leftist and materialist criticism, and no full-length studies of the theme of poverty. The sociological and semiotic approaches more common to the study of French-Canadian literature have produced a greater consciousness of class issues on the whole (for example, see works by Purdy, Shek, Popovic, Guilbert, and many others). Although canon questioning has increased in English-Canadian literary studies, theories of counter-culture, cultural production, and social power are seldom employed to question the canon on its representation of classed subjects as opposed to those of minority racial and ethnic groups, regions, gender, or sexual orientation. In Robert Lecker's anthology, *Canadian Canons: Essays in Literary Value*, to name just one example, the only sustained discussion of *class* refers to how professors of Canadian literature are still second-class citizens in English departments. Lucie Robert's *L'institution littéraire au Québéc* considers the formation of a national literature in the context of cultural theories such as Bourdieu's and Dubois's, but more as an epistemological and historical challenge to the canon than as social critique. There are exceptions, of course. In the more recent anthologies of criticism, such as *New Contexts of Canadian Criticism* by Ajay Heble and colleagues, the newness of vision is once again characterized largely by concern for race and gender, but with an emergent radical reflection on class issues in Canada. What we seem to have produced surprisingly little of in either French or English Canada is engaged criticism of literature which takes into account economic and social inequality based on poverty and class. I will return to the paucity of class analysis in the appendix under the heading 'Transgressing the National Canon.'

Before leaving the subject of radical knowledge, I would like to attempt to explain my own complex relation to poverty and a community of the poor. Although I admire the oppositional voices of theorists and critics who have inserted their own class or racial subjectivities within their academic discourse (for example, Barbara Christian, bell hooks, Richard Hoggart, Raymond Williams, Arun Mukherjee, Himani Bannerjee, and Carolyn Steedman – to name just a few), I have not been able to find a voice to bring together my academic knowledge and the empirical and subjective knowledge from a childhood in poverty. I do not know the reason for this, whether it is fear of being ridiculed, or perhaps because there was almost total silence and isolation around the issue of poverty as I experienced it in a small town in northern Ontario. Whatever the reason, I have not found an appropriately 'outlaw' voice in which to refer strategically to my own memories of poverty or to assert my coalition subjectively. Also, my positioned reading is affected by the fact that I was a lecturer at university at the time I wrote this study and no longer poor. Currently, I am a professor and live with a highly skilled, working-class man. Nor is my family any longer poor, for my sisters and brothers have all moved up the social scale through jobs or marriage, and none of them would ever consider themselves 'working class.' In fact, I am sometimes afraid that the community of opposition which I imagine is one of ghosts from my past more than of the people living poverty today, since I have grown so far from that community.

When I was a child at school in a small town, the children from poor families were more often than not relegated to 'slow' groups where they were treated as objects of scorn and sometimes real physical violence by teachers. I myself was put into the slow group when I was seven and taken out only when there were visitors to the classroom (inspectors, other teachers, parents, et cetera). The following year, with a different teacher, I ranked first in the entire class, with no change in performance. This made me suspicious of school and teachers from the outset. I watched very closely to see when students from poor families were treated differently. In the same year, a classmate was regularly belted across her bare legs and arms with a leather strap at the slightest error: for instance, for faltering when she read, for turning a faulty faucet too far, for forgetting her homework. She cried so often and for so long that her eyes were permanently bloodshot. When I saw where her family lived, in a rickety trailer perched on the side of a gully, I feared for myself and all the poor children in the class because I had suddenly comprehended that we were all vulnerable to the teachers' whims because poor parents could not protect us in the same way that the other parents could. I was and still am haunted by the look of utter terror in my classmate's eyes, by my powerlessness to stop the unfairness, and by my guilt at escaping the worst punishments because I did well at schoolwork. My younger brother's cries from strappings also tormented me as I listened from an adjoining class, powerless to help, and trying to hold back the hot tears of powerlessness. Poor kids without parents fared even worse. A boy from a foster home was chased through a field for running away and dragged back to school to be strapped fifty times on each hand by the school principal. The boy's brother, also in foster care, was forced to help give chase and to hold the younger one down for the strapping. I followed them back to the school as they dragged the boy along the road. But I stopped outside the door, listening to his screams, afraid to be strapped myself, yet ashamed once again of my cowardice. Such violence was never directed at the children from wealthy farmers' or merchants' homes. Watching these and other more subtle versions of poor children's victimization, I was powerless to intervene but promised myself someday to expose the unfairness, the blindness, and the ignorance – in short, to bear witness. Well, I have not been able to bear witness as I promised and have trouble reducing these home truths to anecdotes; but I have since decided that there may be a more strategic task at hand for me. That is, to find a way to make other testimonies public and to question what these stories mean in relation to what we value from generation to generation as cultural heritage. When we celebrate local memories and identity through national culture, where are these stories of poverty and how do they figure in collective memory? For me this is what it was like growing up in Canada, and I recognize in poverty narratives by Maria Campbell, Hugh Garner, Margaret Laurence, David Adams Richards, Laura Goodman Salverson, and many others, the symbolic and social violence that a wealthy nation visits upon the poor of many races and ethnic groups. But the fact remains that my own relation to this study is problematic. No matter how sophisticated my theoretical methods of fictioning a literature become, for me this project has more to do with telling the truth than with fiction.

Chapter 2

Visits and Homecomings

Given that English-Canadian criticism has been preoccupied for decades with the primacy of place as a cultural determinant, sustained explorations of the place of the poor and the working class in Canadian literature are long overdue. Northrop Frye's provocative question: 'Where is here?' largely overshadowed concern for social differences and set us on the road, instead, to discovering idealist nationalist constructions which posited a more or less homogeneous collective imagination made coherent through its relation to nature, nation, or region. In this chapter I would like to disturb such liberal notions of cultural inclusiveness and nationalist notions of collective, imaginative experiences of place by raising the issue of an inside/outside paradigm which positions poverty and the poor beyond the bounds of civil society. Also, I will go outside the traditional, anglo-majority construction of Canada by probing a French Canadian's perspective on poverty and identity. The writers whose works I will discuss, Susanna Moodie, Nellie McClung, and Gabrielle Roy, have little in common – not their generation, not their style of writing, not their class background, not even the language in which they wrote – only the fact that they made quite detailed statements, as professional authors, about their projects to visit poverty through narration or to write their way back home to that place. Where applicable, I look beyond these individually stated strategies to ask how such author/subject positions might be partly fashioned by the writers' social, historical, or ideological position(s), especially in respect to inside/outside paradigms of poverty in social discourses of their time.

These writers' projects to narrate poverty come together in their representation of poverty as an imaginative space which is somehow inhabitable through narration or reading. Despite their differences, their stated intentions are explicitly tied to beliefs that either the experience of poverty or the poor themselves may be transformed directly or indirectly through the socially and personally therapeutic process of narration and reading. However, the psychosocial space of the poor is quite different in each, depending on the author's respective class identification and ideology; poverty appears variously as a dark immoral space to descend into, a state to rise above, or a daily reality to survive. Thus it may be relevant to interpret to what extent the speakers/narrators are looking or speaking from the outside in or from the inside out in respect to their own configurations of social boundaries. But the *inside* of their own social paradigms will rarely be stable; they may be defined by a number of configurations or sites of poverty: a class of people, an experience, a sensibility, a poor woman's body, a house, a home, a social curse, a neighbourhood, a memory, and so on. The goal of indicating subject positions in respect to these narrative configurations of poverty would not be to know the authors' class identification or to judge the relative authenticity of their various accounts, but to consider how different positionings of poverty assist in the construction of meaning around that place in the narrative and how these different constructions of meaning may ultimately be related to issues of social power, empowerment, and resistance.

Before studying particular constructions of poverty in these narratives, however, I would like to review briefly Ruth L. Smith's philosophical reflections on the subject. Her article 'Order and Disorder: The Naturalization of Poverty,' which appeared a few years ago in *Cultural Critique*, argued that the logic excluding the poor from civilized society is masked as natural in liberal humanist discourse and that, consequently, the first task in exposing the conceptual practices 'through which we pigeonhole the poor, denying their subjectivity and denying our complicity in ideology-making' is to expose and deconstruct this paradigm (210). Smith exposes the highly rationalized contradictions of a liberal discourse which may express concern for the poor (women and children, in particular) but which actually maintains societal boundaries based on class status and also on gender. She observes that liberal discourse maintains a seemingly 'natural' boundary between the poor and civilized society through three main clusters of images: first, images which construct market society and the concepts of autonomy, rights, and individualism as *good, orderly nature* while exiling poverty and need to an outside position as *bad, disorderly nature*. This dualistic notion of two natures, inherited from seventeenth- and eighteenth-century world-views (Baudrillard), takes attention away from poverty as a social construction and projects the inherent disorder and deficiency of market society – in that it is unable to provide all its members with the rights and subsistence it promises – onto those who are designated as naturally outside. Second, images of naturally disorderly bodies create a strong link between women and the poor via symbolization. And third, welfare systems in late capitalism have provided images which institutionalize 'disorder' into symbolic order by bureaucratizing and naturalizing the poor into monolithic order and making boundary maintenance more transparent – in other words, by regulating the poor.

Thus, a long genealogy of assumptions in current liberal discourse explains why similar associations (about inside/outside, order/disorder, good nature/bad nature, civil society/women and the poor) recur in poverty narratives from different periods. On the other hand, in more concrete terms, it is necessary to remember that imaginative models of exclusion which recur in discourse are acted upon as practices of power in everyday life, so that the deconstruction of an inside/outside paradigm – for example, linking women and the poor to the outside – is not merely a cerebral game but actually can tell us something about how lives and identities are lived out on the margins. As Smith observes: 'To be on the margins is to be both inside and outside. These positions are fluid and unstable, resisting the boundary definitions that the liberal view assigns. But the fact that marginality involves inside as well as outside, that it defies its peripheral location, should not mask the fact that, as Sidel notes, to be poor is in many ways to be outside of a society that isolates the poor' (Smith with reference to Ruth Sidel, *Women and Children Last* [9] 213).

2.1 Susanna Moodie: Poverty and Vice

In her essay 'A Word for the Novel Writers,' appearing in *The Literary Garland* (August 1851), Susanna Moodie encouraged novel writers and readers alike to step imaginatively into scenes of poverty in order to 'acknowledge their kindred humanity' (61, 60). Although noting that readers were apt to be 'insulted or offended at being seen in such bad company,' Moodie as author/critic was defending the novel as a genre and was advocating that the novelist's moral mission was to emulate the 'realism' of Dickens and Sue in order to lead readers into 'dirty hovels' and 'neglected abodes,' to expose the 'wretched lives' of the poor and the criminal, whom she lumped easily together within her discourse of judgment (61). Realistic scenes would, she proposed, shock complacent readers into paying 'for the instruction of these poor creatures.' However, the images of the poor in her own essay are not so much realistic or shocking as they are predictably stylized and iconic: 'starving brothers and sisters,' 'beds of straw,' 'tattered garments,' 'famishing children sobbing around your knees for bread' (61) – which calls into question not only the humanitarian effect but also the liberal intent of these proposed literary visits to the poor. Carole Gerson has remarked that although Moodie's call for realism constituted the most radical departure of its time from the strongly romantic trends in Canadian novels, its radicalism was primarily aesthetic, advocating no social action stronger than 'a change of heart on the part of the rich' (1989, 31–2).

Obviously, the invitation to 'imagine' our way into the psychosocial space of the poor presupposes that readers are from outside that circle of experience – an assumption reinforced each time Moodie addresses her readers as 'you' and the poor as 'they.' Despite the title 'A Word for the Novel Writers,' most of the text is addressed to the readers. Interestingly, authors do not seem in as much need of moral reminders to be charitable, for Moodie accords them the place of highest moral good in the article, likening authors to voices from the pulpit, 'missionaries in the cause of humanity,' even associating them with '[o]ur Blessed Lord, himself,' as story-teller and teacher (60, 63). Thus it is 'we,' the readers, who will visit the poor under the moral direction of the author who maintains a distant, bird's-eye view, so to speak, from the pulpit. Moreover, two opposed discourses – one redeeming the poor and the other insulting them – find expression in one breath: 'Give them a knowledge of their unrecognized Christian duties and healthful employment, and these victims of over-population may yet prove beneficial members of that society by which they are only recognized as a blight and a curse' (61). One discourse (Malthusian) positions them naturally at an extreme place on the outside of civil society, likened to animals or disease, while the other (Christian) welcomes them within – conditional on the process of conversion. The rapid oscillation between these two positions has the effect, ultimately, of placing the poor at the mercy of the author's own rhetorical powers.

The imaginative distance to travel is itself stylized according to the conventions of the urban walking tour (at one point she admonishes us for hesitating upon the doorstep), fashionable among the bourgeoisie and writers in late-nineteenth-century Europe and America, to discover both the picturesque and the horrors of slums within cities. As described by Carrie Bramen in a paper given recently at the Popular Culture Association's annual meeting, the genre of the narrated walking tour aestheticized the poor in the form of the picturesque while, paradoxically, expressing repulsion at the physical proximity which shattered that picturesque image. Once again, the contradiction between this double discourse of moral distance and humanitarian proximity becomes blatant: Moodie denies any danger of moral contamination by realistic novels portraying the poor because of the irreducible qualitative distance between them and us: 'You need not fear contamination from the vice which they portray. It is depravity of too black a hue to have the least attraction ...' As her passionate invective controls and fixes the subject, the extreme dualistic imagery, paradoxically, eclipses the poor as the essay advocates bringing them into view: 'Vice may have her admirers, when she glitters in gold and scarlet, but when exposed in filth and nakedness, her most reckless devotees shrink back from her in disgust and horror. Vice, without her mask, is a spectacle too appalling for humanity ... and breathes of the corruption of hell' (62).

Poverty as feminized and dirty and licentious can be kept at a safe distance because it is naturally, as the worst imaginable evil, deserving of exclusion. The symbolic use of the female body to designate the worst evil suggests the author's need to distance herself, as a proper lady, from a gendered association with poverty and corrupt wealth, stigmatized places upon which she could then project the cumulative evils of the 'other.' As Cora Kaplan has noted, such projection was characteristic of eighteenth- and nineteenth-century constructions of gender: '"True womanhood" had to be protected from this threatened linguistic contamination, not only from the debased subjectivity and dangerous sexuality of the lower-class prostitute, but from all other similarly inscribed subordinate subjectivities' (360). In addition to the contradictions of a liberal discourse on the poor which haunted Moodie's text, then, there were also the contradictions naturalized by patriarchal ideology. Moodie's attempt to resolve these tensions imaginatively resulted, rather predictably, in exaggerated claims of privilege, virtue, cleanliness, and subdued language and movement, or, in other words, what Mary Poovey has termed 'the shadow of the proper lady' cast across her text (x–xiv).

A year after Moodie's essay on realism was printed, her collected travel sketches appeared as *Roughing It in the Bush: Or Forest Life in Canada*. Here again she portrayed the poor in a judgmental light, recounting how she and her husband were forced into closer contact with the 'squabbling crowd' on entering the New World (on board ship and while detained on Grosse-Ile for quarantine purposes [27]). When Moodie herself is embodied in the autobiographical text, located on the brink of the New World, in the institutional holding place of Grosse-Ile where possible infection is to be surveilled and controlled, the poor and the ethnic (Scottish and Irish), and especially the women, appear to her as fundamentally different and uncontainable, 'infected' not only by disease but by 'insubordination and misrule' (25). Clara Thomas and Carole Gerson have both commented, in the context of biographical criticism, that Moodie's assertion of distance from the working class, domestics in particular, seems to have been all the stronger as a result of the shock of declassing inherent in the immigrant experience combined with the reduced circumstances of Moodie and her husband (a pensioned officer) which left them, in Moodie's own words, among 'the well-educated sons and daughters of old but impoverished families' (xv).

The Grosse-Ile scene has come under increased scrutiny recently in Canadian criticism, most notably by John Thurston and Robert Kroetsch, largely because of Moodie's style of reporting the temporary dissolution of social boundaries experienced on arrival in the New World. Thurston remarks on Moodie's subject position in this sketch in regard to genre; ultimately, he explains, she failed to keep the people around her at a distance or to have her Old World, monologic voice assert itself over the dialogism of the New World voices (200). Thurston maintains that the class-mixed experiences and 'dialogic force of the discourse' which Moodie encountered in Canada 'could not be contained by any generic framework,' and so she tried to capture all, 'with little sense of form,' in her life-writing (202–3).

I would add that the parallel between uncontainable voices and forces of utter disorder in this scene reasserts the inadmissible *nature* of these voices and reinscribes social exclusion under the guise of realistic inclusion. Moodie naturalizes exclusion when she constructs the poor and ethnic as outside good and orderly behaviour and associates them with uncontrolled sexual appetite and bad hygiene, a crowd mentality versus an individual one, and a profane and incomprehensible noise instead of civilized language – for example, 'the confusion of Babel ... all talkers and no hearers ... uncouth dialect ... incomprehensible to the uninitiated ... as insolent and *noisy* as the rest ... out of sight, but, alas, not out of hearing of the *noisy*, riotous crowd' (emphasis added, 25). Her implication that disorderly behaviour and licentiousness were *worse among the women in the group* also expresses as natural both patriarchal and bourgeois ideologies which have so often associated the poor with women and wild, unruly nature (27). As Smith points out '[w]omen and the poor are on the outside, not as a result of external order and rule but as a result of their own nature, their bodily nature ... Within the logic of this ideology, the "natural" extends into the interior of the person, erasing essential signs of order, control, and rule ...' (222). According to Moodie's descriptions of the women, their class was so naturally different that it was reflected in their physical appearance: 'I shrank, with feelings almost akin to fear, from the hard-featured, sunburnt women as they elbowed rudely past me' (25).

Despite the din of alien voices and unruly behaviour, however, Moodie reports having tried 'several' times to tell members of the lower orders what she perceived their position should and would be in the New World. Note, again, how she designates 'girls' as being particularly at fault and out of control, especially on the issue of projected employment:

> I was not a little amused at the extravagant expectations entertained by some of our steerage passengers. The sight of the Canadian shores had changed them into persons of great consequence. The poorest and worst-dressed, the least-deserving and the most repulsive in mind and morals exhibited most disgusting traits of self-importance. Vanity and presumption seemed to possess them altogether ... Girls, who were scarcely able to wash a floor decently, talked of service with contempt ... To endeavour to undeceive them was a useless and ungracious task. After having tried it with several without success, I left it to time and bitter experience to restore them to their sober senses. (31)

This unfair targeting of working-class women is in striking contradiction to the humanitarian concerns Moodie expressed in 'A Word for the Novel Writers' for female workers in England as 'a most deserving and oppressed portion of the population,' whose plight had been exposed by Thomas Hood in 'Song of a Shirt,' and rectified, Moodie claimed, in the attainment of 'liberal employment' on arriving in Canada. But Moodie attributed the working-class crowd's exacerbated rowdiness on Grosse-Ile to their belief in vain promises of opportunity and class mobility in a pioneering society. By virtue of a blatant double standard, she tried to dispel the belief in class mobility in the lower orders while empathizing completely with those wishes in 'persons of respectable connections' (xv). Ironically, however, the remainder of her travelogue shows that 'time and bitter experience' will instruct *her* rather than them, that the boundaries of one's proper *place* are very slippery in a pioneering society where manual labour frequently means survival and where settlers are frequently declassed to some extent. Moodie ultimately acknowledged the greater suitability of workers and labourers over members of her more genteel class to the rigours of Canadian settlement, but she would, nevertheless, generally recoil at any lessening that might cause in the qualitative distance between her own class and her underlings (Thomas 50, 58, 62, and Gerson 1985, 41–2). The narration of the proper 'place' of the poor in realistic fiction, which Moodie advocated in 'A Word to the Novel Writers' might, therefore, succeed, where life-writing could not, by allowing the bourgeois author's voice to penetrate and dominate the space of the lower orders voyeuristically and moralistically yet ward off any possible contamination caused by actually hearing or touching them.

2.2 Nellie McClung: Social Gospel Rescue

More than eight decades later, in 1935, a very different social reform advocate, writer, and feminist activist, Nellie McClung, also confirmed the role of realism in depicting the lives of the poor. McClung's doctrine, however, seems to have been based on an understanding that prior representations of the lives of the poor, especially the rural poor, had been largely excluded from or distorted by high culture. As a remedy, she praised Dickensian 'realism' – but not, as Moodie had, to effect change by educating the privileged classes; rather, McClung implied that literature should make room for the voices of the poor to encourage and inspire the poor themselves as readers. The following artistic creed is from her autobiography, *Clearing in the West*. It exposes the discontinuities between pastoral poetry and McClung's own lived experience of rural life and helps to explain why she will choose to be a writer of popular novels. Importantly, she indicates her intention to circumvent the gap between high culture and everyday life by writing from a different imaginative location:

> But there were times when I wondered how happy the mower and the

milkmaid and the plowman really were, interesting and romantic as they were to the poet, when he was out for his walk and knew he was going home to a warm fire and an easy chair and a good meal which some one had cooked for him. What did he know about them any way? Quite likely the milkmaid had chapped hands and the shepherd chilblains and stone bruises according to the season. And all of them were probably underpaid and over-worked and lived lives of chill stagnation.

When I wrote I would write of the people who do the work of the world and I would write it from their side of the fence, and not from the external angle of the casual visitor who likes to believe that the poor are always happy. (226)

McClung is committing herself to an author position which she locates *inside* rather than outside the sphere of workers and the poor. She claims entry to their world via her choice of subject and style (the popular novel), claiming special knowledge of hardship and shared concerns with the people in this community. Herself a member of an upwardly mobile pioneer family, she had experienced poverty, but very briefly. This brief contact with poverty would become a pattern which was to be reflected in her fiction, where poverty appears framed by an ideology of hard work and the rewards of entrepreneurship and as a step towards something better in this world or the next. Her stylistic choices seem also to have been influenced by a rural educational background which had been fitful and inadequate in its early stages because of her family's material struggle as homesteaders. No one was more acutely aware of her position growing up outside high culture than McClung herself, for she recalls: 'The depth of my ignorance appalled me. I was bound, fettered, gagged in ignorance. What did I know of the world's great literature? My words were but the ordinary workworn words of everyday happenings ...' (281).

One of the few modern critics who has commented on the aesthetic pleasure of McClung's choice of subject and use of rural diction has done so in the context of a reader's guide rather than in the context of high criticism. John Moss, in *A Reader's Guide to the Canadian Novel*, expresses an appreciation for the texture of the experiences and language which McClung represents, noting, however, that her fictional works, now all out of print, are still far outside the institution of Canadian 'literature' (185–7). McClung's best-selling fictional works have been pushed outside the margins of Canadian literature partly because they interpellate readers who are rural, poor, and feminist and are regarded as popular rather than high culture. However, it seems dismissive, or at least reductionist, of critics in *The Literary History of Canada* to state that McClung's 'writing was directed by a necessity for telling the truth, by a moral zeal, and by a strong Christian purpose; she had little use for *any other* artistic standards' (Roper et al., emphasis added, I: 345). Her artistic standards were populist rather than élitist. Her texts were targeted for accessibility, the flavour of her idiom was both rural and feminized, the register of her language would appeal to those who valued plain speaking rather than ornate or elevated language, her feminist heroines struggled successfully against sexual exploitation and economic insecurity, and her plots often functioned as inspirational trajectory for the poor and workers who were ordinarily excluded from high culture. Nevertheless, the fact that she wrote popular art does not guarantee a specific class content, class identification, or oppositional ideology in terms of class, for as Stuart Hall has explained, popular culture is not a site where socialist culture emerges full-blown, but rather a site of struggle between different versions *for* and *against* the culture of the powerful (as quoted in Dentith and Dodd 7).

Such a struggle is evident in McClung's novel *Painted Fires* (1925), whose first sentence – 'It all began with the rustle of silk' – represents a New World promise of social mobility as it was heard by a young Finnish girl. When her aunt visited from the New World and wore a silk skirt which 'seemed to raise the whole family to a higher social level' (7), Helmi decided to follow her path and emigrate in the hopes of making a better living as a domestic and cook. The cycle of work and sexual exploitation which the novel subsequently unfolds exposes the 'rustle of silk' as a false cue in that it has promised a quiet, ladylike, genteel, and almost leisurely ascent to economic security. The duplicity of this and other traps for a young girl alone in a new country is reinforced by frequent allusions to the image of painted fires in the title. Selfish or bigoted individuals (usually from higher classes or public office – a magistrate, a landlady, and the vain and idle doctor's wife whose opium habit places Helmi in trouble with the law) victimize the 'Finn girl,' turning her faithful service, innocence, and penchant for self-improvement against her. Left to face imprisonment, hunger, and homelessness alone, a pregnant Helmi at one point collapses on someone's doorstep. She gives birth on Christmas day surrounded, in Dickensian fashion, by a family of urban poor whose children are both pathetic and precious. Also in Dickensian fashion, she will, in the end, be reunited with her long-lost husband and become heir to property.

All along the way, the author consistently rallies a formidable combination of forces to her heroine's defence – Helmi's own hard work, simple virtue, and strength of character; the help of public-spirited women's and girls' clubs; male and female benefactors; and even divine intervention in the form of a few well-aimed lightning bolts.

Truth-telling, in this novel, is framed by unrealistic melodrama which ultimately depicts power on the side of the downtrodden *if they will persist in their individual struggles and moral righteousness*. The ideological strategy here coincides with McClung's often romantically stated intention to narrate poverty as a source of inspiration (*Clearing* 281) because she sought to uplift the poor, the women in particular, leading them away from their assigned place *on the outside* to greater prosperity on the inside by presenting exemplary models of behaviour which conform to the work ethic and a sense of feminist collectivity. But the naïveté of a world-view in which a congenial universe rights systemic wrongs through unseen forces of good seems, on the surface at least, to run contrary to McClung's stated intention to write realistically and not 'from the external angle of the casual visitor who likes to believe that the poor are always happy.' However, glossed images and improbable plot twists appear as the only possible respite to the darker naturalistic current in the novel, given the author's refusal to occupy a position advocating class struggle.

Although her indictment of systemic wrongs was astute, McClung would not advocate collective social action to reform the capitalist system, not even union action, neither in her fiction nor in her political career. Historian Veronica Strong-Boag has explained in the introduction to McClung's essays, *In Times like These*, that as feminist activist and middle-class suffragist, McClung was actually, despite her feminist views, very distant from the concerns of women workers. Strong-Boag suggests that the author's agrarian bias and middle-class outlook made it impossible for her to portray urban poverty and industrial problems realistically, even though these concerns had led her into politics (xv). In the second chapter of *Painted Fires* there is a cameo appearance of another Finnish domestic worker, Anna, who is jailed for throwing a stone at a policeman during a pro-union rally. Later, law officers will confuse Helmi with Anna, but the reader will not; her presence early in the novel allows McClung to dissociate her heroine and her narrative voice from collective class struggle as a legitimate source of power. (McClung seems to be rewriting history here, for in reality Finnish women in Canada were particularly resourceful in organizing domestic workers' unions and were active in the Communist Party [Prentice et al. 196, 222, 261, 278]). The narrator comments acridly that Anna feels that the 'golden age' of class equality has arrived in jail because she will no longer have to serve breakfast and make beds. The narrator then explicitly links ill-defined socialist goals with other deceptions and misleading paths in Helmi's life by calling them Anna's 'own little painted fire,' in which 'she had not yet found out that there was no heat' (22). Thus, Helmi must be constructed otherwise, through an *individual* struggle for social mobility, her collective spirit being roused not by her class but by other women, especially the girls in the social club and, later, those in the detention centre.

The novel reinforces what an older domestic worker says early in the novel: 'Any girl that will wash dishes and scrub can always find a place, and if she's civil and clean and honest she'll get on' (18). Here the myth of meritocracy is expounded to buoy the heroine up above the distress and despair of poverty. The dream that sustains her tireless domestic labour is to be accepted on the inside, to build her own house and to possess 'the swell suits' and 'the wristwatch' which signify for Helmi the stenographer's status as the new, urban working woman (139). Her sight is so fixed on work and self-improvement that she flees poverty rather than inhabiting it. She never actually mixes with her own class of people for more than brief moments. Presented as an isolated and exemplary protagonist, Helmi fulfils, in many senses, the ideological function of 'representativeness' which Roger Bromley has criticized in his study of popular fictions and autobiographies about working-class women in inter-war Britain: 'They were ... mobilized out of their class not *for* it ... They are published for their *representativeness*, or rather, for the way in which they are constructed within a particular ideology of a representative experience – enterprising, talented, self-educating, resourceful individuals' (40). Thus Helmi may be described as a 'class traveller,' who, according to Bromley's analysis of preferred cultural representations, 'stands on her own two feet' with the aid of 'commonsensical notions of self-help' (48). This interpretation of the novel's class ideology suggests that, although McClung may have crossed the fence, so to speak, to represent workers and poverty from the inside, she occupies that author position just long enough to rescue her heroine from it.

McClung's choice of a white, European, immigrant woman as protagonist for the narrative of individual mobility facilitates the conversion to good order on the inside of civil society by passing over the problematics of ethnicity and race which figured prominently in McClung's own politics. The western-Canadian, Anglo-Saxon suffrage movement, of which McClung was perhaps the most prominent figure, advocated social purity, which included eugenics and selective immigration policies, and discouraged participation by minority ethnic and working-class women (Prentice et al. 185, 193). Thus McClung's novel challenges the inside/outside paradigm in the least radical way possible in terms of class – fundamental changes or extreme effort on the part of one poor (white) individual will make her orderly enough to be admitted into the centre, which implies that similar fundamental changes in the nature of the poor as a class would eradicate poverty altogether and restore us all to order.

2.3 Gabrielle Roy: Everyday Struggle as Resistance

The more radical challenge according to Smith's discussion of order and disorder comes when the concept of society itself is expanded to include the poor. This expanded view of society entails exposure of the contradiction between the realities of market society, with its unequal distribution of goods, and the unrealistic, liberal promises it makes of equal opportunity and rights. In terms of representation of the poor, it means that exposure of the justifiable needs of the poor and the denial of those needs will in turn expose the contradictions and disorder of market society which have been projected onto the outside position as its own inherent natural disorder. Consequently, stories of the poor which function as testimony to the everyday experiences of the poor on the outside may displace the more flattened images of the poor which are fixed by liberal discourse. As I explained earlier, I use the concept of literary testimony rather loosely and metaphorically here, but in a culturally oppositional sense like that suggested by Shoshana Felman and Dori Laub in *Testimony: Crises of Witnessing in Literature, Psychoanalysis, and History*: 'The specific task of the literary testimony is, in other words, to open up in that belated witness, which the reader now historically becomes, the imaginative capability of perceiving history – what is happening to others – in one's own body, with the power of sight (of insight) usually afforded only by one's own immediate physical involvement' (108).

Stories of everyday lives thus have the power to challenge the inside/outside dichotomy in a fundamental way. Gabrielle Roy's *Bonheur d'occasion*, for example, stands in obvious contrast to brief literary visits and rescue missions to the world of the poor, as do other notable poverty narratives which inscribe the daily lives of poor individuals and the logic of their needs (for example, Hugh Garner's *Cabbagetown*, Adele Wiseman's *Crackpot*, Laura Goodman Salverson's *Confessions of an Immigrant's Daughter*, Maria Campbell's *Halfbreed*, and Phyllis Knight and Rolf Knight's *A Very Ordinary Life*, to name but a few). In his remarkable reading, 'On the Outside Looking In: The Political Economy of Everyday Life in Gabrielle Roy's *Bonheur d'occasion*,' Anthony Purdy claims that Roy's novel goes even farther than Orwell's *The Road to Wigan Pier* to denounce the dehumanizing effects of consumer capitalism by showing the economy's regulation of everyday details at the root of all human relations. In a wonderfully lucid discussion too complex to summarize adequately here, Purdy describes the novel's representation of social boundaries based on two conflicting economies: one of the actual need of the poor and the other of the regulated desire of affluent, consumer society. 'No human emotion or bond,' he writes of the novel, 'is proof against the all-pervasive influence of money' (49). Rather than a narrowly economist reading focused on the public sphere, Purdy interprets economy and social exclusion based on economy as a determinant of identity and social relations. Purdy and Patricia Smart are among the few critics of *Bonheur d'occasion* who probe the reciprocal relation between class and gender.

It is curious, however, that Purdy situates Roy as author/witness on the outside looking in at working-class experience (merely because she does not insert herself as observer/first-person narrator in the text and is no longer poor at the time of writing), rather than accepting her own autobiographical positioning in that psychosocial space as a form of homecoming. If two sets of factors are taken into account, it seems to me more appropriate to accept Roy's own positioning of herself as one who narrates poverty from inside rather than outside the place of exclusion: first, the special significance of the motif of homecoming and private space in respect to women's gendered experience of poverty, and second, the idea that psychosocial spaces may be chosen and occupied imaginatively and politically rather than merely by virtue of essence (class origins or actual class status). Rather than offer a rereading of the novel based on such a positioning, I would like to explore just a few of the cultural and textual implications of that positioning.

In *La Détresse et l'enchantement*, Roy recalls that in choosing the impoverished neighborhood of St Henri as the location for her first novel, she was reaching towards a sense of home[1] closely associated with poverty, which seemed to have its own compelling story to tell:

> Ce quartier où, à peine un an plus tard, j'allais délibérément revenir écouter, observer, en pressentant qu'il me devenait le décor et un peu la matière d'un roman, me retenait déjà, ce soir d'avril, d'un curieux voyage, ses odeurs n'étaient pas seuls à me fasciner. Sa pauvreté m'émouvait. Sa poésie m'atteignait avec ses airs de guitare ou de musiquette un peu plaintive s'échappant de sous les portes closes et le son du vent errant dans les couloirs d'entrepôts. Je me sentais moins seule ici que dans la foule et les brillantes rues de la ville. (503)

Although romantic strains are present in her representation (for example, in guitar music and wind in warehouse passageways [503]), poverty moved her in more than simply romantic or nostalgic ways. She identifies it as a world-view: both site (*décor*) and substance (*matière*) of her story and a vantage point from which the world can be viewed more clearly, not from a fixed position but from that of the wanderer: 'il est mieux de ne rien posséder si l'on veut du moins bien voir le monde

---

1 The concept of cultural home has a political dimension in respect to linguistic and ethnic communities which I do not explore fully in this study. The passage above describes Roy, a Franco-Manitoban returning to Canada from Europe and relocating in Montreal, Quebec – a homecoming in the sense of rejoining her French roots in the largest Franco-Canadian city. Yet, Roy chooses St Henri, a bilingual slum area, as a site more closely associated with home than the rest of the city. In this case, poverty seems to override ethnic roots in Roy's imaginative construction of home. In the novel, however, the poor quarter is constructed as French rather than bilingual, a conflation of Franco-Canadian culture with poverty which I discuss later in this chapter.

The assumption that Roy's solidarity with the poor came from her own impoverished background needs to be examined in terms of François Ricard's unflattering portrait of her as a spoiled and demanding child from a prominent family in St Boniface. In *Gabrielle Roy: A Life*, which came out after this manuscript had gone to press, Ricard portrays Roy as someone who scarcely tasted of poverty but deserted her mother and handicapped sister when they began to experience hardship. The family became downwardly mobile when Roy's father lost his job. The process of impoverishment continued when the mother was widowed. Although the truth of a life cannot be fully known, it would be an interesting future project to compare the constructions of self and poverty as they appear quite differently in the two accounts of Roy's life: Ricard's and Roy's. For my purposes here, however, the reading of homecoming described is more an empathic and ideological position adopted in the text than a biographical claim.

que nous traversons en passant' (503). Roy implies that the poor quarter will return her to a sense of belonging which is a necessary element of seeing, not only that place, but *the world*, clearly. This expansive world-view requires that we imagine ourselves looking at the world from the outside, the slum, which we are now inside.

Roy's formulation of poverty and home as a sharpened awareness of social boundaries recalls bell hooks's invocation of her own lived experience of growing up poor and black in a southern town in the United States in *Feminist Theory: From Margin to Center*. Hooks testifies to the heightened symbolic significance of boundaries in the minds and lives of those who are excluded from mainstream society, sometimes even physically, by law and economic constraints: 'We looked both from the outside in and from the inside out. We focussed our attention on the center as well as the margin. We understood both. This mode of seeing reminded us of the existence of a whole universe, a main body made up of both margin and center. Our survival depended on an ongoing public awareness of the separation between margin and center and an ongoing private acknowledgement that we were a necessary, vital part of that whole' (Preface i). The transgressive world-view, unknown to most of their oppressors, was a source of strength to impoverished black women and men because it helped them struggle against despair by strengthening their sense of identity and solidarity – for one of the most significant forms of power held by the weak, according to hooks, is 'the refusal to accept the definition of oneself put forward by the powerful' (90).

The motif of homecoming may be useful to describe a contestatory reinscription of poverty not only because many of the authors of such narratives are writing their way back to poverty as an experience from their past and a way of knowing the world, but also because it draws out the special relationship between gender and poverty as excluded areas. Christine Delphy has argued in *Close to Home: A Materialist Analysis of Women's Oppression* that home is the appropriate place to begin critiquing Marxist formulations of classed identity in terms of gender because it is the site of most of our commonsensical notions about women and unpaid labour in the domestic sphere of production and thus the site where we can draw knowledge about women's special relation to class. By expanding the importance of home and the female body in *Bonheur d'occasion*, Roy has necessarily diminished the span of traditional social realism to a focus on the smaller realm of women's private sphere. But it is here where gender is as important a determinant of destiny as poverty in that the two activate each other. For example, Rose-Anna seems to testify to this through her body itself and her pain when she is about to give birth for the twelfth time and renounces her hope for a girl, for girls will suffer poverty more (323). Moreover, as Patricia Smart has discussed at length in *Writing in the Father's House: The Emergence of the Feminine in the Quebec Literary Tradition* (first published as *Ecrire dans la maison du père*), woman's body is a site of unpaid reproductive labour for the church, a role both accepted and resisted through the novel when female author and characters speak out beyond that silenced space and gendered definition in French-Canadian culture. The detailed life scenes of mother/daughter bonding depicted in the context of material struggle are not as transcendent as sometimes argued (P.G. Lewis), but testify to the paradoxical fact of women's position of weakness and strength, defined by and redefining poverty. Poor women buttress their families against poverty in a world where their nurturing identity becomes the last collective resource for survival. When patriarchal society fails to house and feed the poor and when men flee responsibility or are devoured by the war machine, the story of daily struggle and survival falls to the women to tell.

Smart has theorized that the primary polarization and conflict in the novel is that between mothering and the war machine (160). In formalistic terms this is true, but mothering and poverty meet at more points of tension. As they construct each other they are twisted into a macabre union under the pressure of the social system. Rose-Anna cannot sew clothing fast enough to keep all her children attending school, nor feed them well enough to stave off hunger and illness, nor secure them from the trauma and motion sickness of constant evictions and moves, nor comfort her dying son as well as a paid care-giver in an impersonal institution, nor, like her own mother who bore fifteen children, can she even give gestures of affection freely. As martyr, Rose-Anna constructs her family's experience of poverty by taking it *inside* herself, as far as possible, and transforming its ugliness, its shamefully diseased and grotesque *outsider* nature in a mothering gesture: 'Elle silencieuse, songeait que la pauvreté est comme un mal qu'on endort en soi et qui ne donne pas trop de douleur, à condition de ne point trop bouger. On s'y habitue, on finit par ne plus y prendre garde tant qu'on reste avec elle tapie dans l'obscurité; mais qu'on s'avise de la sortir au grand jour, et on s'effraie d'elle, on la voie enfin, si sordide qu'on hésite à l'exposer au soleil' (153). Rose-Anna's greatest power against poverty, however, is not her martyrdom in internalizing the family's pain, hiding it from public view, but rather the small 'ignoble' acts which follow her throughout the novel: the sewing, the washing, the budgeting, the nagging, the questioning, the house-hunting, the waiting. Through these gestures and this work, the material struggle with poverty is inscribed as a fact of the quotidian and an exhausting struggle for physical survival within a disorder clearly not of her own making.

Janet Zandy has developed the concept of homecoming and an inside/outside cultural paradigm to situate working-class women's utterances as both outside dominant culture and inside their own sphere of experience, class knowledge, and sense of class solidarity. The 'inside' of working-class experience is accessible, Zandy claims, through knowledge made possible through lived experience, empathy, or political commitment, rather than through essence (such as class origins), making the imaginative trick of affirming marginality as home one which is a question not just of identity politics but rather of a sense of political coalition, particularly among women who would otherwise remain isolated and silenced in their private homes. 'Home,' she writes, 'is an idea: an inner geography where the ache to belong finally quits, where there is no sense of "otherness," where there is at last community' (1990, i).

I would like to suggest that Roy's novel be read as a strategy of homecoming in this respect. In her autobiography, Roy stated that she began writing as a strategy to survive poverty. She recalled what it felt like to narrate poverty as one who was living it and drew a strong parallel between her own literary writing and the 'incomparable little stories' which her mother had told them as children to relieve the pain of poverty. Thus the novelist names her mother/storyteller as her antecedent, describing both their art forms as firmly grounded in lived experiences and aimed at similarly therapeutic ends:

> Je ne l'ai jamais vue sortir de la maison, ne serait-ce que pour aller au potager cueillir des légumes pour la soupe et, en passant, parler à la voisine par-dessus la clôture, sans revenir avec quelque petite 'histoire' à raconter, chaque détail à sa place et la place importante accordée à ce qui importait et qui était une surprise toujours. Si bien que nous guettions son retour, à peine était-elle partie, assurés qu'elle allait nous rapporter une fine observation très drôle et très vraie, mais d'avance il était impossible de deviner ce que ce serait. Au fond, chaque pas hors de la maison était pour elle une sorte de voyage qui aiguisait sa perception de la vie et des choses. Elle a été la Schéhérazade qui a charmé notre longue captivité dans la pauvreté. Et, maintenant que j'y repense, je crois que j'étais alors un peu comme elle: un jour accablée par le sentiment que jamais nous ne

pourrions nous extraire de nos dettes à présent empilées jusqu'au cou, et, un jour plus tard, marchant comme sur des nuages parce que, travaillant au grenier, sous ma plume était venue une phrase qui me paraissait contenir lueur de ce que je cherchais à dire. Miracle! L'expression de la douleur vengerait-elle de la douleur? Ou de dire un peu ce qu'est la vie nous réconcilierait-il avec la vie? (*Détresse* 142–3)

Usually credited with having created the prototype of social realism in Canadian literature in French, Roy posits emotionally charged questions about the personal function of narration in the poor home. As these questions imply, she does not turn a distanced and objective eye towards the poor but depicts poverty as home and a place from within which to speak, albeit one towards which she as survivor and some of her characters feel great ambivalence and guilt (Bessette 283–4, Stratford 20, *Détresse* 242–3).

For example, in *All the Polarities: Comparative Studies in French and English*, Philip Stratford observes that the place of poverty in the narrative is one towards which most of the characters feel a great ambivalence, ranging from 'pity' to the 'desire to flee.' 'It is this duality that causes Jean to be both drawn to and repulsed by Florentine ... "She was his own poverty, his solitude, his sad childhood, his lonely youth. She was all that he had hated, all that he had left behind him, but also everything that remained intimately linked to him, the most profound part of his nature and the powerful spur of his destiny"' (Roy [205] as quoted by Stratford 20). Roy's inscription of poverty reads complexly as the reclamation and rejection of home in that it is about the profound sense of guilt and loss associated with escaping poverty while still identifying with the others who are left behind. Jean Lévesque's desire for escape is complexly told from inside the knowledge of both alliance and betrayal. When he hesitates on the threshold of the house he is leaving in St Henri, he remembers loving it because he and the house had struggled together as long-allied forces (30). Told from the outside and according to the logic of the market place, social mobility is often impersonally inscribed as a struggle which is proof of opportunity, self-improvement, and meritocracy of the individual, or merely good fortune. On the other hand, inside stories of mobility and escape, such as Roy recounts through the character of Jean Lévesque and in her own autobiography, accuse the system, as well as the individual, of the betrayal which class mobility entails. Inside stories may insist on the value of those who are thrown away or left behind, such as Florentine and Roy's own mother, and the guilt of the survivors who leave, but hesitate on the threshold of social boundaries seeing how they are caught between different worlds of opposing value.

The novel's strategy of cultural and emotional homecoming should also be read in the context of Franco-Canadian culture, a dimension which I do not explore here, but which intersects with the theme of poverty in that the two are often conflated. That the Franco-Canadian community was often imaginatively and historically constructed in poverty is reflected in Jean's perception of Florentine as a poor girl who represents her people, in Jean's guilt at leaving the quarter to pursue his individual career, in the geographical layout of the city where the rich English neighbourhood of Westmount dominates the city, and in the general form of the novel, which Purdy analyses so aptly, in which the lost agrarian past gives way to an urban economy where so many of the displaced rural French become exploited workers or soldiers in someone else's war.[2]

As many critics have noted, the novel's truth-telling capacity lies not in conventional social realism but in its innovative narrative technique. It is seldom overtly critical of social inequities from a distanced objective perspective and not at all contrived in form to accommodate social criticism. In *Social Realism in the French-Canadian Novel*, Ben-Zion Shek has discussed the possibility and evidence of censorship and self-censorship between the first and second editions, where explicit references to the *exploitation* of the poor were cut or replaced. He also notes that Roy, even in her most explicit references to exploitation, was not an advocate of socialist solutions (82–3). Thus the novel derives its credibility not from a standard form of documentary social realism or from sustained,

---

2 The conflation of the Québécois people with poverty is sometimes a strategy of cultural opposition against English domination, as, for example, in Pierre Vallières's frequent conflation of the proletariat and Québécois in *Les Negres blancs d'Amérique*. A similar conflation is embodied by Antonine Maillet's characterization of La Sagouine, the washerwoman and ex-prostitute who speaks out for both the poor and the Acadians when she invokes the people in her monologue. A conflation of poverty and the Canadian francophonie has also been used as cultural insult in expressions such as 'peasoupers' and 'Pepsi,' both identifying French Quebecers as poor people with a traditional diet of cheap food. Behind the conflation of poverty and the people of Quebec is a complex history of lived systemic oppression by the English and class exploitation among French Quebecers themselves, both of which would need to be explored in a more detailed historical recovery of Québécois and Franco-Canadian poverty narratives.

explicit social protest, but from the appearance of telling truths as people experience them – a narrative *tour de force* that Philip Stratford has referred to as a 'dramatic condensation' of life, achieved through a psychological rather than a documentary way of selecting detail and a contracted rather than a sweeping spatial range. Stratford notes that Québécois critics had to invent a special term to define Roy's narrative stance and special intimacy with her characters: 'Instead of invoking the historian-novelist's description as memory, they choose a more dramatic phrase and speak of Roy's technique as "description *en acte*," the emphasis falling on the dynamic activity of identification rather than on the static function of recall' (25). Here Stratford approaches Felman's concept of literary testimony with its emphasis on the 'imaginative capability of perceiving history' through identification.

In Roy's address to the Royal Society of Canada after the successful reception of her novel, she brings us on a walking tour of St Henri, representing it as a ghetto, but one of universal and enduring proportions: 'the same grey village within our great city, the village that is found in all the great cities of the world.' From this universal vantage point, without the sense of voyeurism or repugnance or distance which Moodie's turn-of-the-century walking tour entailed, Roy has us encounter, once again through a dynamic process of empathy and identification, the inner thoughts of her characters from *Bonheur d'occasion*, and the enduring nature of the social imperatives which constructed them. Poor women are again, as in the novel, singled out for their attachment to home and strong but isolated survival techniques. For example, Roy asks us to empathize with the trauma of Rose-Anna's homelessness as she walks these streets in order to 'see her whole,' a radical phenomenological experience whereby we walk together ('Return' 160): 'Walk, then, keep walking! Rose-Anna still belongs to those thousands of women in our city who are looking for a home. If they all came together in closed ranks, we might understand, or we might begin to fear their determination' (161). Ironically, a cultural home for marginalized women emerges through the contemplation of homelessness and a utopian vision of revolt. The sense of feminist and class-based coalition draws the reader and the writer, as well as the subject, into a circle of cultural inclusion which is not simply a sentimental encircling of the most excluded elements but rather one constructed through political insight into the related function of class and gender as mechanisms of cultural exclusion and a profound sense of social responsibility to see the world otherwise – more expansively.

Chapter 3

'We Live in a Rickety House': Social Boundaries and Poor Housing

Every interior expresses, in its own language, the present and even the past state of its occupants, bespeaking the elegant self-assurance of inherited wealth, the flashy arrogance of the nouveaux riches, the discreet shabbiness of the poor and the gilded shabbiness of 'poor relations' striving to live beyond their means; one thinks of the child in D.H. Lawrence's story 'The Rocking-Horse Winner' who hears throughout the house and even in his bedroom, full of expensive toys, an incessant whispering: 'There must be more money.' Experiences of this sort would be the material of a social psychoanalysis which set out to grasp the logic whereby the social relations objectified in things, and also, of course, in people, are insensibly internalized, taking their place in a lasting relation to the world and to others ...

Pierre Bourdieu, *Distinction: A Social Critique of the Judgement of Taste*, 77

Characters, like their authors, are often acutely aware that poor houses are an important part of the course of lives as well as metaphors for those lives. In Margaret Laurence's *The Diviners*, the complacent façade of middle-class houses reflects the blindness and detachment of class privilege. In spite of the fact that these big brick houses do not wish to see or be seen, Morag (as seer) reads them while riding through the *better* part of town on Christie's garbage wagon: 'The windows are the eyes, closed, and the blinds are the eyelids, all creamy, fringed with lacy lashes. Blinds make the houses to be blind' (37). Laurence's depiction of Morag reading middle-class complacency, like her depiction of Christie reading the townspeople through their garbage, locates the subjective experience of reading culture with economically marginalized subjects. Moreover, these characters do not read the culture of houses and waste whimsically but for survival in a class-divided society. As a young child, Morag reads Prin and Christie's house to comprehend where she has landed as an orphan, in a lower class than her late parents' home. Then as an adult, Morag reads the high-rise of her well-to-do professor husband as a step up the social scale, one that she sought and yet one that imprisons her through both class and gender expectations of what a middle-class housewife ought to be. In each case, reading houses is a survival tactic for the declassed subject and the poor subject who wants more than anything to move beyond poverty. More than just a literary device, reading houses as a sign of material standing is part of the lived experience of subjects who move in and out of poverty.

However, in spite of the fact that poor and working-class people often have an acute ability to read houses and culture from the hyper-vigilant standpoint of the powerless, literary criticism too often teaches us to read living space in high culture as mere setting or backdrop to lives which experience their struggles and desire on a higher level than the material. We are also willing to see the metaphorical meaning of 'blind' houses but not the subjective impact on a child's mind of passing from a house with neat blinds (a middle-class home) to one with frayed curtains (Prin's house).

Besides telling of inner conflicts of shame and attachment, estrangement and class identification, poverty narratives about the living space of the poor often tell violent stories of invasion or expulsion, in which physical boundaries are threatened but social boundaries prevail. Bourgeois living space, on the other hand, is less often disturbed by volatile plots of eviction, coldness, and insects, or doubling up with other families. The private living space of the poor is tightly constructed within the social boundaries imposed by public attitudes, laws, property rights, and 'good taste.' Some people in poor homes wish to act out their difference defiantly by signalling, flamboyantly and without shame, the eccentric taste of the outcast. But beyond such acts of appropriation and defiance is the more fundamental material struggle between the poor and the non-poor over a space in which to be. The following readings will explore the surprisingly short distance between homelessness and poor homes, and the significant distance between the tasteful homes of the well-to-do and the 'disorderly' homes of the poor. Reading the boundaries around homes and their interiors in terms of both material and psychosocial realities, I explore the way living spaces are inscribed in a nineteenth-century poem by

Alexander McLachlan, 'We Live in a Rickety House,' a canonized short story by Alice Munro, 'The Beggar Maid,' and a little-known contemporary story by Nancy Holmes called 'Bugs.'

The narrative strategies in these works both echo and subvert the hegemonic social boundaries they depict. For example, McLachlan's and Holmes's representations of living space subvert bourgeois order through irony and testimony, whereas Munro's hyperrealism and emotional detachment imitate the orderliness and control of the bourgeois houses in her narratives. In order to interpret how the living spaces of the poor are delineated by social boundaries, we need to read these spaces as both material and symbolic sites. We need to recognize the threat of homelessness and that of state institutions set up to enter the poor home and the family to bring the disorder of poverty under control. Whereas bourgeois culture can afford the luxury of interpreting living space according to choices based on the nuances of taste and refinement, the poor and the once-poor might have learned to be preoccupied with quite different aspects of living space – for example, its high price and regulation in a market they do not control, the need for shelter, and the entrapment of self in the visible markings of poverty. How many characters in Canadian poverty narratives are ashamed to walk home in sight of friends or colleagues because their poor homes will expose their origins and lack of status? What social function does this shame perform? How many make of their poor homes a refuge from market society, a place in which to resist by merely surviving and claiming a space to be?

Houses may be read as signs of class habitus, evidence of lifestyles based on ease or necessity. Theories of class habitus and the sociology of taste by the French cultural theorist Pierre Bourdieu are helpful in reading the language of rickety houses because they explain that the taste and arrangement of interiors are not innocent of ideology, but are sites where social structures and class differences are reproduced. This is a less economist and mechanistic notion of class identity than previous Marxist theory offered. Simply put, it bridges the gap between subjectivist and objectivist knowledge by suggesting that identities are not determined wholly by relations to the market or class position, but are educated into a complex and shifting class habitus marked by tastes and everyday practices of dressing, eating, leisure, and lifestyle which they then go on to reproduce. To balance this emphasis on domination and cultural reproduction with a theory of resistance, one can look to bell hooks's notion of 'homeplace' – as a site of possibility for radical knowledge in the domestic sphere. Hooks makes the very conditions of her intellectualizing contingent on the concrete reality and political power of homeplace in her own past, citing the generations of African-American working-class women in her life who made it possible for her to write. Furthermore, she redefines these struggles to reterritorialize houses as an alternative to textual resistance for women who often had no written discourse to explain their position in a hostile world. Hooks's genealogy of resistance underscores the fact that marginalized subjects must first survive poor houses in order to construct their own human narratives and minority theories. Other materialist feminists such as Christine Delphy, Carolyn Steedman, and Pamela Fox – to name only a few – have likewise opened us to broader notions of what constitutes class resistance for lives lived in the private sphere away from the possibilities of organized labour or collective class action.

Oppositional readers of poverty narratives will reach for an understanding of what poor houses mean in terms of material struggle – in other words, as sites of struggle over shelter, property, privacy, and independence in the lives of concrete subjects. Reading poor houses as sites of struggle should expose lived class differences which would otherwise be suppressed as private matters of taste in a culture which masks class divisions. For example, in David Adams Richards's *Road to the Stilt House*, the house emits a constant buzzing from hornets nested within the walls, reminding its inhabitants and the visiting welfare officer of the family's entrapment in poverty and the constant powerlessness and rage which divide them day by day. But the incessant buzzing of hornets also reminds the family of the thinness of their walls, the cold, their physical vulnerability, and the reason why poor people in a cold country may find themselves dependent on welfare for the sake of shelter and emotionally despondent because of this dependence. In Percy Janes's *House of Hate*, the exterior ugliness of the house seems always unaltered despite the mammoth home-improvement projects which the father forces on his sons. The unchanging ugliness parallels the lasting scars of the family's emotional wounds. But the beginning of the novel traces these deep wounds back to a string of life choices based on necessity rather than material ease: migration from Europe and generations of poverty, hunger, and hard, underpaid labour. In Janes's novel, the characters become entrapped by the poor home through incessant labour rather than despondency. Both novels testify to the immovable materiality of poor houses and how they *cause* powerlessness and rage in the lives of the characters as well as symbolizing those emotional states to readers.

The subjectivities of the poor often appear in high and popular culture through representations of their living spaces, probably because houses, like clothing, are strategic sites where public scrutiny and private identity meet, especially in the context of a consumer culture focused on the display of identity through acquisition. Subcultures in consumer societies, hyperconscious of the link between identity and acquisition, may appropriate outward icons and styles and transform them into coherent forms of self-expression and, sometimes, cultural opposition. As discussed by Dick Hebdige in his reading of the flamboyant dress style of street gangs in Britain and John Fiske in his reading of America's grand-scale conversion to denim, consumerism lends itself to appropriation. But houses are less malleable than clothing and more expensive to alter. Michael Harrington noted in *The Other America: Poverty in the United States* that the invisibility of poverty in North America was due in part to the affordability of clothing in late capitalism. The poor and the homeless could be relatively well dressed in sneakers and jeans, thus masking their lack of food and shelter.

A fuller knowledge of how to interpret poor houses in Canadian narratives would acknowledge how concrete subjects experience housing needs, but also, in terms of the genealogy of discursive conventions and social attitudes, a history of subjectivities linked to poor houses – for example, theories of the shame experienced by the poor, the stigma that is reproduced over generations, the evolving public discourses and shifting dominant ideas of poverty and how to control the living space of the poor (theories such as those by Chaim Waxman, Ruth Smith, and Gertrude Himmelfarb). These histories can suggest why earlier structures of feeling and ways of speaking about poverty still have great bearing on the ways in which poor houses are lived in and represented in contemporary times.

In two recent anthologies of essays entitled *Place and the Politics of Identity* and *Geographies of Resistance* (1993 and 1997), radical geographers Michael Keith and Steven Pile have attempted to spatialize politics as a response to the impasse and relativism of postmodern theories of a constantly liquid and floating subject. Keith and Pile signal their dissatisfaction with a recent trend towards spatial metaphors to describe academic work that rarely takes three-dimensional space and concrete subjects into account; metaphors such as 'position, location, situation, mapping ... centre-margin, open-closed, inside-outside, global-local ... the city,' and so on (1993, 1). Keith and Pile caution with reference to work by Soja that 'space (in general) has been misrecognized by contemporary social theory,' a misrecognition which has led to two extremes: seeing space as opaque or transparent – or, in other words, fixed, dead, and undialectical on the one hand, and dematerialized, abstracted, and folding 'into mental space' and 'away from materialized social realities on the other' (Soja 1989, 125; Keith and Pile 1993, 4). The antidote to these extreme views, they argue, is to keep in mind that subjects struggle both materially and symbolically with their allotted space and reproduce the politics of these spaces in both ways as well.

Although people who live in poor houses often experience public meaning as a force which bears down upon them or conspires against their right to private space and threatens them ultimately with repossession and homelessness, the literary interpretation of living space and homelessness has more often than not focused on symbolic rather than material meanings. One semiotic study which interprets the social significance of the homeless beggar or vagabond in oral tradition in Quebec culture, *Pauvre ou vagabond: Le quêteux et la société québécoise*, offers an excellent example of how semiotics may probe the social meaning of homelessness from above (by dematerializing it or treating it merely as discursive space), without including radical knowledge of how homelessness feels from below. This excellent study merits criticism for the limits of its vision only because of the context in which it occurs, the pervasive silence on the subject of poverty and literature in Canada. The authors, Lucille Guilbert and colleagues, have taken texts primarily transcribed from the oral tradition to illustrate how the sign of the beggar has been a popular site of struggle over religiously based values in Québécois culture. Historically, they argue, the character of the beggar in Québécois folk songs has inspired hospitality and private charity in the context of a spiritual test. Steeped in religious values, eighteenth- and nineteenth-century Québécois oral culture produced a prototypical beggar whose appearance at the door subsequently became a testing-ground for how good or miserly the homeowners were, in spite of the fact that the beggar simultaneously inspired fear and repugnance.

Ironically, *Pauvre ou vagabond* is a highly informative study in terms of tracing the genealogy of dominant discourses on poverty from Europe to la Nouvelle France and of social history in Quebec. None the less, it is also complicit, as academic discourse which collapses the place of the homeless into discursive spaces and symbols, by giving the homeless a place as a mere object of their literary study, with little or no discussion of the subjectivities of the homeless themselves or the impact of symbolic boundaries and material need on their actual lives (except in terms of their experience as subjects of the law). For example, it reads the vagabond abstractly as the 'anti-modèle' (3) against which societal norms are defined: 'le non-conformisme, la contre-culture ou peut-être tout simplement la liberté' (ii) – all social constructions which *do* exist and were played out in popular culture but not without impacting gravely on the poor themselves. Should we not also ask what the frequent symbolic inscription of homelessness as freedom means in the context of the lack of choices experienced by the forcibly poor? According to all reports I have read by street workers on the front line, those who choose homelessness are in the minority (Mettrick, Webber, Baxter, Murray). The semiotic study of the beggar in question is also complicit in naturalizing 'la *race* des quêteux' (emphasis added) as a social reality which will *never* disappear, but, as the Bible says, will always be with us. Should we not be wary that academic complicity in the construction of poverty-as-inevitable may, *ipso facto*, limit the possibility of cultural opposition which might contest these dominant social myths? Equally complicit in a distanced view of the poor and homeless as outsiders in *Pauvre ou vagabond* is the authors' romanticizing of the vagabond/beggar as representing both *all* of us and at the same time the prototype of the single, male, unemployed wanderer. Once again, these dominant social constructions are operative; but can we not, as oppositional readers, ask what it means to be the ones pinned to the wall by these generalizations and stereotypes, and if or how these lived experiences are different from the labels which pin people down this way? Culture-from-below may see the same symbols as culture-from-above, but they look different when seen from another angle. Rather than simply report or analyse dominant social constructions as such, the authors of *Pauvre ou vagabond* have embraced them as Québécois culture, neglecting to specify that these are hegemonic versions of culture within a classed society – the vagabond seen from the point of view of those who open the door and own the house, the poor at the door seen as an opportunity for homeowners to exercise morality. Thus, despite its focus on folk culture, *Pauvre ou vagabond*, like most studies of the *idea of poverty* in literature, is complicit in keeping marginal subjectivities and marginal discourses outside the field of perception; the parameters of inquiry into literary and social meaning are simply assumed to be those of a bourgeois vantage point of symbolic space characterized by ease and 'homefulness,' rather than those of poor homes marked by instability and necessity and the ultimate threat of lack of shelter. Behind the unspeakable disorder and vulnerability of poor homes and homelessness lies a further unsayable meaning; that is, that the institutions of market society have a long tradition of legislating intrusion into poor homes so that the disorder of poverty may be controlled and masked. In the name of charity, welfare, child custody laws, rental laws, and the earlier 'poor laws,' the materially privileged members of market society, sometimes armed with good intentions, have traditionally institutionalized control over the private and public disorder created when some members of the community are plunged into poverty. Public housing itself can be read oppositionally as a means of controlling, containing, and segregating the poor from more affluent members of society in an intrusive way that continues a symbolic and institutional violence against the poor begun in the times of the poorhouses in England and the emergence of industrialized and prosperous nation states.

3.1 A Genealogy of Poor Houses

'We Live in a Rickety House'

We live in a rickety house,	1
In a dirty dismal street,	
Where the naked hide from the day,	
And thieves and drunkards meet.	
And pious folks with their tracts,	5
When our dens they enter in,	
They point to our shirtless backs,	
As the fruits of beer and gin.	
And they quote us texts to prove	
That our hearts are hard as stone,	10
And they feed us with the fact	
That the fault is all our own.	
It will be long ere the poor	
Will learn their grog to shun	
While it's raiment, food and fire,	15
And religion all in one.	

> I wonder some pious folks
>   Can look us straight in the face,
> For our ignorance and crime
>   Are the Church's shame and disgrace.   20
>
> We live in a rickety house,
>   In a dirty dismal street,
> Where the naked hide from the day,
>   And thieves and drunkards meet.   24
>
>   (Alexander McLachlan 1874)

In Alexander McLachlan's poem, the motif of living in a rickety house is an especially compelling site for a discussion of the meaning of poor homes seen from above and below. It represents insider knowledge of the 'dirty dismal street' and dehumanizing 'dens,' on the one hand, while offering, on the other, opposing views from privileged do-gooders who judge the poor and prescribe a different lifestyle. Thus, while the focus on ricketiness laments the fact that the poor are jeopardized in their private lives by material need, it may also be read, oppositionally and ironically, to charge that the orderly house of the civil state is jeopardized when the poor make their collective complaints heard. To understand the testimonial value of expressing these tensions and disunities publicly, I do not think we can focus on the rickety house merely as an artfully contrived symbol. Rather, we should locate this representation within a larger social framework of analysis, a brief genealogy of poor houses which makes possible political and cultural questions. How have the psychosocial and material spaces of poor homes and homelessness been shared by poor subjects over centuries and what it has meant to them in terms of identity?

The place constructed for the poor in 'We Live in a Rickety House' is demarcated by stereotypical negativity, but also by oppositional community and anger. In its standard negativity, this discursive space bears the genealogy of negatives associated with the undeserving poor in the nineteenth century, the animalistic 'dens' (line 6) of the 'ragged' and 'dangerous' classes which threatened morality and nation (Himmelfarb 371–400). Nineteenth-century attitudes towards the undeserving poor, which have become embedded in the popular imagination, included the automatic association of poverty with dirt, drunkenness, crime, darkness, nakedness, lasciviousness, and idleness. These attitudes involved a discursive clustering of negatives imported from British and French usage and exacerbated by New World promises of self-reliance, free enterprise, and the invisible hand of market control in capitalist culture.

Although McLachlan's poem unfolds the cluster predictably, the speaker exposes its exclusionary logic through irony and the anger of a silenced 'we.' The angry subtext, belied by the lively tempo of the ditty, exposes 'pious folks' for blaming the poor while force-feeding them with spirituality. Transforming the act of feeding the poor out of charity into force-feeding underscores the dominance and self-interest of the Social Gospel tract which would save souls before feeding them (in both England and Canada). In Dickensian fashion, the poem protests that the poor should not have to stomach salvation in order to be worthy objects of relief. What they will defiantly stomach, however, is alcohol. Beer and gin are a boon to their entrapment and ironically referred to, in the place of labour, as bearing the fruit of shirtless backs (lines 7–8).

This ironic challenge to labour unsettles the easy association between idleness and poverty that had defined the undeserving poor in England in the 1800s, especially according to the doctrine of Puritanism (Himmelfarb 33, 149). According to Himmelfarb's mammoth history on the subject, *The Idea of Poverty*, poverty had become '*the* social problem' in the wake of industrialization because large segments of the working population had been displaced and thrown out of work by the dramatic social shifts and changing attitudes towards community under industrialization and mercantilism (Himmelfarb 18, 137; see also Raymond Williams's more politicized analysis of the transition in *The Country and the City*). Political economists such as Malthus theorized that poverty was necessary to stimulate labour and capital, whereas social aid would result only in further problems of sloth and overpopulation. In response to the 'idle' masses, the Poor Law had enforced labour in the workhouses at a rate of pay lower than the most menial wage to ensure that relief was an undesirable alternative to work. Methodists and Social Gospel adherents balanced the harsh self-help doctrine of capitalism by fetishizing benevolence and envisaging a radical Christian redefinition of community based on care for the poor *if* they converted to the spiritual community (Himmelfarb 129–34, 36–41).

In twentieth-century Canada, it is still socially acceptable for religious groups to 'use' hunger to buy converts, a practice which Alan Mettrick denounces as inhumane in *Last in Line: On the Road and*

Out of Work ... A Desperate Journey with Canada's Unemployed (1985). Mettrick describes how the Salvation Army soup kitchens make 'rice Christians' and 'mission stiffs' out of hungry, homeless people by staging religious testimonials before dinner (157) and having the undeserving poor transform themselves into the deserving poor via testimonies, often false, of conversion (157). He writes: 'My abiding memory, though, will not be of the sermons or the fights or the feeding, but of the men leaving by the back door, walking down that dripping alley in the wet dark through smashed glass and sooted walls running with rain, each man carrying a bag containing a few slices of bread in one hand, like looters stealing away in a wartime blackout' (159). Although subjective and personal, this memory is clearly evoked for counter-cultural purposes to show how the city and the soup kitchen collude in segregating the poor and returning them to the space of stigma and homelessness on the streets. But Mettrick deploys the image of a wartime blackout to call up the notion of a city and state in strife. Likewise, he invokes the unfair image of looting to make us reflect on this type of coercive charity as a form of pilfering the dignity, if not the very souls, of the poor. Thus Mettrick's protest against attitudes towards the poor and charity from the 1980s closely echoes McLachlan's from the late 1800s, giving substance to Murphy's claim in *The Ugly Canadian: The Rise and Fall of a Caring Society* that attitudes towards the poor have not improved much in the past hundred years. The concept of market-induced unemployment came into being only generations after the Poor Laws, but even then it was not accepted by those who preferred to blame the unemployed for joblessness rather than the market. Mettrick's narrative about the unemployed in the 1980s shows that though the means of confinement and stigma may have changed since the 1800s and the days of the poorhouses, prejudices against the unemployed abide as they are systemically excluded and their labour is still extracted at cheap rates in day labour camps or workfare programs. Recent popular support in Ontario for imposing workfare, fingerprinting welfare recipients, and busing the homeless out of Toronto back to their place of origin are legal and political enactments of these abiding prejudices. Canada still seeks to criminalize and control the movement of the disposable poor rather than to work towards full employment or the eradication of poverty. Hence the need to probe past constructions of poverty and homelessness in order to understand current references to the politics of living space.

According to Himmelfarb, the application of the Poor Laws meant that nineteenth-century Britain was regarded as a social laboratory by other European countries reeling from the market shifts and social upheavals of industrialization (5). But the experiment with a highly organized system of public relief was largely perceived as having failed to contain, let alone eradicate, poverty because of the vast numbers caught up in the system and the perception that these numbers were becoming 'pauperized' through relief (153–5, 172–84). Public charges that poorhouses were encouraging idleness by functioning as poor *palaces* were among the widespread criticisms which led to harsher laws and conditions in the workhouse as well as to sharper distinctions between those who were and were not deserving of relief (see Himmelfarb on the New Poor Law of 1837 [147–76]). Under the reformed laws, labour was more strenuous and the terms of residence were clearly likened with those of confinement, suggesting that poverty for the undeserving poor (the idle and drunk versus the sick and the aged) was indeed a wilful crime against civil society:

> [The pauper] might be taken care of, indeed the New Poor Law made elaborate arrangements to take care of him, but it did so outside the framework of the market. Since that framework defined the boundaries of society, the pauper was, by definition so to speak, an outcast – an outcast, not so much by virtue of his character, actions, or misfortunes, but by the mere fact of his dependency, his reliance on relief rather than his own labour for his subsistence. From being an outcast it was only a short step to being regarded as a criminal. Hence the workhouse, the visible confirmation of his status as outcast, was also, in popular parlance, a prison, a 'Bastille.' (183)

Consequently, Himmelfarb stresses, the greatest punishment meted out in the workhouse was not the labour or hunger but the lack of liberty of movement and the stigma of confinement (183–7) – hence the beginning of a symbolic and material violence towards the poor by means of public housing.

It is against the nineteenth-century background of such social attitudes towards housing the homeless, confining their movement, and force-feeding them on Christianity through the Social Gospel doctrine that 'We Live in a Rickety House' articulated its radicalism in 1874. The other important analytical frame for a reading of McLachlan's protest is that of emigration to Canada. The context of McLachlan's poem seems, at first, as urban and British as any Dickensian scene, given its darkened streets and gangs of thieves and the abject status of the poor. None the less, the poem invites at least a moment of ambiguity about the locale of this other street and this other 'we' because it withholds topical references, inscribing instead a universal poor subject whose presence is further etched in the present through the present habitual tense of the refrain: 'we live ...' (rather than 'lived'). The subject 'we,' depicted as living in *one* rickety house, explicitly constructs a closely knit and oppositional community, and yet also, implicitly, the instability of a larger civil society or nation in which a communal 'we' lives. The metaphor of the nation as rickety house, however, draws attention to the instability caused when the poor and the non-poor cannot coexist, with the latter trying to expel and/or master the poor Other. The subtext of 'rickety house' could then be said to construct not only the shared conditions of poverty, but also the *nationlessness* of the poor when they are subordinated within the uncaring and coercive nation.

In *The Oxford Book of Canadian Verse in English* this poem is anthologized alongside others by McLachlan that look either explicitly ahead at the New World or back at England: for example, 'The Emigrant' explicitly directs its social critique back to the Old Country rather than ahead to the new, 'I love my own country and race, / Nor lightly I fled from them both, / Yet who would remain in a place / Where there's too many spoons for the broth' (8). Northrop Frye, Canada's most eminent literary critic, had no compunction about locating the 'tough British radicalism' of that poem in the Old World, arguing that it recalled the radicalism of 'the Glasgow dock worker ... the Lancashire coal miner' or a 'Tom Paine unfit for the American way of life' (1971, 185). In other words, the 'we' of McLachlan's poem seemed incongruent with Canada's political values because of their working-class defiance and collectivity, vestiges of a radicalism which Frye saw as originating in and directed at class oppression in Britain. McLachlan's controlled style and humour, however, Frye would claim as Canadian, for these are the qualities which distinguish Canadian poetry from American poetry in Frye's estimation. Whereas Britain housed radicalism and America housed revolution (with its 'rugged prophecy in praise of the common man'), Frye argued, Canada housed irony and detachment and distance from political tensions. The detached point of view of the observer was suitable, Frye said, to a country which had refused the American Revolution, 'a country with a ringside seat on the revolutionary sidelines.' (Later in a discussion of poverty and nation, I will consider how such evolutionary histories of Canadian culture are still being written, with the effect of reinscribing bourgeois values by locating Canada at a distance from political protest and class struggle.)

Insofar as the poor in McLachlan's poem are concerned, it is perhaps unrealistic to suppose that they would emerge in Canada cleansed of all radicalism except against British oppressors, investing only in humour and detachment at their new Canadian situation. Apparently, McLachlan himself rethought his optimism about New World egalitarianism after initially working as an immigration officer and propagandist for Canada. Since radicalism was a response to the harsh and restricting laws and attitudes against the poor which we know were not shed magically within the settler colony, it is unrealistic to suppose that the capacity for oppositional subjectivity evaporated on the shores of the New World. Frye's construction of Canadian culture prescribes as well as describes a 'cultivated' literary imagination and poetic voice for Canada rather than the everyday language of Canadians, but his insistence on the observer's position with its detachment, irony, and linguistic control would be identifiable, according to Bourdieu's theory of habitus, as a bourgeois subjective position because it can afford to choose distance and restraint over protest and anger. Control and detachment, which Frye claims are typical of Canadian poetry, have been argued by Bourdieu to be more typical of the class habitus of the bourgeoisie. Bourdieu has argued that linguistic control in everyday life and the position of surveying life from a detached position is the ultimate culmination of bourgeois taste:

> Bourgeois respondents particularly distinguish themselves by their ability to control the survey situation . . . Control over the social situation in which culture operates is given to them by the very unequally distributed capacity to adopt the relation to language which is called for in all situations of polite conversation (e.g., chatter about cinema or travel), and which presupposes an art of skimming, sliding and masking, making abundant use of all the hinges, fillers and qualifiers identified by linguists as characteristic of bourgeois language. (174)

Unlike Frye, who dismisses the possibility of New World radicalism, oppositional readers of McLachlan's poem may prefer to read the locale as universal in order to contemplate protest against both the

New World and the Old World order.[1] Because the community behind the 'we' is defined against a dominant class of 'pious folks' and the 'Church,' the rickety house seems to be located in England where church parishes took charge of the welfare of the poor through the highly intrusive and punitive British Poor Laws. But this 'we' could also be located on the brink of a New World where Old World notions of the poor were imported and transformed and radicals looked ahead as well as back in anger.

In *The Canadian Social Inheritance*, Jack Blyth has explained how North America followed England's and France's treatment of the poor in many respects: in restricting their movement and expelling them from non-host communities, in punishing idleness through whipping, imprisonment, branding, and forced labour, in failing to recognize unemployment officially as a social phenomenon rather than inherent idleness, and in basing public charity on a rigid distinction between the deserving and the undeserving poor. On the other hand, Blyth also explains that although much has been written about how Upper Canadian society was founded on British law in 1791, histories rarely mention that there was a rider on the law to the effect that 'nothing in this Act ... shall ... introduce any of the laws of England respecting the poor' – largely because of a reluctance on the part of a settler colony to pay higher taxes for the support of public relief and also because of popular support for the doctrine of Social Darwinism which was enhanced by myths of New World prosperity and egalitarianism (17). As Blyth and others have pointed out, in a settler colony, social community meant largely that one expected to get help from one's neighbour. Not until much later would the notion of institutionalized relief emerge, at first through municipalities and private charities. And not until after the Second World War would Canada see the establishment of the full-scale welfare state with the Marsh Report in 1943.[2]

---

1 I am not suggesting that McLachlan intended such ambiguity. On the contrary, a number of his other poems show how much hope he invested in the New World as a site of mobility and democracy – a position he would later recant, however. Given our knowledge of how class differences were to be muted in the New World, none the less, we as readers may reflect critically on the plight of the poor in Canada as well as in Britain, the New World as well as the Old, as an oppositional reading strategy.

2 See Blyth's discussion of the interdependent but different evolution of relief laws and social attitudes in England, Canada, and the United States, and in different provinces of Canada (1–84, 130–91, 242–72, 329–90); see also the discussion of a long cultural tradition of church charity brought from France to Quebec based on a distinction

Thus, while notions of social policy were imported, they were also adapted loosely, according to regions and social influences, and over time. Until the turn of the century, the poor in Nova Scotia, for example, were auctioned publicly after the fashion practised by arriving New Englanders, and workhouses which practised whipping, shackling, and starvation to curb idleness had been in place since 1763. Domestics who ran away from their masters on arrival in New France were branded with the fleur-de-lis for second offences (Guilbert et al. 11) – a practice which imposed, rather strikingly, the nation's claim on the labour power of the poor. In Lower Canada poverty became secularized much later than in Upper Canada because the church held more sway in matters of both state and community and notions of the religious value of charity were more socially embedded (Blyth 10). Charitable institutions had been established much earlier in Lower Canada than in the rest of North America because of church power over community affairs, explaining in part why the beggar became a popular icon and social space for testing morality in early Québécois songs (Guilbert et al. 12–13).

For some, in McLachlan's time, the 'rickety house' would also have evoked an image of poverty as contaminating due to the etymological association with the disease rickets – the unromantic, unnameable disease of poor people's vitamin and calcium deficiency. My mother taught me about this disease when explaining the bowed legs of neighbours in our farming community in northern Ontario, but I have seldom, if ever, seen it mentioned in studies of Canadian literature. Although the erasure of diseases of poverty by bourgeois literary aesthetics is itself an interesting topic, I am more concerned with how poverty becomes conflated with disease and medicalized as one of a number of mechanisms for naturalizing it and placing it outside the bounds of civil society and nation. As Ruth L. Smith has noted in her essay on the discursive construction of poverty, the constant projection of dysfunction, need, vice, and disease onto the poor is symptomatic of

---

between *le bon et le mauvais pauvre* in Lucille Guilbert et al., *Pauvre ou vagabond: Le quêteux et la société québécoise.* Ramesh Mishra's article 'The Collapse of the Welfare Consensus? The Welfare State in the 1980s' compares the history of public relief in Canada to that of Europe and the United States in terms of public attitudes influenced by economic theories. (See also Leonard on 'postmodern welfare,' Struthers on the history of welfare in Ontario, and Murphy on the evolution of contemporary prejudice against welfare.)

a market society divided against itself and trying to cover up or rationalize its own divisions and deficiencies. The poor are the prosperous nation's Other. The rickety house of the poor as home to disease and crime appears with such intensity because it is the projected image of the divided nation, the excess of its own idealization. But historically as well, in medieval Europe, for example, the transient poor were associated explicitly with carriers of evil and disease and thus naturalized as outcasts – until a point between the fifteenth and sixteenth centuries when their wandering was designated a crime and poverty was conflated with criminality as well as disease (Guilbert et al. 7). According to Blyth, these associations were made clear in Canada when in 1859 the Board of Prisons, Asylums and Public Charities was established to deal with the poor in the absence of the British institutions of the workhouse and the Poor Laws (19). The recent controversy about the 'Duplessis orphans,' who were wrongly classified as mentally retarded and uneducable to heighten funding from the state to church-run institutions, shows how slippery the categories remained in the twentieth century when grouping orphans, the mentally ill, the poor, and the criminal as Others within the nation.

Institutional attempts to control poverty often reflect an embedded social hysteria about the needy within our doors, branding them as intrusive strangers. Intolerance of the movement of the poor, for example, was a means of both keeping social control and extorting labour from the populace. Guilbert mentions this in respect to the forced work of transients during harvest time in Lower Canada and the forced servitude of domestics prohibited from leaving their masters on arrival in New France (Guilbert et al. 5, 7, 11–12). Blyth points out that one of the latest such instances of social control over the movement of the poor occurred in the 1960s when the province of British Columbia shipped poor people back to their place of origin in Ontario despite that province's protests – 'on the premise that they might become public charges' (11). More recently, in the 1990s, attempts have resurfaced to restrict unemployment insurance to recipients who stay in their home province, diminishing the role of the caring nation.

To return for one last time to McLachlan's dark streets and rickety house, it is clear that the images of the nineteenth-century undeserving poor represented there did indeed make the crossing from the Old Country, although it is less clear how radical protest fared in the process. Imported images were empowered by fundamental assumptions in North American society about the strength of the market, the abundance of space and resources, and the promise of individualism, ensuring that they would linger in public policy and popular imagination. As I will discuss in relation to internalized negative constructions of identity, nineteenth-century images still powerfully demarcate social boundaries even in the twentieth-century imagination. Alice Munro's story 'The Beggar Maid' reveals how bourgeois living space in contemporary culture still evokes the received narrative of merit, hard work, pride, orderliness, and good taste, while rickety houses evoke the received story of deficiency, idleness, shame, disorder, and bad taste. In contemporary bourgeois literature, however, these received narratives are subtly transmitted through questions of taste, details of decor, and an evasion of material relations, rather than through consignment of the poor to explicitly blameworthy dens and dark streets.

A fuller knowledge of how to interpret poor houses in narratives should be constructed not only in terms of the genealogy of discursive conventions and social attitudes, but also in terms of how concrete subjects experience housing needs. From the outset, in order to burst the bubble of a national image based on the shared prosperity of western nations, we should note that in *Housing the Homeless and Poor*, George Fallis and Alex Murray point out that by 1990 there were 250,000 homeless people in Canada and over 1.5 million at risk of losing the housing they had, with growing numbers of women, youth, and families joining the ranks. Fallis and Murray also note that 27 per cent of renters and 7.8 per cent of home-owners in Canada are in 'core need,' meaning that they cannot solve their current housing problems or the threat of homelessness without spending over 30 per cent of their income. Instead of becoming overwhelmed by the growing problem as it is reflected in statistics, they suggest we must recognize the connectedness of the poor and homeless to the rest of society, to understand the diversity among those in core need and the complexity of the causes and conditions of their need, and to make more evident the systemic causes which keep people in need in an ostensibly prosperous nation such as Canada.

Fallis and Murray conclude that elevated numbers of homeless people reflect as much both about Canadian society as a whole and about the breakdown of welfare consensus in the 1980s as they do about the poor and the homeless themselves:

> But perhaps homelessness is not so much evidence of people falling through the cracks as it is evidence of a society less willing to help. When

> the sorry plight of a bag-lady is portrayed on our television screens, we all sympathise. However, as her background of lost jobs, failed marriage, and running feud with the public housing authorities is reported, our sympathy wanes. Discussion begins to echo the nineteenth-century distinction between the deserving and undeserving poor. She is author of her own fate. She neither wants nor deserves help. What can be done (because the poor are always with us)? The words are seldom explicit but the sentiments are there. (270)

I believe we fail to ask certain material questions about literary representations of living space, not because these questions are conceptually difficult, confusing, or irrelevant, but because people with power and privilege are implicated by the answers. The middle class in particular prefers to deny poverty and its threat rather than interrogate it. Consequently, oppositional reading strategies of poor housing and homelessness must wilfully transgress the conceptual gap which separates literature from lived experience, and the private woes of the poor from the public image of a country reflected through bourgeois culture. The transgression of that conceptual gap will happen not by our insinuating into it any fixed notion of how the poor experience homelessness and rickety houses, but by our opening ourselves to a wider diversity of tastes, experiences, and narrative styles as part of a shared national culture.

3.2 Alice Munro's Gaze – from a Distance

Few Canadian authors have testified to shame over poor houses to the extent that Alice Munro has. But Munro's sustained, refined, almost luminous gaze at poor houses issues from a safe place of critical observation which she consistently constructs for her narrators and protagonists between the worlds of the rich and the poor, the present and the past, and fiction and reality. I will argue that the canonization of Munro's semi-autobiographic, melancholic view of poverty is based on something besides stylistic excellence; it is also based on a bourgeois ethos, on the way Munro's protagonists – for example, in 'Shining Houses' and 'The Beggar Maid' – visit poor houses and observe them from a position of aesthetic enthralment or moral paralysis. In other words, I am suggesting that the ideology of this aesthetic gaze is not neutral but complicit in the assumption of privilege which Pierre Bourdieu has described as characteristic of bourgeois class habitus. Munro's impeccable prose style and her narrators' detached point of view seem acculturated to the living style of bourgeois art rather than the disorderliness of oppositional culture. Her narrative sympathy initially reaches out to the poor, but only to be wrenched away so that it can be fixed on a surer set of values: aesthetic detachment and sometimes irony.

Having said this, I should be careful to qualify that I am immediately uncomfortable with the implications of this kind of assessment of art as bourgeois or counter-cultural lest it seem dismissive of one and idealist of the other or lest it imply that we can draw clear lines to distinguish ideological positions in literature. Munro's work is evidence of how problematic such categories are. As one of the finest stylists in Canadian literature, her use of a literary form of hyperrealism is probably the most skilful of anyone's. None the less, she is identified as a writer of 'social embarrassment' rather than a writer of the working class in *The Oxford Companion to Canadian Literature* (Coldwell 537), and this, I would argue, is because the ideology of her gaze is not merely neutral or distanced. The style and perspective through which she describes a poor house and poor lives is an acculturated perspective which shows only the distanced view of poverty and never the dignity of class solidarity or the social logic (rather than merely the emotional consequences) of class stratification. However, like many acculturated styles it surpasses its model in the sense that it is able to see beyond the assumptions of the bourgeois detachment. As a reader I enjoy her style and the fact that she draws attention to poverty and cross-class experiences, but I always resist being drawn into the apparent neutrality and powerlessness of a gaze that is so distancing towards the poor. Most criticism of Munro's work identifies the melancholy and distanciation of her gaze as proof of a unique world view and stylistic excellence. For example, Ajay Heble credits the distanced gaze as a skilful use of limited third-person narrative and a subversive innovation on realism. While such readings are convincing in a general sense, most avoid the ideological implications of distance in her depictions of poverty.

I resist (in a way similar to that of Judith Fetterley's resistant reader) the recurring ideological structure in Munro's poverty narratives: first poverty is narrated in translucent prose, then potentially oppositional emotions such as anger, shame, or resentment emerge and are dissipated (usually through irony or ambiguity), and finally a sensation of paralysis is remarked upon, from a distanced perspective, as gentle regret or melancholy. For example, 'Shining Houses' inscribes poverty in the form of Mrs Fullerton living in a ramshackle house and eking out a meagre living from egg money and subsistence farming. In the beginning of the story, the protagonist visits Mrs Fullerton to pay for some goods and smoke and talk. A middle-class housewife from a nearby subdivision, she admires the older woman's self-sufficient, practical, and independent lifestyle. Later, however, when the protagonist is at home in the new subdivision with shining houses, she is unable to defend Mrs Fullerton from the neighbours' collective charges that the shacks are eyesores and have to be levelled for the sake of property values. Recognizing that Mrs Fullerton was there first and that her livelihood, since her husband left her, has depended on the animals in the yard, the protagonist resents the unfairness of the situation – but she does not defend Mrs Fullerton to her neighbours for fear of appearing odd or different.

The question I am raising is not whether or not the protagonist should have acted differently – for the story itself raises this question nicely – but what happens when the focus of the story in this, as in many of Munro's poverty narratives, becomes the middle-class protagonist's preoccupation with the weakness of her voice and her inability to act while the working-class women are consistently written out of the story. Although the lived version of poverty in the narrative is closer to the protagonist's heart than the stigmatized version represented by the neighbours, poverty is, none the less, inscribed as an indefensible space given the moral paralysis of the protagonist. The source of melancholy is not only the indefensible space of poverty, but also the failure of the protagonist to assert female friendship across classes.

One resists the resolution of the story if one is less interested in the protagonist's melancholy than in the unfairness of Mrs Fullerton's predicament. The protagonist is well-meaning and insightful because she can see houses from two class habiti – from a place which recognizes the value of unsightly shacks to a single woman's livelihood and from the place which condemns the same shacks for their intrusion on the orderliness of streets of shining houses. The protagonist is also humane enough to lament her own inaction, but these pangs of bourgeois guilt do not prevent Mrs Fullerton's imminent eviction. The story provides no place for the anger inspired by the scenes of poverty which Munro invokes so clearly in the beginning – unless we, like the protagonist, agree to suspend anger and invest instead in the melancholy. Not only the protagonist, but the ideology of the narrative fails to oppose the class boundaries it describes.

A similar but much more complex ideology of class acculturation and shame emerges in 'The Beggar Maid,' in which the upwardly mobile protagonist is painfully aware of the great distance between her family's poor home (Flo's house) and the houses to which she gains entrance as a university student (Dr Henshawe's house). In the following excerpt, Munro inscribes distance from her poor home in terms of poor taste – a taste for the too bright, the too obvious, the too new: 'Dr. Henshawe's house had done one thing. It had destroyed the naturalness, the taken-for-granted background of home. To go back there was to go quite literally into a crude light. Flo had put fluorescent lights in the store and the kitchen. There was also, in a corner of the kitchen, a floor lamp Flo had won at Bingo; its shade was permanently wrapped in wide strips of cellophane. What Dr. Henshawe's house and Flo's house did best, in Rose's opinion, was to discredit each other' (67). That the two homes seem to exist mainly 'to discredit each other' is an enigmatic statement whose potential subversiveness in stating class difference is diffused, as in much of Munro's fiction (in particular 'Privilege,' 'Thanks for the Ride,' and 'Who Do You Think You Are?'), and safely lodged in ambiguity. It is as though the impasse between the rich and poor home in the narrator's psyche is the only power balance that matters, as though the reader should consent that the poor house is somehow equal in power to the rich one simply because Rose experiences them both as important fragments of her self, the two being set against each other to be judged aesthetically like tableaux or stage settings.

As Bourdieu suggests, in cases of social mobility, it is often in respect to taste more than income that the subject must alter her social practices (175). Rose is shown gradually learning to distinguish between the professor's imported carvings, the ornaments she had seen in the small-town jewellery-store window, and Flo's knickknacks bought at the five-and-dime (89). She goes on to testify that each of her worlds has been contaminated by knowledge of the other, their differences, and their mutual exclusion: 'In Dr. Henshawe's charming rooms there was always for Rose the raw knowledge of home, an indigestible lump, and at home, now, her sense of order and modulation elsewhere exposed such embarrassing sad poverty, in people who never thought themselves poor' (90). Clearly, however, Rose's negative feelings are reserved for the knowledge of home and not the professor's 'charming rooms' – the former yielding 'an indigestible lump' and 'embarrassing sad poverty' while the latter yields charm, 'order and modulation,' appearing 'small and perfect' (89). It will remain unclear at the end of the story how Flo's world can ever discredit the bourgeois world whose doors are opening to Rose – except, of course, by inserting shameful memories of poverty into her new experiences of bourgeois habitus or by betraying her outwardly as part of her own identity. The balance between habiti is not in Rose's feelings towards them; it is a stylistic feat whereby both worlds are invoked convincingly. The form itself shows a taste for order and control rather than the disorder of the everyday world. One consequence of form here is to bridge the distance between poor homes and bourgeois living space by travelling the distance textually.

Rose veers away from the path of self-transformation set by acculturation to return to the sensations of poverty, its pettiness and envy, its lack of privacy, and incessant 'bad' taste. This psychic return to a poor home, though only momentary, is sensual enough and powerful enough to transmit an insider's knowledge and shame:

> Poverty was not just wretchedness, as Dr. Henshawe seemed to think, it was not just deprivation. It meant having those ugly tube lights and being proud of them. It meant continual talk of money and malicious talk about new things people had bought and whether they were paid for. It meant pride and jealousy flaring over something like the new pair of plastic curtains, imitating lace, that Flo had bought for the front window. That as well as hanging your clothes on nails behind the door and being able to hear every sound from the bathroom. It meant decorating your walls with a number of admonitions, pious and cheerful and mildly bawdy ... (90–1)

Rose is brought out of her memory by the intrusion of a more educated self and the horror that her new husband will see her poor home, her poor self, her poor friends – all of which she conflates with tackiness and shame. The narrative frequently oscillates this way between the two extreme cultural locations in an emotional distancing from both, rather than a political sensibility of how the two might be related. As I will discuss in a later chapter, Margaret Laurence's *The Diviners* also travels the distance between the extreme differences of a poor home and the university, but Laurence's protagonist reflects on how the two extremes are related within society in terms of power and privilege. In Munro's narrative, on the other hand, the public meanings are distilled (or reduced) to private shame or social games – the stuff of 'social embarrassment.'

At university Rose is acutely aware of her difference as a member of a visible 'class' of scholarship students who are branded by their poverty. She understands that, to be admitted to the inner circle of social acceptance and highbrow culture, the poor girl must be selected by a man from within that circle – which means that she must suppress either braininess or poverty, the two being otherwise an insurmountable stigma for a woman. Rose decides to refuse a work scholarship which would have her visibly branded as both poor and brainy:

> Dishing up stew and fried chicken for those of inferior intelligence and handsomer means. Blocked off by the steam tables, the uniform, by decent hard work that nobody need be ashamed of, by publicly proclaimed braininess and poverty. Boys could get away with that, barely. For girls it was fatal. Poverty in girls is not attractive unless combined with sweet sluttishness, stupidity. Braininess is not attractive unless combined with some signs of elegance; class. Was this true, and was she foolish enough to care? It was; she was. (71)

Although the double sexual standard behind the class stigma is exposed, the narrator does not condemn the social text as much as she mocks, rather ironically and in a detached way, Rose's own inability to assert herself against that text. Her individual failing becomes the focus, not the system.

The gap between her husband's very wealthy but emotionally cold home and her poor past is represented as something which can never be resolved. Thus the naming of the gap between habiti proves how lucid detachment is, and how it may be an end in itself. Rose's highly attuned writer's sensibilities register the unlivable class difference between her professor/husband and herself keenly. As their class difference presents itself initially, she assesses the predicament, ironically, through cliché: '"We come from two different worlds," she said to him, on another occasion. She felt like a character in a play, saying that, "My people are poor people. You would think the place I lived in was a dump"' (75). Later, when he finally sees her home, he comments unfeelingly, 'You were right. It is a dump.' The story seems to promise that Rose's heightened sensibilities, her 'good taste,' will extricate her from the impasse of shame and inauthenticity in her marriage.

The story's retrospective glance is aesthetic and refined, as though the narrator and the character have both been transported from the lived situation and are commenting from some safely remote place.

Wherever that place is, it does not resemble poverty or one who is wrestling with a poor past; it seems to be a place where artistic sensibility is in control and able to construct a self by holding up the fragments of memory for scrutiny. The price of that control, however, is that the observer is never wholly able to engage with the aesthetic portrayal of the past, despite the power to name it precisely and sensually, to call it up and scrutinize it through an artistic gaze, to fix it as though in a tableau. This is what I referred to earlier as aesthetic enthralment. The fact that this tableau of poverty is rendered by linguistic control and impeccable prose superimposes bourgeois form onto the experience of poverty, containing it within a more orderly taste and form. This mimetically reproduces the process of acculturation as a bourgeois reframing of the class Other, which aestheticizes her and her shame. Rose ultimately outclasses her high-class husband.

The feminist subtext is much more oppositional than the class subtext, in that Rose will step out of the object role indicated by the title of the classical painting, *King Cophetua and the Beggar Maid* (and of the story itself). It is significant that she must first be schooled by one who possesses the inherited cultural capital to teach her about her own reflection in classical art before she can grasp the implications of the role and move away from them: 'But I'm glad,' said Patrick, 'I'm glad you're poor. You're so lovely. You're like the Beggar Maid ... Don't you know that painting?' (101). Of course, Patrick does not really mean he loves her poverty for he will dismiss her home as a dump; he loves the power imbalance, the vulnerability and the gratitude caused by her class background, perhaps, the narrative suggests, because this indebtedness on her part compensates for his lack of adeptness and confidence as a lover.

The tableau of the beggar maid depicts a sensuous maid before her lover king, 'meek and voluptuous,' whose 'milky surrender' appals Rose. On the surface it blatantly emblemizes the imbalance in their class positions, but beneath it discloses the reverse imbalance in their affection for each other, for Rose is both a grateful and a dissatisfied lover who will eventually turn the tables of power by divorcing her husband. The spectacle of class difference between lovers becomes contained, in the course of the story, by a more modern, feminist, and highly personal subtext of emotional and sexual incompatibility which leads to divorce. The powerlessness of the poor subject is eclipsed by the power of choice given to the woman who listens to female desire – but the story obscures its own material logic: the only reason the woman can listen to her desire and choose divorce without drastic material consequences (often at the root of the feminization of poverty) is because Rose has become upwardly mobile herself. The resolution of the story is that Rose, by now a successful television journalist, meets her ex-husband by chance in an airport and is surprised and shaken by his animosity. This personalized resolution collapses the larger social issues of difference – king/servant, upper-class man/working-class woman, student/teacher, husband/wife relationship – into one intensely personal moment where the narrator must bear what she experiences as the disproportionate hatred of her ex-husband's gaze. The tableau has shrunk – or has it?

The dynamics of power in the story are played out discreetly in a series of gazes: the disapproving gaze of a university student oscillating between her poor home and high culture; the traditional gaze of the classical painting which fixes class and gender relations; the adoring gaze between servant and king; the distanced gaze of the dissatisfied wife; the public gaze which empowers Rose financially and in terms of her personal identity as a successful journalist; and the gaze of the resentful husband – all of which are transcended by the aesthetic gaze of the narrator, who is detached from these lived experiences for the purpose of ordering them through narration. The bourgeois 'sense of order and modulation' which Rose initially saw in her professor's house is thus achieved not merely in the decor of living spaces but inside the orderly narrative itself and the detachment and austerity of both the protagonist and the narrator. The essentially traditional power arrangement of the classical tableau seems somehow still intact – though the power relations are reversed, gendered, and personalized, the frame of class distinction is still in place. The self-made woman/ artist has merely moved into the position of power, a subject looking down at yet another outgrown home from her past and baffled at the disorderly anger of those she has left behind.

3.3 Homeplace and 'Bugs'

> [T]he easiest, and so the most frequent and most spectacular, way to 'shock (épater) the bourgeois' by proving the extent of one's power to confer aesthetic status is to transgress ever more radically the ethical censorships (e.g. matters of sex) which the other classes accept even within the area which the dominant disposition defines as aesthetic. Or, more subtly, it is done by conferring aesthetic status on objects or ways of repre-

senting them that are excluded by the dominant aesthetic of the time, or on objects that are given aesthetic status by dominated 'aesthetics.' (Bourdieu, *Distinction* 47)

For many poor or once-poor women the distance between a poor home and high culture is irrelevant for they have never stopped identifying with a poor home as the most important site of culture in their lives. They do not compare their living space against the standards of a dominant habitus: perhaps because it holds up no realistic escape route to them, or perhaps because their own home-based culture satisfies them and even fills them with a sense of pride. According to bell hooks, for example, houses for black women have traditionally been havens from a hostile world and sites of generations of struggle. As I discussed in relation to Gabrielle Roy's *Bonheur d'occasion*, hooks's description of 'homeplace' as a historical site of cultural resistance for black women may be adapted to the reading of poor and working-class women's lives to interpret home as an alternative to textual resistance for women who often have no written discourse to explain their position in a hostile world:

> Though black women did not self-consciously articulate in written discourse the theoretical principles of decolonisation, this does not detract from the importance of their actions. They understood intellectually and intuitively the meaning of homeplace in the midst of an oppressive and dominating social reality, of homeplace as site of resistance and liberation struggle. I know of what I speak. I would not be writing this essay if my mother, Rosa Bell, daughter to Sarah Oldham, granddaughter to bell hooks, had not created homeplace in just this liberatory way, despite the contradictions of poverty and sexism. (1984, 46)

In addition to redefining the poor home as a site of female power, hooks identifies her own public voice as rooted in the struggles waged in that private space, an articulate voice coming not from a voyage out as much as from a looking back at roots.

In Canadian literature from the twentieth century, however, female characters are more likely to choose leaving the poor home as a means of resistance rather than transforming it through struggle from within. This is not because poor and working-class women in Canada do not occupy homeplace as a site of lived struggle in the everyday world, but rather because the conditions for literary production have not favoured the recording and circulation of these stories as much as those in the bourgeois vein, and by that I mean those stories which aestheticize interior struggles, social mobility, and bourgeois quests for self rather than collective or material everyday struggles. (Of course there are notable exceptions, such as Roy's *Bonheur d'occasion* and 'Bugs,' but these are exceptions rather than the rule.) Yet as Pamela Fox and Carolyn Steedman, among others, have suggested, our very definition of resistance and struggle would have to be altered to take into account the acts of class resistance which occur within the domestic sphere.

Canadian literature has tended to dramatize the individual trajectories of women's upward mobility with an accompanying fixation on self-transformation, rags-to-riches stories, narratives about endless cleaning and polishing as a means of self-definition – at the expense of showing more collective stories of poverty and how women struggle together against hunger, lack of shelter, unfair laws, or intrusive welfare policies. Canadian literature tells few stories about organizing and civil disobedience among men or women, but in exceptions, such as Irene Baird's *Waste Heritage*, the organizing is usually done by groups of men while women are written out of the story as peripheral figures. Baird's historic novel, based on mass demonstrations against unemployment during the Depression, is a realistic, proletarian novel about the march on Vancouver to occupy the post office. Interestingly, the only female character follows a downward spiral from waitress to dancehall 'floozy' to prostitute – until she disappears from the story because her fall from grace rules out the possibility of romance with any of the male strikers (a fate similar to that of the female character in Hugh Garner's *Cabbagetown*). She is consigned to a sphere of total ignominy and exclusion on the outside of society where organizing and resistance is not possible – even, the novel suggests, farther on the outside than the counter-cultural strikers and hoboes who organize themselves into some form of counter-order. If proletarian literature writes women's resistance out of the sphere of the possible, where can we find stories of poor and working-class women's subjectivities and alternative struggles for dignity and daily bread?

On the whole, Canadian women's poverty narratives are not characterized by demonstrations, organized, spontaneous, or otherwise, because one of the most salient features of poverty in the 'First World' is that it falls back on the individual as a subject of blame and deficiency and rarely becomes informed by class-consciousness or overtly anti-authoritarian acts. In fact, the great majority of women's poverty narratives in Canada dramatize the lone heroine's mobility narrative as she 'falls into' or 'rises up' out of poverty. Lillian Rubin has noted in *Worlds of Pain: Life in the Working-class Family* how even this discourse of ascendancy reinscribes North American cultural values of meritocracy that attach great value to upward mobility by locating individual subjects within a moral and economic terrain which simultaneously values not only economic security but also those who work with their heads and not their hands. Rubin writes: 'The words we unthinkingly use to describe the process of moving through the class structure reinforce that judgment, for we move *up* or *down*, not just through. And when we speak of that movement between classes, we don't speak simply of *going* up or down; instead we *climb* into a higher class or *fall* into a lower one.' (9). Ehrenreich has further probed the 'fear of falling' in her book by that title as characteristic of the inner life of the middle class by examining the source of dread of poverty in North American culture. Ehrenreich concluded that the dread is not of poverty alone, but of the lack of value and stability at the very basis of our market society and consumer capitalism. Yet the spatial metaphors for poverty and mobility suggest that poverty is not merely a monetary state in the popular imaginary of wealthy nations; it is a moral terrain as well.

Not surprisingly, then, women's poverty narratives which focus on upward mobility often entail a story of bringing the disorderly body of the woman under control. Furthermore, behind the individualist story of self-transformation and cleansing of the poor self often lurks the threat of contamination by the disorderly poor as a group. It is small wonder that group organizing and demonstrations do not figure prominently in North American poverty narratives when the hegemonic form of poverty narrative is that of the individual escaping contamination by that group. The Canadian canon abounds with plots based on individual social mobility in which a lone woman chooses to work her way out of poverty through various degrees of drudgery, class acculturation, and self-transformation. For example, Ethel Wilson's 1952 classic, *Lilly's Story*, is a prototype of the mobility narrative in which the protagonist runs from her poor past, consciously fashioning a new identity for herself by styling her speech, clothing, hairstyle, and social habits after bourgeois women. When she finds refuge as the housekeeper of a wealthy British family, Lilly begins to dress her daughter according to their European style and to encourage her to speak like them, 'quiet-like,' so that her daughter will sound more 'like folk' (182). The narrative abounds with words like 'molded' and 'styled' to describe the process of the make-over, first of Lilly as a young mother, then of her daughter, and then of a middle-aged Lilly (227). Finding a home after years of being homeless and abandoned initially 'conferred a dignity upon her,' but her claim to dignity will not be complete until she makes herself over from without and within (191). Eventually, Lilly's suppression of her own class-marked idiom and tell-tale marks of class behaviour is so extreme that she loses the habit of speaking or socializing freely. Ironically, Lilly's daughter remarks on her mother's lack of humour and beauty, saying that her mother appears to know nothing of the 'disorder' and wildness of beauty. Lilly's employers, on the other hand, remark on her cleanliness, how she 'leaves order wherever she goes' (197) and how 'order flows from her finger tips' as she cleans their houses and hospital and hotel rooms. In this prototypical mobility narrative, dignity is bought at a high price: isolation from others, denial of a past and shameful self, hard labour, and denial of sexual or romantic feelings that would compromise the cleansed body through sexual contact. Many other stories of mobility mirror this individualist struggle by poor women to cleanse themselves of the disorder and outward markings of poverty. Female protagonists in Margaret Laurence's *The Diviners* and Alice Munro's 'The Beggar Maid' use the university as a site where poor women learn to remake themselves according to the more dignified mould of middle-class women who have not fallen outside the bounds of civil society and thus qualify for a plot of 'marrying up' to professional men.

The proliferation of stories about poor and working-class women who become socially mobile by means of domestic work is worthy of note. It is uncanny how live-in domestic work, waitressing, and housecleaning are so lucrative for women in fiction that they have become a conventional stepping-stone towards 'a better life' in many canonized Canadian texts (for example, *The Stone Angel*, *La Rivière sans repos*, *Swamp Angel*, and *Lilly's Story*). While it is true that before 1900 domestic work was the primary source of employment available to women outside the home in Canada (Prentice et al. 123), its appearance as a conventional plot mechanism in mobility narratives in the postwar period misrepresents the actual wage level and status of work that places many domestics among the working poor in Canada.

Oral histories of black domestics in Canada, such as Makeda Silvera's *Silenced*, testify to the profound sense of powerlessness and homelessness experienced by women who 'live in' as domestics and are, thus, without a site, a 'homeplace' in which they can construct familial and generational bonds of resistance in the traditionally female ways described by bell hooks. Fictionalized testimonies as well as oral histories such as Maxine Tynes's short story 'In Service' and Makeda Silvera's 'Canada Sweet, Girl' reveal a profound sense of homelessness which extends to a feeling of nationlessness among live-in domestic workers in a wealthy nation whose laws do not protect them adequately, but whose bourgeoisie extracts their labour and emotional commitment cheaply and sometimes their sexual services as well.

One explanation for the misrepresentation of domestic work probably lies in the symbolic power of cleaning in respect to the debased psychosocial space of poor women whom the popular imagination constructs out of dirt, idleness, and sexual promiscuity. Janet Zandy has underscored how working-class women themselves have used cleaning as a form of both symbolic cultural expression and concrete self-definition: 'Working-class women have not found a home in middle-class America. Not really. Recalling the struggle against the dirt and filth of poverty, they try to make of their small and modest homes safe, clean places. The curtains are changed; the glass doors polished with vinegar; the front stoop swept. They tend the walls of self-definition' (1990, 1). The genealogy of the discourse of poverty discussed by Gertrude Himmelfarb in *The Idea of Poverty*, Chaim Waxman in *The Stigma of Poverty*, and Ruth Smith in 'Order and Disorder: The Naturalization of Poverty' teaches us that vermin, lice, plague, licentiousness, and idleness have been assigned the same discursive space as the poor from the Middle Ages onward. Consequently, work based on cleaning can obviously exert a magical power over this multiply stigmatized space. More recently, in postcolonial studies this notion has been popularized by Ann McClintock in *Imperial Leather* as she packages the discursive struggle in a personal history of sexual fetish based on dirt and low-class titillation between a gentleman secretly wedded to his cleaning lady.

Antonine Maillet has harnessed the symbolic power of cleaning over class and set it on its head, extending the discourse of cleanliness to a larger social critique. In her full-length dramatic monologue, *La Sagouine*, which begins with the cleaning lady talking to her pail of dirty water, which she notes represents half a century of all the dirt of a country – the amplification of the public meaning of cleanliness gives this character the epic proportion of a Mother Courage, caught not in war but in a daily struggle of domestic work and class and ethnic differences. Having gone from prostitute to cleaning lady, la Sagouine has few illusions about the real differences between the rich and the poor, the dominant and the dominated, and men and women. She ironically challenges rich women who have washed their hands dutifully in buttermilk and lotion to compare the whiteness of their skin to her own hands, white through years of scrubbing (22).

The struggle over cleanliness is, like that over housing, played out on both a symbolic and a material level where the poor individual attempts to define himself or herself in more authentic ways than social stereotypes permit while claiming a material space within which to survive as a concrete subject. The paradox that homeplace, as a site of resistance, must often be fashioned from an inadequate living space emerges as a crucial element in the construction of female identity in many poverty narratives, as noted earlier in the reading of *Bonheur d'occasion* (*The Tin Flute*) by Gabrielle Roy. In Nancy Holmes's short story 'Bugs,' the close link among female strength, domestic work, cleanliness, poor housing, and class stigma is problematized within the private sphere. The poor immigrant mother in this story cleans against the instability of rented lodgings to restore order and privacy to a homeplace threatened by market society. At the centre of the story are bugs, inserting themselves not only as a nightly horror in an immigrant family's lodgings, but also as a source of domestic conflict between family members as they struggle over dignity and self-definition. For the daughter/narrator, bugs are a shameful icon of the immigrant family's economic powerlessness, confirming the stigma of dirt and poverty assumed in the school children's ethnic slur about her Polish/Ukrainian background, 'Dirty Bohunk!' Insults based on negative constructions of identity become both internalized and amplified, keeping her awake late into the night: 'I was squeezing my eyes shut, trying to blank out all memory of my first day at school in the new town. But instead of fading, the ugly whisper grew louder until it rang like a shout in my head' (192). Later, insults directed at her long skirts and different dress style intrude in the same way: 'Even in my sleep I seemed to hear a constant whispered titter that made me squirm' (196). Thus, the material reality of a bug-infested home meets the debased psychosocial space of insults to impinge on the feeling that homeplace is safe.

Bugs remind the narrator's father of his powerlessness against a landlady who refuses to fumigate and who says instead that the 'Bohunks' have brought bugs to her house, so they will just have to be cleaner: 'You're living in town now, not on the farm' (195). Out of pride and anger, both father and daughter refuse simply to move out of the house or hire fumigators at their own expense, despite the mother's pleas. After pulling up floor boards and other futile attempts to find 'substantial proof' of bug colonies, the father borrows a camera and tries vainly to photograph them at night. Rather ironically, he will instead capture his family, fixing in time, for the adult narrator, the memory of her torment over identity: 'I still have that photo – slightly over-exposed, grey and grizzled like the weather that autumn. Mom looks unusually stern, and we children are shyly dishevelled. I, the eldest, am tall and adolescently weedy, wearing a wilting aster in my hair, which at the time I thought looked chic. The next day I wore one to school, but after enduring the giggles of my classmates all morning I tore it out of my hair and threw it in the garbage' (195–6).

As the father's obsession with the bugs becomes more determined and focused ('"Evidence," he went around the house muttering, "Proof."' [196]), it is as if their integrity, their identity as a family, and his position as patriarch depend on this type of scientific testimony. Unable to construct a powerful enough case, however, he heightens the nightly conflict in the home by insisting that they stand on principle and remain in the bug-infested house until they clear their name. At this point, the crisis in terms of testimony is evident: the harried pursuit of ideal rational or eyewitness proof thrusts the home into further crisis and confusion, and further discredit. Instead of acting as understanding audience for each other's authentic testimony, the members split and act out the trauma of not being able to address 'the Other' in the Other's terms. As Shoshana Felman and Dori Laub have observed, the trauma of symbolic and physical violence is exacerbated when the powerless cannot address their oppressors. Since powerful oppressors are often 'un-addressable Others,' social therapy often depends on testimony after the fact to an audience who will share knowledge of the trauma. While the story of bugs itself may function as testimony and social therapy for the daughter/narrator and readers after the fact, during the action the family struggles with divisions based on credibility.

The narrator confesses to having identified with her father, because of his ostensibly more active and principled method of resistance, rather than with her mother, whose daily resistance took the form of cleaning: 'Mom began to hate the house ... Now she spent every day cleaning, cleaning, cleaning. She changed the sheets on our beds each morning, washed the walls, beat the rugs. I remember thinking resentfully that we always had potatoes and sausages for supper. And I remembered Mom always looked tired' (196). The narrator also recalls her mother's furious cleaning as demeaning at the time because it seemed a weak and shameful response to the landlady: 'I was angry with Mom, too, for nodding so eagerly, for being so fearful' (195). Instead of threatening and challenging the landlady during her visit, the mother scrubs her trail of dirty footprints from the floor. The daughter's identification with her father's more aggressive projects and ways of knowing (for instance, photography, carpentry, open confrontation with the landlady, rational proof, evidence) suggests a desire for a more publicly valued sense of self, one that can testify to itself in a public and rational way, rather than a domestic and emotional one. Dissociating herself from her mother's image, her 'long skirts,' and her domestic role in the family becomes a way for the daughter to escape a psychosocial space which is devalued by gender as well as by poverty and ethnicity.

As a more mature narrator looking back, however, the daughter has developed more sympathy for her mother. This emerges in the overall form of the story as it focuses its ending on the mother's point of view, her labour, her muting, and her ability to bring the family together again through an alternative form of resistance. It also emerges through a double-voiced discourse. Two converging but contrasting versions of 'home,' which become the shifting frames for the story, are narrated through this double-voiced discourse: the poor house as entrapment and stigma and the homeplace as safe haven. The first line of the story relates the daughter/narrator's memory in a flat, detached tone – 'It was raining the night I discovered the bugs' (192) – which alternates throughout with a richer, more sensuous diction used to narrate family and ethnicity – 'I buried my face in Mom's faded pink nightgown ... She clucked and cooed, her voice husky with her Ukrainian accent, her breast full of her scent: a mixture of yeast, cabbage, and rose perfume' (193). The daughter's deep bonding with the mother and respect for her mother's struggle to maintain a safe 'homeplace' is communicated in the repeated use of the intimate address, 'Mom,' and in affirmative depictions of their physical closeness – 'I slipped back under the covers and fell asleep immediately, as if I had absorbed sleepiness from my mother's soft skin' (193).

The final tapestry of the narrative is a messy one, which, in its very messiness, testifies to the mother's anger, her limitations, and her drive to shape both into testimony. One morning, the family finds the mother asleep at the kitchen table after another all-night vigil. Behind her, the kitchen bears: 'hundreds of dead black bugs pinned to the wall ... each brittle black body was stuck to the wall with a thin pin' (197). The grotesque tapestry signifies the mother's sense of rage and triumph through a mode of resistance within her means. In effect, she has reappropriated bugs as the icon of poverty which insinuates dirt and sloth upon the immigrant poor, and reworked them instead into a more truthful tableau about her own industry and the family's entrapment in an exploitative rental space. The family's sense of priorities is re-established according to the mother's quest for privacy and the safety of home, and the father will apologize for having held the family hostage to supposedly higher values. Although the parents embrace over the extremity of the moment, the narrative itself ends simply on a flatly reported statement – 'We moved a few days later' (197) – showing that although the mother's testimony was unassailably truthful and effective in reuniting the family, it was still impotent outside the domestic sphere and the emotional circle of the family. Given the unfair practices of a market economy whereby the 'might' of the landlord 'makes right,' matters of truth may be subsumed by that law. (Although rental laws in many cities in Canada would allow tenants to fumigate and then present the bill to the owner, from my experience, few new immigrants would be aware of these rights, would risk the wrath of an angry landlord by asserting them, or would wait for rental board hearings months away when landlords often appear backed by lawyers anyway.) The material position of the family has not been directly altered by testimony. None the less, in affirming for them who they really were and what their home meant as private domain, the mother's non-verbal protest gives them the courage to make demands beyond the public, legal, and market definition of rented space.

The daughter's narrative gives audience and utterance to the mother's non-verbal testimony. But as the narrator reinscribes lived struggle, she admits that the mother's outrage and circuitous strategy of resistance had frightened the daughter into turning to her father for a 'sane' response. Thus, in the tradition of wall-reading begun by Charlotte Perkins Gilman in 'The Yellow Wallpaper,' the walls of the home in this story demarcate, both materially and semiotically, the limits of a housewife's powers to posit herself as a credible subject beyond and even within the home. Her resistance is taken for madness. The mother's testimony in 'Bugs' has a limited reach in contrast to the insults which amplify and intrude upon their private space. The wall stands itself as signifier to the work of an ordinary woman who needed foremost to report her reality transparently rather than decoratively or artistically. Her daughter will pick up the raw material of that testimony from which to spin a more crafted story. The generational and domestic link between utterances is established – the writer/daughter reinscribes the worker/mother's otherwise incoherent and devalued mode of resistance and pays tribute to her simple mode of expression by keeping the unaesthetic title 'Bugs' as proof of the unadorned, raw material of their everyday struggle.

If, as the epigraph by Bourdieu to this discussion of 'Bugs' suggests, a spectacular way to 'shock ... the bourgeois' is by 'conferring aesthetic status on objects or ways of representing them that are excluded by the dominant aesthetic of the time,' Holmes's story effectively shocks by resisting and reinscribing meaning around poor housing and by inserting bugs as the title of the tale.

Chapter 4

Theories and Anti-Theory: On Knowing Poor Women

For feminist critics to study the practical, ordinary narratives of poor women beside literary poverty narratives is as problematic as it is challenging, given the context of current literary criticism. Tony Bennett has noted in *Outside Literature* that there is a struggle, a 'wresting' of discourse materials needed in order even to begin to speak from or about a place outside literature: 'There is no ready-made theoretical position outside aesthetic discourse which can simply be taken up and occupied. Such a space requires a degree of fashioning; it must be organized and above all won ...' (10). Whereas Bennett would suggest we win that place by scientifically analysing and exposing a hierarchy of discourses within the academy, a political activist such as Paulo Freire has a more narrativist and populist approach to understanding ordinary voices. Freire's concept of cultural struggle urges academics to look beyond the limits of academic perception and academic hierarchies of knowledge to engage actively with oppressed groups to help them achieve subjecthood and to learn from them.

Speaking from the field of social activism and radical pedagogy rather than literary criticism, Freire has urged that shifts in theory be grounded in human narratives. Since these narratives are a location where the oppressed may imagine liberation in the context of their own experiences, Freire notes, they yield knowledge about the particularities of people's suffering and the multiple possibilities for their emancipation (1993, xi–xii). Especially in the context of a postmodern world where subjectivities have become unmoored from previous narratives of social justice, Freire encourages academics to listen to and ground our own educational praxis in the language of everyday experiences (1989, ix–xi). However, given the demands of established literary discourse, of which mainstream feminist criticism is now a part, populist feminist critics cannot move directly beyond theoretical exclusions towards marginal subjects; we must learn to move consciously between the theoretical positions we inherit and sometimes oppose and those I call, for the purposes of this discussion, anti-Theory.

This chapter discusses the importance and difficulty of understanding poverty narratives by women through theories of gender and class. Considering the mechanics and ethics of collecting voices within feminist criticism, this review chapter also reflects on some of the larger debates about representation and subjectivity which have determined our perception of gender, class, and poverty. In the absence of one over-arching Theory to order the present study, it draws on challenges narrativists and populists have posed to Theory when it fails to valorize everyday voices as sites of alternative knowledge.

4.1 Anti-Theory, Anti-What?

> Whereas the dominant position requires acts of self-deconstruction, the subordinate position entails collective self-construction. (Radhakrishnan 277)

By 'anti-Theories' I do not mean anti-theoretical discourse which mistrusts all theoretical formulations or anti-intellectual discourse or even the resistance to post-structuralist theory described by Paul de Man as a generalized 'resistance to theory.' Anti-Theories, as I see them, question the exclusions of Theory when it assumes its own primacy – for example, through scientific, homogenizing, or totalizing abstractions – above other ways of knowing culture and marginality. By 'anti-Theories' of marginal women's subjectivities, I mean those discussions about reading and interpreting marginal voices, often quite theoretical themselves, which steadily work towards political agency in the form of populist goals or coalition politics. These ideas comprise an oppositional force within academic feminist criticism by trying to bring feminist literary criticism back to a more direct interest in community and everyday life – or, in more political terms, back to praxis. While some anti-Theories reach beyond Theory into the area of experiences and particularities of concrete subjects, others scrutinize Theory to expose its own subjective blind spots which sometimes reduce the complexity of the marginal women as subjects or eclipse them altogether. Finally, these critical gestures towards greater community alliance are not simply an act of faith;

they often include, as part of their own political self-reflexivity, questions about the nature of political coalition and the claim to know and include marginal subjectivities as an alternative form of knowledge.[1]

In the early days of 'authentic realism' in American feminist criticism (during the 1970s), the problematic of moving back and forth between androcentric Theory and women's everyday experience was resolved by a veering away from theory and towards a direct assertion of the pre-eminent truth value of experience and subjectivity. As Sara Mills has observed in *Feminist Readings / Feminists Reading*, at that stage in experientially based criticism, the claims on the text were unabashedly prescriptive, privileging authenticity as a measure of the social effect of the text to challenge the status quo by correcting misrepresentations. Authentic realism implied an anti-theoretical stance because, as it sought to make literary texts accessible to more women, it also encouraged a more plain-speaking, less jargon-ridden form of critical inquiry and the received values enshrined in that discourse. In 'unacademic' language, grassroots discussion groups probed the transformational power of autobiographical and confessional texts in respect to the lives and experiences of ordinary women readers, an act which by its very existence raised important questions about knowledge claims in critical discourse and the social effect of literature (Mills et al. 51–82). But current poststructuralist debates on knowledge claims and experience across the disciplines have developed more complex attitudes about knowledge, attitudes which mistrust the representationist assumption that we can capture a concrete reality that is simply out there waiting for a purer, truer form of representation.[2]

Chris Weedon has critiqued the earlier strains of anti-theoretical and experiential criticism in *Feminist Practice and Poststructuralist Theory* through a deconstruction of the fiction/reality dichotomy and a more complex understanding of the relation between texts and everyday reality. But the emergence of more complex representationist theories has sometimes resulted in our neglecting realist texts altogether and privileging only those texts which consciously experiment with postmodernist forms and playfully deferred subjects. Rita Felski, among others, has expressed a concern with this neglect and has argued for

---

[1] For examples of such self-questioning around populist or radical goals, see Linda Alcoff's 'The Problem of Speaking for Others' and John McGuigan's *Cultural Populism*.

[2] For example, see Joan W. Scott's 'Experience,' Mary E. Hawkesworth's 'Knowers, Knowing, Known: Feminist Theory and Claims of Truth,' and Linda Alcoff and Elizabeth Potter's anthology *Feminist Epistemologies*.

reasserting the value of realist texts in the shadow of a postmodernist feminist canon. In *Beyond Feminist Aesthetics: Feminist Literature and Social Change*, she argues at length that, out of both political need and theoretical efficacy, the value of realist literature should be reinstated as a vital part of an oppositional feminist discourse. Felski has observed that certain types of feminist literary theory, especially those influenced by poststructuralism, have carried the implicit assumption that a concern for subjectivity based in lived reality is anachronistic and naïve. She concludes that there is, consequently, a need to defend the theoretical validity of a culturally based feminist criticism:

> it becomes possible to see [that] the debate between 'experiential' and 'poststructuralist' feminism does not lend itself to simple resolution by adjudicating their respective validity as theories, but springs from conflicting ideological interests: on the one hand a populist position which seeks to link texts to everyday life practices in the hope of affecting direct social change, on the other the emergence of an academic feminism with often quite different affiliations and professional commitment to more rigorous and intellectually sophisticated, and hence necessarily more esoteric, forms of analysis. (11)

Bella Brodzki and Celeste Schenck have also noted that the complex theorizing practised by feminist deconstructionists may have served to legitimate feminist discourse professionally, but that it may be time to 'uncouple' feminism and deconstruction in order to look at other forms of feminist theorizing and the politics of theory itself. As another critic has so succinctly put it, once again linking theoretical schools to subject positions grounded in power relations: 'Whereas the dominant position requires acts of self-deconstruction, the subordinate position entails collective self-construction' (Radhakrishnan 277). Yet those of us who prefer the ideological positioning of collective self-construction and populist feminism – and I use the term 'populist' here, as Felski does, in an affirmative sense[3] – still need more wide-ranging theories and reading practices to help us make these links between everyday life and theories of subjectivities and representation. More recently, the critical pendulum within feminist criticism has had time to recuperate from a dominant postmodernist swing, which invested heavily in theory as the language of knowledge and resistance, to produce more

---

3 See Jim McGuigan's discussion of the complex etymology of the term in *Cultural Populism* and my earlier discussion of the notion in chapter 1 under 'Populist Motives.'

community-grounded and self-reflexive reflections such as those found in Rosemary Hennessy and Chrys Ingraham's *Materialist Feminism* and Theresa Ebert's *Ludic Feminism*. Critical of the élitism of postmodernist feminist theory and its failure to posit subjects grounded in the material world, in history, or in minority groups – except on the level of discourse – these works call for a broader understanding of the feminist subject and a more diverse notion of women's subjectivities.

4.2 Subjectivities

The plural form 'subjectivities' is now fashionable within the context of postcolonial and poststructuralist debates because it invokes, paradoxically, both a sense of inclusiveness of other identities and a sense of playfully deferred identities. One notable exception to this generally blurred invocation of the term is Regenia Gagnier's astute theoretical introduction to a recent study by this title, *Subjectivities: A History of Self-Representation in Britain (1832–1920)*, which begins by stating that 'subjectivity' according to cultural studies is broader than the subjectivity previously known within the realm of literary studies. Not only did literary studies tend to limit the choice of texts to those which reflected bourgeois subjectivities, Gagnier observes, but the questions it asked of those subjectivities were not broad enough or probing enough to reveal the full cultural role of subjectivity. She reviews a wide range of definitions now circulating actively in academic discourse: first, 'the subject is a subject to itself, an "I"'; second and simultaneously, it is a subject to others appearing as the 'Other,' which often leads it to construct itself, especially in the case of groups, communities, classes, and nations, in opposition to others; third, the subject is one of knowledge, especially in terms of 'the discourse of social institutions which circumscribe its terms of being'; fourth, the subject is a body separate from others (except in the case of a pregnant woman) and dependent upon its concrete environment; fifth, the subject is often identified, despite challenges by deconstructionists, as the site of subjective knowledge as opposed to objective knowledge, in other words with the partial and particular view of the world rather than the Cartesian and hypothetical universal view; and finally, the subject is also a textual convention or, as Gagnier describes it: 'the "I" is the self-present subject of the sentence as well as the subject "subjected" to the symbolic order of the language in which one is writing' (8–9).

Gagnier's is not an exhaustive list, but it is complete enough to hint at the complex theorizing of subjectivity in the context of current academic discourse and to show how precisely defined the use of the term should be to avoid blurring and slippage among these applications. For example, marginal women's subjectivities are represented in current academic discourse, more often than not, in terms of the second definition listed above: how working-class and poor women are defined as 'other' in terms of both class and gender. But increasingly, some of the more radical critics aligned with these women are willing to ask, like the proponents of a Marxist history-from-below tradition, how working-class and poor women experience themselves as 'I' as well as 'other' and also according to any of the other applications above (for example, according to Gagnier's fourth definition we might also ask how the working-class or poor subject might experience her body differently because it is classed as well as gendered). As Patrick Brantlinger notes, however, rendering the subject more theoretically complex is not in and of itself an oppositional act, and therefore the cultural critic who claims to be critiquing dominant culture must posit more than increasingly complex ways of representing the subject or exposing hegemonic misrepresentation; she must also posit through her critique alternative social orders (145).

Interestingly enough, populist feminist critics seldom spend publication time rigorously defining their precise theoretical application of the term; they usually focus instead on the importance of listening more closely to the heterogeneous and complex composition of classed and gendered subjectivities as it is represented by the voices of marginal subjects themselves and the problematics of listening to and speaking for others. For example, populist critics such as Barbara Christian, bell hooks, and Janet Zandy, whose anti-Theories I will discuss shortly, urge the valorization of the voices of marginal women as the first and primary step in gaining access to their subjectivities. These feminist critics, whom I would term populist critics, look to the voices and the concrete subjects in their communities as more than objects of study, and above all as subjects capable of imparting knowledge about their own meanings and imaginings.[4] That is not to assume that we can gain access to these subjectivities purely and simply

---

4 Some might not appreciate this categorization because of associations between right-wing movements and populism. But I use the term in its broader, cultural studies context, which includes the possibility of left-wing populism as well as right-wing movements such as Reaganomics, the Common Sense Revolution, or Thatcherism.

through good faith and solidarity, but to recommend that we listen closely to the idiom, the texture, and the testimonial function of the stories where subjectivities are expressed.

Understanding marginalized subjectivities in terms of class, race, and gender should involve a radical critique of our own categories of analysis, as well as the context of our inquiry and how we invoke marginalized subjects from our relatively privileged positions as academics. For example, it is important to remember that current inquiries about class and gender come after an embattled era when Marxists and feminists vied for the primacy of their respective categories of analysis: class and gender – with socialist feminists caught in between. The following excerpt from 'The Very Last Feminist Poem,' by the little-known Canadian writer and propagandist for Marxism Sharon Stevenson, dramatizes a socialist feminist's struggle with conflicting subjectivities. On the one hand, the speaker mistrusts a feminist subjectivity as less politically potent than a man's and more bourgeois in its self-absorbed nature. On the other hand, she fears that a Marxist subjectivity will not make room for a woman's private and corporeal concerns. Yet the poem affirms the concreteness and emotional texture of a woman's experiences of her body against the backdrop of history:

> if I were, for instance, Chris Marlowe
> (dead soon after)
> I might be thinking a great deal of the future
> of possibility
> of how to affect change
> if only I were a man.
> instead my mind runs in argument
> over & over again
> with the husband
> the lovers
> the absence of child
> held small in the womb
> seeming lack of purpose
> chaos in day-to-day life
>
> & subjectivity
> rushes soft & clinging
> along the thighs

before nestling in the brain
as the strongest weapon
of the bourgeoisie.

(ll. 9–28)

The sensuous diction reveals ambivalence over womanly subjectivity, rejected as alien and invasive on the surface but 'clinging' and 'nestling' none the less, in a softly sensual way. The Marxist despairs of her lack of focus on the public sphere and her distraction from a historical mission, a distraction which leaves her wanting beside Marlowe, remembered by history as both artist and political agent. But this guiltily confessional moment does invoke a different scene of historical struggle, a gendered scene: the early stage of socialist feminism when highly politicized women experienced their subjectivities (and their political souls and physical bodies, for that matter) as contested territory.[5]

This historic tug-of-war with the fundamentally conflicting notions of public and private subjectivity in Marxism and feminism warrants more careful study because the assertion of the primacy of one category over the other was more than theoretical 'nit-picking,' as Josephine Donovan noted in *Feminist Theory: The Intellectual Traditions of American Feminism*. The conflict implied questions of loyalties to various communities and different 'revolutionary strateg[ies]' (87). In the early days of socialist feminism in American academia, revolutionary strategy depended not only on where one's primary loyalties lay in terms of theory, Donovan notes, but also on how theory extended into strategy – especially, how one perceived the formation of revolutionary consciousness in oneself and others as subjects of history – for example, whether working-class women would be brought to class-consciousness through the efforts of an educated élite or through their own insights into oppression, a debate over agency long raging in Marxism itself.

When the object of study shifts from class and gender to poverty and gender, there is much less of a theoretical basis from which to study subjectivities. As I mentioned previously, the concept of the feminization of poverty is very recent and has not been applied to literary study as theories of class and gender have. Furthermore, the change of focus to poverty and gender may upset alliances with working-class men and their writing communities which were previously encompassed in

---

5 For a good overview of the theoretical dilemmas of socialist feminists, see Louise C. Johnson's summary 'Socialist Feminisms' in *Feminist Knowledge: Critique and Construct*.

feminist studies of class and gender. On the other hand, recent sociological studies of the feminization of poverty in North America are more available than those on class and gender. In the past, the latter studied women as classed subjects in respect to their husbands' or fathers' occupations. It is significant that poor women's and working-class women's subjectivities appear through different types of academic discourses with their own ideological implications. It is significant, and worth repeating, that poor women often appear as objects of study in sociology and ethnography rather than as subjects of their own stories in the field of literary analysis.

4.3 Theories of the Classed and Gendered Subject

> It is equally necessary for feminist theory to acknowledge that gender is only one of the many determining influences upon subjectivity, ranging from macrostructures such as class, nationality, and race down to microstructures such as the accidents of personal history, which do not simply exist alongside gender distinctions, but actively influence and are influenced by them. To define gender as the primary explanation of all social relations, to speak of the male and female subject in abstract and ahistorical terms, is in fact ultimately counterproductive for feminism, in that such an account can offer no explanation of how existing forms of gender inequality can be changed. (Felski 59)

Although the present study fashions a category of poverty narratives in order to interrogate narratives about cross-class experiences of poverty, it is also informed by feminist critiques of class theory in order to interrogate different representations of poverty on the subject of class and gender. Until the advent of feminist scholarship, social critics rarely interpreted the link between class and gender, partly because Marxist theory itself did not adequately address 'the woman question.' In the past three decades, feminist materialist critics have begun to articulate theoretical concerns which can guide our reading by helping us interpret class and gender as reciprocal constructions – critics on the international scene such as Cora Kaplan, Lillian Robinson, Michèle Barrett, Judith Newton and Deborah Rosenfelt, Paul Lauter, Janet Zandy, Theresa Ebert, and Rosemary Hennessy and Chrys Ingraham; and in Canada, Sara Diamond and Madeleine Ouellette-Michalska. Common to most of these theoretical discussions is a newly forming definition of class and an understanding of women's experience of poverty based on a consideration of employment ghettos and unpaid domestic and reproductive roles and the feminization of poverty. Recently, debate has surfaced around the notion of the feminization of poverty. Some critique the concept for blurring class distinctions among poor women by failing to situate the experiences of working-class women in relation to those of bourgeois women and working-class men. For example, Johanna Brenner cautions in 'Feminist Political Discourses: Radical versus Liberal Approaches to the Feminization of Poverty and Comparable Worth' that a social campaign against the feminization of poverty in the United States is ideologically suspect in that it usually focuses on women's domestic role, implies that the nuclear family is the solution to women's poverty, creates a false image of the deserving and the undeserving poor, invites the intervention of the welfare state, and fails to distinguish between bourgeois and working-class women's experience of the dissolution of the family while severing consideration of working-class and minority women's poverty from that of their male counterparts. These objections to certain applications of the term are valuable as qualifiers. It seems strategic to retain the term in this expanded and critical sense, however, rather than discard it, since it is the only expression describing increased poverty among women already on its way to becoming a household word, at least in feminist households.

It is also important to remember that slippage between the terms 'poor' and 'working-class' women and the terms 'poverty narratives' and 'working-class writing' cannot be avoided completely because of the present theoretical climate in feminist theory. As I mentioned in the introduction, the slippage by contemporary feminist critics is often willed and oppositional, in order to show their dissatisfaction with previous class theories for failing to take into account the gendered realities of women's experiences of class. I try to distinguish between the terms when I do not mean to include both these overlapping groups of women, but many contemporary theorists whom I discuss do not make these distinctions and do not consider the cross-class phenomenon of the feminization of poverty. On the other hand, some are very much aware of these issues and thus choose to apply the term 'working-class women' very loosely in response.

Most schools of feminist theory are now demanding that the theoretical basis of feminist coalition has to be more historically and socially informed than an idealized category of gender. And the inclusion of marginal subjectivities is central to this project of informed coalition among women. But the great majority of academic feminists are still theorizing from a position of privileged status (of several types: economic, racial, ethnic, educational, social, professional, and cultural), a position which tends to idealize the relation of a pluralist feminist discourse to lived marginality and lived rifts among women. An idealist feminist discourse claims to transcend élitism and to unfold truths about female subjectivity which apply to all women no matter how different their stories may be. For example, Elaine Showalter's pioneering essay 'Feminist Criticism in the Wilderness' (1981) posited a theory of culture whereby all women were represented as culturally marginalized and thus part of a binding reality. Furthermore, Showalter claimed, '[i]t is in the emphasis on the binding force of women's culture that this approach differs from Marxist theories of cultural hegemony' (27). Showalter may be seen as having posited, first, an idealized concept of collective female culture as a rallying cry to theory and, second, a theory which by its very nature would not make a significant place for the knowledge that marginalized women have of difference and hegemony in their everyday lives. As evidenced by Donna Perry's later overview of the discipline in 'Procne's Song: The Task of Feminist Literary Criticism,' mainstream, academic feminist criticism still posits the concept of a community of female readers and writers which ultimately transcends class and race. Through the rather optimistic notion that the feminist critic is one consciously 'writing to and for the converted,' Perry claims that dissenting voices and differences among feminists are able to emerge and challenge what those shared concerns are (302–3). As anyone knows from looking at the class and racial make-up of student and faculty populations and attendance at academic conferences, however, women do not all speak with one transcendent and homogeneous voice – we are not all being heard through 'the voice' of academic feminism.

High theorists as well as populists are increasingly arguing that the assumptions behind gender-specific categories of analysis may detract from theoretical rigour by failing to recognize women's different group and individual social locations and subject positions.[6] For example, Jeanne Costello's 'Taking the "Woman" out of Women's Autobiogra-

---

6 For further critiques of gender as a category of analysis, see Joan Wallach Scott's chapter 'Gender: A Useful Category for Historical Analysis'; Rita Felski's chapter 'Subjectivity and Feminism'; and Sandra Harding's 'The Instability of the Analytical Categories of Feminist Theory.'

phy: The Perils and Potentials of Theorizing Female Subjectivities' calls into question not only the homogenizing of the female subject through disregard for social forces such as class, gender, and sexual orientation, but also the whole strategy of still creating gender-specific categories of texts at this point in feminist criticism. Costello criticizes recent theories of women's life-writing, in particular those based on the application of psychological gender theories such as Nancy Chodorow's and Carole Gilligan's, showing how essentialism often creeps into feminist practices of reading and questioning women's texts. Judith Butler's *Gender Trouble* suggests dismantling the gender paradigm as a gesture towards greater theoretical rigour. As an antidote to the homogenizing aspect of heterosexual feminist identity politics in high theory, Butler prescribes even higher theory: 'a critical genealogy of [feminism's] own legitimating practices' (5). But Butler's own genealogy is historically lopsided on the side of academic feminism, leaving out the dissenting voices, the 'anti-Theorists' among feminism's populist critics and activists who have traditionally exceeded 'Theory' in their capacity to embrace heterogeneity by going outside the academy among those very women whom 'Theory' has excluded. Consider, for example, Sheila Baxter, activist and welfare mother, who in 1998 compiled a collection of interviews with poor women in Vancouver, *No Way to Live: Poor Women Speak Out*, and included women of diverse racial and ethnic groups, lesbian women, elderly women, single women, married women, handicapped women, and so on.

Although populist critics may be as falsely idealistic about a common community of women as practitioners of high theory are in invoking unproblematized claims of identity and macro-political goals, populists do not need to rely exclusively on increasingly complex theory to invoke the heterogeneity of subjects in their community because the very practice of their cultural critique is linked to recovering and exploring the particular and heterogeneous voices of concrete subjects. With our eyes on the complexity of everyday life, we are more likely to see that alliances between a given individual and various communities and subcultures, with their accompanying constructions of identity, are tentative because they shift with material circumstances, age, sexual orientation, race, ethnicity, and so on. (For more detailed theoretical discussion about coalition politics and reading practices see 'Resisting Autobiography: Outlaw Genres and Transnational Feminist Subjects' by Caren Kaplan and 'Negotiating Subject Positions in an Uneven World' by R. Radhakrishnan.)

In the last two decades, in particular, feminists have advanced beyond the dispute over the primary identity designation (class or gender?) and refined the discussion by asking how class, race, and gender work as interacting contexts which construct the subject. This challenge has arisen partly from anti-Theories such as Janet Zandy's when she asserts empirically the importance of women's gendered difference within the working class: 'the boundaries and texture of working-class women's lives are not the same as men's. Not separate, but not the same' (1990, 7). And the relation between class and gender has also been problematized by theorizing class differently. For example, Christine Delphy in *Close to Home: A Materialist Analysis of Women's Oppression* (1984) has challenged the Marxist conception of class identity with an alternative theoretical formulation; instead of class identity based solely in market modes of production (the public sphere), she posits the construction of working-class identity within the domestic mode of production (the private sphere). Of particular interest in Delphy's challenge is the method of bringing her own empirical observations of rural women in everyday life to bear on intellectual Marxism – but not in a scientific or even a methodologically systematic way, rather in a descriptive way which shows the complexity of lives which exceed Theory (9, 43–6).

Materialist feminists, especially in British feminist theory, have also called for greater rigour in theorizing the classed and gendered subject through consideration of a more psychologically complex subject. For example, Carolyn Steedman has described how necessary it is to allow an unconscious life to working-class childhoods in order to understand the individual formations of class-consciousness and the different textures of classed and gendered experiences. She attributes the devaluation of the unconscious in class theory to gender bias. What Steedman terms the 'refusal of a complicated psychology to those living in material distress' has come about, she suggests, not only because of the privileging of experiences of working-class men as a source of knowledge about class identity, but also because of the generally debased position of mental life in Marxist philosophy and the fact that the theory of emotional and psychological selfhood was executed by people in a central class relationship to the dominant culture (285).

Materialist feminists have been discussing subjectivities recently in two significantly different ways: while some generate what I call 'anti-Theories' to explain the utterances of working-class and poor women as subjects of oppositional culture, others have approached class and gender through high theory as inscriptions which need to be decoded by engaged critics applying oppositional reading practices to texts. In other words, while some feminists write anti-Theories to locate the agent's potential for cultural opposition in marginal women's voices themselves as subjects of knowledge, others are working on new theories to refine how we read class and gender in these voices and more traditional canonical texts as objects of knowledge, thus locating the agent's potential with intellectuals in the act of critical analysis itself. The purpose of the discussion here is not to valorize one method over the other, but to show how anti-Theories often function to balance theories and bring them back to political praxis and a more concretely inclusive sense of community and culture.

In 'Pandora's Box: Subjectivity, Class and Sexuality in Socialist-Feminist Criticism,' Cora Kaplan suggests that we reframe the theoretical debate about whether one social construct – class or gender – should contain or take precedence over the other by studying texts in terms of how the speaking subject is constructed by class and gender given that these constructs interact reciprocally and in a complex way upon the speaking subject (346, 364). Class and gender work upon the subject as reciprocal processes, she argues, rather than fixed contents or static territories which can be located in and around the subject definitively. Kaplan suggests that fiction in general can reveal subjectivities if we study it as 'the ordering of the imagination,' as the site of expressions of 'hidden' or taken-for-granted ideological beliefs about the self and other classes of women, especially in respect to a history of conventional formulations of femininity: 'Literary texts give these simultaneous inscriptions narrative form, pointing towards and opening up the fragmentary nature of social and psychic identity, drawing out the ways in which social meaning is psychically represented. It is this symbolic shaping of class that we should examine in fiction' (359). In addition to identifying the 'construction of dominant definitions of the inner lives of working-class women,' Kaplan suggests, therefore, that we learn 'how dominant definitions of both class and gender are lived by these women' (361). She implies that taking class and gender into account in 'a more complex way' would mean – in addition to the appropriation of semiotic and psychoanalytical methodologies by materialist feminists – turning to 'non-literary sources, to the discourses in which [working-class women] themselves [speak]' (361). But she adds that the integration of these voices falls beyond the theoretical scope of her own essay, perhaps because at this point her theory necessarily heads into the uncharted area of anti-Theory.

Catherine Belsey, on the other hand, does not discuss the possibility that counter-hegemonic knowledge can emerge from the utterances of ordinary subjects in her essay 'Constructing the Subject: Deconstructing the Text.' Belsey implies that the power to challenge ideology lies in the hands of a reader/critic who can discover contradictory subjectivities by deconstructing the canonized text: 'Having created a canon of acceptable texts, criticism then provides them with acceptable interpretations, thus effectively censoring any elements in them which come into collision with the dominant ideology. To deconstruct the text, on the other hand, is to open it, to release the possible positions of its intelligibility, including those which reveal the partiality (in both senses) of the ideology inscribed in the text' (58, 51). Belsey's use of the term 'subjectivity' may be partly explained by the concept of ideology to which she subscribes, that of the Althusserian school, which defines ideology as a determinate and dominant force of misrepresentation acting upon all subjects to create false and partial consciousness. Given this context, Belsey refers to subjectivity as though it were an ideologically determined location which is knowable or partially knowable through discourse analysis, historical analysis, psychoanalysis, and deconstruction – in short, through scientific or objective means. This implies that a woman's own narratives about herself and her lived realities are not potent enough to challenge the misrepresentations (and thus hegemony) which ideology imposes – unless, perhaps, the subject herself is capable of applying a method of deconstruction to open her own utterance and see how ideology is operating within it.

By comparing Kaplan's and Belsey's theorizations of the subject, we can see that Kaplan's discussion of subjectivity implies more faith in individual agency and in personal formulations of lived experience as an additional source of knowledge in challenging oppressive ideologies. Kaplan's use of the term valorizes subjectivity as a way of knowing, as politically grounded perspectives and sensibilities through which we can know and feel, rather than merely deconstruct and map, the female subject. Thus, as noted earlier, Kaplan invites emergent voices into the process of oppositional analysis as epistemologically valid subjects, though she stops short of theorizing how this might be done. The nuances between the two theorists' concepts of subjectivity illustrate how materialist feminists must struggle with residual and somewhat divergent Marxist theories about ideology and subjectivity while striking out with new feminist theory to explore subjects which have previously been off the map. (On gaining access to women's subjectivities through fiction, see also Weedon 74–113; Felski 51–85; and Rabinowitz 97–136.)

I would agree that it is useful to be vigilant about the dangers of mystifying subjectivity and prioritizing it above other forms of knowledge, practices which Chris Weedon links with assumptions in humanist discourse of the free, self-determining individual and those of certain radical and essentialist theories of gender (78–9) and which Catherine Belsey also links with assumptions of autonomous agency (1988, 51–2). But the fact remains that theories which are not informed by these subjectivities, even when acknowledging the voices of working-class women as worthy *objects* of study, have tended to be too abstract or too idealist to bring us much closer to any 'inside' knowledge of what Zandy referred to as 'the boundaries and textures of working-class women's lives.' It seems that the mundane and messy sphere of material struggle, class identification, complicity, and the complexity of life in the concrete world have not been able to emerge through the highly abstract language and theory of literary discourse – whereas these subjectivities are palpable in testimonies about the lived experiences of class and poverty.

4.4 Understanding as Opposed to Mapping Subjectivities

Among the theories and anti-Theories of materialist feminism, there emerge nuanced but significant differences between projects to map marginal women's subjectivities and those which claim to experience them as knowledge and cultural exchange. These projects are not necessarily separate, and sometimes one critic will attempt both in the course of a particular work; but it is interesting how the choice to 'map' subjectivities often signals that the critic is about to write a theory from a more distanced, bird's-eye view, so to speak, rather than from the more closely identified position of coalition with the marginalized community itself. Although both of these projects are invaluable to feminist criticism and cultural studies, anti-Theory is the more devalued of the two in academia. Critics who place greater value on the power of marginal voices to inform reading and writing practices are often seen by the literary establishment, at worst as anti-intellectual, and at best as less academically rigorous than those who confine their methods to archival research or abstract theorizing about these voices as objects of study.

I have already mentioned that Janet Zandy's introduction to *Calling*

Home: Working-class Women's Writing: An Anthology constitutes what I would call an anti-Theory based on recovering working-class women's voices and reading them 'from the inside out.' Zandy has suggested that working-class women in late capitalism in America experience a special kind of cultural exclusion which is so pervasive that it denies us a 'cultural home.' This severe experience of muting requires, more than the academic mapping of difference, the cultural recovery of stories, memory, and subjectivities specific to this community of women. Cultural recovery projects assume that the phenomenological potential of reading will allow texts to play a role in social therapy and in identity construction. For example, Zandy calls for an intertextual rather than theory-oriented cultural criticism which would allow us to bypass complexly exclusionary Theory and claim access to a 'cultural home' through a process of recognition and retrieval, a collaborative process between reader and writer.

Zandy is pragmatic and respectful in her discussion of working-class women's utterances, expressing a great faith in the internal coherence of these voices and their potential to inform the oppositional reader: 'To try to fit this literature into the neat academic categories of genre or period is like squeezing a wilderness into a cultivated park. Despite its diversity and unconventional literary forms, working-class literature is not a mass of dangling parts but a collective body of work. To see these connections, one has to look from the inside out, that is, through the impulses and intentions of the literature itself' (1990, 9). While affirming the coherence of working-class texts as a body, Zandy also affirms the uncontainable nature of these utterances in the image of the wilderness. This motif recalls Showalter's paradigm of cultural muting in 'Feminist Criticism in the Wilderness,' but stresses heterogeneity, class differences, and lack of cultural access as realities within a non-idealized cultural wilderness. Furthermore, Zandy implies that access to the inside of working-class women's experience of cultural wilderness is possible by assembling voices which come from the inside of these experiences not in terms of essence but in terms of point of view: 'I looked for pieces from the inside of working-class experience either by virtue of the author having been born into the working class or through close political and cultural identification with working-class life' (ibid., 8). Thus, the inside of this community is determined by a sense of coalition based on empathy, political analysis, or an insider's knowledge of experience, rather than on essence.

In her brief discussion of 'intentionality,' Zandy gives the impression that she has been selective in drawing together narratives which express subjectivities based on collectivity and struggle. This selectivity makes the project of reading 'from the inside out' one partly dependent on the inside of a consciously idealist (as opposed to idealized) category of narratives which has been fashioned by the critic for, by, or about a particular group of working-class women or women who empathize with this position – all of whom have achieved an awareness of the importance of struggle (ibid., 10). What I am saying here is that the claim to read from the inside, in this case, is more a politically demarcated space than a theoretical one; it comes to mean reading from the inside of a community of women writers and readers who are brought together through political coalition. To use Zandy's own distinction, then, she implies that we strive to read not only from inside a space (a cultural home) of class knowledge but, more specifically, from inside a space of willed class solidarity: 'Class knowledge comes from experience and story, history and memory, and from the urgency of witnessing. Class solidarity is born from perception of common struggles and common enemies' (ibid., 8). By distinguishing between the search for class knowledge which tolerates heterogeneity and the search for class solidarity which wills commonality, Zandy avoids having to idealize the stories of working-class women, as earlier categories of proletarian literature did.

Although she avoids the word 'populist,' probably because of its negative political implications under Reaganomics, Zandy's populist goals are overt; they outweigh any merely ethnographic concerns for broader representation and are the clearest aspect of her 'anti-Theory.' When she gives priority to a reading practice and a form of critical discourse which 'would not alienate working-class people from their own texts and would not privilege the critic at the expense of the writer,' her commitment to make her own theory more accessible, relevant, and serviceable to a community of readers and writers among working-class women signals a stronger bond with the concerns and sensibilities of this community than with the abstract notions of class and gender (ibid., 10). This bond is perhaps one reason why her concept of reading from the inside out remains inadequately theorized for academic consumption (especially on the point of intentionality) – inadequate, that is, given the bourgeois tradition that literary discourse speaks an academic insiders' language.

The exclusionary aspect of theoretical language and theoretical practice has been eloquently challenged by Barbara Christian in 'The Race for Theory.' For example, Christian maintains that African Americans have always had to theorize as a strategy for survival. Although their theories have not been academically sanctioned, they have always been a race who theorized their own oppression to make sense of their world. In the present academic climate, however, Christian argues that African-American critics and other radical critics often feel pressured by the institutional exigency of creating and prescribing one Theory which will contain or homogenize the voices under study: 'Some of us are continually harassed to invent wholesale theories, regardless of the complexity of the literature we study ... I consider it presumptuous of me to invent a theory of how we ought to read. Instead, I think we need to read the works of our writers in our various ways and remain open to the intricacies of the intersection of language, class, race, and gender in the literature' (570).

Christian's solution to the race for theory, which she sees as taking place at the expense of recognizing difference, is twofold: first, to valorize theoretical formulations other than those of 'high' criticism by learning to listen to the theory couched in the ordinary or the poetic language of the people themselves; and second, to ground theory constantly in the practice of reading the literature of people who are not usually heard, because, Christian notes, 'theorizing is of necessity based on our multiplicity of experiences' (577). The bottom line she sees for engaged critics from oppressed groups is that we must always interrogate our own praxis ethically by asking, 'For whom are we doing what we are doing when we do literary criticism?' Grounding our inquiry in feelings of coalition and our own subjective experiences of class and gender – as well as our concepts of these forces – will bind us more faithfully to the community about whom we write and help us to resist acculturation in an academic community which often pressures us to deal in the currency of theories and authorities which are alien to our subjective experiences.

Though the current fashion is to engage in critical discourse about marginal subjectivities, we may still devalue those same subjectivities through institutional discourse and reading practices. In *Yearning: Race, Gender, and Cultural Politics*, bell hooks has noted: 'Too often, it seems, the point is to promote the appearance of difference within intellectual discourse, a "celebration" that fails to ask who is sponsoring the party and who is extending the invitations. For who is controlling this new discourse? Who is getting hired to teach it, and where? Who's getting paid to write about it?' (54). Hooks suggests that white academics refuse to perceive the existence of a special psychosocial/cultural space based on black sensibilities and experiences: '[T]he tendency to overvalue work by white scholars, coupled with the suggestion that such work constitutes the only relevant discourse, evades the issue of potential inaccessible locations – spaces white theorists cannot occupy. Without reinscribing an essentialist standpoint, it is crucial that we neither ignore nor deny that such locations exist' (55; see also both Steedman and Mukherjee on the topic of informed and subjective reading by insiders in marginalized groups). Yet stepping forward and signifying difference subjectively in the academy provokes negative feedback, according to hooks, as long as it occurs within a feminist movement where well-intentioned, but none the less privileged, white women impose a transcendent and idealized 'notion of friendship and sisterly bonding ... based on principles of seamless harmony' and an unacknowledged code for 'nice, nice behaviour' (89).

Without making subjectivity the exclusive or even the pre-eminent source of knowledge about life and culture on the margins, populist critics such as Zandy, Christian, and hooks are beginning to present us with a clearer image of how the academic world pushes marginal voices to the outside via theories and institutional practices which actively, though often unintentionally, assert a hierarchy of subjectivities. Anti-Theories show feminists how the wilderness of female culture has already been colonized by classist and racist values and that the way back to a history of that colonization should include, as well as a collection of muted voices inscribed in narratives, the critic's own subjective knowledge and even her or his own oppositional idiom. For example, Christian has described how gaining knowledge through texts is a way of feeling connected with her own community of women and men and a means of cultural survival: '[W]hat I write and how I write is done in order to save my life. And I mean that literally. For me, literature is a way of knowing that I am not hallucinating, that whatever I feel/know is. It is an affirmation that sensuality is intelligence, that sensual language is language that makes sense ' (578). And bell hooks recalls that her attempts to use language from the vernacular invariably met with editors' corrections, which she herself accepted until she realized how 'disempowering it was for people from underprivileged backgrounds to consciously censor our speech so as to "fit better" in settings where we are perceived as not belonging' (90). Similarly, writing about the politics of representation in Canadian Native women's writing, Barbara Godard has noted that the literary institution has asserted 'its authority monologically by refusing to engage in dialogue with these alternate discourses' (1990, 186). Godard explains that so few subject-positions are left open to Native writers, given the literary institution's enforcement of a limited author-position, that their subjectivities and idiom are sometimes rejected by publishers – in Lenore Keeshig-Tobias's words, for sounding 'too Indian' or 'not Indian enough' (ibid.). An English literature professor of South-Asian origin in Canada, Arun Mukherjee, has reported that students may also discourage a discourse of cultural difference by reasserting a dominant apolitical and ahistorical humanist discourse in their analyses. Mukherjee explains how students may resist oppositional readings of texts and embrace instead a 'prophylactic view of literature,' described by Richard Ohmann as filtering subversive content from even the most provocative texts (Mukherjee 27–8). Important steps in oppositional criticism are, therefore, not only the recovery of marginal subjectivities but also the exposure of a hierarchy of subjectivities within theoretical discourse and the exposure of academic discourse as an insider discourse subjectively formed in the interests of that reigning group. For, as Terry Eagleton noted in *Literary Theory: An Introduction*, you may speak a 'regional dialect' of critical discourse, 'but you must not sound as though you are speaking another language altogether' for '[t]o do so is to recognize in the sharpest way that critical discourse is power. To be on the inside of the discourse itself is to be blind to this power, for what is more natural and non-dominative than to speak one's own tongue?' (210). There is a terrible irony here. Pronouncing difference within a tightly policed formal discourse risks pushing populist critics farther towards the margins, yet in order to move closer to marginal women's subjectivities, we must speak different critical languages through which we can construct a more radical subjecthood. And so we move between theories and anti-Theory, not so much playfully as critically – not celebrating detachment, but looking for a home.

Chapter 5

Subverting 'Poor Me': Negative Constructions of Identity

To dare an adventure I cannot afford is the tension I experience in realizing myself as a writer. A question of identity. To step out of my heritage as a member of the working class to attempt to say something of importance is the adventure. I was not meant to do this. As a woman. As a working-class woman. Writing is an act of defiance, rebellion ... arrogance.

'A Question of Identity,' Cy-Thea Sand, 61

Self-representations by poor and working-class women are an adventure for writers and readers alike because they often raise previously unspoken questions of identity. They defy the class and gender imperatives which would otherwise keep these women invisible or contained within representative images. In many cases, these life stories expose the social mechanisms of exclusion. But the act of self-representation for poor women is often, paradoxically, shameful as well as defiant in that it is so often accompanied by the shame of being made visible and admitting powerlessness. In the quotation above, Sand represents writing as a life choice requiring daring through the appropriately economic image of 'an adventure [she] cannot *afford.*' This image draws attention not only to the heightened economic stress of a writer's existence for a working-class woman who already occupies an economically precarious position but also to the psychosocial danger of stepping beyond the place of a silenced subject. Studies of shame and redefinitions of shame as potentially resistant (Fox) have recently emerged as alternative ways of reading working-class identity, especially individual identity, in the absence of strong social movements that affirm collective goals and subjectivities. In this discussion, however, I have chosen to focus on two women who move beyond shame to a place of resistance. In terms of genres, this chapter focuses on the resistant potential of autobiographical testimony, whereas the next will interrogate the hegemonic element of autobiographic memory. I hope to problematize both theories of autobiography with reference to specific life stories to show how, ultimately, the form and content of poverty narratives, not to mention the reading experience, determine the ideology of the story, never the form alone.

In Cy-Thea Sand's personal essay 'A Question of Identity' and Maria Campbell's full-length autobiography *Halfbreed*, more than the angel-in-the-house mechanism of feminine self-censorship identified by Virginia Woolf and other feminist critics, we see class- and race-based, as well as gender-based, negative constructions of identity, all of which function as compelling sources of cultural muting. For example, one such negative construction of how Sand experiences herself as a writer turns 'rebellion' into 'arrogance' in her formulation, quoted above. In *Halfbreed*, the subject reflects less on the act of narrating or self-censorship than she does on the events and family members in a long life of struggle. As both survivor and witness, Campbell testifies in a seemingly transparent style to the material consequences of racism and poverty and to the despair and self-destruction triggered by internalized negative constructions of her people as 'halfbreeds.' Both writers venture the risk and shame of self-representation in order to defy dominant definitions of the self. Moreover, it is through the confronting and telling about a shamed self that their oppositional voices emerge.

I use the term 'constructions' of identity in opposition to 'strategies' of identity to imply the palpable and received nature of negative images (despite complicity on the part of marginalized subjects). I use the term 'negative' when constructions of identity reflect exclusionary practices by people at the centre against those on the periphery – practices such as stereotyping, blaming, disbelieving, misrepresenting, or silencing – or when these constructions of identity result in feelings of shame, self-blaming, passivity, or powerlessness. These references to received, negative constructions of identity are tentative working labels which are subjectively unfolded in the narratives themselves rather than rigorously theorized here. What is central to my exploration, at this point, is not how to isolate or categorize these discursive events or present a taxonomy of them but, rather, how autobiographical subjects report them as complex, lived experience of exclusionary discourse and how we may interpret them as readers.

If writing is for poor and working-class women, as Janet Zandy has suggested in *Calling Home,* 'a way of locating oneself, a way of finding a home in an inhospitable universe,' then one of the crucial processes in that search for a sense of cultural belonging is navigation through exclusionary discourses and negative definitions of the self (1990, 1). As autobiographical subjects, poor and working-class women frequently call on negative constructions of identity as markers of past selves in order to position themselves as subjects even when they report conversion to more self-affirming or more oppositional discourses on their own marginalization. To position themselves in this way, subjects may testify directly to the lived consequences of a rhetoric of exclusion, they may unfold a shameful 'I' who experiences powerlessness and muting in the face of internalized negative definitions, or they may subvert the negative identity through defiance or the use of a collective 'we.' Negative constructions of poor and working-class women are generated culturally in both simple and complex ways: for example, through popular myths about the poor, through a liberal discourse that is covertly exclusionary, especially towards poor women, and through representative narrative forms which often misrepresent lived experiences of poverty. Sand and Campbell report experiencing insults and stereotypes, internalizing such constructions, and defying them – but not necessarily in a linear progression whereby the subject's relationship with negative constructions of identity resolves itself in any definitive way. These readings of Sand's and Campbell's subjective experiences are exploratory. I want to suggest that it is not enough to study the genealogy and dissemination of negative definitions of the poor; we must examine, also, how these definitions are lived by concrete subjects themselves as a significant part of their personal histories.

5.1 Cy-Thea Sand's Cultural Smuggling

In Cy-Thea Sand's personal essay 'A Question of Identity,' the writer testifies to classed experiences which fixed her sense of identity and contests these limiting definitions by speaking out about how it feels to be fixed in this way. The essay begins with a number of tropes representing limited physical and psychosocial space: 'narrow-halled Verdun flat,' 'crowded flat,' 'close city quarters,' 'squeezing me into a psychic corner,' and '[my] father's irritability marked the boundaries of my childhood like the fence of our tiny backyard' (55). The sensation of physical restriction quickly passes to one of linguistic restriction as Sand describes her fear of publicly occupying the author position in order to tell her own story: 'I cannot call myself a writer without hesitating' (59). She also relates her frustration with a muted class language: 'I want the garbled and hesitant language of my life to become intelligible' (62).

Sand's most formidable barrier to sharing fully in the dominant culture is not her lack of social opportunity or leisure, as in many stories by poor and working-class women, but her learned fear of partaking publicly in a culture which she had learned was not rightfully hers. Her family's greatest fear, she explains, was to be laughed at, and their lives were consequently 'choreographed' by shame and fear. Her first and often repeated lesson is 'You are nothing without money ... impressed upon [her] memory as regularly as rent-collection day' (55); this negative construction of identity is always in the narrator's memory telling her that despite publishing successes, she is never safe from complete nervous collapse – as though speaking out of place and with a sense of self-importance as a working-class subject would project her immediately into a place of contradiction to which the only response could be madness.

If read on the level of social allegory, Sand's account is of a marginalized self confronting dominant culture in a sombre struggle over language, culture, and identity. When read on the level of personal history, the details are just as sombre. Sand grew up in a crowded flat in Verdun, a residential area for factory workers in Montreal with a significant anglophone population. Her father's angry presence dominated their daily lives along with a sense of financial insecurity. Her uncle, a war veteran and indigent drunk, and her aunt, a domestic worker, both loved literature and were formative influences. Sand began suffering from 'emotional and mental distress,' however, when she confronted the middle-class milieu of the university as a scholarship student. She turned to drugs and alcohol to assuage her acute sense of alienation and when expected, as a scholarship student, to speak in public, she attempted suicide. Without finishing her degree, she moved to British Columbia where she 'came out' as a lesbian, worked part-time as cleaning staff, and wrote and published only intermittently while in recovery.

'A Question of Identity' first appeared in 1987 in a small feminist magazine, *Fireweed*, and was reprinted in Janet Zandy's *Calling Home: Working-class Women's Writing: An Anthology* in 1990. (Sand did not write for publication from 1987 to 1995 [Zandy, 'Working-class Studies,' 1995].) It was written when she was in recovery and resembles the sort of piecing together of fragments and trauma with key figures and causes which might constitute part of the process of personal recovery as well as that of a political awakening. As literary testimony, however, the essay has the potential to transcend confession and to recover, explain, and reconstruct fragments of lived experience for the purpose of making individual identity more coherent and legitimate as the basis of social action.

Among the formative experiences which Sand relates, besides that of reacting to her father's sense of economic and personal powerlessness, are two important types of exclusion which ultimately converge in her life story: the sense of symbolic exclusion revealed through her troubled relation to language, and the sense of lived exclusion from high culture revealed through anecdotes about cultural isolation. Like people colonized by external powers, generations of Sand's family had been exploited and silenced and unable to participate fully in the dominant culture either of their country of origin, Scotland, or their country of destination, Canada (or the francophone city where they settled). For example, she remembers her shell-shocked uncle quoting Yeats to passing cars in a pained, drunken stupor and her aunt reading 'great literature' late at night after her domestic work, a stolen act beyond her station:

> Did she want to write? Did the cultural authority which breathed its history and power into the very room in which she sat convince her of the impossibility of that notion? The gender and class of writing are not embodied in an off-duty cook scribbling in her room. What would she write about? What pronouncements on philosophy, history, society, God or Nature would a woman with sore feet have? Did she try to write and then judge her work to be mere footnotes to the real world of writing? Did she think of her nephew Steve as a poet? Did she connect his inebriated attempts at coherence to her own desire to write? (56–7)

Here Sand echoes and reframes within a sense of class difference Virginia Woolf's famous questions about women's limited access to the literary profession, adjusting the bourgeois woman's question of 'a room of one's own' to the limited, borrowed spaces of a domestic worker's life. Her aunt's limited access to high culture and literary voice resulted from gender as well as class imperatives that are echoed later in the words of Sand's doctor when he defines her university studies as 'a secretarial asset to any boss' (60). The mirroring between these two generations of women stresses the contradiction between the subject/author position of high culture and the object position of women as well as the enduring social script according to which generations of poor and working-class women must accept their place as doubly silenced subjects.

Sand's aunt and uncle, although partly thwarted in their access to high culture, were the only models for her cultural aspirations and her turn to literature and libraries as nourishment and escape. The improving, enlarging psychosocial aspect of culture is dramatized in the quotation above through the image of cultural authority 'breathing' life into a room, an image in direct opposition to the squeezed spaces and symbols for working-class flats, cited earlier, which concretized material limits and those of a culture of poverty, as well as the oppressive authority of the family patriarch. As art lovers, her aunt and uncle saw beyond the materially and emotionally limited life of labour which her father led. The desire to see beyond also figures largely in Sand's inner landscape. But the out-of-place nature of literature and the expansive spirit it engenders in these restricted working-class lives resulted in images of breakage, public humiliation, madness, or a particular type of defiance which we might refer to as 'cultural smuggling.'

The aunt's form of 'smuggling' was to absorb the cultural capital of her employers' huge libraries voraciously in her off hours and to leave the country a retired domestic, homeless but with 'a trunk of first editions, her most cherished possession' (56). Her uncle's form of 'smuggling' was to appropriate high culture from the Old Country (Wordsworth, Coleridge, Yeats, and Burns) in order to import them and graft them on everyday life in Canada, orally and in street scenes. However, though he seemed to master poetry, which 'slipped off his tongue' while he was 'lecturing away,' he was also 'shell-shocked and broken'; relatives referred to him as 'poor Stevie' (56). The contradiction of his association with beauty, mastery, and high art, on the one hand, and rank smells, stupor, and indigence, on the other, constitute a form of transgression whose illegality is echoed in the oxymoron which Sand uses to describe his precarious balancing act as 'inebriated grace' and in the irreverent synecdoche which explains that 'poetry had become the language of his twenty-six ounce addiction' (56).

There is a parallel to his 'inebriated grace' in Sand's own daring self-disclosure and cultural smuggling. In opposition to her working-class father's internalized rage, limited choices, and resentful labour, the daughter has externalized her anger and shame through public testimony. Her search for cultural coherence through class politics and working-class literature and her choice to try to be a writer admit her to a dance which is not 'choreographed' puppet-like from above, like that of her family for generations back, but is performed on the thin, sliding edge between the worlds of high culture and subculture, where she must balance with her own genre of 'inebriated grace.' The fissure between cultures climaxes in her experience at university where the exclusion from language and high culture come together. Her fear of public speaking, of being shamed by the negative self as it steps into the public subject position, precipitated a suicide attempt: 'At the moment I swallowed that bottle of pills I collided with the most negative messages of my working-class childhood: who do you think you are? Who do you think you are getting all this education and trying to be one of them?' (60). The question alludes to Alice Munro's semi-autobiographical work by that title: *Who Do You Think You Are?* and opens the narrative to the testimony of distance between a poor home and the university. As in one of the stories in Munro's collection, 'The Beggar Maid,' discussed in chapter 3, Sand's testimony reveals the impact of class barriers to education on the writer's identity:

> I walked those Concordia corridors high on pills and was told by professors and peers that women waste their time getting degrees. I walked those corridors as my father's daughter, 'that conventional Sunday-best type of working-class person who cannot bear to be seen even carrying a parcel or doing anything that might attract attention to himself' (J.R. Ackerley) ... My ambition defied my gender role but I was the daughter of a class and a family which is echoed in Alice Munro's words: 'ambition was what they were alarmed by, for to be ambitious was to court failure and to risk making a fool of oneself. The worst thing ... the worst thing that could happen in this life, was to have people laughing at you.' (60–1)

Importantly, the method Sand chooses of finding a 'home' in high culture and its institution is by creating a sense of community, by assembling kindred working-class voices which render her isolation and feelings of inferiority comprehensible as a shared class and gender phenomenon. Assembling these voices in her head, she is able to counter the messages with which the academy silences her and to see a place inside her silence for an oppositional culture and an alternative vision of reality.

But there is no neat, magical conversion from 'poor me' to 'defiant us,' for Sand also identifies more readily with the cleaning staff at the university than with well-spoken academics, with the institution for drug addicts and madwomen than with the institution of higher learning. After mapping a family history, generational in scope, of the frustrated impulse to share fully in literary culture, Sand confesses intimately, painfully, how her writing voice and her core of identity are constructed from this history of silence and broken voices: 'Speaking and writing do not come easily for me' (59). She explains the ways that she is divided from a bourgeois woman she befriends at university: 'Your father was a writer who made quite a name for himself. My father's stammer made it difficult for him to say his and he worked as a supplies clerk in a school board basement office' (58). And another refrain is added to her story, distinguishing her own classed female identity from that of a female friend: 'We are divided in terrible ways' (58–9).

In 'Modernism and History,' Lillian Robinson and Lise Vogel have argued that members of the working class who attempt to absorb 'high culture' are described by the semantics of acculturation as 'improving' themselves. Working-class people who allow themselves to be acculturated by university study do so at a high cost to their own identity by submitting to a process as unnatural as 'changing race' (30; see Tokarczyk and Fay, and Bourdieu [1977]). However, they also note that few submit to acculturation because the 'irrelevancies' of high culture do not offer enough incentive to be co-opted in this way. In Sand's essay, we see her remaining on the fringe of university life, roaming the halls high on drugs, attending classes but not speaking, later befriending lecturers and artistic types but cleaning toilets for a living, identifying with cleaning ladies and institutionalized women rather than professionals. In a longer reading of Sand's essay, her extreme outsider position in the academy as lesbian and working-class woman could be considered alongside more traditionally gendered plots of heterosexual working-class women who experience the university as a site where they can 'marry up' through the academy to professors or men from higher classes as an alternative form of social mobility and acculturation (for example, I discuss both *The Diviners* and 'The Beggar Maid' in respect to these mobility strategies).

Of all of the marginal positions which are dramatized as contours of Sand's inner landscape, the most highly dramatized is that of her symbolic relation to language as a colonized subject. In the primary position more ordinarily given to circumstances of birth, Sand's first sentence relates her slowness to speak: 'I spoke not a word until my fourth year of life and then language came out garbled and hesitant' (55); and later she admits identifying with the muted speech of institutionalized women: 'Few of them speak. The ones who do usually shout or force the odd syllable from drug swollen tongues' (59). At university, the exclusion from high culture and from language converge. Significantly, Sand dramatizes her experience of education as stage fright: 'To get up and speak before people, to make a public statement of any kind, sometimes even to state my name became unbearable, impossible, terrifying. I asked not one question, spoke not one classroom word in four years of university' (60–1). The two stages of silence and growth, the first four years of life and four years of university, converge to suggest that cultural and linguistic initiation is, for a working-class woman, initiation into exclusion.

As I discuss in more detail later (chapter 8, 'The Long View: Contexts of Oppositional Criticism'), Pierre Bourdieu has suggested in 'Cultural Reproduction and Social Reproduction' that the university, despite its promise to offer a means to social mobility, is actually the place where the working class are often discreetly but ultimately excluded. Bourdieu argues that working-class youth are subtly excluded from the word games of examinations and classroom discussions because they enter university without the necessary 'cultural capital' to decode the objects of high culture or to express themselves like people who have a claim to that culture. In stressing the role of social definitions and judgments of competence in cultural struggle, Bourdieu exposes the special power of language and academic discourse to convince the working class of their own cultural deficiency and exclude them anew. Despite the fact that Bourdieu's positivist research on this score has been controversial, the enduring value of his theory, according to many supporters, lies in the connections he suggests between culturally reproduced inequality, cultural capital, working-class identity, and university methods of teaching and recruiting, connections which expose the logic of this form of institutional exclusion but which have been 'systematically neglected by recent sociology' (Jenkins 179–80).

As a result of a profound, internalized sense of cultural exclusion that rippled outward from her working-class home to the university, Sand continues to express self-consciousness towards the subject position throughout her essay, her narrative culminating dramatically in the final sentence which not only posits a collective and politicized 'we' but also dramatizes how silenced subjects may demand the position of speaker and witness:

> Fear of poverty made us tiptoe around life's possibilities, around authority and even around our anger at our own compliance. My father could not externalize what he understood so clearly ... But some of us are daring to dance along the edge of economic and social uncertainty to challenge self-oppression. We know who paid for those avenues of brick and to the ruling class we join with David Fennario in saying 'We shall walk backwards and applaud no longer. We shall celebrate ourselves. We will create a forum for our thought. We will have it out with you.' (62)

The closing passage of the piece reveals a self-consciously divided identification between the 'us' of her family and a new, more powerful 'us' of a politically aware working-class community. This public avowal of divided identification places the 'I' between the invisibility of the forgotten working-class figures in her family and the small but visible community of working-class intellectuals writing in Canada. This subject shift marks her identity conversion whereby the fragmented and damaged 'I' of her past meets others who have been silenced and excluded, across the interdiscursivity of texts. Through quotation, again in the form of cultural smuggling, but smuggling she now flaunts and legitimates, the 'I' of her personal story transforms into the 'we' of David Fennario's text from *Blue Mondays*. (Fennario is an anglophone author from Pointe-St-Charles, Quebec, a working-class neighbourhood that adjoins Sand's. The absence of the majority francophone culture in Sand's essay is an ambiguous political frame for her own inscriptions of language and exclusion.) Together, the two authors' voices redefine their position of invisibility and subordination as one of solidarity, historical insight, and cultural opposition.

The stylistic nuances – the tropes of restricted space and movement, the fixed, local setting of brick buildings and narrow halls of a factory neighbourhood altered by historical knowledge, and the shifting referent to indicate shifting identification, from 'us' (family) to 'us' (class), from the individual 'I' to the collective 'we' – all reflect the enclosed and expanding parameters as Sand dances discursively through and around negative constructions of identity. The speaker dares to dance upon the very notion of the margin, not to erase it but to call attention to the nature of such boundaries and their importance to her sense of who she is and how she speaks. This dance upon the margins begins when she posits herself as speaker, no matter how tentatively, and as a literary witness who joins the assembled collage of oppositional testimonies (Fennario, Munro, Ackerley) which testify to the oppression and yet still celebrate class difference. Given the need to testify beyond the silencing of her class and her personal voice, she does not dance upon the margin in a postmodernist celebration of fragmentation and deferred meaning, but with the use of psychological and social realism, concrete metaphors, and a transparently testimonial voice.

Thus from the fringes, Sand smuggles out 'cultural capital' for illicit ends. She has learned how to assemble quotations and a muted literary heritage around and behind her own voice in order to invoke a renewed sense of identity based on difference and class solidarity. Quoting here and there from working-class authors, she allows us to glimpse this new identity and the possibility it holds out for her, not instead of, but beside, the ever-present negative images. The prose of Sand's essay is simple but eloquent and resonant with a longing for familiar silence and invisibility. Her 'garbled language' has obviously been refined by education. But when we learn how culturally excluded she felt at university, we receive the refined prose as smuggled goods. And with the smuggled cultural capital comes knowledge of the systemic causes of her poverty and her shame. The brick buildings of Verdun are no longer confining in the same way; the landscape is filling out through Sand's trick of seeing beyond, not only through, literature and of learning her own collective history. She writes: 'The messages are deciphering. I am walking through the geography of my childhood and my family's history is coming into focus. The narrow hallways of Verdun were built to contain and control its working class and their children ... We know who paid for those avenues of brick ...' (62).

5.2 Maria Campbell's *Halfbreed* and Alternative Status-Honour Groups

Among working-class women's autobiographical writing in Canada, Sand's essay is an anomaly, for very few of these narratives use Marxist class discourse to reconstruct identity from the margins. There are other class-conscious women's autobiographical works, of course, such as those by Helen Potrebenko, Joy Sykes, and Phyllis Knight (*A Very Ordinary Life*, transcribed by her son), but very few. Contrary to what one might assume, among Canada's marginalized groups – the poor, Native people, blacks, Asians, minority ethnic women, and so on – it is those marginalized by working-class or poor status who are least able to recuperate positive self-images as members of that class. On the other hand, negative discourses on poverty and class are often countered by positive identity strategies recuperated through other subcultures, especially race and ethnicity: for example, in works by Maria Campbell and by Mary John (transcribed by Bridget Moran) through Metis culture, by Laura Goodman Salverson through Icelandic culture, by Dionne Brand and Maxine Tynes through black culture, by Gabrielle Roy through Franco-Canadian culture, and many others.

This trend of expressing positive identity through subcultures other than class is in keeping with Stanley Aronowitz's thesis in *The Politics of Identity: Class, Culture, Social Movements* (1992), which examines the erosion of working-class identity in contemporary North American society, given the decline of Marxist discourse and the weakening of union power under deregulated capitalism, and given, as well, the global and local policies of the dispersal of capital and workers by corporate management. Aronowitz claims that, for the past fifteen years especially, North America has seen a loss of dignity associated with working-class identity and a growing identification among other subcultures based on race, ethnicity, religion, gender, et cetera. Workers, he claims, have become invisible in public representation, their oppositional 'subject position' being occupied now by other emergent social groups. Although few self-representations by poor and working-class women in Canada employ a discourse on class, most address the experience of classed exclusion in the context of a strongly felt absence of community, which is addressed, if at all, by forms of group affiliation other than class or by close personal ties.

Waxman, in his study of poverty as stigma, has explained that the poor and working class from ethnically and racially stigmatized groups may sometimes convert negative status into positive status through a strong sense of group affiliation:

> Where the stigmatized group is an ethnic minority, the fact that it is a more or less homogeneous group makes it considerably more likely that that group will develop and retain its own unique status-honor and value system as a reaction to the stigma. When, however, the stigmatized group is an economic unit rather than an ethnic unit, unless that lower economic class can 'unite' to the point where it is in the position to reject the existing economic and value system and replace it with another, it will have to seek other means for adjusting to the stigma ... [W]ith a heterogeneous lower class – that is a lower class which does not share a common positive ethnic and/or religious heritage and identity or a common physical char-

acteristic – there is little basis from which may be formed an alternative system of status-honor ... (94)

Consequently, among the heterogeneous poor, Waxman argues, the negative and self-defeating traits described as the culture of poverty are most likely to take hold precisely because of the absence of alternative status-honour systems. In the two texts chosen for discussion in this chapter, an alternative status-honour system arises from different sources. In Sand's essay, it arises from a Marxist discourse and working-class literature which redefine class and culture on the fringe as positive rather than negative; in *Halfbreed*, from Campbell's appeal to an alternative status-honour system through the positive redefinition of the Metis racial group, as well as through an elder's teachings and the speaker's activism.

Campbell's struggle for positive identity through a reconstituted sense of racial identification is achieved mostly by internalizing her grandmother's teachings. The narrator depends on these teachings to comprehend poverty, racial discrimination, her people's history of colonization, suppression, and social exclusion, and her resulting feelings of shame. The primary functions of these teachings are to pass on racial pride and a knowledge of racial history. Campbell's own historicizing strategy is unfolded in the first chapters where, instead of her personal beginnings and earliest memories, she unfolds the history of her people, beginning in the mid-nineteenth century (Campbell was born in 1940). She relates the conditions which led to the westward migration of the Metis across Canada away from settlers, and eventually to confrontations with the government in the form of armed rebellions in 1869 and 1885 led by the Metis hero Louis Riel, and his ally, Gabriel Dumont. She also tells of the after-effect of those events on the identity of 'halfbreeds.' The Metis are distinguished from Indians and whites as those of mixed blood, but also, materially and historically, as those who, unlike full-blooded Indians, failed to have their land claims honoured and also failed, through poverty and lack of interest in farming, to meet land-improvement requirements for homesteading claims among whites. Hence, they were exiled as squatters to the narrow strips of government-owned land beside roads and highways and given the pejorative label 'Road Allowance people' (13). From these historical traumas, Campbell slowly begins to construct the more personal details of her own story – but broadly, after having laid out a detailed landscape of her family's history from four generations back.

Her personal story relates some pleasant experiences, such as a happy home and feeling of close community ties in her early childhood, but they soon become remote with the death of her mother and her father's subsequent lapse into despondency and alcoholism. Campbell recalls her struggle to support and care for younger brothers and sisters through extreme poverty, which included dropping out of public school, working long and hard at cleaning and other forms of child labour, scrounging for food, and hiding from the welfare agency. Numerous concrete scenes perform a testimonial function in the narrative: scenes such as feeding a new-born baby out of a beer bottle with a nipple, tying their baby brother to a nearby tree so they could attend school, acting 'ignorant, timid, and grateful' to welfare officials, and working harnessed like horses to uproot trees under a government make-work project. When Campbell tried to protest the biblical adage 'Blessed are the poor in spirit for they shall inherit the Kingdom of Heaven' (Matthew 5, verse 3) because it did not apply to her people or her personal experience of poverty, a teacher punished her by making her hold up the Bible while kneeling in the corner all afternoon. Campbell remembers defiantly: 'I used to believe there was no worse sin in this country than to be poor' (56). Here, the early Christian construction of the poor collides with the child's knowledge of her own twentieth-century identity as an outcast of affluent society. She had to contest institutional constructions of poverty by the church because of what she knew to be true, and later, she had to contest institutional constructions of the poor by welfare agencies because they threatened to break up her family. At fifteen, Campbell married for the sole purpose of becoming legal guardian to her younger brothers and sisters. After the marriage failed and welfare authorities broke up the family anyway, she began a free fall into street life, prostitution, and drugs, which finally ended with the private process of drug rehabilitation and spiritual healing and the public process of political activism.

The literal, unadorned style of *Halfbreed* makes two dominant metaphors for identity conversion stand out in one's mind long after reading. These are couched not in literary language but in the words of the author's grandmother and teacher, Cheechum. The first is a lesson about shame and self-blame. The author remembers returning home from school after being humiliated by the taunts of white children for her poor clothing and lunches of wild game. Insults are a frequent occurrence in her childhood; she and her siblings are called 'dirty Halfbreeds,' 'Road Allowance people,' and 'squatters' by the whites, and by full-race Indians they are called 'poor relatives' and 'Awp-pee-tow-koosons,' meaning 'Half people.' By history, they are called 'madmen and criminals' who rebelled, following the popular but doomed hero Riel, himself branded a madman by whites (10, 11, 13, 26). On this particular day, however, the author returned home more hurt and ashamed than ever by the insults from the white children and began striking out physically at her mother and father, calling them 'No-good Halfbreeds' and blaming them for the lack of good food and clothing (47). At this point her grandmother, Cheechum, stepped in, led the author half a mile from the house, and told her a story about her people before beating her with a willow stick. The author remembers beatings as part of her education rather than as abuse. Here the beating functions ironically, for as well as being a brutal form of discipline and a reassertion of dominance over the child, it also purges racial dominance by externalizing the 'stick' of ethnic and class shame and self-hate and putting it back into the hands of the Metis elder.

Cheechum said that when she was a girl, the Metis had had the chance to follow a great leader who came west and promised to show them the way to freedom, but because some people held back for clothes and horses, and called their own people 'no-good Halfbreeds,' they 'lost their dream.' 'The white man saw that that was a more powerful weapon than anything else with which to beat the Halfbreeds, and he used it and still does today. Already they are using it on you. They try to make you hate your own people' (47). In Cheechum's story, the white culture makes its meaning stick to the subject by eroding collectivity and implanting negative constructions of identity.

Thomas Berger has commented in *Fragile Freedoms: Human Rights and Dissent in Canada* that the problems of twentieth-century Metis are 'not simply problems of poverty, but of a people trying to preserve their cultural identity' (55). Whereas the Metis are now developing a political vocabulary which asserts identity, Berger observes, early generations lacked the language to proclaim their distinctive identity and their rights to land and services. The only political vocabulary they possessed was that of Riel's armed revolution, and this was not enough to combat the passage from hunting and trapping to an agricultural economy. Nor was it enough to combat the ingrained attitudes of whites such as Sir John A. Macdonald, the prime minister who executed Riel for insurrection: 'If they are Indians ... they go with the tribe; if they are Half-breeds, they are White' (52). The 1981 report of the Métis and Non-Status Indian Constitutional Review Commission thus argued not simply for individual integration into Canadian life, but for the collective integration of people with a history (Berger 55–6).

Campbell's political narrative asserts itself over the hegemonic implications of autobiography largely through its testimony of collective identity and history. She uses autobiography effectively to expand our knowledge, not only of the self, but of the people who had been erased by the label as insult, 'Halfbreed,' and who may now reappear beneath the word as title. As I mentioned earlier, her story begins not with childhood scenes but generations back, with the Riel uprisings. She subverts the negative power of 'halfbreed' as insult by using revisionary history in an act of cultural and political intervention. The 'I' of her story is clearly shaped more by her relation to history, to her people and their material oppression, and to her grandmother's spiritual teachings than it is by the textual politics of an 'I' with its European cultural assumptions of a unified and individual self.

Another of Cheechum's teaching images is carried through the text to transform the negative 'I' of racial and class shame to one of inner stability and collective spirit. Cheechum chooses to teach the lesson through the image of a blanket – an apt symbol for colonization, for it is an icon of trade with the whites and also a symbol of the material comfort they promised. Cheechum, who always refused charity and welfare, chose to live by trapping, and dressed in the traditional way, teaches the author a lesson about the incompatibility of the materialistic world of the colonizers and the Metis's spiritual survival:

> when the government gives you something, they take all that you have in return – your pride, your dignity, all the things that make you a living soul. When they are sure they have everything, they give you a blanket to cover your shame ... [Cheechum] used to say that all our people wore blankets, each in his own way. She said that other people wore them too, not just Halfbreeds and Indians, and as I grew up I would see them and understand. Someday though, people would throw them away and the whole world would change. I understood about the blanket now – I wore one too. I didn't know when I started to wear it, but it was there and I didn't know how to throw it away. (137)

In the context of her personal lived experience, the 'blanket' which keeps Campbell from knowing herself and her people with any sense of pride is fast money, drugs, and alcohol. The trajectory of the self in her story is a plot line which too many Native and Metis women have lived in Canada, leading rapidly away from past subsistence in a rural setting to dispossession of land, increased poverty, family illness, underpaid hard labour, the intervention of welfare agencies, dissolution of the family, domestic violence, migration to the city, homelessness, drug addiction, and prostitution (for a contrasting plot of family and collective struggle, see Janet Silman's *Enough Is Enough: Aboriginal Women Speak Out*). The author can cast off a blanket of denial about the destructiveness of her lifestyle only when she joins a collectivity and becomes an activist for her people and against drug addiction. This is not the exemplary, representative life of the upwardly mobile class subject or the assimilated racial other, but the exemplary life of a political radical, and therein lies the secret of the appropriation of the 'I' for political purposes. Campbell does not advocate armed revolution but fosters a dream of an inclusive society and of racial pride and a historically rooted language of resistance. This is how she is able to throw off her 'blanket' and to look without despair at her identity in the context of the ugliness of colonization, class oppression, and racial decimation: 'The years of searching and loneliness and pain are over for me. Cheechum had said, "You'll find yourself, and you'll find brothers and sisters." I have brothers and sisters, all over the country. I no longer need my blanket to survive' (157).

Both Campbell's image of the blanket of denial being thrown off and Sand's of the silenced audience claiming the right of speech recall Franz Fanon's image of colonized subjects throwing off obscurity and silence in order to define themselves and rewrite their own history: 'Decolonization never takes place unnoticed, for it influences and modifies [the colonized] fundamentally. It transforms spectators crushed with their inessentiality into privileged actors, with the grandiose glare of history's floodlights upon them' (Fanon 36). Such dramatic symbols of empowerment through speaking out, however, are more useful as inspiring dramatizations than as theoretical models. They do not allow for the complicity of colonized subjects in their own colonization, for unresolved questions of identity, or for generic constraints which may impose themselves as discursive limitations. Just as the spectator does not become an actor merely by standing upon the stage, so the subject does not decolonize herself simply by occupying the public position of the autobiographical 'I.' As covered in the discussions of 'A Question of Identity' and *Halfbreed*, the autobiographical 'I' and even the collective inscription of 'we' do not automatically displace or overpower negative constructions of identity, although they can convert their negative power into knowledge of systemic oppression and a will to resistance. Identification with the working class or with racial or ethnic groups or other subcultures is often able to empower the poor subject by explaining poverty and exclusion in historical and political terms and by providing an alternative status-honour group to rescue the self from stigma. Above all, a politicized view of negative constructions of identity shows whose interests they serve and allows the subject to free herself from the 'meaning stick' of the master narratives. Thus revisionary historical knowledge, in particular, will often allow the subject to see beyond self-blame and despair and free her for more oppositional forms of self-expression and self-representation.

Not surprisingly, many writers begin to narrate poverty or working-class status in Canada by gesturing towards the silence that surrounds the issue of poverty and class in an affluent society, or report, at some point in their life-writing or oral history, the sensation of speaking through that silence. Also, a significant number relate the sensation of being named by insult and having to find a strategy – self-representation being one possible dimension of that strategy – to escape or come to terms with the shame of having one's identity fixed in that way. Many autobiographical subjects who identify themselves as poor women, or as having been poor at one time in their lives, also identify themselves as witnesses to buried truths and as voices seeking and needing a community of readers/witnesses to affirm their classed experiences and make them credible. Janet Zandy described the task of writing as cultural intervention in the following way: 'Like Lot's wife, the working-class writer must keep looking back. She has to be multi-voiced in witnessing for the silenced many, in negotiating with the dominant culture, and in claiming her own identity as a woman with a particular ethnic and racial culture' (1990, 12). This recalls Freire's radical pedagogy, which similarly emphasized speaking out as a form of cultural agency and decolonization, but speaking out in the form of dialogue rather than speaking out for others: 'no one can say a true word alone – nor can we say it for another, in a prescriptive act which robs others of their words' (1970, 175).

5.3 The Poor as Colonized Subjects

John Porter began *The Vertical Mosaic* (1965), his cornerstone study of the correspondence among class, racial, and ethnic stratification in

Canada, by stating: 'the most persistent image that Canadians have of their society is that it has no classes' (3). More than thirty years later, a volume of essays in tribute to him, *The Vertical Mosaic Revisited* (1998, Helmes-Hayes and Curtis, eds), agreed that whereas Canadians had become more sensitized to racial and ethnic stratification in the interim, class rifts in Canada had not only widened but were still largely denied within the popular imagination.[1] Furthermore, one contributor claims that class rifts may have heightened in postindustrial Canada: 'Class formation has changed, but it has not disappeared as a real factor in the dynamics of contemporary Canadian society. In many ways, the restructuring, reducing, and diminishing of the state have caused a resurgence of class struggle with new challenges for the labour movement' (Wallace Clement in *The Vertical Mosaic Revisited* 37).

Poor and working-class women's self-representations depict their lived experience of subordination to popular myths which erase or misrepresent these class tensions in Canada, including individual subjectivities and the actual, concrete presence of the poor within the wealthy nation. As mentioned earlier, Mary Daly, in *Women and Poverty*, has identified the power of popular myths to discredit claims of the poor on market society. In her summary, these myths are: that there is no poverty now like that of the 1930s and 1940s, that no one needs to be poor anymore because of welfare, and that people are poor due to some fault or failing of their own (6–7). Likewise, Michael Harrington, in his pioneering work *The Other America: Poverty in the United States* (1962), identified the most familiar form of social blindness as the myth that the poor do not work and that they cheat on welfare. Although Harrington's political beliefs have been the subject of much criticism from the Left, many of his reflections on the lives of the poor were thoughtful and contestatory. For example, in the following description, he depicts the subtle but definitive cultural exclusion facing the poor who grow up within the United States: '[The poor] are dispossessed in terms of what the rest of the nation enjoys, in terms of what the society could provide if it had the will. They live on the fringe, the margin.

---

[1] The essays in this collection address the issue of changing class realities and class concepts in Canada in more complex ways than I can indicate here. Among their concerns are the factor of today's high unemployment (six times higher than in Porter's time), which upsets traditional class positions, the mediation of class and power by gender issues, and the changing face of the nation and the welfare state itself as crucial contexts for the experience and the notion of classes.

162 Remnants of Nation

They watch the movies and read the magazines of affluent America, and these tell them that they are internal exiles' (178). Such observations suggest that telling their life stories truthfully sets the poor at odds not only with popular myths but with the national imaginary itself.

The long genealogy of moral judgments against the poor in Anglo-Saxon society has been summarized in *The Stigma of Poverty* (1983) by Chaim Waxman, along with corresponding genealogies of legislative controls, charitable movements, and social work, and their discourses. Popular myths have shifted over the centuries, Waxman explains, first constructing the poor as morally righteous under early Christianity, as a negative status group with a collective and morally suspect identity in fourteenth-century Europe, as increasingly immoral but more and more individualized after the sixteenth century, and then, from the nineteenth century on, as naturally deviant and deficient (with the advent of Social Darwinism) rather than simply morally culpable. The stigma of poverty in North America in the twentieth century is characterized by the inherited and recycled European labels and categories 'deserving' and 'undeserving' poor, the further individualization and psychologizing of poverty, and a close association between welfare and the poor (72–92). Waxman argues that these popular myths representing the poor as prolific breeders, welfare cheats, unemployable, lazy, dishonest, criminal, and so on, spill over into scientific concepts and social programs and function as the rationalization for the dominant group's material exclusion of the poor. In the following passage, he adapts Erving Goffman's theory of stigma (*Stigma: Notes on the Management of Spoiled Identity [1963]*) to expose the social logic of exclusionary discourse: 'The effect of all of these labels is to stereotype the poor, to isolate and distort their position by concealing their roles in terms of their interaction with both themselves and the non-poor. These legitimations and rationalizations serve what Goffman (1963) calls "stigma-theories," or ideologies which "explain his (the stigmatized's) inferiority and account for the danger which it represents," and thus justify our "exercise [of] varieties of discriminations, through which effectively, if not unthinkingly, [we] reduce his life chances" (5)' (75).

A striking dramatization of how popular myths, stereotypes, and labels become nuanced and personalized as they are internalized by the poor is the following passage which appeared in the introduction to *The Real Poverty Report*. Written by four men who had resigned from Canada's Special Senate Committee on Poverty in the early 1970s because they could not agree with the censorship imposed upon their findings, *The Real Poverty Report* survives as an important historical document in the construction of the poor in Canada. The passage below gains imaginative power by dramatizing the colonization of the subject as a series of acts of discursive violence:

> From the very beginning, when you are still a child, you must learn to undervalue yourself. You are told that you are poor because your father is too stupid or too shiftless to find a decent job; or that he is a good-for-nothing who has abandoned you to a mother who cannot cope. And as you grow up on the streets, you are told that your mother is dirty and lazy and that is why she has to take money from the welfare department. Because you are poor, the lady from the welfare office is always coming around asking questions. She wants to know if your mother is living with a man, and why she is pregnant again.
>
> If as a child you are going to survive, you must close these violences out of your mind and retreat into a smaller world that you can handle ... If your parents are Indian, black or Eskimo [sic], then all these strikes against you are multiplied. (Adams et al. 1971, xi)

The passage goes on to describe more of these discursive 'violences,' the myths of failure and personal responsibility for poverty, which intrude on the subject's consciousness at each new stage in life. On the one hand, this dramatization of the subject's psyche stresses the unrelenting quality and the pervasiveness of popular myths. Their repetition and commonsense taken-for-grantedness give discursive power to negative constructions of identity, making them intrusive and capable of flattening the psychosocial space which houses our sense of identity. On the other hand, the above dramatization may oversimplify the process of colonization, in that the subject shows no complicity with, or resistance against, the messages she receives about herself, but seems, rather, to passively internalize them.

Yet the complicity of subjects, their passivity and resistance, and their recycling of hegemonic representations has been at the core of theoretical discussions about how class inequality gets reproduced as culturally acceptable, generation after generation. Among such leading theorists of cultural reproduction as Pierre Bourdieu, Louis Althusser, Antonio Gramsci, Paulo Freire, Theodor Adorno, Raymond Williams, and Stuart Hall, the discussion has focused on how able subjects are to extricate themselves from entrapment by culturally disseminated ideology and what the role of intellectuals can and should be in mediating popular discursive fields outside the traditional bounds of academic discourse. There has been fundamental disagreement about the degree to which education and the media maintain structures of class domination over subjects. For the more populist theorists, such as Freire, Gramsci, Williams, and Hall, the power to resist socialization belongs to the subjects themselves, as well as to intellectuals and political theorists, largely because populists refer to models of class oppression and cultural reproduction which are agent-centred. These agent-centred models are constructed in such a way that the subjects' complicity and resistance must be factored in. According to subject/agent–centred models of cultural reproduction, emergent forms of art, popular culture, and radical pedagogy may help subjects contest popular myths and stereotypical identities and thus decolonize themselves. Such complex accounts of cultural reproduction depend on models of interaction which show that popular myths and stereotypes construct subjects, but that subjects, as agents and readers, may also participate in shaping their own relationship to dominant myths.

As well as the complicity and resistance of poor subjects to misrepresentation, a further complexity of their colonization as subjects is multiple stigmatization, whereby an individual may be constructed by exclusionary discourses based not only on poverty, but also on racial, ethnic, or religious stigma, on physical differences, on gender, and so on (Waxman, 71–3). Because the double stigmatization of poverty and gender has only recently been brought into the field of academic discourse, especially through the paradigm of the feminization of poverty (see, for example, Diana Pearce [1978], Gertrude Schaffner Goldberg and Eleanor Kremen [1990], Ruth Sidel [1986], Barbara Gelpi and Nancy Hartsock [1986], and Morley Gunderson et al. [1990]), this expert discourse has not trickled down to offer masses of poor women the means to redefine themselves more positively, nor has it significantly increased the cultural access and visibility of poor women as agents and subjects of their own oppositional discourse, speaking among themselves or on behalf of themselves oppositionally. Apart from the occasional collection of these voices in ethnographic oral histories, only limited attention has been given to the details of poor women's position of multiple oppression and stigmatization in cultural studies and to how to read these voices in literary studies. One reason why the academy has been slow to recognize this position of double stigmatization is because of the blind spot around the subject of gender in Marxist discourse, which I discussed earlier in respect to the classed and gendered subject. Marxist paradigms of class identity were never adequate to make visible or coherent poor and working-class women's gendered experiences, as we are increasingly being made aware by feminists critiquing and adapting Marxist paradigms of culture (see, for example, Christine Delphy, Michèle Barrett, Cora Kaplan, Lillian Robinson and Lise Vogel, and Karen V. Hansen and Ilene J. Philipson). Class identification among working-class and poor women has been weakened by the fact that many women in these groups could not see their experiences of oppression as being meaningfully represented by a political discourse based on market relations and wage labour. Yet silence on the subject of the gendered specificity of women's experiences of poverty and class has reinforced the naturalized link between the stigmas of class and gender in the popular imagination.

Ruth L. Smith's linking of poverty and female identity in liberal humanist discourse shows that language itself tends to construct both on the outside of civil society. As objects of an exclusionary liberal discourse which projects disorder and deficiency onto the poor and women as a means of naturalizing difference, poor women are socialized to see themselves not as members of a market-based class of workers or the poor, but as somehow inherently and individually deficient. Smith writes: 'Characterized by the lack of even potential symbolic power, the poor appear to be without the capacity for intent, belief, or value. They are desire that has no creativity, the necessity that cannot become historical, the hostility that cannot be bent into the preconditions for revolution' (219). In my view, Smith overstates the outsider status of the poor to the point of denying agency. As my discussion of Sand's and Campbell's narratives shows, autobiographical subjects may subvert 'poor me' and harness the symbolic power which is a precondition for cultural opposition.[2] None the less, Smith's discussion of the naturalization of poverty explains in part why it is so difficult for poor women to make demands on society and speak out collectively, why even academic studies of the working class will often overlook the poor and their lived experiences as naturally outside the bounds of civil society, and why civil society can rationalize interventionist policies into the lives of the poor, and poor women in particular,

---

2 As a recent CBC radio series attests, many anti-poverty activists rise from the ranks of the poor to protest authority and the status quo (*Fighting Back* May 1999, hosted by Pauline Grey and Karen Wells).

via a welfare machine which polices those on the outside of the market.

The narrative form of self-representation itself may exercise a subtle form of distortion or misrepresentation on the subject's story. Roger Bromley's call for reading practices to challenge iconic perceptions of poverty maintains that cultural images of poverty have become 'sepia-tinted,' fixed in icons of 'four in a bed, bugs, tuberculosis, poor relief, raggedness, stylized forms of the unemployed' (7). Bromley argues further that these extreme versions of poverty are now considered as 'authenticating data' for contemporary claims of poverty. As I discuss in some detail in the next chapter when exploring the hegemonic aspects of the autobiographical genre, Bromley posits that conventions for representing poverty in popular autobiographic forms mediate history in such a way as to also mediate the present. Instead of seeing current experiences of poverty in terms of what they mean historically, collectively, and politically, Bromley argues, we see them uncritically in the shadow of icons from a remote and discontinuous past, far from the present. Bromley also maintains that popular autobiography tends to remember the poor in the form of representative figures such as hard-working, upwardly mobile individuals who travel through poverty and are represented apart from their class. In short, this theory of colonization and cultural exclusion scrutinizes the terrain of cultural memory. It argues that more 'authentic' or subversive versions of poverty have been 'lost' through a cultural process of 'organized forgetting' in representation and in reception, especially of popular versions of poor and working-class women's life stories.

Exclusion of the poor from society is naturalized in discourse and narrative form, but also through the absence of widely disseminated counter-narratives which could convincingly contradict exclusionary attitudes. Although the poor have been described as having their own culture or subculture, it is both muted and isolated, having less access to public discursive space than the discourses on the poor generated by the non-poor. In North America, the poor and the working class often experience themselves as alien and powerless in the context of an affluent society where working-class identity and organized solidarity have been sufficiently eroded that they have been replaced by what both Michael Harrington and Oscar Lewis conceptualized, in the early 1960s, as a 'culture of poverty.' Harrington observed that the poor in 'developed' countries had become another nation: 'alien citizens' (10), 'the invisible land' (17), 'the underdeveloped nation within a nation'

(158–9), 'the internally exiled' (178–9). But behind this invisibility, Harrington maintained, there lay a different culture, one that was both alien and effectively colonized:

> There is, in short, a language of the poor, a psychology of the poor, a world view of the poor. To be impoverished is to be an internal alien, to grow up in a culture that is radically different from the one that dominates the society. The poor can be described statistically; they can be analyzed as a group. But they need a novelist as well as a sociologist if we are to see them. They need an American Dickens to record the smell and texture and quality of their lives. The cycles and trends, the massive forces, must be seen as affecting persons who talk and think differently. (17)

Harrington is calling for more knowledge about the lived experience of poverty and the subjectivities of the poor, 'the smell and texture and quality of their lives,' which he sees as being somehow available (perhaps rather unproblematically) through literature.

Criticized for locating the cause of poverty internally in the subjects themselves, rather than situationally in the external market forces or attitudes of the non-poor (Waxman 1983, 27–68), Harrington's view of the 'other' culture was largely negative and monolithic, in that he saw it as reproductive of poverty and 'immune to progress.' Hence, he assumed that the 'internally exiled' could best become visible through representations by experts – sociologists, novelists, et cetera – rather than through their own cultural interventions or utterances. This view of a wholly negative content to the culture of poverty was different from Oscar Lewis's fuller conceptualization, which attributed both positive and negative content to the culture of poverty as he observed it in several countries. Lewis, one of the first anthropologists to experiment with transcribing the taped voices of the poor as oral histories (*The Children of Sanchez* 1961), also described the culture of poverty as a subculture, but one which constituted a creative response to the destruction of a traditional community by capitalist and imperialist society and a means of coping and surviving in hostile circumstances. Noting its counter-culture potential, Lewis allowed that the culture of poverty could be acted upon, if not eliminated by, revolutionary or nationalist movements with an alteration of its ideological basis – without, necessarily, having first to alter the objective state of poverty. At the same time, however, Lewis claimed that a mere change in material circumstances would not undo the cultural isolation of the poor, for it was generational in scope.

David L. Harvey and Michael Reed, examining a wide range of academic paradigms for studying poverty, endorsed Oscar Lewis's concept of an adaptive 'subculture of the poor' over Harrington's view of negative content because Lewis's is 'sensitive to the survival enhancing immediacies which the culture of poverty has for everyday life, while, at the same time, acknowledging the role which such a culture plays in reproducing the overall structure of capitalist social relations' (278). 'Like all cultures,' Harvey and Reed write, 'the subculture of poverty has simultaneously creative, oppositional elements, as well as constraints which in the larger picture reinforce existing class relations' (278). This larger relational view of the subculture of poverty situates the subject's reactions to negative constructions of identity within a more complex schema that explains resistance and complicity as more than matters of solely individual choice.

Waxman also favours the relational theories which focus on the connections between the non-poor and the poor, especially on the level of discourse and attitudes. Once again adapting Goffman's theory of stigmatized identity, Waxman writes: '[J]ust as the reaction of normals to stigma must be understood within "a language of relationships," within the societally established "means of categorizing persons and the complement of attributes felt to be ordinary and natural for members of each of these categories" (Goffman 2), so too must the reactions of the stigmatized individuals be understood within the context of culturally derived techniques of adjustment to situations where the stigmatized individual is interacting under a disadvantage' (93). According to Waxman, seeing the subcultures of poverty as a variety of responses to the stress of stigma within a relational view of the poor and the non-poor facilitates a deeper understanding of those responses as strategies arising both from social practices carried out in the interest of dominant groups and from individual and collective identity construction among the poor. He explains that strategies for coping with stigma may entail isolating oneself from 'normals' and forming solidarity with other stigmatized members, hiding one's identity through acculturation, or 'managing' the stigma itself in an adaptive way by appropriating its power for other uses (93). According to this theory of strategies within a relational context, negative constructions of identity are not internalized directly but entail a number of choices on the part of the poor (both conscious and unconscious, and collective and individual). Waxman also notes that the relational context of the construction of poverty allows us to see identity itself more profoundly. In respect to normative constructions such as the 'American dream,' Waxman notes that poor subjects, due to cultural isolation, may not internalize 'the goal of success' fundamental to capitalism and affluent society:

> [O]ne of the harshest effects of the stigma of poverty is that it results in the isolation of the poor from not only the material provisions of the society, but also, and perhaps equally important, from the cultural provisions as well. It is from the society and its culture that each member receives his social self, his sense of identity and self-identification, and it is only when the individual is part of the society and identifies with it that he internalizes its normative system, its values, and its definitions of reality ... unless [the poor] have a different cultural system with which they identify ... [t]heir 'me' is quite different in nature from that of the real members of society. They do not completely internalize the normative system of society. This does not mean that they are unaware of the norms and values of society. They are very much aware of them, but these have not become part of their subjective consciences to the extent that they adhere to them because they really believe in them. (97–8)

Although Waxman's reference to 'real members of society' is misleading and his representation of 'the poor' seems unnecessarily homogenizing, he does, at least, strain for the words to explain how the identity of the poor and hence their cultural participation is shaped by stigma, taking care to establish relational connections between cultural differences and situational causes. But I would like to posit further that the complexity of the lived relation between marginalized subjectivities and stigma may rest, in part, with the subjects themselves to relate. In the details of individual and subjective testimonies, we can find hitherto silenced knowledge about marginal experience, and such insider knowledge may inform our reading practices further than any single theory of socialization or discourse analysis, especially on the subject of agency.

5.4 Decolonizing Poor Subjects through Autobiography

> She wanted things. Politics and cultural studies can only find trivial the content of her desires, and the world certainly took no notice of them. (Steedman 109)

Just as theories of poverty differ according to how much cultural agency they attribute to poor subjects, so theories of autobiography also dispute how much agency the genre attributes to the marginal individual as autobiographic subject. Having examined two autobiographical poverty narratives which subvert 'poor me,' I turn in the next chapter to two more autobiographies which tend to 'forget' poverty, rather than resist it. At this point, I would like to review a few theories of the potential of autobiography as a genre to colonize or decolonize subjects, or in other words, to help poor subjects resist or conform to the class hegemony that devalues them.

Recently the motif of 'decolonization' has been used to describe the shared cultural project of liberating 'colonized subjects' not only in postcolonial studies, but also in culture-of-poverty theories, feminist theories, cultural studies, African-American and other diasporic studies, and multicultural studies in general. In *De/Colonizing the Subject: The Politics of Gender in Women's Autobiography*, Sidonie Smith and Julia Watson have discussed, at some length, this extended use of the term 'colonial subject' in respect to internally marginalized groups (xiii–xvii). Smith and Watson borrow from Abdul R. JanMohamed and David Lloyd the notion that colonial subjects speak from a shared position as a possible clarification of the shared circumstances of oppression experienced by externally and internally colonized groups who experience widely varying degrees of physical violence and restrictions of movement as 'a position of damage, one in which 'the cultural formations, languages, the diverse modes of identity of the minoritized peoples are irreversibly affected, if not eradicated, by the effects of their material deracination from the historically developed social and economic structures in terms of which alone they "made sense."' (xvi–xvii). No matter what we call it, the effect of this shared 'position of damage' is usually, according to Chandra Talpade Mohanty, the suppression of the heterogeneity of the subjects (as quoted by Smith and Watson 1991, xvi). Hence the oppositional potential of autobiography to decolonize the subject lies partly in its power to demystify the experience of cultural others and to reconstruct the identity of those others according to their own sensibilities and heterogeneity. In other words, the autobiographical utterance holds out the possibility of repairing cultural damage by enabling marginal subjects to represent identities closer to their experiences, hence decolonizing them as subjects of others' definitions – whether this colonization occurs between North and South, West and East, or different class, ethnic, or gender groups within one nation.

Conversely, the colonized 'other' who steps into the politics of the 'I' in order to represent herself is, according to Smith and Watson, unwittingly collapsed into an essentialized 'other.' Rather than gaining access to this privatized and privileged subject position, 'others' remain outside because they cannot be accommodated by such a position in all of their heterogeneity. Smith and Watson thus observe that the genre of autobiography itself may function imperialistically to reassert meaning over the subject. Autobiography may make 'meaning stick' through the genre's own discursive imperatives, through its resonant ideology and a particular genealogy of privilege (xvii–xviii). The colonized subject will always have a troubled relationship to the genre, they claim, because the generic conventions are based on patriarchal and Eurocentric assumptions about the 'I,' including a cult of selfhood, rationality, and uniqueness which ultimately erases or filters difference and collective resistance by giving priority to individual consciousness.

Although the ideological implications of genre are important to consider, I am wary that theorizing about ideal forms of oppositional autobiography leads to prescription: for example, that new, self-reflexive (especially postmodernist) modes of autobiography are necessary to combat the imperialism of the old genre. Recent prescriptions for postmodernist forms of autobiography which are self-reflexive and demand a knowledge of the textual mechanisms of representation rarely reflect concern for whether or not marginal subjects actually have access to knowledge of these esoteric forms of expression or whether or not their stories and traditional relation to language are best reflected by these forms. This is the case with Sidonie Smith's implicit prescription for postmodernist expression and *jouissance* in 'The Autobiographical Manifesto: Identities, Temporalities, Politics' (1991) and Dentith and Dodd's prescription for 'complex ways of seeing' in 'The Uses of Autobiography' (1988). Both are pioneering essays in their own right and show a strong spirit of resistance to hegemonic imperatives on the subject, but both assume quite simply that the autobiographical subject is educated enough to have access to postmodernist discourse and to bring distance and style to bear on her life story as an appropriately subversive technique of telling. Neither can claim to democratize the subject, because both prescribe forms of resistance writing which are too esoteric to be accessible to all people. Such theorizing rarely considers texts by uneducated or materially disadvantaged subjects and thus fails to show how these prescriptive forms of utterance challenge dominant discourse by democratizing the subject.

Moreover, implicit prescriptions for postmodernist styles of life stories fail to heed the need for different strategies of resistance among subjects who are marginalized to varying degrees by gender, class, and ethnicity. We might recall again that succinct phrase by R. Radhakrishnan quoted in the last chapter: 'Whereas the dominant position requires acts of self-deconstruction, the subordinate position entails collective self-construction' (277). Likewise, recent theorists of testimony and social realism have cautioned that truth claims, textual reality construction, and group identity may be more valuable strategies for self-identification among imperilled subjects of extreme marginalization than word play and *jouissance* (Sommer, Foley).

On the other hand, prescription of mediated forms of autobiography whereby educated writers transcribe the words of marginalized people in oral histories and testimonies sometimes fails to allow that marginalized subjects, even uneducated subjects, can subvert and appropriate traditional author positions through their own innovative styles and their own language. Such theories about testimony often suggest that mediated forms such as testimonio and oral histories are somehow inherently more oppositional because they eschew the author position altogether (Sommer, Beverly). Rather than debate which forms of autobiography best challenge hegemonic values discursively, I feel we should turn to a variety of individual life stories and discover the uses to which autobiography has been put by concrete subjects, given the details of their concrete lives and the subtleties of their own lived relation to language. We might ask, for example, how in each life story the fact of telling that life subverts or reproduces the specific negative constructions of identity experienced by the subject from her own standpoint.

According to Carolyn Steedman in *Landscape for a Good Woman*, although we cannot hope to restore a complete picture of excluded lives simply by writing and reading working-class women's personal stories, we can hope to make the fragments more meaningful by restoring fullness to the landscape of this subculture through the specificities of history and place and through a more receptive attitude to the psychological differences created by material distress and social exclusion. Steedman proposes that working-class women as autobiographical subjects can make sense of their deracinated and culturally muted lives by re-using the past and interpreting it through social information, in other words, 'what people know of a social world and their place within it' (5). She suggests, for example, that we look at the development of class-consciousness as a process which may occur, especially for women and children, in relative isolation and in private rather than through organized public struggle, and which may also involve the formation of a class-marked unconscious that would be discernible by looking at loss and desire in terms of social exclusion.

Steedman goes on to say that the adventure of making women's working-class experience visible does not end with the writing, but is also present in the reading. The muted meaning of the text and the class-marked 'I' at its centre often elude the 'central interpretive devices' of a culture designed to receive and decode bourgeois subjectivity, so that even working-class women have difficulty *seeing or decoding* the meaning in autobiographies of other women in their class, including their own mother's stories, though they may *experience* them on an empathic level (284–5). What Steedman seems to be arguing here is that working-class women's life stories cannot be decoded through available categories of collective symbolization, but must be studied, instead, in terms of their own internal logic and personalized metaphors and signposts. Moreover, she suggests that we can better come to terms with the fragmentary nature of our own knowledge and of the lives represented by reading these stories in tension with master forms or master narratives, rather than by trying to absorb them into these categories for forced coherence. Thus Sand's and Campbell's personal subversions of 'poor me,' discussed earlier, emerge in tension with at least two forms of master narratives, the negative constructions of class, racial, and gender identities circulated through popular myths, insult, stereotypes, and so on, and the master form of autobiography itself.

Chapter 6

'*Organized Forgetting*'

Autobiography is a site for both the suppression and the recovery of collective memories. The fate of collective class memories in less openly resistant poverty narratives than Sand's and Campbell's is often subtle or total eclipse by individual stories. In Edna Jaques's *Uphill All the Way* and Fredelle Bruser Maynard's *Raisins and Almonds*, the subjects indeed blur or erase collective class memories as they rely, instead, on the individualized trajectories of upward mobility and the professional writing career to restore dignity to the shamed subject. When discussing how Sand's and Campbell's life stories were a site of decolonization where collective memories were summoned to buttress the pride of the poor subject with a sense of class identification or racial community, I also noted that their sense of class opposition and collective memory were quite anomalous to Canadian poverty narratives, where more often than not the poor subject chooses upward mobility or identification with alternative status-honour groups to recover dignity. Both the life stories discussed in this chapter under the rubric 'organized forgetting' erase collective class memories or denigrate them in order to free their subjects for class mobility. However, while one subject (Maynard) distances herself willingly from local people and the poor, the other (Jaques) romanticizes her connection with the common folk to tell the tale of a rural woman's upward trajectory.

Not surprisingly, many of the critics who have developed autobiographical theories of gendered working-class experiences (for example, Regenia Gagnier, Carolyn Steedman, Rebecca O'Rourke, Cora Kaplan, and Roger Bromley) write in the context of British society, where class identification is much stronger on the whole than in Canadian society. As I have stressed throughout this study, the cultural erasure of class in North America has been exacerbated by what Stanley Aronowitz has described as the effects of social movements, corporate power, decentralized labour pools, declining unions, national agendas, and competing marginal identities. In this cultural context, class history is not only forgotten and then (possibly) remembered in preferred ways, but is also eclipsed by stories of individual mobility, by anonymous statistics, or by shamed denial. In returning to the discussion of autobiography and the poor subject, I focus here not on the recovery of memory and pride as a strategy of resistance, but on the culturally dominant erasure of collective memories of the poor within wealthy nations as a strategy of assimilation and denial. Furthermore, I consider in the case of both *Raisins and Almonds* and *Uphill All the Way* how poor subjects consent to forgetting as a means of dissociating themselves from the poor as a class or from class politics.

6.1 On Autobiographical Memories of Poverty, Class, Gender, and Nation

In *Lost Narratives: Popular Fictions, Politics and Recent History*, Roger Bromley observes that popular autobiography is often complicit in hegemonic forms of 'organized forgetting.' Bromley explains how significant class absences and the blurring or erasing of collective memories may function as narrative strategies which dehistoricize the self in order to reinscribe an idealized notion of popular national history and individual struggle. Despite the risk of distortion in transcultural borrowing, it is possible to apply knowledge from Bromley's theorization of popular autobiography in Britain and its cultural implications to interrogate life stories of poor women in Canada. By adapting his concept of organized forgetting to Canadian subjects and cultural contexts and critiquing his discussion of the dehistoricized autobiographical subject from a feminist perspective, I will interrogate the strategies of remembering and forgetting poverty and class in *Uphill All the Way* and *Raisins and Almonds*. This does not mean that Jaques and Maynard fail to illuminate the *true* history of class behind their stories of poverty, but rather that they remember individual mobility at the expense of collective memories and, furthermore, that this way of remembering is not simply a narrative frame created or preferred by these individual writers, but a dominant cultural phenomenon in the way poverty is remembered as separate from classes of people, history, and systemic causes. These forms of organized forgetting around the experience of poverty buttress the cultural belief that the individual is responsible for poverty in a meritocracy.

To return to the issue of the hegemonic function of organized forgetting in late capitalism, we can look more closely at how Bromley has theorized the colonization of popular memory under Thatcherism in England before adapting it to the reading of Canadian texts:

> *Forgetting* is as important as remembering. Part of the struggle against cultural power is the challenge to forgetting posed by memory. What is 'forgotten' may represent more threatening aspects of popular 'memory' and have been carefully and consciously, not casually and unconsciously, omitted from the narrative economy of remembering. Part of this structure of amnesia is the recurring ideological sense that the representative individual replicates the essence of the society's experience. This is offered as the 'logic' of the period – its unvarnished truth – rather than a comment on cultural hegemony. (12)

According to Bromley's theory of 'lost narratives' under Thatcherism, representations of class and poverty have been subjected to a process of 'organized forgetting' whereby popular perceptions have been dominated by the 'flattened' 'still shots' of the Depression era. As noted earlier, Bromley criticizes extreme media images – of soup lines, bugs, and disease, for instance – for colonizing popular memory in Britain and fixing poverty in a discontinuous and distant past, far from the present (7). Importantly, the result of using extreme versions of poverty as 'authenticating data' for dismissing contemporary claims is that poverty is projected onto the past in order to preserve an idealized, evolutionary version of the contemporary nation and current prosperity.

The idea that the colonization of memory is vital to national culture is not, of course, unique. In the late nineteenth century, Ernest Renan observed, in the context of his discussion of nations and their often brutal beginnings, that 'it was good for everyone to know how to forget' even when the inscription of historical inaccuracies is involved (16). And Franz Fanon also remarked that national culture often builds upon an idealized past and forgets parts of the present in order to fashion a mask of national unity that will cover class differences and poverty along with other forms of internal colonization (225, 159). Other historiographers have shown the narrative function of forgetting as inherent to the telling of history. In an analysis of history as discourse, Michel de Certeau has created the striking image of history as a master text consorting with corpses and making of marginalized subjects ghostly presences who have been excluded and written out of memory. And Daniel J. Boorstin, in his essay 'The Historian: A Wrestler with the Angel,' represents the contemporary historian's struggle with obstacles and trends, which range from the lack of ideal material conditions for retrieving information to the temptations experienced by the historian herself to celebrate heroes and success stories and to feign knowledge beyond ignorance. Forgetting and remembering are thus inspired by many motives: nationalist, narrative, and epistemic.

Bromley's version of the political implications of struggling with history draws on works by Michel Foucault, Antonio Gramsci, Agnes Heller, Haydn White, Raymond Williams, and Patrick Wright. His unique contribution is the idea of how 'organized forgetting' takes place when *popular culture* colonizes our memory and our consciousness of the present *in respect to poverty and class*. He argues that the life-writing of working-class women, in particular, is complicit in reproducing representative images as preferred memories of poverty. Thus, Bromley calls into question the whole role of popular literature in the construction of cultural memory. Singling out working-class women's autobiographical accounts of the postwar period in Britain as especially nostalgic, ahistoric, and iconic in their representations of poverty, he names them the primary category of 'lost narratives.'

Bromley identifies these narratives as particularly representative in that they typically show the working-class woman emerging as a highly mobile individual who struggles alone and against all odds to transcend her poverty. Significantly, she is mobilized *out of* rather than *for* her class and becomes a class traveller in her own narrative. The highly mobile representative individual thus consigns collective history to a background position as 'demobilised' landscape. In keeping with Bromley's observations of 'lost narratives' is a set of absences and presences which makes a certain type of popular autobiography particularly marketable: the primary absences are representations of structural poverty and historical continuity, and the overwhelming presences are quantitative scenes of extreme poverty and the qualitative triumph of the human spirit through hard work, enterprise, independence, and self-determination.

According to Bromley, then, lost narratives are 'lost' both in the sense that they do not record collective class experiences or individual experiences in terms of Marxist conceptions of a continuous progression of history and also in the sense that they are flattened, iconic versions rather than detailed and, he implies, authentic (xiii). As I mentioned earlier, feminist theories of class have problematized the idea of a continuous master historical narrative in the public sphere, and feminist theories of women's autobiography have also problematized the relevance of collective frames to what are sometimes secret memories. Building on Bromley's theory of forgetting by adding such feminist insights, I think it is possible to interrogate popular working-class autobiographies by Canadian women with respect to their own narrative economy of absences and presences.

In my own life story, I have seen an example of how dehistoricized and selective memory operates culturally in the place and time in which I have been speaking about. The flattening of cultural memory through 'organized forgetting' was brought home to me recently when, as part of my research on Canadian women's 'poverty narratives,' I asked my mother about her own experience of poverty – over twenty years of living on welfare with a house full of children and she and my father both physically disabled and housebound. She answered me with shocked silence and then asked: 'Were we poor? I never thought of us as *poor*! We never had to stand in line or anything. Did *you feel* poor?' This was the first time the subject of poverty, as such, had come up between us, and I was shocked that we remembered things so differently. By calling up the Depression scenes of soup lines – '*We didn't have to stand in line or anything*' – my mother was confirming Bromley's cultural theory for me in a very personal way. She was using the extreme 'still shots' of a distant past as authenticating data for our own shared experiences of poverty.

It is now a standing joke in our large, now financially secure, family that I have actually said we were once 'poor,' with everyone disagreeing on the way we should account for the past. The joke heightens to nervous laughter when I suggest, by way of explanation, that we moved from working class to lumpenproletariat after my father's illness. The joke now goes: 'Have you heard the latest? Now we're *lumpen*!' – and I laugh too at our complex lives collapsed into the negative connotation of Marx's own category (*lumpen* meaning 'ragged' and *lumpenproletariat* receiving its classical definition from *Das Kapital* and *The Communist Manifesto* as a class distinct from the thinking proletariat: including thieves, beggars, prostitutes, street people, the ill, and the handicapped – in other words, the poor without labour, the parasitical classes).[1] The personal challenge of negotiating some agreed-upon version of the past with my family has impressed upon me how subjects in contemporary Canadian society must struggle to find ways of either affirming or suppressing class in order to construct a more socially coherent sense of self. It has also impressed upon me the complicity of working-class and poor subjects in their own historical erasure and the need for recognition of such complicity in order to decode their ideological renderings of personal history. In other words, not only does the audience in our culture prefer to remember and credit stories which represent poverty in certain ways – individualized, distant, extreme, ahistorical, and apolitical – but the tellers of these stories are also often complicit in this 'organized forgetting' by living their lives and telling their stories in a way which erases class connections among people and across time.

The challenge of reading working-class women's stories entails seeing beyond the strategic absences in the text itself, which may constitute a politics of erasure, including the gender absences in master historical narratives, Marxist or otherwise. This challenge to recover forgotten aspects can be described as a patching and piecing together of what Rebecca O'Rourke has termed, 'the not done, not thought of, not there history' (53). It is not simply that we have few public records of these women's lives and how and why they did or did not write their stories; the cultural project of forgetting also resides with the subjects themselves in the way they told and the way they lived their stories, and with the audience in the way these stories are received or overlooked. O'Rourke observes that members of the working class, especially women, have been regarded as 'most fully of their class when silenced' (52). In her essay 'Were There No Women?: British Working-class Writing in the Inter-war Period,' she observes that, ironically, as soon as these women do speak out by writing autobiographies, they are often perceived as no longer working class. And Tillie Olsen, herself the author of one of the most lyrical and revealing unfinished novels of the twentieth century, lamented the pressure on the working-class writer to conform to dominant narrative strategies: 'Coercions to "pass"; to write with the attitude of, and/or in the manner of, the dominant. Little to validate our different sense of reality, to help raise one's own truths, voice, against the prevalent' (288).

---

1 See Gertrude Himmelfarb's discussion of the genealogy of the term before and after Marx and Engels (386–94).

Working-class poet, critic, and teacher Tom Wayman exposes the contradiction between lived class rifts and the bourgeois, national myth of an inclusive, democratic culture in the title of his most recent book, *A Country Not Considered: Canada, Culture, Work* (1993). In a personal testimonial, Wayman protests that he does not feel defined by the high culture we have come to recognize as Canadian national culture:

> I hear from time to time ... that Canadian culture defines who we are. When the 'we' is not specified here, this argument to me seems absurd. I certainly do not feel defined by Karen Kain's dancing, or Margaret Atwood's new novel, or Bryan Adams's new record, or some video artist showing her or his work to a group of fellow artists at a state-supported gallery. All these artistic productions may be dazzling, accomplished, innovative, or may be less successful artistically. But I personally do not know anybody who considers their lives, their identity, defined by such activity. (21–2)

Dominance of the bourgeoisie over the production of national culture and national identity ensures historical amnesia of how the poor and working class experience culture and nation by controlling access to representation. Porter's study *The Vertical Mosaic: An Analysis of Social Class and Power in Canada* concluded that Canada had 'a very long way to go' in order to become a 'thorough-going democracy' (557) in that the decision-making apparatus and the educational system which shape its development are based on élites rather than the structures of a 'liberal citizen-participating democracy' (558). Porter's assessment explains a contradiction at the very basis of both academic and popular constructions of Canadian culture, one which arises when democracy and capitalism are conflated and a nationalist myth of a developed, prosperous, inclusive, democratic nation cloaks the stratagems used by its cultural élite to exclude, forget, or exploit the poor and the working class. But the problem is much deeper than that, as Bromley suggests, reaching into the very forms and texture of life stories to inscribe distance and fragmentation where experiences of class might otherwise be remembered. In the following readings of poor women's autobiographies I intend to illustrate the absence of collective memories and the hegemonic function of these absences. At the same time, however, I intend to draw on the insights of feminist scholars about the necessarily fragmented nature of poor and working-class women's history in order to interpret absences, fragments, and individualism differently from the way Bromley has.

Before analysing the fate of class memories in specific autobiographies, I would like to discuss feminist theories of cultural memory. Feminist theories of history, politics, and autobiography have exposed many layers of misunderstanding and misrecognition arising from gender bias in the way class history has been constructed through Marxist analysis. At the same time, there has been a great deal of apathy on the part of many feminist literary critics towards classed memories and class subjectivities among women. The latter may be another cultural instance, this time in the academic sphere, of the 'organized forgetting' which Bromley sees inscribed in popular texts (22). Some of the greatest indifference arises from the assumption that class-conscious readings merely seek to reproduce an idealist master narrative (from class exploitation to solidarity, to class struggle, to revolution, and, eventually, a classless society) by illuminating its shape in the text or by showing where the text falls short of reproducing it. This concept of the reading strategies available to recover class history is dated and unnecessarily limited, particularly in light of the way feminist materialist scholars and cultural critics have problematized class history to make it a more challenging and meaningful interpretive device. Moreover, few would deny that skilful Marxist and post-Marxist readings of culture and text, such as those by Raymond Williams, Cora Kaplan, Pamela Fox, Catherine Belsey, Roger Bromley, and Carolyn Steedman, to name just a few, have demonstrated that much more is involved in decoding class in a text than merely matching it to a grid of Marxist history. Before considering how certain popular narratives erase collective memories of class, I would like first to mention how our understanding of class itself and of class memory has been expanded through materialist feminist theory. Here, although I take up and build on my earlier discussions of the gendered class subject (chapter 4) and of the resistant autobiographical subject (chapter 5), the focus at this time is on memory and the way class, gender, and nation are remembered through the construction of poor and working-class women's identity.

Feminists have shown that collective amnesia regarding gender in the Marxist construction of history constitutes a conceptual trap that serves patriarchal interests. For example, Joan Wallach Scott, in *Gender and the Politics of History*, maintains that, when the reciprocal relations of class and gender are not taken into account, patriarchy is reinscribed. More specifically, Scott explains, Marxist discourse on class exploitation, class struggle, and class history has tended to situate itself in the public sphere as the site where 'workers' experience their lives, thus often excluding or devaluing the classed experiences of many poor and working-class women who lived out their lives in largely private spheres. As Scott explains, the 'presumed "social reality" of the working class' has been constructed according to gender assumptions and is made coherent through the same assumptions – for example, the assumption that labour is more important in forming class identity than other formative experiences such as culture and domestic life (83). Moreover, Scott observes that although Marxist class history has provided clear categories and definitions through which we can recall a linear past made coherent through theories of economic causality, gender and race defy such clarity of collective memory. Herein lies one of the conceptual problems in recognizing how class, gender, and race construct each other reciprocally in everyday life and history: that is, sheer complexity (30).

The Marxist preference for memory of the public sphere of wage labour and market practices has also been critiqued by Christine Delphy in *Close to Home: A Materialist Analysis of Women's Oppression*. As mentioned in my discussion of the classed and gendered subject (chapter 4), Delphy theorizes women's domestic and reproductive work outside the wage-labour marketplace within the category of 'the domestic sphere of labour' in order to redress conceptual problems around how class identity is understood based on gender assumptions. Delphy advises materialist feminists that we cannot expect to find the answers to women's gendered class experiences in Marx's writings; rather, in order to disentangle ourselves from the conceptual trap of seeing class through men's experiences exclusively, we must ourselves reapply Marxist principles to women's everyday experiences and empirical knowledge of the domestic sphere of labour (154–81). This would demand remembering class history by expanding our field of knowledge to include the private sphere, which was previously designated as an insignificant, depoliticized sphere of activities.

Another cornerstone critique which finds Marxism inadequate to the task of recovering memory of working-class women's experiences is Carolyn Steedman's *Landscape for a Good Woman: A Story of Two Lives*. Steedman challenges the way male scholarship has understood class history by revealing how the contradictions, the secret stories, and the gendered significance of her mother's life and her own childhood are not recoverable through Marxist concepts of class. Through interdisciplinary play between autobiographical theory and history, Steedman focuses less on the political reconceptualization of labour than on the need to reconceptualize class history through its personalized and subjective nature, which, she argues, has often been suppressed as politically naive or insignificant. Steedman demonstrates how, in her mother's and her own intertwining stories, material need and class identification were lived out not as collective history but rather as deeply internalized, subconscious, and secret stories, crystallizing in anecdotes around personal markers: a wished-for dress, anxiety, moments of exclusion and loss, 'a revolving door, a full skirt, some flowers' roots' – markers which can be made sense of only through the history of private lives (98).

Taken together, these critiques of a gender bias in Marxist theories of history suggest considerable adjustments in how we remember poor and working-class women's stories, asking us to re-examine the categories through which we remember, the way we see these women situated in terms of their own class and patriarchal society as a whole, and the way we make sense of fragments of personal lives. Despite such recent developments by materialist feminists, however, 'class' and 'history' are, more often than not, 'bumped' (or included only nominally) in current feminist discussions of autobiographical subjects in Canada – while race, ethnicity, and gender usually emerge as the primary categories for discussions of the colonized female subject. It may be that 'class' will continue to be overlooked in discussions of Canadian women's autobiographies for a number of reasons. First, there is resistance to the new-found complexity of considering class and gender as reciprocal forces in the construction of identity because of a strong institutional trend to valorize textually based readings of autobiography-as-literature (as opposed to autobiography-as-history). Second, many theories of female autobiography tend to homogenize all female subjects, regardless of class, within a category of gender or race. And third, the cultural context of our readings of these autobiographies in Canada favours the sort of erasure of class-consciousness and historical memory described by Roger Bromley as 'organized forgetting' (22).

6.2 Poverty as Distant Landscape: Edna Jaques

> I didn't know they called it poetry, I only knew it sounded nice and after that, now and then the flash would come, like the echo of a voice singing somewhere, or something you kind of remembered. (Jaques 11)

Uphill All the Way is the autobiography of one of Canada's all-but-forgotten folk poets, Edna Jaques, written when she was eighty-six to tell of her *rise* from uneducated farm girl to highly successful poet. On numerous speaking tours, Jaques emphasized women's work and domestic space as part of the celebration of the local. According to her own description, her 'common, ordinary poems' ranged in topics from 'a clothesline full of nice clean clothes to the coronation of the queen' (79). She had a refreshingly irreverent way of speaking about poetry as both community property and a tidy source of private revenue. At forty-one, she would earn what she called her 'first easy money' by publishing a collection of poems which had previously been sold individually by the poet herself in the marketable size of small greeting cards (Jaques 80; Gerson 1993, 66).

In an important gesture towards recovery of Jaques's popular poetry in *Canadian Literature*, Carole Gerson has supported the author's claims by confirming that she was 'Canada's most popular poet through the middle decades of this century' and 'had published nine volumes of verse between 1934 and 1946' (62). Gerson focuses, however, on how Jaques's popular poems have since been excluded from the canon due to 'high-brow' hostility towards 'low-brow local versifiers' and decades of prejudice against female poets on the part of Canada's canon-makers (63). Gerson notes that the parodic version of Jaques as the 'Bad Canadian poetess' (67), the comical character of Sarah Binks in Paul Hiebert's book by that title (1947), has become better known in Canadian culture than Jaques herself (64–5). And, indeed, a 1994 CBC radio special on Sarah Binks featured academics discussing the fictional poetess's 'bad, bad poetry' without any mention at all of Jaques as the historical counterpart nor of the unusually large popular following the 'bad, bad poetry' had inspired due to the 'low-brow' tastes of the Canadian public.

Gerson observes that public ridicule in literary circles did not concern Jaques (and the chapter 'Successes' in the autobiography confirms this), but that the exclusionary process obviously concerned Canadian canon-makers and the literary élite who saw their own national literary agenda threatened in multiple ways (for example, in terms of class, gender, commercial success, and popular support). Gerson's valuable archival work and observations on the cultural context of canon formation establish the factual basis for reinserting Jaques's popular texts into an expanded notion of national literature. In recovering Jaques's persona and her works as historical artifact, however, Gerson seems to gloss over the ideological nature of class absences in Jaques's relation to 'ordinary women' and in her construction of herself as a folk poet.

Whether Jaques's verse for ordinary women constitutes a working-class voice should be questioned because, even among the few critical commentaries available, there is disagreement as to whether her 'ordinariness' was closer to a middle-class or a working-class ethos. Northrop Frye sneered at the nostalgic poetry and its tendency to 'flatter the collective memory' with a 'smoothly edited and censored transcript of wholesome food, happy children, simple virtues, and, of course, mother dear,' and E.K. Brown was equally dismissive, saying that her work was falsely valued because of its 'coziness' on the subject of '[l]ove, patriotism, even religion itself.' Brown dismissed Jaques's work for its ordinariness, in the worst sense of the word, calling it 'an expression of the ordinary self of the Canadian *middle class*, that is to say, of the immense majority of Canadians' (Frye and Brown as quoted by Gerson 68, emphasis added). That the popular poet's class ethos has become contested ground is not evident from Gerson's insistence on the oppositional feminist and rural quality of Jaques's work: 'Unlike Nellie McClung, who was a personal friend and who also wrote heart-warming, optimistic words to cheer the hard lives of women, Jaques did *not* speak down from *a middle-class perspective* but directly to her peers in the kitchens of the country' (67, emphasis added). Gerson's conflation of 'ordinary women' with working-class women and domestic farm work with working-class labour may itself be oppositional in that it assumes a more flexible definition of 'working class' which would accommodate women's experience within the domestic sphere. However, many middle-class women as well as working-class women occupied the rural kitchens of the country, and Jaques was from the middle class not the working class. This conflation may also result from the notion that the popular defines itself against high culture and is therefore necessarily the vessel for working-class perspectives. Rather than unravel this conflation in respect to Jaques's poetry, I would like to suggest that the contested terrain of Jaques's class affiliation and her 'ordinariness' could be broached in respect to her construction of self in *Uphill All the Way* and the class ideology the autobiography deploys in its way of remembering the past.

True to Bromley's theory, what is overwhelmingly present from the first page is the triumph of the independent human spirit and hard work, both of which stand out in relief against the distant landscape of poverty. Although there are references to class, money, and labour in the following excerpt from which the book takes its title, the archaic diction used for these subjects ('queen,' 'guinea gold,' 'galley slave') places them even farther in the past than the subject's own time and gives them an extreme and fanciful ring: 'from the day I was twelve and started to herd cattle, I've worked like a galley slave and it's been uphill all the way – very uphill – steep and rocky, with hard slugging. Although I wouldn't trade places with the queen, I wouldn't go back over the trail I've come for a million dollars in guinea gold' (Jaques 1). Later, when Jaques places material struggle once again in the distant background as landscape, she is assuring us that poverty is a road already travelled, a hardship one can and does escape. Whereas Jaques expresses strong beliefs about self-help and the democratization of art and poetry, her beliefs are never radical enough to challenge the social system or to lead her to advocate social change. Instead, poverty recedes to the discontinuous past as landscape, made coherent mostly through the speaker's ability to 'go it alone' and rise above hardship: 'I can see the valleys I travelled alone, the little hills that I toiled up, the meadows where the going was easy for a short time, and then the hills again. How wonderful it is to see where you made the right turn, and the other times when you took the crooked mile, yet came out triumphant at the end' (243). As the title and this metaphor suggest, the speaker is as resigned to the inevitability of life's setbacks – poverty included – as she is to the 'lay' of the land. The necessity for personal and spiritual struggle among the poor is figured in the received image of life as an individual journey through rough landscape and the Self as a lone, struggling pilgrim. The formula of absences and presences here establishes the work as popular and marketable, according to what Bromley has suggested, because it reduces anxiety around the prospect of poverty by placing it in the context of personal history and in the realm of the temporary rather than in systemic structure or social history.

The motif of the road may also be situated within an older discourse of *classlessness* which used the country road as a trajectory for collective folk memory. Regenia Gagnier has described this earlier tradition and its use of the road and folkloric time as an ordering principle which often replaced the unified 'I' as subject in working-class writing of the 'commemorative' or storytelling genre (156). Poverty recedes temporally in Jaques's story, existing as a backdrop to an idealized picture of a folkish and fanciful agrarian past, and more importantly, to her representation of a highly spirited, hard-working, and upwardly mobile self whose 'I' orders narrative events and time itself in respect to class mobility, class travelling, and the move towards public recognition as a national poet and public speaker.

The details of Jaques's life journey unfold chronologically around these main life events: at a young age, she moved with her middle-class family from relative ease in small-town Ontario to a rough-hewn homestead in Saskatchewan – thus undergoing an experience of 'declassing' not at all unique in Canadian pioneer narratives (compare, for example, Susanna Moodie's *Roughing It in the Bush*, Laura Goodman Salverson's *Confessions of an Immigrant's Daughter*, and Nellie McClung's *Clearing in the West*). But Jaques, writing retrospectively, recalls no sense of privation at the experience of declassing. Although she received only a grade-eight education, she seemed content with that and did not yearn after high culture and education as some of her writer contemporaries such as Salverson and McClung did in their homesteading stories (hence Jaques's ties to local folk and the local culture). Unlike Nellie McClung, whose attendance at school was also interrupted to permit her to tend cattle, Jaques enjoyed the freedom of studying away from the schoolroom. In solitary hours, she recited poetry to the cows and depicted those summers close to the land as spiritually nurturing and a source of inner peace to be summoned during the hardships to come (59–60).

Jaques's recollection of life on the family homestead is unfailingly nostalgic, stressing the plentiful food, the house always full of company, and pleasant chores. Hard work is always cheerfully undertaken, and any mention of physical fatigue is followed by an uplifting remark. The cheerfulness is unrelenting, but not monotonous as in other, even more idealized accounts of homesteading life such as Nina Moore Jamieson's *The Cattle in the Stall* (1932) and Kathleen Strange's *With the West in Her Eyes* (1937). Jaques's story is saved from tedium by a refreshing and unaffected use of local idiom and a lively and concrete narrative style.

The rural poor as a group, however, do not figure at all in the narrative – the only report of poverty occurs as part of Jaques's own story. Following the chapter on her wedding is one titled 'We Go Broke,' which reports how the young couple went east to homestead in Ontario after a business failure. Jaques was distressed about the move, for by now she knew of her husband's aversion to work and wondered how they would fare on uncleared land. The portrait of her life at this point becomes gruesomely rugged as she uses the autobiography as testimony to personal trauma. With her husband frequently absent, Jaques and her baby were left alone for days and weeks at a time in a doorless and windowless log shack. As winter came on, she became the object of concern to her closest neighbour, a woman who lived a

188 Remnants of Nation

mile away through uncleared forest. The neighbour woman lodged Jaques and her baby and asked her own husband to put a door on the shack and make it habitable for winter.

Although this helping gesture would not register as historically significant according to traditional concepts of class struggle in the public sphere, it is a significant fragment for feminist historians, representing one of many forgotten but vital acts of support among pioneer women and neighbours, acts which helped sustain poor women and their children, but which remain part of the 'not done, not thought of, not there' history referred to by Rebecca O'Rourke. It is also a significant fragment of Canadian history, when considered along with what Jack Blyth describes, in *The Canadian Social Inheritance,* as the attitude taken towards poverty given the context of a North American pioneering environment: 'poverty was seen mainly in terms of a "help thy neighbour" policy' because of the reluctance of the pioneers to take on tax burdens associated with the Old Country and its costly Poor Laws (9). As Blyth also notes, when public-relief laws were instituted later, they carried with them the moral assumptions of earlier times. This meant that, in the 1920s in Ontario, Jaques as a single mother would not have been eligible for relief under the new laws – only widows and the wives of the completely disabled were judged deserving, not women and children who had been deserted.[2]

For four years, Jaques stayed on the homestead with only minor

---

2 Blyth does not specify, but this suggests a moral refusal to subsidize unwed mothers as well as deserted wives (28). For a more complete discussion of the politics and practices of welfare in this period, see James Struthers, *The Limits of Affluence: Welfare in Ontario, 1920–1970* (1994). Struthers relates the paradox of how welfare grew out of a concern for mothers and children (rather than the unemployed, the disabled, or the elderly) and yet a moral discourse of social control severely limited which mothers and children were eligible for relief and how they had to live in order to remain eligible. For example, only widows and their children were considered eligible because the idea of including the majority of single mothers (deserted and unwed mothers) was rejected by advocates for mother's allowance and women alike on moral grounds. The concept of subsidizing unwed mothers, according to Struthers, was too controversial even to debate. Despite the findings of public hearings in 1919 that most poor women and their children were deserted, not widowed, social support was not offered to the majority, who were judged undeserving for moral reasons. Moreover, those widows who did obtain social support were severely regulated to ensure their worthiness to be caretakers of their own children *on behalf of the state*. For such distinctions and exclusions, Struthers maintains that welfare functioned as social control more than simply public charity (Struthers 19–49).

improvements, spending her savings from jobs before her marriage for basic food items. By the time she finally left her husband for the life of a single mother, she was in her mid-thirties, she weighed less than one hundred pounds, her hair had turned white, and she reported that she had lost the ability to cry – rather extreme and concentrated images of poverty but not merely iconic (157). Extreme poverty and isolation of the individual woman is inscribed here as a testimony to her husband's failure and unwillingness to provide for their baby and her, and also as evidence of the lack of systemic support for deserted mothers and children. Jaques stresses the spirit of independence which allowed her to leave an exploitative situation and go on to support her daughter and herself by working as a domestic, a factory worker, a secretary (none of which are described in much detail), and, finally, as a commercially successful poet and speaker. It is important to contextualize this individual struggle by acknowledging that it was partly thrust upon her through lack of social support. Jaques does not mention social support or going back to her family as possibilities, but instead insists on faith in God, luck, and finding courage as the means of sustaining one's spirit and coping with poverty alone.

Uphill All the Way is complicit in bourgeois cultural hegemony, according to Bromley's theory of 'organized forgetting,' through the image-making of a representative poor woman struggling alone in a nostalgic and discontinuous version of the past; but it is also, paradoxically, oppositional to patriarchal hegemony in the way it remembers a gendered experience of poverty by a single mother and the details of women's domestic sphere of labour. Bromley's account of the representative working-class subject as a class traveller cut off from her roots temporally and spatially would not adequately describe Jaques's self-portrait because underlying her individual struggle is a strong affirmation of solidarity among women and among the rural community. Rebecca O'Rourke observes that working-class women often employ the motif of voyage in their life-writing in order to stress the class mobility which moves them out of and away from their class (unlike working-class men whose stories more often include actual travelling and displacement). This move towards social mobility gives poor and working-class women a story worth telling according to hegemonic values in that it bolsters the bourgeois concept of meritocracy and provides the working-class woman's life story with a plot aligned to bourgeois conventions. (Regenia Gagnier has also discussed how working-class subjects attempted to force their life stories into bourgeois plot lines in the nineteenth century, even at the expense of an ungrounded sense of identity and disintegration of the narrative [41–6, 52]). In the stories of poor and working-class women, actual isolating conditions of abandonment, single parenting, and social stigma may also account for the female subject's individual striving towards mobility, not only on the level of narrative trajectory, but as a survival strategy.

In *Uphill All the Way*, whereas the realities of gendered experiences are remembered, much of the reality of personal economic struggle is simply not. Although Jaques alludes to such hardships briefly when she endorses religion as a source of comfort and inner strength – 'through danger, poverty, being homeless, out of work, out of money, in big cities, or on the homestead, on planes or ships at sea, in situations that would make your hair stand on end' (12) – what is remembered is how the words of two evangelist women who visited her childhood home and urged trust in God helped her triumph over these hardships, not the hardships themselves. None the less, within the context of a pioneering ethos, Jaques's capacity for hard work and self-determination signifies more than one woman's struggle for class mobility, for feminist independence, or for survival. It also signifies a community's striving after idealized notions of local and national history through the values of individualism and free enterprise. Consequently, the collectivity in *Uphill All the Way* is not divided by class or historical struggle. It is the imagined communities of women's groups, rural folk, and nation which are all invoked nostalgically, without class rifts. In the way Jaques's autobiography remembers community nostalgically, it stands in direct contrast to an overtly class-conscious work such as Laura Goodman Salverson's *Confessions of an Immigrant's Daughter*, which interrogates nation each time it dips into social realism about the sweat shops in early industrialized cities and shows poverty to be systemic despite New World promises for social mobility. As I will discuss in the last chapter, Salverson refuses to limit her inscription of self to the private sphere of women or to reproduce received notions of the New World as a homogeneous community with equal opportunity for all.

Jaques, on the other hand, is resistant in the way she constructs popular art, prairie life, and women's domestic sphere at the centre of culture. But she is also complicit in class hegemony in remembering nation nostalgically through a mask of unity. At the lowest point in her personal motivation, when she is alone in the backwoods of Ontario, she invokes nation to give her sustenance when God seems to have forsaken her, venting her loneliness and anger at the moon: 'I leaned against the little pole fence surrounding the cabin and looked up at the sky and talked to God. "All right," I said, shaking my fist at Him up there in the heavens, "It's your turn now, but some day," I sobbed, "I'll stand on Parliament Hill in Ottawa and they'll honour me"'(150). Then she goes on to recount how such an honour came to her when her poetry was celebrated by women of the national press on the site of Canada's parliament.

Historical amnesia in *Uphill All the Way* is all the more evident because Jaques conflates her role as popular poet with that of national historian. She speaks with a collective and commemorative as well as a personal voice, for example, when she states that one of her reasons for writing 'common, ordinary poems' and telling about life on the prairies in Canada is to combat forgetting: 'no child will ever grow up in the pioneer conditions that we did and so much of what we experienced might be lost forever' (79).[3] Yet generally, Jaques's narrative contains and flattens historical representations of the public sphere while simultaneously inscribing a preferred version of local history and the private sphere. This can be seen through the following sample of chapter titles: My Ancestors, My First Memory, Our Homestead, The First Furrow, The School, Buckwheat Pancakes, Seed Potatoes, My First Editor, The Munitions Plant, The War Goes On, The War Ends, My Grandchildren – which suggest the containment of world and political events *through* the celebration of the personal and the local. For instance, the Depression is contained in a one-and-a-half-page chapter called 'The Drought' – where it is localized and naturalized as a series of natural disasters: the drought, infestations of army worms, and freak storms. Absent from Jaques's representation of the Depression are market causes and class confrontations such as those depicted by other Canadian writers who firmly resisted idealist local and national constructions through documentary realism of the Depression era – representations such as Hugh Garner's *Cabbagetown*, Irene Baird's *Waste Heritage*, and Mary Quayle Innis's and Dorothy Livesay's short stories and reportage.

---

[3] It is not within the scope of this discussion of autobiography to analyse the construction of class, gender, and nation in Jaques's poems. I am concerned here only with her autobiographical construction of self as national poet and her claims that the poems are a site of shared memory.

A further example of how Jaques subscribes to nostalgic nationalism is the way she remembers the Second World War primarily through her own job in the munitions factory and the strong sense of zeal and solidarity felt around the war effort. Her sentimental account differs greatly from oral histories in Dionne Brand's *No Burden to Carry: Narratives of Black Working Women in Ontario 1920s–1950s* by women who recall racial divisions among the workers in munitions plants and how black women were assigned the heaviest and most dangerous tasks.[4] An oral historian interested in documentarism, Brand purposefully asked questions which would make women consider how events in public history related to their own personal stories.

To the class and historical absences in Jaques's popular mythologizing of 'common people,' are added the absence of ethnic and racial tensions which have been brought to light in other autobiographical reports about minority ethnic experiences in prairie communities between the wars. For example, Fredelle Bruser Maynard's *Raisins and Almonds*, Bridget Moran's *Stoney Creek Woman: The Story of Mary John*, and Maria Campbell's *Halfbreed* remember the fissures among the common rural folk, fissures springing along ethnic and racial, as well as class, lines. They offer more than a transparent reporting of the experiences of 'others' by speaking through subjects with wounded identities and using autobiography as both a site for testimony to the trauma of exclusion and for an identity strategy aimed at piecing together a damaged sense of self. These accounts are culturally oppositional constructions of race and ethnicity; but, as in Jaques's autobiography, oppositional memory of certain aspects of the self and society does not ensure opposition to all forms of cultural hegemony.

6.3 Class Travelling with Fredelle Bruser Maynard

Fredelle Bruser Maynard's *Raisins and Almonds* is better known in Canadian literature than Jaques's *Uphill All the Way*, most probably because of its literary bent and because we possess more reading strategies to decode and aestheticize the construction of an educated and

---

4 An alternative means of inserting a frame of public history around private narratives was skilfully applied by Rolf Knight in transcribing his mother's autobiography, *A Very Ordinary Life*. Knight supplied encyclopaedic end notes on class and world history to render his mother's personal *ordinariness* more coherent in terms of other lives.

cosmopolitan Self. Maynard, like Jaques, tells of hard economic times between the wars, but inscribes distance from that time and those communities, not only as an economically mobile subject who expressed distaste for the uneducated and for labourers, but also as a Jew who was ostracized repeatedly. 'Difference,' Maynard writes, 'was in my bones and blood, and in the pattern of my separate life' (27). Once again, as with Jaques's uphill motif and Bromley's prototype, the subject looks back on her difficult past as distant landscape, but this time clearly as an isolated visitor in a *foreign* country: 'They are not all happy highways where I went. What, then, drives me down them again, after all these years and another life? The effort, I suppose, to understand. Somewhere, in yon far country, lies the answer to the question that confronts me with increasing urgency. Who am I?' (181). The travel motif returns her to the distant site of trauma to witness and testify to the experience of exclusion and to repair a damaged self. The motif of the wanderer derives from a representational tradition of the Jew as wanderer, as well as from that of the class traveller in a mobility narrative. But although Maynard is able to identify with others who are isolated due to ethnicity, she does not identify with those among the poor and working class. Unlike Jaques, however, she does not erase class differences; she merely defines the lack of economic status negatively by reporting only the indignities and privations of her family's relative poverty – the result of her father's many business failures – and by frequently implying a distaste for labourers as the narrative of her own life unfolds.

It is evident from her description of her parents' clothing and their first house and possessions that, despite their downward mobility and her father's peasant roots in Russia, they identify themselves as middle-class store owners rather than as working class – or from Maynard's point of view, 'though we might be poor we were not common' (23). When the Depression forces them into Winnipeg to try setting up yet another business, Maynard remembers the shame in that, as well as every other, step towards reduced circumstances: '[a]s for our new city business – it didn't seem like a real store at all. Papa had bought – how diminishing – a neighbourhood candy store' (71). Maynard stresses that her mother saw to it that 'without money, [they] lived rich' and kept a garden, used silver napkin rings, and ate jelly from crystal as 'assurances' (185); and she also remembers her father's 'nobility' and how 'something invincibly aristocratic shaped his features till the end' (177). Her deep aversion to the working class emerges indirectly through her admiration for anything bourgeois. For example, the description of her father's superior physiognomy may be an attempt to rationalize his difference and his vulnerability to market fluctuations by stressing his refined sensibilities:

> I had always admired his beautiful hands. Mine are stubby-fingered, suggesting a certain peasant coarseness ... (178)

> His skin was whiter than I would have believed possible, and strangely smooth – the skin of a man who lived indoors and never used his body except for love. (174)

> [H]is clear nobility provided a standard of value in my life. (185)

But curiously, despite Maynard's disdain for poverty and for signs of peasant blood, the poor as a group are not as absent from her reconstruction of the past as they are from Jaques's *Uphill All the Way* – they are depicted fleetingly as Other, as hoboes and Gypsies passing through town or romanticized as part of the distant past (the Jewish ghetto in the Czar's Russia of her father's past) (21). As to her own identity, she admits that the poverty of the Depression left its mark – '[f]rom a thousand penny-pinched situations I breathed in frugality' – and then goes on to itemize in detail the survival lessons about food and clothing which she learned from the Depression as well as some of her more compulsive saving habits (186). However, the conclusion of *Raisins and Almonds* asserts that the landscape and education, not poverty or ethnicity, left the strongest mark on her identity. This is not surprising in the context of conventions of Canadian writing which recognize landscape but rarely class as formative principles on literature and identity.

Maynard's inscription of her past as 'yon far country' distances her writing Self from more than poverty as landscape; it also inscribes a sense of otherness within a national community divided along ethnic lines, thus implying an ambivalence towards nation. On the other hand, Maynard inscribes her Jewishness positively as collective tradition, a shared way of life, and a special gift. Moreover, when she suffers from blatantly anti-Semitic attacks, her sense of ethnic exclusion extends beyond the private into the systemic. She remembers the prairie farm communities and cities alike as exclusionary not only to Jews but to Native people, Chinese, and blacks as well. For example, when she wants to be accepted into the inner circle of school girls from the dominant ethnic group (in this case Norwegian immigrants) in a certain town, she must agree to participate in ostracizing the local Indian, and when he cannot be found, they torment a Chinese storekeeper instead (56–9). The incident shames her as much as the family's economic decline does; the guilt that she, too, can torment outsiders tears at her identity and explains a central metaphor for breakage in her life story: 'the needle of glass that pierced my heart' (60).

Yet class melds complexly with ethnic tensions in Maynard's story, for the family's reduced financial circumstances render them more vulnerable to the sting of anti-Semitism by separating them from the Jewish neighbourhood and school and by exposing Maynard and her sister to the openly anti-Semitic attacks of aggressive school children. Poverty for Maynard means a host of negatives: more vulnerability to anti-Semitism, a house on the sidewalk always open to public view, neon signs flashing in her window, longer work hours, sexual harassment from her father's customers, disappointment in her father, public shame, and inferior teachers who spitefully hold her back in school. The distant landscape she describes does not gloss over poverty but places it negatively at a shameful distance from her writerly, educated, remembering Self. She revisits the local landscape and the Depression era across this shameful expanse, remembering more the contents of the mail-order catalogue and her school readers, the world on paper that piqued her desire to move beyond 'yon far country,' than the specifics of the family's material need. Commodities and received versions of the past take a preferred place in the narrative as the details of a past landscape because they represent the acquisition of material and cultural capital and the desire for a bourgeois lifestyle which would move her beyond need and necessity into the safety of a new landscape.

Through this brief comparison of Maynard's and Jaques's autobiographies I have tried to illustrate that the convention of consigning poverty to landscape, which Bromley identified as symptomatic of organized forgetting in British culture, may also be operative in Canadian culture. None the less, I have also tried to show through contrasts between Jaques's and Maynard's life-writing how poverty may be constructed differently in that distant landscape with respect to different imagined communities and shifting, if not actually contradictory, ideological values. The remaining question, I feel, is a theoretical one about whether or not popular forms of autobiography are more susceptible than other forms to organized forgetting, as Bromley suggests, or, conversely, more suited to oppositional memory. Is it true, for example, that popular autobiography is especially apt to reproduce the representative forms and icons that induce collective amnesia about poverty and class? Are certain forms of autobiography more likely to particularize the landscape of working-class women's lives and thus accelerate the recovery of their classed and gendered histories?

Bromley's formulation of organized forgetting carries the underlying assumption that popular culture in its shared and remembered aspect is particularly susceptible to hegemonic formulations. It is in the automatic, unpolished, 'remembered' aspect of popular art as well as in its commercial success that it is subject to charges from quite divergent circles: from high-brow critics as culture of inferior aesthetic value and from certain political critics as culture that perpetuates received values and hegemonic ideology. (As I noted earlier, for example, Jaques described her verse as a form of popular memory: 'I didn't know they called it poetry, I only knew it sounded nice and after that, now and then the flash would come, like the echo of a voice singing somewhere, or something you kind of remembered' [11]; and Frye criticized it because it 'flatter[s] the collective memory.')

Tony Bennett, however, in *Outside Literature*, has observed that Bromley devalues popular art just as surely as élitist critics do, though in a different way – that is, he devalues it by ascribing to it hegemonic qualities and by measuring it according to classic Marxist aesthetics. Bennett charges that many traditional Marxist critics, Bromley included, prefer forms of writing associated with high culture because they assume that forms such as the historical epic are more able to transcend cultural hegemony and achieve oppositional insight. Bennett argues, however, that the series of absences and presences postulated by Bromley as representative and hegemonic are not exclusive to popular narratives in any way. (Bennett's indictment fails to acknowledge that Bromley is analysing certain dehistoricizing strains of popular memory rather than popular culture as a whole.)

Just as Bromley suspects the limited oppositional value of popular autobiographies, other cultural critics have cautioned against the conflation of popular culture with oppositional culture. In 'The Uses of Autobiography,' Dentith and Dodd have cautioned that popular culture is 'not self-defining but is in part what high/literacy/élite is not' (7). They invoke Stuart Hall's definition of popular culture as a 'site where the struggle *for and against* a culture of the powerful is engaged

... not a sphere where ... a socialist culture – already fully formed – might be simply expressed' (7). Furthermore, the conflation of the popular with working-class and oppositional culture is often exacerbated by a fundamental confusion around the subject of working-class identity. Folk heroes or uneducated speakers in rural areas, for example, are not automatically conscious of class in their lives, nor are they necessarily members of the working class, poor, or critical of dominant cultural values. Many middle-class people in rural areas cultivate a 'down-home' type of idiom as part of their community image, but the shared aspect of that local idiom obscures differences in class position rather than explicates them. Thus, popular autobiography does not recover class history simply because the writer is unschooled and speaks in colourful, local idiom about rural subjects, or because she celebrates work and popular culture. The celebration of work, for example, may stem from the nostalgic, the georgic, the bucolic, or from the puritan work ethic and the right-wing doctrine of self-help.

As Rebecca O'Rourke observed, not all working-class writing conveys a socialist ideology, a distinction she urges us to keep in mind when considering the difference between men and women and their access to politics and writing (50). Class history such as that recovered by Carolyn Steedman challenges the notion that political class-consciousness or even objective class position need be a part of working-class identity. After their mother's death, Steedman and her sister found that she had saved quite a sizable sum in the hope of buying a house and escaping the working-class surroundings she resented so much. Steedman concludes that their complex, working-class history could not have been recovered through theories of their relation to the means of production or of their solidarity with members of the working class. Her mother's struggle with class envy was a private and secret one, and her repeated message to her children that they cost her too much money could be understood only through the personal markers in her own story. A personal history such as Maynard's *Raisins and Almonds* may be read in order to recover a class history of a similar negative ilk, one which inscribes a repugnance at the lower status of labourers and at material need itself, even in one who has shared that position.

Given that the range of identities and cultural strategies encompassed by a flexible notion of 'working class' is wider than we would want to fix with certainty, it would seem futile to prescribe which narrative forms would be best suited to recovering memories of poverty and class. Yet debates about the ideological implications of various forms and subject positions often supply us with the clues to reading history across various types of autobiographies. As I noted in a discussion of how autobiography may subvert negative constructions of identity, certain critics have voiced concerns about the limited oppositional value of all autobiographical subject positions which posit a unified 'I'/eye – with its hegemonic implications – arguing that the 'I' becomes a filter for social observations and historical memory. Theorists of Latin American testimonio, such as Doris Sommer and John Beverly, suspect that the author position itself is too hegemonically contrived, too egocentric, to allow truly oppositional ways of expressing collective experience. Conversely, other critics have expressed mistrust of the mediated forms of discourse, such as the oral histories and testimonial literature that Sommer and Beverly advocate, in that intellectuals and activists have tended to distort voices for their own purposes, if not merely by the distance between their own lives and those of their oral subjects (O'Rourke 52; Rimstead 1996). Still others have argued that the subject herself must mediate between discourses through more complex or more postmodernist means of narrating a life in order to oppose the homogenizing and containing nature of the unified 'I.' (See, for example, Steedman on a case study approach to recovering history, Dentith and Dodd on 'complex ways of seeing,' Sidonie Smith on the 'autobiographical manifesto,' and Domna Stanton on 'gynography.')

Practically applied, however, no one theory alone can account for the diversity of writing styles which the poor and the working class have experimented with or collaborated on – or for the diversity of historical fragments lodged in personal lives. Our ability to see the full range of forms and subject positions available to us as a means of recovering history rests partly in the way we construct categories and theories of analysis through which to study these subjects and their stories. Regenia Gagnier has made this point convincingly regarding working-class autobiographies in nineteenth-century Britain by insisting that one can identify certain recurring strategies – such as the opening apology and disclaimer on the part of the subject, the traumatic first memory, the truncated childhood, the zest for education, the forced bourgeois plot, or the political or religious conversion – but that the variety of forms and subjectivities remains limitless and uncontainable by any one theory of identity and representation for the poor and the working class (150–67).

On the subject of gender-specific categories for the analysis of autobiography, Jeanne Costello has lamented the trend to contain the particularities of women's history within theories of the gendered subject. This has led her to speak of our 'responsibility to "history"' (127) and to urge more attention to 'the whole range of material conditions that have historically determined female subjectivity and ... to the various institutional relationships that have constructed identity' (125). 'Perhaps even more important,' Costello writes, 'we must accept that our theories will be provisional and limited in certain ways. It is only by suspecting definitive theories and accepting the limitations of our own theorizing that we can prevent severely limiting our sense of the complicated variety of women's writing practices and the range of female subjectivities' (125).

A similar cautionary attitude towards theory came earlier from Philip Dodd, who observed that a theory of autobiography-as-literature has sought 'to rescue the self from history' by stressing the exceptional individual and the narrative techniques by which the self is constructed as exceptional rather than historical context (65). The self in these theories emerges as a product of art, not of history. On the other hand, Dodd cautioned, autobiography-as-history, without theory, stalls the reading of the text on the level of transparent document or fragments. Thus, what he is calling for is a balancing of the reader's claims to perceive the Self in respect to textuality and claims to perceive identity in respect to history.

What I have been trying to emphasize in this discussion of 'organized forgetting' is not only how received narrative techniques erase poverty and class history, but also that the oppositional reading practice can situate the self and its story within an interpretive frame that refuses, despite the narrative's own ideology, to forget history. However, this interpretive frame must itself be responsive to the idiosyncrasies of the text and its own particular cultural, national, gender, and ideological groundings and also to the provisional aspect of its own usefulness as practice. The working-class female subject can be encountered through such a reading practice not only as one who is interpolated by existing discourses of history, art, class, gender, and nation but also as one who acts as an agent, a complex subject of history, upon the discourses and genres available to her. Even without complex styles of self-representation, a marginalized subject can inscribe her life according to complexly lived experiences of alliances, identification, needs, and desires. What the writer forgets, the engaged reader can sometimes interpret and recover.

Chapter 7

'Remnants of Nation'

Although postcolonial criticism has examined the relation between poverty and nation in emerging nations or between worlds (that is, 'First' and 'Third Worlds'), little has been written about how Western nations colonize the poor, and poor women especially, within their own borders. Aijaz Ahmad has critiqued how a Three Worlds model of development conceived in the West projects lack of 'progress' and poverty on the Third World. Similarly, Franz Fanon and Partha Chatterjee have critiqued bourgeois nationalism for reproducing the abuses of colonization in emerging nations by condoning the subjugation of subaltern groups internal to those nations after an initially liberatory and inclusive independence movement. However, while postcolonial theories have been untangling the symbolic and political practices of exclusion and domination between West and East, North and South, and dominant and minority groups in postcolonial nations, the problem of the internal colonization of the poor in the West remains largely unexplored territory in theories of nationalism as a colonizing discourse.

Yet the West continues to colonize its own poor, and poor women in particular, through certain discourses of nationalism. New World/First World myths promise opportunity and progress; political myths of Western prosperity claim classlessness and market stability; and, more subtly, North American cultural myths promote individualism and meritocracy together as an ethos that presupposes a lone, class-mobile subject. These social myths (or fictions, depending on one's standpoint) construct dominant versions of nation based on, at best, a blind spot concerning the poor or, at worst, the symbolic and lived expulsion of the poor to the outside position of blame or natural deficiency. Given this cultural context of denial and distancing and the relative silence of postcolonial theory on the subject of class in Western nations, it is very difficult to begin questioning if and how a national literature in the West might be complicit in the internal colonization of the poor. Likewise, we are unused to reading nation and poverty side by side in specific works of literature even when the literature itself problematizes the position of the poor as remnants of nation. In non-literary texts, as well, we need ways of making the two subjects, the poor and the national imaginary, appear side by side in order to see how a discourse of bourgeois nationalism colonizes the poor by containing them or by excluding them from the imagined community of a wealthy nation.

7.1 Poverty and Nation as Reciprocal Constructions

Postmodernist theories of nation which stress the shifting quality of a collective imaginary (Bhabha) would seem to imply that we are not looking for a fixed historical or political relation between poverty and nation. Postcolonial theories stress the role of narration in the construction and maintenance of a dominant paradigm of nation. According to the concept that the nation comes into being and maintains its power partly by virtue of being narrated and narrating itself, we have come to expect that those in power in a particular nation will manipulate internally and materially colonized groups by nationalist discourse in the form of a dominant imaginary fixed on unity and set against internal and historical differences. For example, Ernest Renan claimed that nation defines itself not by the obvious characteristics of race, religion, language, geographic boundaries, military necessity, dynasty, or material interests, but by the more ephemeral cultural forces such as collective will, sentimental and spiritual interests, and a common history and future project. Similarly, Benedict Anderson also prepares us for the cultural eclipse of subalterns as internally colonized Others with his observation that nation is an imagined rather than a known community (hence the eclipse of internal and lived heterogeneity for the sake of homogeneity), a community with deep horizontal (often homosocial) comradeship, and a community which defines itself and limits itself relationally in respect to Others.

These definitions indicate why forceful and repeated, though also shifting, narratives are essential to the survival of nation as a social and political force and why narratives of collectivity and unity position different groups as internal or external Others. They also suggest why wealthy nations need to exercise discursive dominance over the poor within their borders by intruding upon less powerful narratives and formulations of identity. Before examining the reciprocal relation between the wealthy nation and the poor more closely, I want to clarify that not all discourses of nation within the West seek to colonize the poor. Certain left-wing nationalisms, for example, argue to include the poor by critiquing the practices of an uncaring, market-driven, or authoritarian nation. For example, Barbara Murphy's *The Ugly Canadian: The Rise and Fall of a Caring Society,* Linda McQuaig's *The Cult of Impotence: Selling the Myth of Powerlessness in the Global Economy,* and Alan Mettrick's *Last in Line: On the Road and Out of Work ... A Desperate Journey with Canada's Unemployed* are three examples of critiques of bourgeois nationalism (and/or global, corporate-driven postnationalism) which suggest alternative, more humane and inclusive imagined communities as a better possible project of nationhood. Each interrogates the notion of public good in Canada on its treatment of the poor to reveal and critique the shared values behind the bourgeois national community. My oppositional reading strategies are similar to these interrogations of nation in that they refuse to consent to the blind spot around the relation between the wealthy nation and the poor, but my approach is more analytical and less sweeping in its claims about social myths. I am interested in tracing the tension between national discourses and the poor in specific works in order to pry open the reciprocal relation between the two in each work and finally to show how these constructions of nation and the poor influence the ideology of particular texts, literary or otherwise. This means being able to distinguish between different discourses of nation – those that are dominant or hegemonic and those that are counter-cultural.

Since literature can be understood as a site where collective as well as individual identities are constructed and contested, we can ask questions about the narrative strategies of inscribing marginal identities in respect to dominant paradigms of nation. But rather than anticipating a fixed historical or political relation between poverty, gender, and nation as interacting discourses, politics, or fixed fields of knowledge and experience, it may be useful to ask how these forces act upon particular subjects in a reciprocal way. Here, I borrow from and extend Cora Kaplan's theory of class and gender as reciprocal elements. Kaplan suggests that we reframe the theoretical debate about one social construct – class or gender – *containing* or *taking precedence* over the other by studying texts in terms of how the subject is constructed by class and gender given that they interact reciprocally and in a complex way upon the speaking subject (346, 364). As discussed in some detail in chapter 4, Kaplan argues that class and gender work upon the subject as reciprocal processes rather than fixed contents or static territories which can be located in and around the subject definitively. Each narrative becomes a site where social boundaries and social constructs can be recognized as forces acting upon the subject and, thus, on each other reciprocally through the subject. We encounter these forces through a story of a particular subject grounded in the specificities of place and time rather than as abstract fields or politics. The push and pull of national discourse on the cultural space and identity of the poor (and vice versa, as the two are reciprocal) can be seen when selected novels, autobiographical works, and press clippings juxtapose poverty and nation in order to represent everyday lives. Studying identities in respect to discourses of poverty and nation will also explain in part why certain stories and images become preferred as part of a given national culture.

The subtext of Margaret Laurence's *The Diviners*, for example, is a personal and liberatory form of nationalist discourse, though also a critical one. One of the reasons for her standing as one of English Canada's best-loved authors may indeed be that Laurence's protagonist struggles with class as well as racial divisions in order to achieve a stronger, more humane vision of nation than the one in which we live. More than liberal pluralist humanism, this personally liberating nationalism refuses to forget colonial violence; it recognizes colonial guilt (in particular, in respect to the Metis) and illuminates current divisions based on class, race, and gender. By emphasizing cultural memory and cultural roots, *The Diviners* unearths a reconstructed, inclusive ideal of nation, not only *despite*, but *because of* differences. The novel suggests how the individual and the artist are both ethically and morally responsible for coming to terms with the violence of social boundaries around or within the ideal of an imagined community, whether those social boundaries are maintained against class or racial Others.

In addition to tracing the push and pull of class and nationalist discourse on subjects in novels, I will also look at how these discourses construct poor subjects in non-fictional representations. In press clippings from *Maclean's* magazine I will interrogate various subtexts on nation which subtly, but forcefully, construct the poor outside of Canada (mainly in the Third World) or dehistoricize and psychologize poverty as a means of naturalizing the poor as the deviant, deficient class Other within the nation. These strategies of projection and denial become more coherent when read beside Partha Chatterjee's critique of bourgeois nationalism and Aijaz Ahmad's critique of the 'Three Worlds' theory of development because such postcolonialist theories stress the essentialist character of progressivist nationalist myths. Whereas Chatterjee and Ahmad protest the homogenization of peoples in 'Third World' countries, I wish to draw attention to how these paradigms homogenize the peoples of the 'First World' by distancing the poor, symbolically containing them, or merely erasing them.

Although Canadians know objectively that there is poverty within the nation, the progressivist and rationalist ideology of Western nationalism subtly and irrationally denies connectedness to and responsibility for that poverty. A long-standing conceptual strategy for denial is the two-nations motif, which is not a New World myth but one imported and adapted from nineteenth-century England and France. As discussed at length already in chapter 3, 'We Live in a Rickety House,' this paradigm represents the rich and the poor as co-existing in two separate nations-within-a-nation. This inscription of distance from the poor has long shaped the discourse of bourgeois nationalism in the West and is still being culturally recycled. For instance, North American concepts of the culture of poverty (Oscar Lewis, Harrington, and Rubin) tend to depict the poor as an *inherently different* smaller community within the larger prosperous national community, one that reproduces its own conditions of poverty with little room for agency.

In a more resistant vein, the final section of this chapter examines diverse testimonial voices and how they often challenge, either explicitly or implicitly, bourgeois constructions of nation. They also challenge readers to find oppositional reading styles to detect these counter-cultural variations on nationalist discourse. For example, the two-nations myth emerges as a residual form even in works by journalists wishing to gain more detailed knowledge of the experiences and subjectivities of the poor (I mean 'residual' in keeping with what Raymond Williams identified in *Marxism and Literature* as residual cultural forms which adapt and incorporate earlier hegemonic narrative forms for different purposes [121–7]). Along with this reworking of the two-nations motif, a variety of innovative strategies have given a testimonial voice to the poor, and poor women in particular. Our reading strategies need to be open to these alternative visions of poverty and nation.

7.2 Saving the Nation: *The Diviners*

Critical readings of the classic work *The Diviners* have tended to focus on racial rather than class rifts within the nation. This is not surprising, since there have been no major recovery projects for literary images of the social identity of the working class and the poor in Canadian literature and hence limited training and theoretical works available on decoding class identity in literature, especially in terms of newer theories of complex class identity based on class habitus, stigma, and ideology (Bourdieu, Delphy, Steedman, Laclau and Mouffe, Stuart Hall, Dimock and Gilmore, and Balibar and Wallerstein) rather than on modes of production and economic status.[1] These critical trends are reflected in the reading of canonized texts in Canada, even when the subject is quite obviously classed. In critical responses to *The Diviners*, there has been a general blind spot about, or only a tacit awareness of, the way class identification cuts across racial barriers and produces a profound affinity between Morag and Jules. Furthermore, Morag's own classed identity is often reduced to non-systemic terms: for example, to personal feelings of shame at being brought up poor and of ambivalence about past alliances with colourful characters from Hill Street (Christie, Prin, Eva Winkler, and others). Morag's individual story of mobility is often interpreted as a rural/urban or feminine/feminist trajectory with little reference to the class journey – for example, to the story of the small-town girl who 'made it' in the city – or that of the spirited woman writer who refuses the confining wifely role she originally sought in order to 'make it' on her own. Even the 'grittiness' of the novel itself and its inclusionary gesture towards social outcasts, especially Metis characters, has often, of late, been labelled romantic nationalism – but the idea that a class subtext runs throughout as one level of social commentary aimed at critiquing nation is rarely given serious consideration. Despite the fact that other works by Laurence such as 'Horses of the Night' and *The Stone Angel* also dramatize poverty and collective class interests through the site of personal and family identity, overviews of the criticism of her work (by Lorna Irvine and

---

1 With the exception of a few isolated readings of the politics of *A Jest of God* by Kenneth Hughes and of the *The Stone Angel* by Michael Peterman. As I discuss shortly, Frank Davey's reading of *The Diviners* in his book on postnationalism is more conscious of class than most, but differs significantly from my own conclusions about the cultural politics of inscriptions of class and nation in the novel.

Hildegard Kuester, for instance) identify no trends towards reading class in her *oeuvre*. In rereading *The Diviners* as a poverty narrative, we might address these blind spots and suggest why the issue of class identity is so contentious to readings of a novel preoccupied with reconceptualizing cultural memory and national community.

When we devalue the resistant class ideology of Morag's story we are effectively parallelling the blindness of the houses in the 'well-to-do' streets of Manawaka, houses which refuse to see their own ease and privilege. To repeat a citation discussed earlier: 'Cream coloured blinds, all fringed with lace and tassels. The windows are the eyes, closed, and the blinds are the eyelids, all creamy, fringed with lacy lashes. Blinds make the houses to be blind' (37). In contrast to this blindness is Christie's insistence on seeing the town's culture from below. Christie's 'garbage telling' transforms the margin, the place of 'nowhere,' into a privileged place of class knowledge about the complacent façade of middle-class identity. But his second sight does not reveal a political protest against class exploitation so much as it vents class anger and exposes the illusory superiority of the middle class maintained as proof of difference and distance from the poor in the everyday matters of taste and consumption. Although critics have oftened interpreted Laurence's protest against the blindness of the centre to the periphery as social critique against small-town propriety, hypocrisy, and ethnocentrism, the issue of classism on the streets of Manawaka remains a buried truth of the novel which we recognize when we read about it but rarely discuss openly.

It is granted that racial stigma is more silencing than class stigma to the characters within the world of *The Diviners*. For example, Morag, as a college-educated writer, will be able to narrate her ancestral history and personal experiences in novel form – to divine self-knowledge – whereas Jules Tonnerre as a Metis is less free to narrate his life publicly. Ironically, Jules will be made to ape country-and-western traditions in bars and dress like a flashy cowboy while keeping his oppositional songs of Metis history for private consumption. However, I want to argue that class is the more contentious identity when this novel is discussed in the context of a national literature, precisely because we tend not to see the poor in relation to a nation like Canada even when a writer like Laurence clearly inscribes them thus. While studies of *The Diviners* discuss the divisions between Metis and whites in the world of the novel as it relates to racial history and tensions between racial groups in everyday life in Canada, few critics broach the class divisions between Morag and Brooke as representative of the tensions between different classes of Canadians, and fewer still interpret the affinity between Morag and Jules as one based on a shared class habitus, since their racial differences are highlighted, with the basis for affinity usually being identified as Morag's expansive feminist or postcolonial consciousness.[2] My partial rereading of *The Diviners* is based on decoding the everyday practices of class identity in the novel which signal more profound sources of class distinction: that is, cultural memory, class knowledge, cultural capital, class roots, counter-culture community, and so on.

Working against the disclosure of links between poverty, class, literature, and nation in a work like *The Diviners* is the logic of a category of national literature itself, a category shaped by nationalist interests and committed to positing a common basis for culture within national boundaries rather than a common culture built upon the recognition of the political significance of internal differences. Of late, that category has opened to the recognition of differences based on race, ethnicity, gender, and sexual orientation. But the subject of Canadian literature as it is consumed and studied as an institution has yet to be democratized enough to highlight class differences. In fact, the silence around the issue of class in Canadian high culture may well explain why we have had such a great longing for more humane and inclusive visions of nation such as Laurence's. A discreet, liberal-humanist discourse of nationalism makes us believe that nation can be saved from the harsher implications of its own exclusions through the practice of individual ethical responsibility rather than systemic reform, through the novelistic inclusion of social outcasts in one protagonist's life and art.

In *Postnational Arguments: The Politics of the Anglophone-Canadian Novel since 1967*, Frank Davey has given the class subtext of *The Diviners* more sustained treatment than most:

---

[2] Recently, the Canadian canon has been challenged in terms of its exclusions and (mis)representations of Native people, and a number of prestigious publications and scholars have, in the last two decades especially, turned their attention towards decoding cultural representations of Native people and including more Native history and voices (works, for example, by Penny Petrone, Leslie Monkman, Marjory Fee, William H. New, Barbara Godard, Julia Emberley, Terry Goldie, and Gail Valiskakis, to name just a few). But literary studies have been more willing to acknowledge the burden of postcolonial violence and dispossession of indigenous people and the Metis than the ongoing marginalization of class Others within the nation, an exclusion which cuts across ethnic and regional groups.

> Among the middle classes are the variously empowered of the town: the doctor, who can decide whether or not to make the special effort needed to cure someone like Piquette of her TB; the teachers, who can decide which children are encouraged or promoted; the lawyer, who can decide whether someone like Jules can also have the opportunity to become a lawyer; and the newspaper editor, who decides whose activities enter into print, in what words, and with what exclusions. These people and the institutions they represent enforce class privileges. (32)

Although Davey's analysis of class in the novel and its connection to other forms of marginalization is more detailed than many, his conclusions about the ideology of the novel, in particular its inscription of poverty and nation, are harshly critical. He charges that the shaping motif of the 'river of now and then' is humanist and idealist, subsuming oppositional discourses and absorbing them into a symbol of unity. Furthermore, he concludes that the novel ends weakly by proposing an individual rather than a social solution to the problem of several levels of oppressions identified within the nation:

> It is strange that a novel which declares so emphatically its dismay at the exclusion of women, Métis and the less-educated from power and influence should end so weakly. While it is able to see these oppressions as socially constructed rather than 'natural,' it can imagine only individual, rather than social, solutions to them and in the end finds itself poetically and humanistically envisioning them as 'natural.' Although it can illuminate group issues, it can focus only on the well-being of a single individual, an individual who by the end of the novel is a university-educated, land-owning, published novelist with little in common with the small-town working class that ostensibly inspires her writing. This class remains as alien to power as when the novel began, despite having been sympathetically 'represented' by Morag. (41)

I would argue with Davey's interpretation for a host of reasons,[3] only a

---

3 More often than not in Canada, class is lived individually, and this is a painful reality of the North American ethos of classlessness, meritocracy, and national prosperity. This is partly why Canada has not had a tradition of proletarian fiction to voice collective interests and to dramatize collective solutions to class rifts. But Davey is not calling for these types of narrative representations of social solutions (incidentally, he also blames David Adams Richards, one of Canada's most class-conscious writers,

few of which are of concern here. First, do we really want to demand that realist depictions of poverty and the working class end with social solutions? Isn't it more realist, given a strongly individualist culture where people usually struggle against class stigma alone, to depict isolated rather than collective struggles? Furthermore, from a materialist feminist position, the personal is a viable site for acts of class resistance when collective movements are undermined or unavailable to certain subjects, women in particular (Fox, Steedman, Kaplan, and Ebert). Second, Davey is not really critiquing individualism in the novel, nor the individual's failure to act on behalf of the group; he is critiquing the idealism of the modernist, individual subject who tries to make the fragments of nation coherent enough to imagine an alternative national community. This critique is apparently based on Davey's tacit preference for fragmented, postnational subjects and postmodern forms of resistance, not a nostalgia for proletarian fiction or collective subjects. Having reduced class issues to the level of discourse (despite the fact that examples from the novel, such as those Davey himself cites, show that power relations between the classes are lived out in concrete and material as well as discursive ways in the everyday world of the characters), Davey goes on to measure the realist text against a postmodernist yardstick that judges discursive resistance as the ultimate measure of political or 'social solutions.' According to this evaluative process, Davey reduces Morag's inclusive vision of community to romantic nationalism[4] and aestheticized oppression, partly because it does not celebrate fragmentation and the impossibility of unified community. This is a way of tacitly suggesting that the novel would have been more resistant, more pluralist, if it had ended otherwise – in other words, had the subject been postnational or postmodernist (and relinquished moral solutions for rifts within the nation). I think it is more interesting to identify how the novel actually ends by asking more nuanced questions about the type of nationalism it inscribes.

---

for depicting the poor and unemployed as despairing). On the contrary, Davey champions the types of resistance offered by postmodern and postnational texts and those subjects who transcend nation and the concrete lives of the characters to resist authority discursively.

4 Marjory Fee's discussion of the use of Native lovers in the expression of romantic nationalism helps to tease out the strains of romantic nationalism within Laurence's work, especially in respect to a tradition of such romantic unions in Canadian literature. But, once again, as with class identity, it is possible for a work to deploy romantic images beside politically critical realism without the one subsuming the other.

As writer, Morag magically and painfully gathers all the fragments of nation together to create a more inclusive narrative which legitimates the popular, the everyday, the fragmentary, the ethnic, the marginalized, the obscene, the grotesque, and the spoken and sung words, as well as the written ones of high culture, at least within the protagonist's growing postcolonial, feminist, and class-consciousness. This inclusiveness should not be dismissed as mere romanticism, humanism, or idealism, for it unfolds its own oppositional ideal of common culture[5] beyond the dominant paradigm of bourgeois culture. I will argue in the following rereading of *The Diviners* that the text and the protagonist do not aestheticize oppression for merely romantic purposes as Davey suggests, but that each struggles with various levels of silencing and oppression as a means of understanding and realizing community. This is how the collective imagination works; when individuals internalize myths of nation and reimagine them, the nation is renewed or sometimes reformed.

In critiquing the homogenizing tendency of nations, Etienne Balibar claims that modern national formations use writers, journalists, and politicians as 'social actors' who speak the language of the people in order to translate between different levels of language and thus relativize social difference within the nation. In other words, Morag's hegemonic function may be to dissolve differences by offering us an inclusive national narrative that makes us feel more at home within the nation – one which we can all internalize in order to rewrite the boundaries of nation more humanely in respect to the poor and the Metis and the local, small-town culture. '[T]he "external frontiers" of the state have to become "internal frontiers" or – which amounts to the same thing – external frontiers have to be imagined constantly as a projection and a protection of an internal collective personality, which each of us carries within ourselves and enables us to inhabit the space of the state as a place where we have always been – and always will be – "at home"' (Balibar, 'The Nation Form' 95). Having acknowledged the

---

5 The democratic ideals of 'common culture' (Eagleton, Williams) as a basis for counter-nationalism are discussed in detail in the conclusion of this study. Suffice it to say at this point that common culture points to the need to valorize all levels of culture and all cultural subjects, not just in the mind of the artist, but in education and the everyday practice of culture, so that high culture may be informed by popular culture and so that national cultures may embrace both. It is not homogenizing but pluralist and inclusive, not idealist but pragmatic.

hegemonic function of the novel to save the nation in this way, however, I feel we also need to take account of the oppositional strains in its counter-national imagining. Morag's resistant function is to re-imagine nation more humanely and more inclusively as a way of challenging bourgeois nationalism. (The river of now and then has more to do with life cycles, mothering, generations, aging, and spiritual knowledge than with the life of the nation. It does not overpower the realist accounts of class divisions or suggest a solution to enclose them; it merely frames political consciousness in the context of a larger spiritual consciousness.) In this way, the novel tries to critique nation through a moral discourse rather than by transcending the local and the national through a global or shifting subject who abandons an interest in nationalism. This form of resistance (closer to left nationalism than to romantic nationalism) is as valid as the postmodern or the postnational, since it inscribes cultural memories of silenced groups – classed, gendered, and ethnic – within a narrative project to challenge and re-imagine nation. The many transgressions of form, history, and social boundaries within the novel ensure its oppositional function despite the narrative solution, the coming-to-consciousness of one individual within the collective.

> Morag loves this song ['The Maple Leaf Forever'] and sings with all her guts. She also knows what the emblems mean. Thistle is Scots, like her and Christie (others, of course, too, including some stuck-up kids, but her, definitely, and they better not forget it). Shamrock is Irish like the Connors and Reillys and them. Rose is English, like Prin, once of good family. Suddenly she looks over to see if Skinner Tonnerre is singing. He has the best voice in the class, and he knows lots of cowboy songs, and dirty songs, and he sometimes sings them after school, walking down the street.
> He is not singing now.
> He comes from nowhere. He isn't anybody. She stops singing, not knowing why. Then she feels silly about stopping, so sings again.
> (Laurence, *The Diviners* 70)

In this scene, the divisions of civil society are exposed through the unfolding of oppositional subjectivities: Morag's subjectivity as poor white and Jules Tonnerre's as poor Metis. In Laurence's social critique, the larger structure of civil society is not ambiguously located but explicitly constructed as Canada by the humorous misquoting of lyrics of two national anthems mentioned in the text or echoed in a subtitle.[6] In its misquoted version, the anthem/title inscribes Canada as a homogeneous community of three, entwined, white ethnic groups (English, Scottish, and Irish) but, ironically, the chapter exposes a multitude of divisions and tensions within the lived community – tensions between the Scottish and the English ancestors who battled over songs as well as borders, between forgotten Gaelic and dominant English cultural heritage, between the French and the English in Canada, between Metis and white, between poor Metis and poor white, between poor children and 'stuck-up kids' and the teachers' attitudes to the two groups, between the normal and the mentally deficient or disturbed, between healthy and crippled children, between bullying patriarchs and their battered children, between pre-pubescent boys and girls, and so forth (61–70). Even a twelve-year-old child like Morag suspects that the Anglo-Saxon emblems and national anthems are not inclusive enough to admit poor whites, such as Christie and her, along with the 'stuck-up kids.' She joins the dominant group singing of nation, but her need to protest silently – 'and they better not forget it' – betrays anxiety around her own admissibility to the 'fictive ethnicity' (Balibar) on class grounds. This dominant, ethnic alliance offers Morag what Waxman referred to as 'the alternative status-honor group'[7] which helps her override the stigma of her poverty as the garbage collector's foster daughter. But the shakiness of that common past and the imagined, shared blood roots emerges in her need to buttress and mythologize them through the Piper Gunn stories about highlanders. Christie, who seems to recognize her need for heroes and pride, not to mention a sense of belonging somewhere, will help her mythologize the past of her ancestors, and that of her father's war experience as well – even when it means deflating his own part in that past to do so. Ironically, the way Morag and Christie use the past subtly exposes ethnically based imagined communities and shared national projects like war efforts as products of selective memory and thus a matter of choice and will rather than birthright. By capturing the shifting and arbitrary nature of national community, Laurence challenges both the ethnic and class assumptions of the dominant national imaginary and opens the

---

6 'Memorybank Movie: The Thistle Shamrock Rose Entwine the Maple Leaf Forever.'
7 See the discussion of Chaim Waxman's theory of alternative status-honour groups from *The Stigma of Poverty* earlier in chapter 5, section 5.2, 'Maria Campbell's *Halfbreed* and Alternative Status-Honour Groups.'

narrative to the possibility of reconceptualizing the imagined community on the basis of class as well as race and gender.

Although Jules and she share a stigmatized class position, Morag knows, even as a child, that he is more radically stigmatized as a half-breed. She notices his holding back from singing the popular anthem because he is from this place outside the symbolic boundaries of nation: being 'not anybody' from 'nowhere' means that he is so far outside the imagined community of town and nation that his difference is unbridgeable and unsayable: 'They are part Indian, part French, from away back. They are mysterious. People in Manawaka talk about them but don't talk to them. Lazarus makes home brew down there in the shack in the Wachakwa valley, and is often arrested on Saturday nights. Morag knows. She has heard. They are dirty and unmentionable' (69). What stands out in her description of Jules's stigma are the battery of institutional and symbolic practices which enforce social boundaries and distance him from community as an irretrievable outsider– 'from away back ... mysterious ... don't talk to them ... down there in the shack ... often arrested ... dirty and unmentionable.' But they are virtually the same shame-based, distancing strategies as those used 'to other' the town poor. Hence, Morag's strategy to recover from the shame of being excluded as poor, the positioning of the Other as nobody from 'nowhere,' is to remake herself for a place on the inside. As Jules charges later in life, 'Yeh. You married a rich prof after all. I told you you would, didn't I? Jesus, you sure wanted to go *somewhere*' (265). In the context of a wealthy capitalist nation, 'going somewhere' means more than leaving Manawaka; it also means becoming mobile, a class traveller who leaves behind the shameful sense of not belonging and all those who are identified as such. The novel clearly inscribes class mobility as a shared, dominant narrative of the Canadian dream of 'making it,' of going 'somewhere' by drawing attention to this ethos of meritocracy as part of the everyday, local idiom and the characters' life choices. There is, for instance, the story of Eva Winkler's brother, who escapes the small town and a poor and abusive home, changes his name, and sends only the odd Christmas card back to the foreign country of Hill Street. Morag herself shuns other escapees, the poor scholarship students at university: 'She has seen the worse-off ones walking alone, and quietly, or else trying to ingratiate themselves, clownlike, into the brazen multitude. These walking wounded she avoids like the plague. It might be catching' (177). When we neglect to read the discourse of poverty and class in the novel as a coherent subtext, it has the effect of naturalizing Morag's social mobility as an exercise in meritocracy as she herself initially sees it: 'But if you work, really work, and get educated, something will come of it, maybe. Like being able to get out of Manawaka and never come back' (120). Escape from the stigma of poverty is conflated here with escape from Manawaka. (After all, in a small town, people's class positions are known and not easily forgotten, making it tremendously difficult to 'pass' for middle class even after one makes oneself over from outside and within.) But the novel problematizes Morag's class acculturation to bourgeois class habitus by having her evolve beyond the mere desire for escape from poverty. As she grows dissatisfied with acculturation and critiques bourgeois culture, the novel takes on a less hegemonic form than the mobility narrative suggests by turning back on the values and assumptions behind 'making it' to explore the more democratic and resistant possibilities of cultural memory and oppositional art.

Morag's empathy for Jules and her willingness to see him across racial boundaries grows out of her own experiences of class stigma as the foster child of Christie Logan. Whereas Jules's family shack is set well outside the town in the forest, Christie's house is on a disreputable street in town, demarcated by class rather than race or ethnicity, but demarcated, none the less, by the psychosocial place of insult and outsider status. Note Laurence's symbolic and ironic use of the hill and 'the sturdy maple' to inscribe class hierarchy once again within her critique of the imagined community as it is lived out in the landscape of the small town:

> Hill Street was the Scots-English equivalent of The Other Side of the Tracks, the shacks and shanties at the north end of Manawaka where the Ukrainian section-hands on the CPR lived. Hill Street was below the town; it was inhabited by those who had not and never would make good. Remittance men and their draggled families. Drunks. People perpetually on relief. Occasional labourers, men whose tired women supported the family by going out to clean the big brick houses on top of the hill on the streets shaded by sturdy maples, elms, lombardy poplars. Hill Street – dedicated to flops, washouts and general no-goods, at least in the view of the town's better off. (28)

Critical readings of Hill Street have tended to reassert that looking away from poverty which Morag herself initially enacts out of a sense of shame, but which the novel refuses to reproduce ideologically.

Though numerous critics will identify Hill Street as a class-marked zone in the town and the character's life – for example, Hildegard Kuester, Barbara Godard, W.H. New, Frank Davey, Marianne Rocard – their gaze does not rest long on the class subtext. It is as if we are willing to admit that the dots demarcating class identity are there and arranged to mark a class habitus, but not willing to connect them in terms of the cultural politics of the novel as a whole or the formation of character and construction of subjectivity.

Morag's lament, 'Away is here. Not far enough away,' which becomes the leitmotif for the whole novel, is focused on the superficiality of the distance she has tried to put between her acculturated self and her poor home as well as the distance between her wifely self and her wilder, womanly, writerly self (175). Although this lament has profound class implications about Morag's character and about her novel as art form, the potentially subversive act of reading poverty as a past which asserts itself critically against high culture was too often, in the course of university seminars that I attended as a student, abstracted to 'The-Concept-of-Time-Handled-as-Narrative-Retrospection' or simply 'The-Development-of-the-Artist.' More recently, debates on identity in the novel have tended to focus on the issue of gender and ethnic identity and the cultural politics of coming to terms with a local and colonial past. Yet the novel also exposes the political significance of the cultural gap between a poor home and high culture. It travels the distance consciously through a highly retrospective narrative which 'calls home' again and again, in feeling and in texture and with growing class awareness that calls into question the social construction of class difference.

Contextualizing her protagonist's personal experience of class stigma in terms of the similar experiences of a whole community (Hill Street and the Tonnerres), Laurence renders these cultural memories of poverty and class stigma as matters of political importance and community alliances, rather than of primarily personal shame, melancholy, or aesthetic enthralment as Alice Munro does with visits home in the 'The Beggar Maid.' In other respects, the two plots are remarkably similar as poverty narratives: both portray a young working-class woman's personal evolution as professional writer, the distance between a poor home and high culture as it is experienced by a working-class woman through university education, and a working-class woman's experience of 'marrying up' to a university professor. (In both cases, marrying a professor will serve as a means of gaining access to alternative status-honour and cultural capital as well as capital itself.) But Laurence constantly grounds personal mobility in her narrative in the explicit contexts of cultural memory, nation, and community. Unlike Munro, whose gaze moves the reader ideologically away from social criticism and a systemic understanding of stigma, Laurence urges the reader to inhabit the emotional spaces of marginalization through empathy and understanding of systemic injustice and to share a sense of moral indignation and defiance with the outcasts through social critique. Whereas Munro scrutinizes poverty from an aesthetic position which seeks ultimately to control and survey the scene of poverty for its representational and aesthetic impact, Laurence enters those scenes more viscerally and more politically to show how complex survival is on the margins and to confer as much dignity on these everyday struggles as she does on the artist's struggle for expression. In fact she makes the two struggles, the artistic and the everyday, inseparable, partly through an aesthetics of populism that breaks through the rarefied air of literary representation and its detachment from life to include disparate and mismatched voices from other levels of culture: local legends, everyday voices, country music, folk songs, gossip, department store advertisements, and so on. Shortly, I will examine the ideology of this populism in respect to theories of national form.

As part of Morag's journey of self- and social discovery, the book dramatizes how acute the struggle for cultural instruction, self-improvement, a literary education, and class mobility may be for the poor and the once-poor. Yet Morag's journey to self-discovery is more complicated than this, since she inherits class knowledge of culture-from-below from Christie. Very early on, Morag experiences the Otherness of herself and her home when the outside perception of shabbiness and difference is thrust at her during her first contact with school children: 'Christie Logan's the Scavenger Man / Gets his food from the garbage can!' and 'Morag! Morag! / Gets her clothes from an old flour bag!' (38). To shield herself from the insults, she learns a highly inflated but bizarrely eloquent form of verbal defiance from Christie, defiance with a cavalier and self-defeating quality all the same: 'I say unto you, Morag, girl, I open my shirt to the cold winds of their voices, yea, and to the ice of their everlasting eyes' (47). Christie's ranting, his class anger, is not aimless though it is often self-destructive, for it is buttressed by his knowledge of the underbelly of town life, signified through his 'garbage reading,' a form of behind-the-scenes class knowledge that cleaners and servants have about privileged people's lives. From her foster mother, Prin, Morag learns the other-worldliness of victimization, an innocence and resignation which transcend meanness, the ability to shelter any finer sensibilities behind mountains of flesh, mental vacancy, and complete social isolation. Yet Morag is never able merely to transcend class difference. Her initial class defiance has her echoing Christie's words and behaviour (behaviour that later re-emerges as the Black Celt in her); but defiance eventually subsides as she commits her whole conscious will to a striving towards social acceptance and, most of all, escape. More transforming than the identity strategies practised by Christie and Prin are those Morag learns from the social scripts around her – namely that Taste in clothing, furnishings, speech, and even in literature are the best way out of nowhere into somewhere. Working part-time at fourteen, she buys Prin a new coat but still cannot wish away the shame of being seen with her in public (108). Morag's commitment to self-fashioning according to 'good taste' (learned incidentally while in high school and working in a department store where, she finds, 'good taste' is 'learnt' [111]) means that in the market defined space of community in consumer capitalism she will be included if she forgets Christie's brand of class knowledge (garbage reading and truth telling) and learns instead the class knowledge of the bourgeois or middle-class habitus (taste, cultural capital, manners, verbal control, and so on). After the gradual process of having 'smartened herself up' in the eyes of the townsfolk through studied changes in clothing and mannerisms, Morag is disgusted by Eva Winkler's failure to follow suit: 'Eva's dresses are still the same old cotton things like potato sacks. Eva hasn't smartened up any. She is no longer in Morag's grade at school but has failed two grades ... Morag is ashamed to be so glad they are in different schools' (113). Throughout the novel, good taste in clothing and material items is carefully layered beside knowledge of literature and language. This layering suggests that cultural capital is all around, there for the taking, but the common-sense idiom 'smartened herself up' creates a distance from the process of acculturation whereby working-class habitus is shed in order to mimic bourgeois values. The novel suggests that everyday values about dressing and speaking are relative to class interests, and it also hints that the borders around cultural capital are maintained simultaneously in stores and schools. But the female body as a site for performing class identity by dressing up or down to marry up or down also accounts for the way cleanliness and class become conflated in women – and the ordered image of the bourgeois habitus becomes imprinted on and naturalized in the woman's choice in shoes, clothing, hairstyle, and manner of speech.

When Morag wins a scholarship and enters university, she discovers that shedding her past has actually enhanced her attractiveness to her literature professor and future husband: '"Perhaps it's your mysterious nonexistent past," he says, "I like that. It's as though you were starting life now, newly"' (195). Morag's husband, Brooke, is excited by the imbalance of power caused by their different social positions because of the advantage this gives him to rewrite her story and reshape her in his own eyes as a well-groomed, soft-spoken bourgeois faculty wife – although he also uses the erasure of the past as a form of romantic rescue and emotional comfort (198). But the denial of a working-class woman's personal past in *The Diviners* has more political implications than in Munro's 'The Beggar Maid,' where the bourgeois professor/ lover is also excited by the power imbalance caused by class difference and the possibility of rewriting the working-class woman's past. Since Laurence has shown how cultural memory and history, in the form of Jules Tonnerre's Metis heritage and Christie's Highland tales, have the power to sustain the dignity of subaltern groups despite the violence of social exclusion and erasure, Morag's personal class history is contextualized as an important part of identity and survival, not only hers but that of a whole class of people who were invoked as the ne'er-do-wells and failures of Hill Street. They have by now faded into the distance in the novel, but resurface from time to time as reminders of the conflicting values of different class locations (for example, Eva's kindness to Prin as she lies dying calls into question Morag's desire to distinguish herself from Eva's poverty and shabby appearance). When Morag, like Munro's protagonist, is only too happy to comply with her husband's wishes and suppress her personal poverty narrative and even her style of speech as a means of denying her 'home' or class habitus in the name of embourgeoisement and feminine submission, she cuts herself off from the class roots which would otherwise offer her sustenance, as both artist and individual, in the alien environment of bourgeois culture: 'she will conceal everything about herself which [Brooke] might not like' (196) means more than simply denying the wild side of her female identity; it also means suppressing her personal poverty narrative, her class anger, and even her style of speech as a means of remaking herself. This suppression of class memory in the novel is more compelling and formative than Morag's loss of memory about her birth parents, and it is one of the main reasons she needs the Piper Gunn stories to buttress her sense of self with an alternative status-honour group.

As Morag bridges the distance of social rupture by travelling from the outside to the inside of accepted social space by altering her appearance and manners, the novel appears to conform to a hegemonic narrative form of mobility based on individual effort and hard work. However, Laurence uses the mobility narrative only residually, in Raymond Williams's term, because the character is never comfortable with the acculturation process. Since Morag refuses to forget the exclusion of the poor in a classed society and since she also refuses to embrace bourgeois space or transcend class conflict by retreating to a distanced, aestheticized perspective, her mobility highlights how both material and imagined class differences cause unbridgeable ruptures within the larger social fabric – unbridgeable, that is, unless the individual reconceptualizes self and community.

When Morag returns to Hill Street for Prin's funeral, she finds the old house stinking, oppressively small, and full of ghosts – but she feels even less at home on returning to the highrise apartment she inhabits as Brooke's wife. She experiences the apartment as a desert island, a cave, and then as a tower from which she, as Rapunzel, must escape by metaphorically 'letting down her hair' (refusing to be coiffed as Brooke instructs). This is not only a feminist fantasy of liberation, but also a fantasy of returning to the crowded people, in Raymond Williams's term, and the sense of community in a common culture where high and popular tastes can enrich each other. For what Morag rejects in the tower, in addition to patriarchal control, is the confining aspect of the bourgeois habitus for a working-class woman, the taste for Danish-modern furniture, polite speech, sterility, sexual control, high culture, isolation, and coiffed hair that she can no longer abide.

All that Morag is, has been, and would be, simply cannot be contained within the limits of bourgeois culture, Anglo-Saxon puritan morality, the wifely role, or bourgeois language. The sense that acculturation has somehow emptied her of previous value while giving her a new 'glossy painted shell' is reflected in her alienation from the language of high culture, from the discourse of 'well modulated grammatically correct voices' in graduate seminars – which she finds 'devoid of epithets and bland as tapioca pudding' (255). Her friend Ella helps her to see beyond the culturally and ethnically biased definition of literature and reading practices taught in English departments, and Morag is able to see for herself how male writers in a patriarchal culture have inscribed women as listeners and objects of beauty rather than speaking subjects. Her feminist resistance is evidenced in seminars where she protests, as a woman reader (perhaps a misreader), John Donne's 'For God's sake hold your tongue and let me love,' and Milton's 'He for God only; she for God in him' (191–2). Culture as it is presented to her from a male bourgeois perspective in the university requires a highly rational, controlled, and accurate language based on received values; but the poverty in her life has expressed itself through a highly emotional, living language issuing from orality, shared struggle, local idiom, and personal meanings, all coloured by obscenities and grammatical deviations, a quaint idiom that titillates her professor/husband (119–20). It is socially significant, therefore, and not merely humorous, when Morag's frustrations with her husband explode into obscenities. And it is socially significant, rather than merely poignant, when she revisits Manawaka as a faculty wife and remarks upon her linguistic sense of alienation from her past and her sense of emptiness as an acculturated subject. Yet many critics read the following passage on a sense of self as a 'polished shell' to represent urban transformation of a small-town girl or as alienation from local cultural roots, rather than class transformation of a once-poor subject.

> Had it been wrong to want to get away? No, not wrong to want to get away, to make her getaway. It was the other thing that was wrong, the turning away, turning her back on the both of them. *The both of them.* As soon as she got back to Manawaka, she even began thinking in the old phraseology. Extraneous 'the,' yet somehow giving more existence, more recognition to them than correct speech could have. Escapist, Wordsmith, forging screens. 'You're looking smart, Morag,' Christie says.
>
> She is dressed in a fairly pricey cotton dress and light blue summer coat, her hair short and swept back and upwards. At this moment she hates it all, this external self who is at such variance with whatever or whoever remains inside the glossy painted shell. If anything remains. Her remains. (248)

Ultimately, through an intense struggle to redefine herself and include the Others from her past, Morag will claim an oppositional sense of cultural home that allows her to hold on to the meaningful 'remains' of herself. These 'remains' are the forgotten fragments, the excluded excess of a classist, sexist, and racist society as they fall back upon one individual within the community. These are remnants of a nation that can be gathered only through a more inclusive vision of community.

When Morag rebels against Brooke's paternalistic use of 'Little One,' she is making much more than a feminist statement about her female independence and strength. Insisting on telling her 'long past' is an oppositional act that affirms Morag's class difference and her ancestral heritage, but also the way these differences connect her to other excluded groups within the nation. This politicized construction of her personal past as a *long* significant past is an implicit construction of a more inclusive nation outside the usual rhetoric of nationalism. Yet Morag's act of reaching back through memory is generally interpreted as a historical/personal coming to terms with Canada's colonial past more than a coming to terms with class divisions that cut across ethnic and racial groups. At the end of the novel when Morag travels to Scotland in search of a sense of home and belonging at the ancestral site of Christie's Piper Gunn stories, her revelation that her true home is 'Christie's country' is usually interpreted as a complex but affirmative construction of Canada as home to both the individual and the writer. Yet 'Christie's country' is also defined by class boundaries within Canada, an interior form of colonization reproduced by the state ideological apparatus of school and university and by the social stigma of Hill Street just as surely as the Tonnerre shack is excluded and defined by racial boundaries. As a deeply politicized individual, Morag refuses to forget ancestral ties and colonial violence – but she also refuses to forget the everyday experiences of symbolic violence against the poor and working class and against women. She is, thus, a thinking and critical political subject, unlike the one usually interpolated by more simplistic discourses of nationalism. She identifies with the many fragments and loose 'remains' of her community as part of her deepest sense of personal identity because she refuses to forget violence and exclusion, no matter what social script the dominant culture gives her to live.

Significantly, as with nation in the novel, class habitus is represented as a matter not of birthright or essence but of material and empathic location relative to social boundaries that define cultural Others. Morag is not born into a poor family but is adopted by one when she becomes orphaned and an object of charity. This makes poverty a matter of situational, material, and relational experience through which any subject can move rather than a place that only naturally deficient subjects fall into. This is nowhere better illustrated than when Christie acts out class difference as madness in front of taunting school children and then tells Morag: 'Only showing them what they thought they would be expecting to see ...' (38) to underline that identity is performed.

We should not be overly concerned with which class Morag was born into before being handed over to Christie and Prin at the age of five, since the novel itself is not. The early period of her life is condensed into the first nineteen pages of a 467-page novel, with Morag reflecting on the blurriness and unreliability of the memories she constructs from 'memorybank movies' and a few sepia-tinted photographs. Her cynicism about this distance from her birth parents is registered in phrases like 'Once Upon a Time There Was,' 'totally invented memories,' and 'I remember their deaths, but not their lives,' along with the realization that she remembers her imaginary friends from early childhood more than she does her own parents (19, 13). In many of Laurence's other works, the class positioning of the protagonist's families (for example, Hagar's and Vanessa's) is more developed than that of Morag's. Here, rather than any essentialist notion that one is necessarily formed by the class or family one is born into, Laurence is exploring the pain and anger of subjects who are fixed as Others by class identity (that is, Morag's shame of being associated with Prin and Christie, her defiant identification with other social outsiders like Jules, and her rejection of the role of middle-class faculty wife to Brooke).

When Morag is first brought to Christie's house on Hill Street as a small child, she has already learned the sense of propriety associated with her birth parents' higher class status and can thus blame Christie and Prin for their slovenliness and poverty through a child's eyes: 'The room is hers, this one thin bed, a green dresser, a window with a (oh-ripped shame on them) lace curtain' (30). Her earliest impression of the house is the dirt: 'It smells like pee or something, not like a barn. Worse.' Her second impression is the physical oddity of her foster parents: 'Can people look like that?'(29). Yet the novel problematizes class identity and refuses to naturalize social positions. All we know of the class position of Morag's birth parents is unfolded before she begins a lifetime of class travelling. They owed such a heavy mortgage on their solid but plain two-storey farmhouse that it and the land and furnishings had to be sold after their deaths to pay off the mortgage. While they experienced hardship and illness (dying from polio) during the Depression (situational poverty), they had some china and other family heirlooms (long, lacy dresses, books, vases, and plates) tucked away in a cupboard as reminders of former prosperity within their respective families. It is hinted, in Morag's musings, that her mother, a music teacher, may have 'married beneath her' in choosing a farmer for a husband (18). Several of the memories of furnishings and everyday practices, however, indicate the orderliness and abundance of a middle-class home, none the less (ornaments, carpets, a piano, leather-bound books, a living-room 'not for everyday,' a dining-room for formal Sunday dinners, and so on [8, 10]). Although the novel invokes only blurred, fragmented memories of the family's class habitus, it turns its attention, instead, to the role of creative memory in the protagonist's evolving consciousness and her developing class-consciousness and class struggle as she grows up with Christie and Prin. The thinness of her bed at Prin's house, the shabbiness of the curtain, the grime and disorder contrast directly with the memories of an orderly, well-furnished bedroom in her parents' farmhouse: 'It has a white dresser with a pale leaf-green ruffled curtain around the bottom, and underneath there is a white (cleaned every day) chamber pot for her to use during the night if she has to go. This is nice because it means she never has to go outside to the backhouse in the winter nights. There is also a white-painted bed, with a lovely quilt, flowers in green and pink on a white background, very daintily stitched, maybe by a grandmother' (9). The class subtext to Morag's memories of space, furnishings, smells, everyday practices, and values sugggests that in her parents' and grandparents' middle-class lives there was time enough to practise music and do fine embroidery, and money enough for the new technology of photographs. When Morag goes to stay with Prin and Christie, however, the photographs and refined pastimes abruptly end. The novel shows that the everyday lives of the poor and the working class are not recorded in heirlooms, possessions, or family albums, but simply in the more affordable cultural space of storytelling – namely, the pages of a novel or the oral tales about Piper Gunn – where the past of outsiders (like the Scottish Highlanders, the Metis, an unwed mother, the town gargage collector, his simple wife, a broken-down country singer) can be testified to creatively.

Although Morag's feelings of alienation in passing into poverty at the age of five are strong and immediate, the bridging of the gap in the other direction, from the poor home to the university, is much more subtle. By this time, Morag's poor home, as location of shame and difference, but also of affection and identity, cannot be publicly divulged to anyone – not, that is, until Morag meets Ella, a warm, politically aware young woman at the university (incidentally, whom many believe was modelled on Laurence's real-life friend, and one of Canada's most class-conscious writers, Adele Wiseman).[8]

Ella, who comes from a Jewish leftist home, will teach Morag the concept of 'lumpenproletariat.' Although Morag feels the class label somehow unfair, thus calling attention to the inadequacy of class theory to explain the whole truth of Prin, Christie, the Tonnerres, Mrs Crawley, and herself, naming the stigma and theorizing it frees her to tell her life story and to show her writing to a peer for the first time (180). In this central chapter, called 'Halls of Sion,' often shortchanged in critiques of the novel, Morag fortifies her class and gender identifications and discovers in Ella's woman-centred, ethnic, leftist home emotional openness, female bonding, and a flexible, complex, lived version of class politics.

Important to a subtext on culture and canon, Morag also discovers a new source of cultural understanding: namely, literatures outside the English canon (174–210). Ella's mother sends Morag home with volumes of Russian naturalism by Dostoyevsky, Tolstoy, Chekhov, and Turgenev (and later the *History of the Communist Party in the Soviet Union*), a cultural borrowing which subtly suggests that these works describing social classes from a different cultural and political perspective lay the groundwork for Morag to grow into her own class history and her own authorial voice more smoothly (186). Significantly, in the beginning of this chapter, when Ella and Morag first meet, they are both hiding their writing entries for a literary contest in heavy, canonic volumes: Ella's is *Das Kapital* and Morag's is the first volume of Taine's *History of English Literature* – an intriguing contrast which subtly foreshadows the profound cultural and canonical challenge later in the chapter. The cluster of awakenings in 'Halls of Sion' – class, gender, emotional, literary, and cultural awakenings – are significant in that they offer Morag cultural alternatives through which she can construct a more oppositional self and a more oppositional, inclusive art. The community has shifted from the closed, exclusionary, Anglo-Saxon imaginary of small-town Canada to the open, expansive possibilities of other European cultures and woman-centred community. However, working against this woman-centred, cultured home, Morag's literary education and the tightly closed community of academia lead her farther away from her working-class past, her writerly aspirations, and

---

8 Wiseman's *Crackpot*, 'Memoirs of a Book-molesting Childhood,' and *The Dollmaker* attest to an expansive, politically charged, and iconoclastic sense of cultural populism.

her independence as a woman through a series of exclusions. The *double entendre* 'Higher Learning – The Lowdown,' the title of a subsection on education, ironically signals the bourgeois exclusion of working-class lives in the academy and the linguistic colonization this entails (174).

Claiming the right to be a speaking subject rather than merely a colonized subject necessitates a struggle with a language that is a classed and gendered medium. Christie has lived out a similar tortured ambivalence towards language: incoherent in his private rages and monologues, eloquent in his condemnation of all the world as garbage, defiant in his feigned ignorance and wilful use of substandard language, and richly imaginative in his oral stories of Piper Gunn. The heritage he passes on to Morag is not only the cultural content of the Piper Gunn stories, but also this stubborn struggle with a language and a culture that do not accommodate one's own experiences, real or imaginative. Thus, an important aspect of Morag's spiritual return to roots in *The Diviners* is a linguistic escape from the potential prison house of exclusionary, academic language which is both bourgeois and masculinist. This linguistic escape allows her to rediscover the utterances and alternative artistic formulations taking place on the fringes of society beyond high culture – Christie's tragic, twisted eloquence, Jules Tonnerre's rejected Metis songs, Prin's protective inarticulateness, Ella's Old World ethnicity and political insights, and Pique's youth culture.

As Timothy Brennan has theorized in 'A National Longing for Form,' the genre of the novel provides a site for the composite representation of culture, where various discourses and histories are brought from the external reality into the internal world of an individual. Brennan suggests that the novel has been the preferred vehicle for national imagining or for the national longing for form, precisely because of its bourgeois roots, but he also points out that the genre has been appropriated for oppositional formulations of nation more inclusive to the working class. I am suggesting that Laurence's novel has both hegemonic and oppositional strains. In the end the protagonist's humane revisioning of nation is indeed a nationalist narrative that saves us from the lived ruptures it testifies to. Rather than censure this illusion of rescue, however, I think we should go on to ask ourselves why we need it and to what use it may be put. We are comforted by Laurence's protagonist's quest for a more humane form of national community because when she imagines it, we too can imagine it. These imaginative acts are vital to changing the nation.

By studying *The Diviners* in relation to other poverty narratives in Canadian culture, we can make the class ruptures in the novel reappear less individualistically and less neatly. And we can look at other strategies we deploy to transcend class ruptures in order to inscribe a bourgeois sense of peoplehood or, conversely, to call attention to class ruptures in order to testify to the need to reconceptualize nation. Coming to consciousness about class blindness is not necessarily a form of blind idealism. For example, what *The Diviners* shares with other counter-cultural re-imaginings of nation by the poor or by left-wing critics is a depiction of alternative forms of local and community support. These images of support among the poor defy the stereotype of the poor as dependent and inherently deficient. It is, after all, Christie the scavenger man who takes charge of the penniless orphan, and it is Eva, the girl who refuses to 'smarten up' and dress 'properly,' who nurses Prin when Morag has left to 'marry up.' These radical reformulations of community loyalties call into question the definition of progress within the nation and show that no master narrative of systemic reform or systemic domination can sum up or contain the lives of the poor. Social agency is possible and can spring up in everyday relations among the poor. Granted, we do not all have the wordsmith's power, like Christie Logan or Morag Gunn, to remythologize our relation to nation. But we can be conscious of how we use their stories and other poverty narratives in our own construction and reconstruction of national culture.

7.3 Strategies of Containment and Exclusion

In *Nationalist Thought and the Colonial World: A Derivative Discourse*, much of what Partha Chatterjee critiques about assumptions behind Western nationalism can be adapted to understand the position of the poor as an internally colonized group within Western nations. Narratives about the poor in Canada often reproduce assumptions about New World/First World progress, prosperity, equality, and meritocracy or define themselves oppositionally against these dominant values. Chatterjee has argued that nationalist thought, even when liberatory in respect to Third World countries, derives from deeply rooted colonial assumptions about the inherent superiority of the West and Western styles of rational thought in relation to the 'underdeveloped' nations. Although Chatterjee is discussing the East more than the West, his critique of Western nationhood provides a good springboard for this discussion because, though nationalist discourses vary widely, he argues, they often share underlying evolutionary assumptions that nationhood equals development, progress, and freedom and that the Western nations are 'pacemakers' which the developing world needs to catch up with and emulate. Furthermore, he claims, postcolonial concepts of nation often share a *faith in theory* which, he argues, is itself a European rationalist heritage that ultimately devalues the lived, heterogeneous experiences of marginalized Others and their alternative ways of knowing nation as a shared collective project.

According to Chatterjee, postcolonial theory becomes entangled in a paradox by positioning the colonized in the Third World as poor Other, as objects of both study and charity according to nationalist discourse. Whereas postcolonial theory would liberate the Third World poor through a liberal doctrine, it simultaneously fixes them within an evolutionary model of history that assumes their inferior epistemic status. I would like to suggest that this liberal doctrine and cultural essentialism, which Chatterjee has identified so aptly as being at work in the Three Worlds model, also operates in the way the West constructs internally colonized groups as either outside itself or as naturally inferior and thus inherently incapable of sharing in the progress and wealth which define Western nations as pacemakers. In the West, however, the liberal doctrine of progressivism is applied internally, not through an overt discourse of nationalism as much as through the discourse of cultural assimilation and individual mobility (the Canadian/American dream).[9] When the mobility narrative or the narrative of assimilation are conspicuously absent, the voices of the domestic poor are usually studied like those of foreign Others – as *objects* of anthropology or ethnography rather than as literary *subjects*. The inferior epistemic status of the poor within the West is assumed when they are fixed as objects of study in one field (social work, ethnography) but overlooked as subjects in another (literature, cultural studies). One step to restoring epistemic status to the poor is to recognize the importance of subjectivity and radical knowledge among the poor and lay bare the mechanisms which silence those subjectivities in Western society. (I am thinking, for example, about studies of the representation of

---

9 Lest there be doubt that Canadians, like Americans, have generated a dream of mobility as part of a shared national project, see a collection of narratives on the subject in *Making It: The Canadian Dream*, ed. Bryan Finnigan and Cy Gonick (Toronto: McClelland and Stewart, 1972), many of which contest the viability of the dream.

the poor as varied as Peter Leonard's *Postmodern Welfare* and *Personality and Ideology*, Sheila Baxter's *No Way to Live: Poor Women Speak Out*, and Bryan Green's *Knowing the Poor*.)

As an example of how myths of affluence and progress generate a national identity that excludes the poor, consider the following two items from a 1993 edition of *Maclean's* magazine (1 March): the first item is an appeal for donations to fight poverty in the 'developing world,' and the second is an article discussing the high suicide rate among an impoverished Innu community at Davis Inlet. Both texts project poverty onto the Third World while simultaneously erasing or rationalizing poverty in Canada.

The appeal for donations deploys a dualistic form of representation through the language of the advertisement, the photo-image of a white baby and a black baby, and the title, 'Open & Shut,' as part of a rhetoric of simplicity in order to convince Canadians that fostering children in the developing world is both a pragmatic and a readily accessible project (see figure 1). The types of simplification chosen are effective, however, because they activate a chain of acceptable assumptions regarding the poor, racial differences, and the Third World: for example, that the poor are distant and not here, them and not us, black and not white, geographically specific and not historically created. Furthermore, the way to open the door to opportunity for the oppressed is clearly within the existing market system without redistributing the wealth of rich people in those countries or this, except to ask them voluntarily to give gifts of charity.

That Baby Jordan, '[l]iving here in Canada,' has a future like 'an open book,' 'an easy path' with 'every opportunity to shine' is an acceptable homogenization of Canadian babies, given the assumption of extreme contrast with baby Monzon, whose script for the future is 'deprivation, hopelessness and even death – a life shut off before it really ever began.' The extremity of Third World poverty is thus deployed with the effect of automatically cancelling or inauthenticating claims of poverty in Canada. This is similar to the logic whereby extreme scenes of poverty from the Depression function to discredit present claims of poverty (as discussed in respect to Bromley's theory of organized forgetting in the last chapter). Furthermore, the language used to describe baby Monzon's deathlike future invokes, beyond the image of the closed door in the title, the horror of uncontainable poverty as a deathlike abyss, a received image rooted in the Victorian idea of poverty as an encroaching abyss (Gagnier, Himmelfarb). The low-key pragmatic lan-

Figure 1   *Maclean's*, 1 March 1993

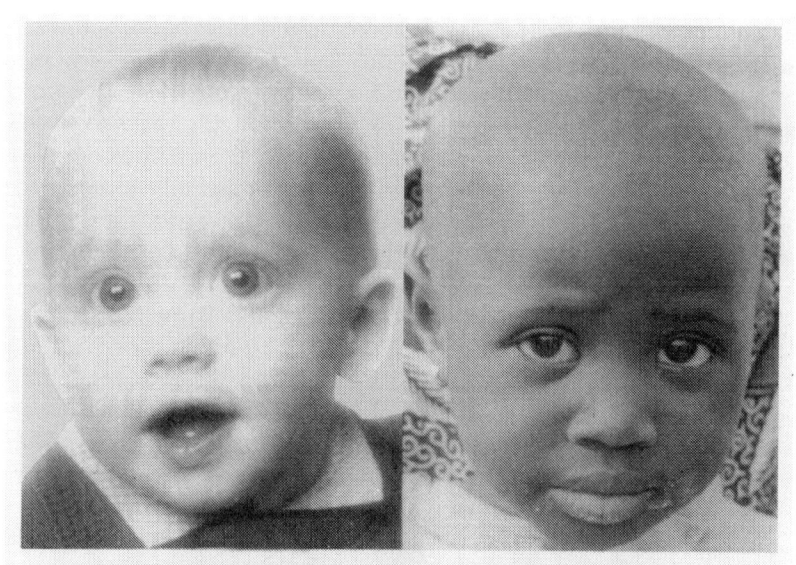

guage describing the capitalist solution, on the other hand, is soothing and concrete – 'Less than a dollar a day can open closed doors to medical care, education, clean water and so much more.' Charity overtly promises to open the door for the poor but implicitly seeks to close it, thereby soothing us with the impression of having contained or at least temporarily controlled poverty without fundamentally altering systems of distribution or political power. Whereas the explicit text offers a solution to the difference between the two worlds: 'There shouldn't be a difference. There doesn't have to be,' the hidden text affirms the insoluble 'nature' of that distance as unbridgeable. Baby Monzon will receive minimal support to keep death at bay, not 'an easy path' and 'every opportunity to shine,' conditions which are reserved for children in the developed world. Consequently, where it is written 'his share of a bright tomorrow,' we understand this as his *naturally* smaller share according to a neocolonialist conception of the contained, Third World 'Other' in a 'naturally' uneven world.

Besides the erasure of Canada's domestic poor there is also a play on the accepted notion that poverty happens out there to other races. Note that the countries listed for donations have white, red, and yellow babies as well as black ones, as does Canada itself, but that the advertisement invokes the preferred image of the poor as non-white and geographically distanced and of Canadians as white and ensured a safe future. Furthermore, the emphasis on the future uproots poverty from any suspicion of causality in domestic class relations or imperialist history and supplants it by a notion of disparity between nations which is geographic, naturalized, and dehistoricized – in other words, a product of a neocolonialist world view of a naturally uneven distribution of the world's resources.

Thus the hidden text behind the appeal for charity reveals that symbolic containment goes on behind the back of philanthropy,[10] that the way we go about opening doors to the Third World poor through charity may imply closing doors to the actual or different potential of the East and the South and, similarly, restricting knowledge of the *lack* of opportunity for the poor within the progressive West. Chatterjee has argued at some length that our intellectual apprehension of the Other

---

10 I do not mean to denigrate all acts of charity. But we do need to be sceptical about whose interests private and public charity serve within a state system unwilling to share goods, services, capital, and technology in a more regulated, socially democratic way.

in the West is fraught with the same paradox: the Western world has set up the East as object of both charity and study through a doctrine of cultural relativism which actually reinforces distance while claiming to understand and tolerate difference (11–17).

Elaborating on Said's theory of symbolic containment in the process of Orientalism, Chatterjee speaks of the symbolic containment of rational and intellectual cultural relativism as a paradox – whereas functionalist, structuralist, relativist, and rationalist anthropological approaches to the 'Other' argue for their own generosity of vision due to a sympathetic and imaginative understanding of other cultures based on a 'principle of charity,' what in fact takes place is the same deep-rooted cultural essentialism fundamental to rationalist sciences in the West; knowledge is implicated as the means of dominating the world through images of the Self and Other, with the Self gaining power over the Other through knowledge (15).

However, whereas minority ethnic groups outside and even inside the West may be studied and accepted through this doctrine of cultural relativism, a charitable attitude of cultural relativism is rarely extended to the poor within the West. According to progressivist myths of development, New World myths of opportunity, and capitalist myths of meritocracy, the poor in the West are irremediably stigmatized in a position of blame and shame that cannot be validated by any notion of cultural relativism. Furthermore, as Ruth L. Smith has argued, this stigmatizing of the poor as Other within the West is necessary to myths of market stability and civil society as a place on the outside where systemic contradictions and weaknesses can be projected and rewritten as natural disorder rather than as internal, systemic political disorder and sanctioned inequality.

Aijaz Ahmad critiques the conceptual categories of the emerging field of postcolonialist theory for reproducing progressivist and essentialist assumptions. Ahmad argues that the Three Worlds concept of development reinforces differences between the East and the West while suppressing differences within nations:

> Even in cultural theory as it has developed in the metropolitan countries, an exclusive emphasis on the nation, and on nationalism as the necessary ideology emanating from the national situation, has been a logical feature of Third-Worldist perspectives. For once the world is divided into three large unities, each fundamentally coherent and fundamentally external to one another, it is extremely difficult to speak of any fundamental differ-

ences within particular national structures – differences, let us say, of class or of gender formation. One is then forced, by the terms of one's own discourse, to minimise those kinds of differences, and to absolutize, on the other hand, the difference between, say, the First and the Third Worlds. (92)

Such essentialist assumptions emerged recently through the media coverage of severe domestic poverty and a high rate of childhood suicide in the Innu community of Davis Inlet. Television and press reports regularly described the horror of the poverty, in distancing and alarming terms, as 'Third World conditions in Canada!,' as though Canada knows no severe poverty – except, that is, in pockets that resemble the Third World. An article on Davis Inlet in the same issue of *Maclean's* in which the charity appeal appeared repeats some of the methods of projection and rationalization, but also develops others more characteristic of the rationalization which takes place when poverty is undeniably located within the West: for example, psychologizing and dehistoricizing poverty.

Once again, as in the appeal for donations to the Third World, monetary rather than political solutions are emphasized – the Innu are being 'treated ... all at Ottawa's expense' – while historical causality is effectively erased. The only historical explanation given for the community's desperate poverty is euphemistically stated in a modifying phrase of one sentence: 'But in the case of the Davis Inlet Innu, removed by Ottawa from their traditional hunting grounds in 1967 and resettled on an island off the remote northern coast of Labrador, clinic staff members acknowledge that they face a special challenge. "Twenty five years need to be reversed"' (16). The euphemisms are not subtle: 'removed ... from' their land, not 'dispossessed of it;' 'resettled on' a remote island not 'exiled to' it. There is no mention that the Innu lost their livelihood, nomadic hunting, when moved to the island; nor is there any mention of the long dispute over government services and housing which has left them without running water or sewage systems. Instead of focusing on the subhuman conditions of poverty and isolation, the article medicalizes the problem as internal to the Innu, who are presented as being sick as individuals and as a culture – the subtitle reads ('Davis Inlet Innu begin their treatment'). This strategy of rationalization is in keeping with what Chaim Waxman observed in *The Stigma of Poverty: A Critique of Poverty Theories and Policies*, that in North America in the twentieth century the stigma has been characterized by the further individualization and psychologizing of poverty (72–92). A focus on the symptoms of poverty manifested in individuals – personal problems of drug addiction, gasoline sniffing, suicide attempts, and despondency – sanitizes the report of colonial history and culminates in the preposterous spectacle of medical staff struggling to 'reverse' history in order to erase its effects on the minds of the Innu ('Twenty five years need to be reversed'). If there is any political problem at all, the article suggests, it is that Ottawa does not have enough money or an efficient enough distribution method to help all of these sick people on all of these reserves. The objective problem of their poverty is never addressed analytically, it is merely invoked as an unavoidable horror and trauma which they must steel themselves against – implying that once they are better, stronger, individuals they will be able to help themselves out of their poverty. The picture accompanying the article shows the Innu, not surrounded by the objective evidence of poor housing and the dismal site of their historic resettlement, but framed within the affluent treatment centre which they have been sent to through the benevolence of the national government (see figure 2). The massive architectural structure, with its columns, stonework, and fireplace, emblemizes the solid nation which seeks to save them from themselves.

The present national government of Canada is shown to include and valorize, rather than exclude and deprive, its racial 'Other.' Although brief mention is made of previous governments' use of residential schools to wipe out Native languages, the long history of economic deprivation and racial discrimination is consigned to absence in the text along with the harder questions about material and cultural survival. The historically rooted problem is collapsed into the present and the tabloid dynamics of a tolerant national government tending to an ailing racial 'Other.' The solution to the problem, once it is posed as psychological, is inscribed through a preferred image of aboriginal people as exotic and spiritually strong. The title of the article, 'A Sweetgrass Ceremony,' refers to a purification ceremony and stands as a public gesture of tolerance and respect for Native difference. Accordingly, abdication of federal responsibility for the material conditions in the community is rewritten as respectful distance and presented as an act of racial tolerance. A clinician's opinion – 'Indian people can best help Indian people' – draws racial difference into the rhetoric of cultural relativism, self-help, and support groups for drug addiction (14).

Figure 2   *Maclean's*, 1 March 1993

This preferred image of inclusion and acceptable difference occludes the lived practice of excluding and segregating Native people and the economic consequences of appropriating their land and legislating against their lifestyle. The Native population has been the poorest in Canada since the formation of white government over First Nations people. They have suffered from suicide rates and infant mortality rates up to seven times higher than those of other Canadians since the time of European contact. To represent one community's psychological experience of poverty without discussing the history of the impoverishment of the indigenous peoples is a significant erasure of colonial history and the systemic cause of their racially rooted poverty. Likewise, the failure to discuss the prosperity of certain Native communities after oppositional court or political action to reclaim land serves to homogenize and naturalize Native people as poor.

The barrage of media reports psychologizing the Davis Inlet situation were followed a year later, not surprisingly, by reports that the initial positive results of treatment had not lasted and that children had again begun sniffing gasoline and publicly talking of suicide. Most media capsulizations of the follow-up story ignored the issue of the Innu's demand for resettlement altogether and the nation, by now familiar with Davis Inlet as a site of illness and social decay, listened to reports on the community's tragic problems with mental health. There was some talk of whether or not Ottawa should construct a treatment centre in the middle of the community. Only in early September 1994, when the Innu themselves moved politically to block and expel federal court officials from their community, would CBC radio finally report on community unrest in terms of political causes. But even then, the discourse infanticized the protesting community by reporting, in the discourse of parental discipline, that if they continued to block planes carrying newly appointed federal court officials, the federal government would refuse to talk to them about the subjects 'closest to their hearts': relocation, land claims, education, health, et cetera. Subsequent reports focused on whether or not the national police would be called in and the criminal discourse escalated, finally making links with other Native communities, *but only* in respect to civil disobedience, not to historical disenfranchisement (for example, references to the armed conflict between Native people and police at Oka and how such a showdown and national embarrassment could be avoided this time).

When the nation narrates the poor as inherently different, isolated, and dehistoricized, it rationalizes class tensions within its own house and affirms unity and stability. The poor, as an internal Other, may experience Canada as a profoundly divided house despite the domination of this liberal rhetoric of unity which repeatedly affirms the classlessness of Canadian culture. But as John Porter observes in *The Vertical Mosaic*, '[i]mages which conflict with the one of middle class equality rarely find expression' on the national scene in Canada, largely because 'the literate middle class is both producer and consumer of the image.' Thus, apart from the lack of access to cultural production by the poor, another silencing force of alternative views of nation is the authoritative power of bourgeois images of nation which derives from the frequency of transmission and the familiarity of conventional messages. Bourgeois nationalism cannot simply silence the poor but must also reinscribe poverty in ways consistent with its own narrative of consensus and community. For example, one of the most traditional motifs for signifying the inherent difference of the poor within the otherwise homogeneous unity of bourgeois nation is the two-nations image which portrays the poor as living completely apart from the majority and its shared project of progress and prosperity, though within the same geographical borders.

As discussed earlier, Gertrude Himmelfarb in *The Idea of Poverty* shows the evolution of the two-nations motif in nineteenth-century Britain to be the logical culmination of a nationalism which depicted the poor as either aliens or victims within a progressive, industrialized nation. From earlier philosophic preoccupations with poverty and nation in the realm of moral philosophy, as reflected in Samuel Johnson's adage – 'A decent provision for the poor is the true test of civilization' – to later popular concerns for the reputation of Britain as Europe's first industrialized nation, the two-nations concept of England took root as a popular method of symbolically containing the poor and urban decay within the idealism of nationalism and industrialization. The two-nations model also naturalized the poor as inherently different in order to rationalize the failure of the England-as-social-laboratory experiment with Poor Laws and workhouses which was itself part of the idealism of industrialization (3–5, 18): 'With predictable and monotonous regularity every parliamentary report, social novel, and journalistic exposé announced itself, and was hailed by reviewers, as an excursion into "distant lands," "dark and unknown regions," populated by "aborigines" and "unknown tribes" as peculiar as the "people of Lapland or California," their tales as "strange and new as the wildest dreams of fiction"' (404). Henry Mayhew had first won the title of the 'discoverer of the poor' by chronicling the extremities of street life of the London poor in the 1860s. Mayhew described himself as a 'traveller in the undiscovered country of the poor' who would bring back reports from a people about whom less was known than 'the most distant tribes of the earth.' Himmelfarb documents that reviewers recycled the image, and from her citation we can see that they also reworked and dramatized the motif to the point where the poor themselves became the unknown tribes: '[h]e travelled through the unknown regions of our metropolis, and returned with full reports concerning the strange tribes of men which he may be said to have discovered' (332). According to this symbolic containment, street folk became naturalized as a race apart who were predisposed to and thus responsible for their own self-perpetuating culture of poverty. This emphasis on inherent difference suggested that the other nation was simply a pocket of society left behind by progress, 'an archaic, anarchic, barbaric people' (362), rather than a corollary to progress. It occluded the systemic causes of their poverty (for example, that workers from the pre-industrial economy were displaced, that workers from the market economy were excess or exploited labour, or that urban growth was creating class-marked ghettos without sufficient housing or planning).

Himmelfarb herself is essentially conservative on such points. Although she exposes the distance and strangeness reinscribed by Mayhew and his contemporaries in the two-nations theme and notes a correlation between that theme and current theories of the culture of poverty which tend to 'overwhelm the prosaic image of the ordinary, conventional working poor,' here as elsewhere in her book, she advocates the description of the ordinary poor but stops short of researching their lives and subjectivities rather than dominant ideas (370). In other words, Himmelfarb reinscribes containment through an analytical paradigm, though to a lesser extent than the two-nations model, by stopping short of a radical political questioning of the uneven distribution of wealth and the systemic causes of poverty (I agree with Harvey and Reed's description in 'Paradigms of Poverty: A Critical Assessment of Contemporary Perspectives' that Himmelfarb's work is politically conservative in that it fails to question the market context of poverty [270–1]).

Through a long tradition of reaching out to poor and working-class subjectivities in British culture – from Mayhew's journalistic accounts which exoticized the poor while chronicling them, to Charles Booth's more scientific attempts to fix the London poor as objects of study, to George Orwell's commissioned study of industrialized towns and the homes of coal miners in England, to Richard Hoggart's analytical return as academic to the scene of the working-class culture of his youth – many have bridged the gap between bourgeois and working-class cultures through the conventional motif of visiting the poor through the eyes of a traveller in a strange or distant country, a motif which both dramatizes and subtly reinscribes distance. Whether traversed by the class traveller who seeks to escape poverty or the voyeur who wishes to capture it in all its sensational squalor, the distance is none the less exaggerated as a means of maintaining the distinction between classes.

In *The Other America: Poverty in the United States*, Michael Harrington adapted the two-nations theme for the deconstruction of the homogeneous version of nation implied by American myths of prosperity and opportunity. Accordingly, Harrington deployed the traditional two-nations model in a new way to define the 'new poor' in the context of twentieth-century cultural practices and attitudes: 'But the new poverty is constructed so as to destroy aspiration; it is a system designed to be impervious to hope. The other America does not contain the adventurous seeking a new life and land. It is populated by the failures, by those driven from the land and bewildered by the city, by old people suddenly confronted with the torment of loneliness and poverty, and by minorities facing a wall of prejudices' (10). Harrington claimed that the 'new' poor were more invisible than ever, because of a wall of affluence and the media image of America as the most prosperous nation in the world, the ghettoization of the poor in the inner-city slums and the simultaneous exodus of the middle class to the suburbs, and the masking of need by false fronts of prosperity such as urban renewal projects and an increased availability of affordable clothing without commensurate benefits to the poor in housing, education, medical care, and a healthy diet. Most importantly, he claimed, the 'new' poor suffer from political invisibility, which stems from a lack of membership in unions, fraternal organizations, political parties, lobbies, et cetera, and results in the poor having no face and no voice; they were not even the subject of conservative political concern, he noted, because slum organization was no longer a threat. Deploying the two-nations theme, he attempted to *re*cover the poor, rather than *dis*cover them: 'The problem, then, is to a great extent one of vision. The nation of the well-off must be able to see through the wall of affluence and recognize the *alien citizens* on the other side' (emphasis added, 159). Although his deployment of the two-nations motif is consciously executed as a challenge to the homogenizing claims of First World progress, it subtly reinscribes essence as the problem in both the Third World and the culture of poverty: 'the United States contains an *underdeveloped nation*, a culture of poverty. Its inhabitants do not suffer the extreme privation of the peasants of Asia or the tribesmen of Africa, yet the mechanism of the misery is similar. They are beyond history, beyond progress, sunk in a paralysing, maiming routine' (emphasis added, 158). This culture-of-poverty theory has been articulated differently by many sociologists, most notably Oscar Lewis, but has been critiqued for attributing the cultural reproduction of poverty to inherent qualities among the poor rather than systemic market causes (see my discussion of the culture-of-poverty debate in chapter 5 in respect to stigma). When seen in juxtaposition with the earlier two-nations conceptual model, Harrington's culture-of-poverty paradigm betrays its essentialist assumptions by showing how compatible the two images are. For example, he writes:

'Poverty should be defined psychologically in terms of those whose place in the society is such that they are *internal exiles* who, *almost inevitably*, develop attitudes of defeat and pessimism and who are *therefore* excluded from taking advantage of new opportunities' (emphasis added, 179).

The implications of such essentialist conceptual models on the possibility of political agency should be obvious. The logic of containment is circular: the poor are assumed to be incapable of action because they are poor, and they are assumed to be poor because they are incapable of action. Moreover, having denied agency to the poor, these conceptual models rationalize the intervention of science or state or nation to save the poor from themselves.

7.4 Counter-national Testimonies

> O Canada! Our home and native land!
> True patriot-love in all thy sons command.
> With glowing hearts *we see thee rise*,
> The True North, strong and free,
> And stand on guard, O Canada,
> We stand on guard for thee.
>
> O Canada! Where pines and maples grow,
> Great prairies spread and lordly rivers flow,
> How dear to us thy broad domain,
> From East to Western Sea,
> *Thou Land of hope, for all who toil!*
> Thou True North, strong and free!
>   (R. Stanley Weir, 'O Canada!'; emphasis added)

A number of recent popular books about poverty in Canada reflect the two-nations tradition by presenting poverty narratives as travelogues that relate journalists' visits to the poor as trips to another land or another layer of civilization akin to an underworld. Like Harrington's use of the paradigm, these are residual, in Raymond Williams's sense of the term, in that they do not merely reproduce archaic cultural formations but reactivate them in different ways. Linda Lee Tracey's *On the Edge: A Journey into the Heart of Canada* (1993) recounts a journalist's cross-country trip, from east to west, to meet poor people in each province as well as to understand better her own working-class past. The 'heart of Canada' in the title signifies the author's strong sense of identification with the perspectives of poor people while also implying that true and essential, and possibly oppositional, knowledge about the nation will be revealed through the inside view of the poor. Tracey reworks the two-nations theme oppositionally to place the outsiders closer to the heart of a nation, thereby challenging the dominant paradigm that Canada's identity or essence as a western nation lies in its prosperity.

Similarly, Alan Mettrick's *Last in Line: On the Road and Out of Work ... A Desperate Journey with Canada's Unemployed* (1985) reports a journalist's travels with the unemployed and his *fall* into that lifestyle in the early 1980s ('dropped off the world' [ix]). The book's cover copy stresses the 'other-worldliness' of poverty by reporting: '[f]or over two years he travelled in a world of two-bit hostels and flophouses, temporary labour pools and mission soup kitchens.' Mettrick himself ponders the implications of the travel/other-world motif and concludes that what he has experienced is so violent that it cannot be described as anything but another world:

> This business of putting on old clothing and venturing into the underworld, so to speak, is a literary tradition that goes back at least as far as the Arabian Nights. Originally, I had not planned anything so melodramatic. I had been reflecting for some time on those stuffed figures in old pictures: logging bums, gold rushers, furmen, cowhands, blanket stiffs. Drifters. And how much we seemed to despise their wandering counterparts now. I saw more and more men and women displaced from waning traditional industries, and I wondered how it would be to have no roots now that the tall buildings are everywhere and the wild horses are gone. I took one tentative step and then another, and ultimately was overwhelmed, not only by the horror of the sub-world in which I found myself, but also by the tragedy of a recession. (ix)

While Mettrick rather romantically includes and befriends the homeless as 'fellow travellers' and drifters, he also resists glossing over poverty by asserting the seriousness of the 1980s recession against the more extreme icons of the Depression of the 1930s.

Mettrick's use of the two-worlds/nations motif is consciously oppositional in that he insists that poverty is a 'national story.' He claims national status for his eyewitness reports about the poor and homeless in the western provinces because many have drifted there towards the warmer weather from other parts of the country where, he documents, homelessness is also a problem. He challenges nation by talking about government's unfulfilled responsibility towards the poor, the suppression of the story of the impact of the 1980s recession by North American mass consumer culture, and the systemic conditions sometimes responsible for trapping people in poverty and then allowing them to be exploited as cheap labour by the country's wealthy (Mettrick's descriptions of his own experiences of the temporary labour pools and welfare bureaucracy are particularly revealing as to how systems may entrap the poor). Mettrick observes how, in the absence of awareness and concern from the national community, the Salvation Army and Alcoholics Anonymous construct an alternative sense of community for the homeless. Although the prose is uneven, Mettrick's reportage is by far the most interesting of the Canadian 'journey' poverty narratives I have read because he stylizes characterizations, connects his own narrative to a long tradition of philosophy and reportage about the poor (a distinctly masculine tradition, albeit, but socially engaged), and politicizes as well as personalizes the discourse. By dressing up as poor in the tradition of Orwell's *Down and Out in Paris and London*, he is able to report the standpoint of the poor for a time and offer his own testimonies alongside theirs.

Reportage reworks the motif of a visit into the 'underworld,' the 'other country' of poverty, with widely varying political and stylistic motives and with varying degrees of distance. Whereas it is no longer acceptable to report on the poor and homeless as another *race* or as the undeserving poor of the nineteenth-century urban walking tours which sought to visit them in their 'dens' (as discussed earlier in respect to Susanna Moodie's 'A Word for the Novel Writers'), the conventional two-nations form of representation is recycled even by sympathetic, self-reflexive, and politically aware journalists and participant-observers like Tracey and Mettrick. Another example is Marlene Webber's *Street Kids: The Tragedy of Canada's Runaways* (1991), which presents a journalist's travels onto the streets as a journey into the underworld, with street workers and the homeless themselves as 'guides' (Marlene Webber is also the author of a book on food banks in Canada, *Food for Thought* [1992]). Webber's best-selling book on street kids includes transcripts from interviews as well as social analysis of a growing phenomenon of teenage runaways and 'throwaways' from all classes. *Street Kids* dispels the social myth that the homeless are men who choose the life of the vagabond, a popular conflation fortified by

Mettrick's representation of today's homeless as a later generation of male drifters. Alex Murray challenges the conflation of the homeless with men in his essay 'Homelessness: The People' (1990, 36–7), and Webber and Baxter both report that, according to front-line workers and the homeless themselves, there are fewer women on the streets because many sell their bodies for a bed just for one night, partly because the streets are much more dangerous for women. Women's reports of the voyage into the underworld of street life frequently include testimonies of sexual threat, violence, or exploitation from the outset, in keeping with Murray's observation that domestic violence is a major cause of homelessness among women. Murray also notes that bad hygiene and madness are strategies of self-protection for 'bag ladies' who are otherwise easy targets for sexual and physical assault on the street (42). The picture that emerges of women among the homeless is that although their numbers are lower (but increasing), their lot is harder.

Evelyn Lau's highly publicized *Runaway: The Diary of a Street Kid* (1990) – 'Now a CBC television movie!' the front cover advertises – relates a fourteen-year-old, middle-class girl's travels into the *underworld* of prostitution, drugs, welfare, and institutionalization. This book is an example of how the traveller's gaze is not always cast from without but can be turned on the homeless by themselves, in this case through the writerly eye of a young Asian-Canadian girl from a middle-class immigrant family looking for writing material, escape from an abusive home, assimilation into North American youth culture, and a more viable sense of self. Lau's testimony constructs a unified self despite mental breakdowns by focusing steadily on her interior world and her goal to become a writer. There are few reports about other poor people; also lacking are any sense of community with them or any political or social reflections on street life and poverty. One wonders if that is why this work, rather than collective testimonies, gained such popular success. It constructs poverty, street life, and prostitution uncritically as personal choice rather than necessity.

Although the tradition of travellers' accounts has spurred great interest in visits to the strange country of the poor and homeless, insider accounts of the politics of everyday poverty have not been numerous enough or powerful enough to establish their own set of conventions – or is it, rather, that they have not been studied as a body of texts related oppositionally and intertextually to dominant representations of poverty? Unconventional literary testimonies, autobiographies, and oral histories employ a variety of innovative narrative forms as they reach for new, oppositional ways of representing the poor from their own standpoint. These various forms of testimonies about the lived experience of poverty often describe the exclusions and symbolic violence of a national community which will not imagine the poor as part of the 'shared project of nation.' But in addition to showing the trauma of exclusion and symbolic violence, they may challenge nation in other ways: for example, by witnessing to ways of surviving poverty, re-imagining nation as a more inclusive ideal, and making demands which will move nation towards that ideal. The relationship between poverty and nation does not need to be fixed as one of exclusion or victimization if nation is not automatically synonymous with progress and prosperity and can be re-imagined otherwise. In other words, the voices of the poor and critical reflection on poverty can inform our idea of nation.

A few published narratives by poor people and political activists address an oppositional community and give voice to it as a means of informing this community about political possibilities and encouraging them in their struggles. For example, Sheila Baxter's *Under the Viaduct: Homeless in Beautiful B.C.* and *No Way to Live: Poor Women Speak Out* are loosely structured to gather fragments which include oral interviews, demographics, anecdotes, political strategy speeches, reports by social workers and activists, and Baxter's own personal testimony. She calls it a 'patchwork' of everyday truths, and it is difficult to read because of the lack of attention to style and form, the largely unedited nature of the transcripts, and the intrusiveness of statistics. But both books are unique in that Baxter consistently allies herself, as a political activist and a welfare mother and child of poverty, with the poor and homeless rather than with the role of detached observer or traveller. None the less, political activism is revealed as a space with its own differences. The poor and workers are represented not as a monolithic community but as complexly different and related individuals struggling alone and in groups. These people's knowledge of the complexity of everyday struggles, of multiple political possibilities, and varied strategies of survival inform these books and construct them as a few of many alternative sites to the dominant culture's fascination with the extremity of poverty and the romance and aesthetics of the outsider position.

Baxter's own narrative of immigration, along with others of downward mobility in her books, dispels the myth that Canada is a land of opportunity 'for all who toil' – as the song goes. In *Under the Viaduct*, she recounts her experiences of homelessness in England and then in Canada as a result of a series of misfortunes beginning with life as the abused and neglected child of alcoholics; living through housing shortages and in rat-infested apartments in 1950s London; emigrating to Canada to end up in Montreal in another slum area and then being evicted by the government when the land was expropriated; having her daughter contract a fatal disease when there was no medicare; moving to Vancouver and having a house burn down; being turned out on the streets by the YWCA with her children and no possessions or money; returning to Montreal with one child, their few possessions in bags, and having left her teenage children behind. At this point in her life, Baxter describes herself as 'giving up' and living on welfare. Shame and self-blame punctuate the narrative of these events, so that 'Sheila's Homelessness' not only describes the construction of her own identity as a poor woman but also establishes for the homeless she interviews that she is an insider who has felt the stigma of homelessness and learned to see beyond it. Later in the book, Baxter reports how she recovered hope by becoming an organizer and establishing Chez Doris, Montreal's first homeless women's shelter. She also encourages the Grey Nuns to rekindle earlier charitable works by their patron saints and open a sister shelter for francophone women. Testimonies to activism pose a profound challenge to narrow definitions of nation by witnessing alternative views of community and alternative definitions of what it means for a culture to progress in the West.

Baxter frames *Under the Viaduct* between her memories of growing up poor in London and the testimony of a black woman recently arrived from Thatcher's England in order to warn that political inaction and conservatism may lead Canada as a nation towards a condition of increased poverty and civil tension like Britain's. Similar warnings are made by shelter workers that Canada is following the American way of homelessness – less and less government aid and more and more crime. Instead of imagining Canada breathlessly keeping up to the 'pacemakers' of Western nationhood, these testimonies show that it is possible to imagine Canada otherwise, as choosing to opt out of the models set by Britain and the United States and looking elsewhere for cultural ideals to emulate. For example, a section of *Under the Viaduct* contributed by a squatter compares information about attitudes towards and strategies of squatting in Germany, Holland, and England in order to put into a more political perspective the philosophy and tactics of organized squatters in Vancouver.

These squatters (like fictional characters in Diana Collier's *The Invisible Women of Washington*, Irene Baird's *Waste Heritage*, and Helen Potrebenko's 'The Interview' [1989]) are aware that their activism and their claims on Canada as a nation are distorted and depoliticized by mass media which promote cultural assimilation to a specific social ideal: 'Part of the reason the coverage was so positive was, I think, because we were presented as the "helpless homeless," driven to desperate acts by the housing crisis. We were very much "victims," and therefore acceptable. That we squat also out of choice, that squatting is powerful action, that we are trying to create something better and to empower, all that was ignored, and if stressed would have turned us into "radicals" (i.e. *bad*) rather than "helpless homeless" (i.e. *acceptable*)' (Keith Chu, quoted by Baxter 84). Testimonies to radicalism and political possibilities challenge nation by trying to reframe the shared project of community to respond to the needs of these muted members.

Another highly contentious form of testimony is that which reveals the causes of poverty to be situational or relational rather than inherent in poor people themselves. Given that the image of Canada's prosperity is so intimately tied to the notion of meritocracy ('hope for all who toil'), the idea that one can be poor in Canada even though one is willing to work challenges the promise of market society to regulate economic relations. The most startling difference that I have seen between people who have lived experience of poverty and those who have not is that the latter often perceive the world through a bubble which tells them that poverty could not happen to them. For women, this bubble is particularly deceptive because the feminization of poverty means that more and more bourgeois women are slipping into the ranks of the poor and homeless. Precisely because the identities of the poor and homeless are multiple and shifting, they pose a threat to bourgeois nationalism and its members by showing that middle-class status itself is not a securely fixed identity but a situational one.

National boundaries are frequently blurred or at issue in poverty narratives because of the nationless status of the poor. Whether or not a national government will intercede on behalf of its own poor to shelter them from poverty or will simply extract their labour power is a question which challenges our assumptions about social rights and obligations and continues to be debated in the arena of cultural criticism, political and economic theory, and journalism (see works by John Ralston Saul, John Kenneth Galbraith, Linda McQuaig, and Barbara Murphy). Stories of immigration tend to highlight the relation between poverty and nation because many people are declassed by immigrating and also because the poor from abroad can compare their treatment in Canada with their lives in other cultures. As Arnold Itwaru has theorized, immigrant literature in Canada – such as *Under the Ribs of Death*, *Crackpot*, and *Confessions of an Immigrant's Daughter* – reinvents nation by testifying to the clash between the immigrant dream of social mobility and the reality of systemic class and ethnic barriers to integration.[11] In some cases, the immigrant poor can call on reserves of self-worth and imported social theory to buttress themselves against the negative construction of the poor in North America. In the case of Laura Goodman Salverson's *Confessions of an Immigrant's Daughter*, the downwardly mobile subject calls on astute social criticism as well as an Icelandic past rich in oral and written literature to protest the lot of the immigrant in a new land that had promised them prosperity.

Salverson's poverty narrative directly challenges nationalist myths of prosperity and opportunity. While Laurence's *The Diviners* resolved in novelistic fashion the class tensions which it exposed, Salverson's *Confessions* critiques nation in the autobiographical and testimonial mode, and thus cannot save Canada from the ideological implications of its own practices. Instead, Salverson offers detailed proof of exploitation of immigrant workers in the form of salaries, living expenses, and working conditions, but at the same time uses narrative strategies of appeasement to soften the blow for Canadian readers. Relating how poverty inspired mass exodus of her people from Iceland to Canada and the United States but then awaited them on the shores of the New World, Salverson offers testimony as well as confession to class distinction in the New World. Perhaps the contentiousness of her representation of a New World divided by class may have caused the text to be overlooked in the context of the study of national literature; it was out of print for many years even though it won the Governor General's Award when it first appeared in 1939. Salverson's autobiography has received little critical attention despite recent feminist recovery projects in Canadian literature, perhaps because of her depiction of two classes of women divided by social boundaries.

Confessions covers roughly the years from 1880 to 1923. K.P. Stich's

---

11 Itwaru's first study was more analytical of class divisions among minority and majority ethnic groups than his later works in which he openly announced his growing lack of empathy, as an ethnically Othered Canadian, with the class plight of white working-class subjects in Canada.

introduction to the later edition argues that the text can be read as a 'psycho-history of nation-building in the multi-ethnic west,' partly because Salverson rejected the American 'melting-pot' model of assimilation of immigrants in favour of the Canadian mosaic. Stich identifies Salverson's two main social themes as immigration and feminism, without taking into account her historical and political insights into class and poverty in the New World. Yet even the chapter headings indicate the importance of class discourse and an insider's knowledge of poverty – 'A kitchen-view of society, ' 'Job-hunting,' 'The working world,' 'Readjustment and the righteous few,' 'False security' – along with open indictments of unfair labour practices: '"Servant, be obedient unto your masters, as unto the lord your God." What a glorious whip that had been in the hands of pious exploiters!' (319).

Salverson's materialist feminism is also openly critical of the divisions between women and especially of bourgeois women's insensitivity to their material and moral privilege. The following, from her standpoint as a domestic servant, is one of several intimations of her outrage at the double standards used to define two classes of womanhood:

> How scandalised [the mistress of the house] would have been to read my thoughts! ... every beautiful thing in that house intensified my resentment against the cruel inequalities of life. It was not that I coveted any of these domestic trappings. Things in themselves meant little to me, for all my yearning centred in the world of books. It was the atmosphere these things created, the sense of security and well-being, that made gracious living a matter of course. It was the contrast of this home as against [a poor friend's] dead dwelling that set me thinking. Laura had brains and ability and a burning desire to better herself. To what good? She was starving in a cheap little room, for the sake of peace! Exaggeration? Well, I wondered how Miss Vera would manage her placid graces on ten dollars a month, six of which went for a bed, a patch of hall carpet, and a pine bureau! I wondered then, as I wonder now, how the fine moralists expect a girl to feed and clothe herself on ten dollars a month, in honour! (327)

Salverson critiques the idleness and 'gracious living' of bourgeois women, their naiveté about the limited choices available to working-class women, and their numerous small affectations which signal privilege (such as the manner some had of pulling back their skirts so as not to be contaminated by touching servant women). She also calls into question the universal application of bourgeois standards of feminine morality to women who are too poor to be protected within a patriarchal class system.

Relatively negative assessments of the book by recent feminist critics indicate that Salverson's challenge to bourgeois constructions of gender may still be sufficiently contentious to irritate or at least confuse. For example, feminist readings have assessed the autobiography according to idealized notions of feminist self and ethnic communities while devaluing the impact of class-consciousness and class anger on female identity in *Confessions*. Barbara Powell's 'Laura Goodman Salverson: Her Father's "Own True Son"' criticizes the writer for being too male-identified, for disdaining childbearing, and for failing to bond with her mother: 'She never did learn an *authentic woman's tongue* to tell her own story' (emphasis added, 78). Powell's unspoken standard for an authentic woman's tongue seems to be at odds with many of the class aspects of Salverson's subject position. For example, Salverson was estranged from her mother partly because she disliked the sombre pragmatism that befell her mother as a result of constantly having to 'make do' on so little and pick up house and move. Similarly, Salverson's disdain for childbearing grew directly out of her fear of not having enough to go around and awareness of how unplanned parenthood could exacerbate family problems – and not, as Powell suggests, merely out of fear of her female body. Kristjana Gunnars's 'Laura Goodman Salverson's Confessions of a Divided Self' identifies the autobiography as a site of negative recollections of Icelandic life and the inability of the author to unite the writerly and ethnic selves into a *coherent* self. Gunnars neglects to explain to what extent these negative scenes are based on social realism that exposes economic exploitation of the Icelanders in their own country. Each of these critiques interprets the autobiographical self by holding it up beside a tacitly invoked feminist or ethnic minority self against which they measure it and find it somehow different or wanting. Yet both overlook poverty as a root cause of this 'divided identity' and an alternative source of identification which may override ethnic, gender, and national loyalties. Salverson's oppositional class discourse in *Confessions* is subtly downplayed in such critiques despite the fact that it is blatant and crucial to the construction of identity. (More recent articles reverse this trend by discussing Salverson's controversial politics and class identification.)

Salverson's family was declassed by the immigration experience, and although she eventually became a successful writer, most of the experiences recounted in *Confessions* centre on working-class people and struggles with poverty, though not in any strictly politicized or Marxist sense of class-consciousness. Salverson's critiques of unpaid domestic labour and childbearing operate within this class-conscious ethos which abhors the fact that two classes of women have different experiences and choices in the matter of reproductive rights, a class difference she witnesses while working in her aunt's midwifery and abortion clinic (332–3). Her personal fear, bordering on repugnance, of being tied down by an unwanted pregnancy and what that meant to her in terms of impoverishment and lack of life choices could be better understood if it were read alongside other working-class women's autobiographies, such as Agnes Smedley's similar account of an American poor woman's reluctance to mother children in *Daughter of Earth* or Carolyn Steedman's account of limited and resentful mothering in *Landscape for a Good Woman*. This is not to say that mothering is always compromised by poverty, for other works, whether autobiographical or fictional, have dramatized the heightened importance of mothering when the system fails to care for the poor (consider, for example, *The Women of Brewster Place* and *Bonheur d'occasion*).

The problem which I am trying to signal here is that reading practices may overlook marginal sensibilities situated in the experiences of poverty or tend to devalue these oppositional strains according to a limited aesthetics based on bourgeois assumptions about gender, ethnicity, or nation. I have already addressed the issue of class division in respect to feminist theory in chapter 4. Now, however, I would like to argue that *Confessions* is an important text to be recovered by Canadian literary study (it was out of print again at the time I wrote this book) precisely because it challenges bourgeois constructions of nation and gender through testimonies of classed experiences.

Viewing history with an epic sweep, Salverson's autobiography relates individual experiences within the context of broader historical events and conditions such as mass Icelandic migrations to Canada, Canadian immigration propaganda, homesteading laws in Canada and tenant farming in the United States, the crowded living quarters of early urbanization, the sweatshops of early industrialization, and the advent of the First World War. Despite the title's suggestion of a private exploration of identity, the most engaging narrative strategy in Salverson's autobiography is not the construction of a private, writerly Self (which she often achieves through stilted romantic language), but her social testimony. In a personal and reflective voice, Salverson testifies to the disappointment of impoverished immigrants who did not have the equity to buy into the promise of New World prosperity.

Interestingly, K.P. Stich interprets the 'confessions' in the title as an implicit challenge to early feminist fears that the arrival of non-British immigrant women would dilute the ethnic frontier society in the West with moral laxity and ethnic inferiority (vi–vii). Stich also implies that Salverson's position as a 'stranger within our gates' enabled her to see more clearly the systemic injustices in the New World (which Stich himself euphemizes as the 'male-oriented aspect' of New World 'materialism' rather than class exploitation). It is also possible that Salverson's refusal to be shamed or defeated by poverty and thus her ability to critique it in the New World came from a different cultural perspective. Certainly, she valorized the spirituality of poverty in a way uncharacteristic of North American and British culture since the Middle Ages.

The first edition of her autobiography is dedicated to a doctor who treated her through a dangerous childhood illness: 'for his devotion to the poor.' She also admired a male boarder who ate bread and milk after every meal as a ritual to symbolize his connectedness with poor ancestors. Furthermore, according to Salverson's Icelandic culture, the role of national poets was to sustain people's spirit against 'the inertia of woeful poverty' – hence the inclusion of the poor in the national imaginary and the national culture (75–6). This different cultural view of poverty, which located it on the inside of the national paradigm, insisted on the importance of a common culture of literacy, a knowledge of folk and high literature, critical reflection and articulation, and cultural access for all members of the community, no matter how poor. In contrast to this ideal, Salverson saw insularity, racism, classism, crass materialism, and inadequate education in the New World culture.

But Salverson also indicted the inhumanity of economic systems which exploited labour around the world – beginning with the German-owned trade monopolies in Iceland which constituted the severe 'economic slavery' that spurred mass Icelandic exodus to Canada, especially to the sweatshops of Winnipeg which were hungry for cheap immigrant labour. Thus an international frame is frequently given to the mechanisms of exploitation and exclusion which she finds in the New World.

But without money, the man who had dependents stood no better chance of attaining financial security in old Winnipeg than his fellow workers in other cities of the world.

> A little plain arithmetic may absolve me from wilful heresy. Mr. Brant's wage scale, it has been seen, made it almost impossible for a piece-worker to earn more than five or six dollars a week. Which, at the most, adds up to twenty-four dollars a month. From that, at least five dollars must be deducted for house rent; another three or four for firewood and kerosene during moderately cold weather, and usually twice that amount in the bitter winter months. At best, then, that leaves only fifteen dollars to spread over the needs of an entire family – that is to say, for food, and clothing, and medical services, and such incidentals as even the poor cannot evade ...
>
> A little quiet speculation on these seemingly low prices, as seen in ratio to the wages paid, will prove, I think, that the average immigrant family that strove to maintain some sort of respectability under these conditions might just as well have dreamed of a mansion on the moon as of sharing in the many profitable opportunities which were open to men of a little means. (86–7)

Salverson's depictions of sweatshops in the early days of Canadian industrialization are rare in our national literature, largely because they are not usually deemed the subject of art. One can see why a nation bound on inscribing its history as prosperous and democratic would choose to forget the daily conditions of a father's hard labour, the shady practices by factory owners to keep profits up and operation costs down, and the paltry buying power of workers' wages. The myth of progress common to the New World and industrialization promised greater prosperity, but it was not until workers protested their lot that the 'progress' would be shared.

Having stated, rather apologetically, at the outset of a chapter called 'First taste of the New World,' that her intention is not 'to recount all the melancholy privations through which [her] family struggled,' Salverson self-consciously rejects the conventional form of extreme icons and a sequence of hardships, and turns instead to a highly detailed and thoughtful depiction of how the systems of power and social boundaries ensnared her family and their neighbours, especially women, in poverty (88). She goes to great lengths to substantiate her claims as a strategy of testimony: the mathematical calculations, the detailed descriptions of food rations, the explanation of employment policies, anecdotes about class prejudice – all contribute to proving the systemic causes of poverty. Yet Salverson just as frequently apologizes for the negative reports as a strategy of appeasement. For example, the title of the conclusion, 'So Dreams Come True!,' echoes the New World myths after having exposed them as fictional (412), but ironically the word 'dreams' here refers to the author's private dreams of cultural inclusion and of having her first book published, rather than to material success. In a gesture of appeasement, she describes her book as a 'burnt offering to lay upon the altar of her New Country, out of the love of a small, passionate heart' (414), but even here she contrasts culture to the nation-building strategies of materialism. Of the difficulties facing a poor immigrant who tries to express herself against the dominant imaginary in the form of a book, she asks, 'How to do it in a strange, new language? How to do it, in the face of poverty and isolation, and the cold indifference of an alien people? How to hold to a purpose that no one counts as precious as a new-turned furrow, a pelt of furs, or a load of grain?' (414). The low worth of art and writing in a materialist, settler culture is called into question here by an immigrant from a highly literate culture, but so is the difficulty of testifying to poverty against the powerful, national dream of material progress when the truth is that progress is not shared equally. Thus testimonies by the poor in Canada must navigate into public view bearing evidence of the underdeveloped side of the developed nation. They can help us to interrogate nation in useful ways by forcing us to see development and prosperity in a more inclusive way.

Chapter 8

The Long View: Contexts of Oppositional Criticism

When reading poverty narratives, how can we will ourselves to see beyond cultural walls that privilege high over popular, bourgeois over working-class, intellectual over everyday culture, and authors over 'ordinary' people? And once we have begun to see beyond cultural walls, how can we avoid reinscribing theoretical mastery over the ordinary voices of subjects who are poor? How can the academic study of the voices of the poor result in meaningful forms of cultural inclusion when so few of the poor will read these studies or have access to this debate? On a purely pragmatic level, it is easy to see that there is a need to improve the visibility of poverty and class in academic discourse in the same way in which gender and race have been elevated to consciousness recently. If teachers are more sensitive to the politics of the erasure and silencing of the poor, the classroom may become a site of public dialogue about lived realities and cultural formations. I know from my own experience that very young children come to know poverty as a site of shame in an intensely private way and could be relieved of some of this burden early on if poverty were openly discussed as a state caused by material circumstances rather than an inherent lack. I also know that adult readers often fail to read poverty when they lack the life knowledge or political imaginary to understand how subjects can be constrained by poverty or contest it. This final chapter takes the long view of oppositional criticism to interrogate academic discourse and, specifically, the field of knowledge known as cultural studies as sites of opposition against poverty. A 'toolkit of theory' might be deployed to explain poverty in a respectful rather than a totalizing way, as we see by reviewing debates about the efficacy of theory to enlighten oppositional criticism.

8.1 Cultural Studies as a Site of Resistance

A very important step in my academic search for oppositional ways of reading poverty was to recognize that I would have to go beyond the approaches offered by literary studies, traditional schools of Marxist analysis, and image-of-poverty studies to model new strategies of interpreting poverty in the broader, interdisciplinary field of cultural studies. Although a brand of cultural studies which focuses on gender, race, consumerism, and media technologies – but rarely on class – is currently emerging as a popular new field in literature departments, in the late 1980s and early 1990s, when I was beginning to conceive of this project, there were no such offerings in most literature departments in Canada. I discovered the possibility of interdisciplinary cultural studies and the British school's interest in class studies only after imagining poverty narratives as a category and having to defend such a category rigorously against criticisms that it was 'too sociological' or 'too negative' a construct.

Moving from literary into cultural studies, with its broadened field of cultural artifacts, however, is not a significant enough change in itself to legitimize a new oppositional, academic space such as poverty narratives. Furthermore, the simple fact of studying images of poverty within the broadened field of cultural studies cannot guarantee a shared political project as the basis of decoding culture. This was brought home to me a few years ago when a cultural studies professor, knowing of my research on poverty, spread before me a pricey art book of avant-garde photographs of the rooms and street corners where homeless people had camped. He thumbed through the black-and-white still shots, earnestly sharing his passion for the stark settings, the empty camps, the scanty bedding, the tin cups: the hyperrealist details of sites of deprivation. To me, however, the book was somehow offensive; the photographs seemed like frozen moments captured, dehistoricized, and marketed for aesthetic consumption in a museum. I was dumbfounded that there were no people in the pictures and depressed that privileged university professors could aestheticize the need and deprivation of others without regard for their subjectivities. (I have been shown rare and pricey art books on poverty and homelessness several times in the course of my study by well-meaning academics and colleagues.) This stylized staging of cultural erasure made a lot of sense to my colleague, whose postmodern theoretical position was that the poor, as subalterns, cannot speak or be represented, but lie outside the dominant symbol systems of language itself, forced to deform their own subjectivities through a language not their own. But the way this glossy artwork was being made to stand in for the subjectivities of the poor clashed with my own knowledge of the radical possibility of cultural agency among oppressed people and the crucial role of intellectuals in facilitating this agency. I also felt like the working-class audience described by Pierre Bourdieu in *Distinction: A Sociology of the Judgement Taste* who resisted reacting to a photo of a worker's gnarled hands aesthetically like the bourgeois audience who saw the photo as 'art.' Instead, Bourdieu observed, the working-class audience empathized with the worker and wondered about the details of his or her life. Out of such contrasts in attitudes and approaches to culture and counterculture the question arises: How can cultural studies, as a broadened field of study, promise to interrogate images of poverty in respect to lived power relations when it houses such conflicting ethical, political, and aesthetic positions?

We can assume no agreement among cultural critics on how they will interpret the politics of the image because cultural studies analyses practices and artifacts with such an array of methodologies and from such different, if not opposing, political positions. The liveliness of the current debate over the nature of this field of knowledge suggests that one cannot guarantee ethical or political self-reflection just because an object of study – in this case, poverty narratives – is located within it. Instead, in order to discern the politics of the image of poverty, one must negotiate a space between the claims of various schools of cultural studies. Cultural studies has tended to construct its own history in the image of a liberally broadened field of academic inquiry, which varies according to particular critics or schools. For example, the editors of the voluminous *Cultural Studies*, Lawrence Grossberg, Cary Nelson, and Paula Treichler, navigate through diverse metaphors of cultural studies – as 'alchemy,' 'process,' 'bricolage,' 'theoretical transplants,' and 'utopian moments' – relating them to different institutional practices in specific historical and national contexts. Although they conclude that the new field defies definition according to traditional notions of disciplinary territory, they do not hesitate to provide a long list of what it most emphatically is *not* and of what it 'calls for' (12–13). They emphasize, for example, that cultural studies is not simply the study of the domain of popular culture, or the erasure of the line between high and popular culture; it is, rather, the interrogation of that line (6). They also claim that cultural studies calls for more than the discussion or recovery of cultural objects and practices; it also calls for their positioning in a broader field that is self-consciously political. Similarly, Cary Nelson's earlier manifesto for cultural studies protested that merely introducing new objects of knowledge into a broadened field of study was not a legitimate concern for cultural studies because the new field should not merely study the artifacts of popular culture, or simply recover subaltern or subcultural voices, but, instead, should self-consciously construct a historical narrative around the act of cultural recovery (31–2). Yet others, such as Antony Easthope in *Literary into Cultural Studies*, have argued that new cultural practices and artifacts should be uncovered but never from a position of mastery that inserts them into a historical narrative. Arguing that the epistemological advantage of cultural studies over literary studies is rooted in the movement away from author-centred analytical paradigms and absolutist aesthetics, Easthope warned that promoting any political/ historical narrative at this point in cultural studies might compromise that epistemological advantage by newly limiting the field of inquiry to yet another master narrative. Similarly, in 'An American in Birmingham,' Grossberg describes a postmodernist conjuncturalist stage in cultural studies that precludes fixed ideological positions and calls instead for an 'amoeba-like' shape-shifting on the part of the critic, who eludes fixed positions, a politics with which I take issue in the conclusion to the present study.

Whereas the culturalist strain, as based on early British class criticism by Richard Hoggart, Raymond Williams, and E.P. Thompson, has always articulated a coherent project for class analysis as a means of democratizing the field of academic discourse, largely because this strain is rooted in a long tradition of Marxist cultural criticism, other, more recent, schools do not necessarily share this political project. For example, the structuralist school of cultural studies reads new cultural voices and artifacts more as a shared epistemological project, as a way of knowing more about the symbolic practices of culture: for instance sports, pornography, music, advertisements, the body, the self, television sitcoms, movie stars, et cetera. Consequently, the reason the culturalist school has had a more coherent political project of recovery of marginalized voices than structuralist or conjunctural schools is precisely because the former extends academic discourse to politically suppressed areas and explores knowledge from these areas as part of a political 'will to know' – for instance, the realm of the everyday and the personal in working-class experience.

Although the inclusiveness of early culturalist works such as Richard Hoggart's *The Uses of Literacy* and Raymond Williams's *Culture and Society* are increasingly open to question by feminist, post-Marxist, and postcolonial critics, they set the tone for engaged forms of cultural studies projects in spirit as well as in theoretical goals by stressing the will to expose hegemony through the detailed and politically engaged analysis of cultural practices. As Simon During and Patrick Brantlinger have both commented, the limitation of the structuralist school of cultural studies has been that it fails to say *why* it was reading new cultural objects or to go beyond the semiotic interpretation of the cultural object's power to signify in the interrogation of cultural practices. The advantage of the structuralist school, on the other hand, has been to renew the culturalist project of recovery by making available more techniques of how to read the recovered voices in ways other than simply as part of a master historical narrative or monolithic categories of class difference which are themselves open to question in a post-structuralist age.[1]

Unfortunately, the emerging field of cultural studies in Canada has begun to inscribe its own evolutionary history as one that *naturally* steers away from class issues, apparently because North American academics are more interested in aesthetic and textual issues than they are in cultural intervention into lived power relations. According to Valda Blundell and the other editors of *Relocating Cultural Studies: Developments in Theory and Research*, although Canadian cultural studies is rooted in the class-conscious British school, its dominant concerns have been renegotiated to fit a North American context – which means the evolution of a less politically engaged critique with more concern for the

---

1 Given increasingly complex theories of political projects and of class formations under global corporate capitalism, however, contemporary studies of the political function of intellectuals (such as those recently mapped by John Guillory, Stuart Hall, Stanley Aronowitz, Pierre Bourdieu, and Pamela Fox) no longer harness cultural studies to a closed, master historical narrative. They take a longer view of intellectual labour than structuralist projects to discern the historical contingency of theoretical choices and how they respond to shifts in lived power relations inside and outside the university. Be that as it may, since class inquiry and cultural intervention are clearly such disputed goals among the various schools of cultural studies, the way academic fields of perception are broadened in respect to class and poverty still depends on the epistemological, political, or ethical choices by each cultural critic involved in specific projects and the specific institutional contexts in which these critics function.

textual construction of identities, especially those of indigenous peoples in white-dominated society. Though I would agree that this overview describes the political conservatism of Canadian cultural studies and its noticeably greater ease with racial, ethnic, gender, and sexual than with class identities, I would argue that these tendencies should not be naturalized as a symptom of transnational global capitalism or the geographic relocation of cultural studies to North America. The 'failure' of Canadian cultural studies to focus on class realities is an extension of that pre-existing 'failure' in Canadian literary studies to form a highly visible and influential school on the basis of class study. This blind spot should not be naturalized as a geopolitical occurrence, for it is in direct contrast to the active engagement with class issues in the social sciences in Canada. Consequently, although as an institution and a publishing industry the literary arm of cultural studies in Canada appears to be as complicit in reproducing the image of the nation as a classless society as earlier literary studies were, this turning away from the subject of class and poverty is a result of conscious critical and institutional choices, not natural evolution or alliances.

In Canada the institutionalization of cultural studies has, regrettably, not strengthened or unified dispersed studies of class relations in Canadian literature and culture (for example, those by Ben-Zion Shek, Robin Mathews, Dorothy Livesay, Tom Wayman, Dorothy Smith, John Porter, Dionne Brand, Makeda Silvera, Arun Mukherjee, and Rick Salutin) into a new field or school. Instead, Canadian cultural studies has invested largely in epistemological questions such as how high theory can be used to decode and legitimize popular culture as an object of study and how sociology can illuminate the repercussions of technological knowedge industries and corporate-controlled media (see Will Straw's overview of Canadian cultural studies that discusses shifting alliances and relative status of disciplines within the university as shaping forces in the content and boundaries of the field). Even among cultural studies critics, feminists, postcolonialists, multicultural critics, and gay, African-American, and Native critics, class still remains the strongest taboo in the academic construction of Canadian culture within the humanities – the word that falls the fastest to the floor at a wine-and-cheese party. During a conference at the University of Toronto in 1994 (Cultural Studies in Canada), although the absence of the Left was the subject of comment in plenary sessions, none the less papers on Oprah Winfrey and mass culture monopolized centre stage throughout the conference, while papers dealing with class were ghettoized into separate, poorly attended panels on 'the Left' in back rooms. Few audience members challenged the way Canadian cultural studies was being constructed in the absence of counter-cultural subjectivities or a more inclusive and radical notion of cultural intervention. The editors of *Relocating Cultural Studies*, on the other hand, have noted a split between cultural studies' analysis of everyday life and those who may not be able to read these analyses even though they grasp the realities of their own lived experiences. To acknowledge this gap between cultural studies theory and those excluded from academia, they suggest we keep asking who cultural studies is for in Canada and if it can make a difference.[2] This book keeps such pragmatic questions in mind by recognizing at the outset that 'cultural invasion' of the poor and working class is a lived reality in Canada as it is elsewhere in the world, and that academic study may be complicit in this invasion and/or serve to counter it, or at the very least, expose it (Freire 1970, 133).

Paulo Freire, the great Brazilian educator, has urged that academics engage in *dialogue* with the oppressed in order to inform theory and praxis and avoid recolonizing the cultural spaces of oppressed people by making them into objects of study. When dominant groups refuse to listen to oppressed people's subjectivities, Freire observed, a form of 'cultural invasion' takes place in support of systemic oppression: '[i]n this phenomenon, the invaders penetrate the cultural context of another group, in disrespect of the latter's potentialities; they impose their own view of the world upon those they invade and inhibit the creativity of the invaded by curbing their expression' (1970, 133). Freire maintained that cultural synthesis will take place not when oppressed people become more familiar to intellectuals as *objects* of study but when they leave behind their status as objects of someone else's cultural imaginings to become the subjects of their own stories. Intellectuals play a bridging role between the oppressed and emerging

---

2 It is important to remember, after all, that the Birmingham School embraced marginalized subjects not only by making them objects of study but also through an extensive university outreach program of adult education that sought to equip working-class subjects with the tools for analysing their own relation to culture (During). In Canada, similar efforts of outreach – say, for example, that of Frontier College to educate illiterate workers on the work site – have not aimed for the same high level of critical analysis. I am not aware that any of the cultural studies programs in Canadian universities are currently invested in adult education outreach programs, unless of course one counts the passive form of TV university.

oppositional culture during cultural revolution, according to both Freire and Gramsci, because they listen to oppressed subjects who are capable of theorizing their own oppression and then lead the oppressed to greater subjecthood and greater cultural power in the public sphere. Freire describes the bridging function as leading others to critical cultural analysis of their own lived experience of oppression: 'Thus cooperation leads dialogical Subjects to focus their attention on the reality which mediates them and which – posed as a problem – challenges them. The response to that challenge is the action of the dialogical Subjects upon reality in order to transform it. Let me reemphasize that posing reality as a problem does not mean sloganizing: it means critical analysis of a problematic reality' (149). The shift of focus from orderly theory to the detailed consideration of disorderly culture is crucial to breaking down the homogenizing image of the poor as Other. For example, it allows us to regard marginalized narratives as alternative knowledge forms that are sufficiently complex in and of themselves as testimonies and minority theories that they cannot be contained or made coherent by theory alone. It also recognizes that many oppressed subjects have not had access to the production of cultural theory in any academically legitimate sense, but that they are, none the less, capable of theorizing their own oppression from their own standpoint. The most critical theoretical position to take in interrogating the politics of representations of poverty is the position that no *one* theory of class or poverty, no single social or literary theory, can explain adequately the complexity of classed experiences as they are lived and reproduced through culture.

8.2 A Toolkit of Theory

The struggle for a new discursive space in which to discuss poverty narratives oppositionally takes place on two levels concurrently: theory, and recovery of works through (re)reading. Seepage of narratives into theory and theory into the reading of narratives is evidence that my own exploratory work came about through the constant cross-fertilization between texts and cultural theory. Yet part of the originality of the study is its refusal to impose one system of theory or one reading methodology to sum up or contain the meaning of poverty narratives. Instead, I use theory as a 'toolkit' in the tradition of cultural studies to avoid reducing the complex, lived, cultural phenomena to oversimplified abstractions, especially when studying the subjectivities of previously silenced people. Indeed, it seems good sense to adopt a praxis-oriented approach to theories of poverty and culture by constructing what Gilles Deleuze and Michel Foucault have described as a 'toolkit' of relevant theories: 'The notion of theory as a toolkit means (i) The theory to be constructed is not a system but an instrument, a logic of the specificity of power relations and the struggles around them; (ii) That this investigation can only be carried out step by step on the basis of reflection (which will necessarily be historical in some of its aspects on given situations)' (Foucault 1980, 140, and 1977, 208, as quoted by Clifford 23). Detailed and praxis-oriented theories and reading practices allow us to bring new knowledge from the marginal standpoints of the poor to bear on the interpretation of culture. A 'toolkit' of theory would include relevant theories on poverty and class along with other forms of knowing about and witnessing poverty. The oppositional reading practices I have proposed deploy minority theories along with the testimonial power of certain minority voices to decode representations of poverty. This results in an intentionally disorderly methodology that refuses to construct linear or master narratives about the poor and cultural representation in Canada, but instead proceeds step by step in a fragmentary way.

A significant breakthrough for me in collecting and reading these narratives was the decision not to impose order on poverty narratives as a group by prematurely trying to identify themes and patterns among them. Instead, a flexible and detailed focus on coherence rather than a broad concern for commonality among the narratives is needed so that the critic is always ready to learn from the various elements of poverty and subjectivities as they emerge. Respect for the disorderly details of culture as a source of knowledge is not new in cultural studies or in Marxist history-from-below. But such flexibility and fluidity, such disorder in an analytical paradigm, made Canadianists in literature departments queasy, and I myself spent painful years ready to abandon the project because I had begun to doubt my ability to make sense of the 'disorder' of considering everyday and popular utterances about poverty beside literary ones. When I discovered that this was a valid and reputable approach to culture, especially culture-from-below (incidentally, within a comparative literature department where international theory rather than national literature framed objects of study), it liberated me to move beyond the censure of more traditional literary approaches to continue reading poverty narratives.

Clifford Geertz theorized that anthropology should keep 'close to the ground,' meaning responsive to the complexity of cultural events themselves: 'Believing with Max Weber, that man [sic] is an animal suspended in webs of significance he himself has spun, I take culture to be those webs, and the analysis of it to be therefore not an experimental science in search of law but an interpretive one in search of meaning' (5). It followed for Geertz that theory should in some sense subordinate itself to culture in order to be informed by it because '[c]ultural analysis is intrinsically incomplete. And, worse than that, the more deeply it goes, the less complete it becomes' (29). Accordingly, although the academic who theorizes about culture should retain self-reflexiveness about his or her own method of interpretation and observation, Geertz argued, this self-reflection should draw attention not to the theory itself or mere theoretical eloquence but to how cultural events are suspended within many webs of meaning, academic theory being only one or two strands of these.

Geertz argued for the 'thick description' of culture according to which academics (in particular, participant/observers of cultural Others in anthropology) question the meaning of cultural behaviour or cultural artifacts from many sides: taking into account more information about the object of knowledge – for example, the relation between subjects and the academic observer. Thick description also includes actor-oriented symbol systems which allow us to base academic interpretations of other people's behaviour according to their own symbol systems – on what their behaviour *means to them*. While Gramsci, Freire, and other radical cultural critics (for example, Janet Zandy, Barbara Christian, Linda Alcoff, and Carolyn Steedman, whose works I discuss in chapter 4, 'Theories and Anti-Theory') have stressed the political, ethical, and epistemological advantages of listening respectfully to cultural Others, Geertz stresses 'informed listening' for primarily epistemological reasons – in other words, not through the 'political will to know' but simply through the will to know more about culture. The control on the problematic passage from microscopic observation to generalizations about culture, from minute details of everyday life and behaviour to larger landscapes and units of meaning such as nation, the epoch, the continent, or the civilization (21), is that theory would not predict meaning but would occur *post facto* of cultural events and only then participate self-consciously in the academic construction of culture (26). This anthropological perspective on listening to details and minority voices and theorizing *post facto* is useful to the reading of poverty narratives or working-class narratives because it trains cultural analysis not primarily on theory as a totalizing system, but on the relation between theory and concrete realities, so that analysis 'will not lose touch with the hard surfaces of life' (Geertz 30). That does not mean that the academic comes to cultural events empty-handed, simply to watch, Geertz cautions, but that we come with many theories in hand, ready to use them or abandon them or even refine them in the process of seeking new, more suitable ones (27); or, as James Clifford put it in his essay on ethnographic authority, borrowing from Deleuze and Foucault, whom I quoted earlier, carrying 'a toolkit' of theories rather than being hemmed in by a system of theory (23).

Earlier calls for more detailed, cultural study of class Others by Marxist critics preceded these developments in modern-day cultural studies. Antonio Gramsci called for the 'integral' and detailed, although *necessarily fragmented*, historicizing of subaltern experience and the contextualization of culture in terms of local, national, and international history (54–6). Later in *The Poverty of Theory*, E.P. Thompson argued at length that theory cannot know everything about the experience of class. He was asserting the value of complex history and experience against the flattening tendency of any one class theory, which always refers back to itself and its totalizing power as a science of political ideology. Thompson's mistrust of theory targeted the Althusserian school of post-Marxism for displacing more historically rooted schools of Marxist cultural criticism and for elevating the power of theory over historical materialism and, by extension, the power of academics who wield such theory over that of working-class subjects to free themselves from the oppressive workings of ideology as agents in their own right. Thompson argued vigorously against elevating theory in this way because he wanted to defend two very important principles of Marxist philosophy: that history matters to how we perceive culture and live it, and that ordinary people are capable both of understanding history and of acting as agents of cultural and historical change. The poverty of theory – and this would apply to theories of poverty as well – is that it does not know as much about the details and feelings of lived power relations as the people who live them.

My own intellectual mistrust of, and also fascination with, theory arises from the fact that my lived experiences growing up poor in Canada have never been adequately explained by any one theory of poverty or class. Instead, I have recognized the texture of my youth in the disorderly details and fragmented nature of poverty narratives as diverse testimonies. The problematic reality of growing up poor in small-town Canada means being cut off from the affirming traditions of working-class culture. To my knowledge, no one in the town I grew up in called her or himself 'working class,' but everyone knew who was poor. And no one I grew up with organized against the exploitation of his or her labour, although people complained about work, or the lack of it, almost every day. In school, our geography and history lessons carefully avoided parts of the map where proletarian revolutions had occurred – we were taught nothing of the Chinese Long March, the Russian Revolution, or Cuban Liberation. In my youth, I never heard anyone speak proudly about class identity based on manual labour. And there was little sense of the 'us' and 'them' described by Richard Hoggart as characteristic of the cohesiveness of British working-class culture, or if there was, we kept it to ourselves.

This lack of a clearly formulated class theory in the everyday lives of many Canadians is reflected in the literature on poverty. For example, in *The Diviners*, Morag finds out only in university what 'lumpenproletariat' means but feels it unfair to label the people from her past in that way; and in *Who Do You Think You Are?*, the protagonist comes home from college telling her stepmother they live in the 'working-class part of town,' and her stepmother comments wryly '*Working* class? ... Not if the ones around here can help it' (Laurence 180, Munro 90). Few Canadian poverty narratives articulate everyday struggle in terms of class politics; instead, many protagonists denounce or sidestep Marxist politics as too extreme or too remote from their own experiences to represent them (for instance, protagonists who denounce collective action or class politics in Hugh Garner's *Cabbagetown*, Adele Wiseman's *Crackpot*, David Adams Richards's *Road to the Stilt House*, Percy Janes's *House of Hate*, and Nellie McClung's *Painted Fires*).

The isolating, unnamed class experiences in many Canadian poverty narratives and in my own life bear little resemblance to the theories of working-class community that have characterized British cultural studies, American studies of proletarian literature, or even Canadian labour histories (that have so often focused on urban, market- and labour-based, and male-centred experiences of class solidarity and class identity). It was precisely the absence of class theory in the lives of poor people in my hometown that left us open to self-blame, low expectations, and complicity in a classist system that most of us could not name. This is not to say that all Canadians experience poverty and class in the same way; a minority of poverty narratives do testify to the ability of poor subjects to see shared class interests politically and externalize blame through class anger or affirm solidarity through class identity (Sand, Potrebenko, Baird). Although an explicitly Marxist discourse is seldom spoken, diverse counter-cultural imaginings help the otherwise stigmatized and isolated subjects to create an 'alternative status-honour group' (Waxman) or an alternative sense of self and community as viable strategies of reconstituting identity (as I have shown in interpretations of Cy-Thea Sand's 'A Question of Identity,' Maria Campbell's *Halfbreed*, Sheila Baxter's *No Way to Live: Poor Women Speak Out*, and Laura Goodman Salverson's *Confessions of an Immigrant's Daughter* in chapters 5 and 7).

To understand the scarcity of images of open class struggle by the poor in Canadian culture it is useful to draw on a variety of sociological theories on the retreat of class identity under consumer capitalism in North America. Stanley Aronowitz's *The Politics of Identity: Class, Culture, Social Movements* interrogates the role of corporate power, the media, and intellectuals in buttressing North American social fictions of universal wealth and prosperity to the detriment of more realistic and politicized narratives of class-consciousness. In *The Hidden Injuries of Class*, Richard Sennett and Jonathan Cobb argue that the injured dignity of the poor and working class in North America which emerges in the absence of class identification serves a logical, though perhaps largely unconscious, function in maintaining class hegemony: 'society injures human dignity in order to weaken people's ability to fight against the limits class imposes on their freedom' (153). As long as people see themselves to be personally responsible for their inability to advance within a meritocracy, they will not feel class anger, but rather, Sennett and Cobb argue, a fiercer competition and commitment to work harder and acquire more material possessions or, conversely, a more docile acceptance of their inherent inferiority. Sennett and Cobb disagree that a higher living standard and better working conditions in North America explain the declining sense of class identification among the poor and working class. It is not that class consciousness has been 'bought off' in North America, they argue, but rather that the injuries of a class system have become internalized, hidden, and depoliticized – largely through social fictions about the ordinary people as 'masses' whose inherent inability keeps them from meriting respect and material success:

> The reason the 'prejudiced' image exists at all is that it serves a purpose, as does this whole scheme of individuals recognized and respected by

virtue of ability. This purpose is to continue the iniquities of the world of nineteenth-century industrial capitalism – on new terrain. And just as the material penalties of the old capitalism fell hardest on the workers, despite the fact that both rich and poor might be alienated by the work, so now the moral burdens and the emotional hardships of class are the thorniest and most concentrated among manual labourers. (76)

Similarly, in *The Other America: Poverty in the United States*, Michael Harrington explains how the invisibility of the poor serves a hegemonic function in consumer society, and a function especially suited to a North American meritocracy in which, theoretically, everyone has the opportunity to achieve upward mobility: 'But the new poverty is constructed so as to destroy aspiration; it is a system designed to be impervious to hope. The other America does not contain the adventurous seeking a new life and land. It is populated by the failures, by those driven from the land and bewildered by the city, by old people suddenly confronted with the torment of loneliness and poverty, and by minorities facing a wall of prejudice' (10). As discussed later, Harrington's image of the poor is complicit in the perspective that the 'culture of poverty' is primarily negative, engendering hopelessness among the poor but little potential for agency.

As previously mentioned, leading academic theories of poverty in the West have been analysed by David L. Harvey and Michael Reed according to whether or not they posit a negative subculture of poverty and whether or not this subculture is blamed before systemic causes for producing poverty. Harvey and Reed conclude that the ideological assumptions behind sociological theories often remain covert but none the less determine which theories will have the greatest institutional circulation in North America. Even at the university level, when the subject of poverty is itself on the table, it seems that there is determined looking away from the market causes of poverty and issues of identity rooted in class differences. There is a predictable tendency, instead, to normalize and legitimize class privilege, if only by leaving class assumptions in literature unquestioned in our construction of culture.

Even though the readings of poverty narratives in this collection are politically engaged, they do not adhere to Marxist or Weberian analysis in either technique or ideology. These readings do not focus on modes of production, historical determinism, or collective identities in the same way Marxist schools of analysis do. For example, I do not interpret images of the poor according to the cultural impact of major shifts in economic history as Marxist studies of the working class have done in such works as Raymond Williams's *The Country and the City*, Richard Hoggart's *The Uses of Literacy*, or Barbara Foley's *Radical Representations: Politics and Form in U.S. Proletarian History 1929-1941*. The majority of the poor in North America do not perceive themselves as a class. For this reason, the *lack* of class identity is usually a more pressing issue in these poverty narratives than class identity. Furthermore, as I discuss in some detail in regard to the distinction between writing about poor women versus writing about working-class women in the appendix, a category of narratives about the poor overlaps with the category of working-class writing, but differs from it significantly. The poor are given a largely negative designation as the lumpenproletariat in Marxist theory because they are defined more by consumption than by production, more by deprivation and need than by labour or political agency. Consequently, although I identify class rifts, class anger, and class interests as they arise in specific narratives, I do not do so as a Marxist scholar who interprets these subjectivities in terms of modes of production and the notion of a historical evolution towards a classless society. Although sympathetic to many of the insights and goals of Marxist analysis, I have resisted devoting my intellectual energy to Marxism precisely because of its marginalization of the poor and of women, but I suspect that I owe more than I fully realize to Marx and his influence on other radical intellectuals who have been formative in this study, such as Antonio Gramsci and Paulo Freire, not to mention the friends and colleagues with whom I have discussed these ideas.

8.3 Representing the Poor within Academic Discourse

As Henry Giroux has argued in *Border Crossings: Cultural Workers and the Politics of Education*, traditional views of education 'lack a language of possibility' to articulate how schools 'can play a major role in public life,' but radical teachers may encourage people to interrogate social forms critically and to imagine alternative ideals that are meaningful to a lived context (11–12). This book has been an attempt to expand the number of questions we ask about textual representations of poverty – but always with an eye to what such academic questions about poverty may mean to people's everyday lives.

Social critics have long stressed the importance of public dialogue in exposing how poverty is lived in private, especially by women and children, but is shaped by public policy and public images. One critic of the gap between needs and services in Canada writes: 'Articulation of need is important because it serves to legitimize these needs. It helps us acknowledge and recognize our needs as real and important. Collective discussion and recognition of need are key steps in the process of translating "private troubles" into "public issues"' (Torjman 42). As a radical teacher, Paulo Freire theorized the role of public dialogue in more radical terms as a catalyst to the liberation of the poor, a catalyst to demystify both power and powerlessness. Freire's belief in the phenomenological power of public dialogue relies upon the link between reflection and action which, simplified, suggests that renaming the world from the standpoint of the oppressed leads to social critique, empowerment, and transformative action: 'Thus to speak a true word is to transform the world' (68-9). But Freire is careful to insist on the communal aspect of transformative dialogue, cautioning that one cannot say a true word alone or *for* another but only in working *with* others towards cultural change.

Claims to use the university, and especially the type of academic discourse spoken in the humanities, as a forum for public dialogue in which marginal voices are somehow recovered or represented must be tempered by consideration of the politics of university education. After all, Freire's theory of transformative dialogue was grounded on direct contact between intellectuals and the oppressed in small groups. In the context of university education in Canada, where academic discourse is highly specialized, privileged, and professionalized, it is both theoretically problematic and ethically suspect for academics to claim to speak for, to, or with oppressed people. As theorists in cultural studies are acknowledging more and more, greater representation of oppressed peoples within literary discourse means little in terms of changes in lived power relations, largely because those who speak or are heard within the academy on the subject of oppression are so rarely the oppressed themselves but are, rather, self-appointed spokespeople for the oppressed (Alcoff, Guillory, Krupat, Radhakrishnan, Godard, Mukherjee).

Scepticism about the nature of cultural intervention and truth claims made by academics on behalf of the disenfranchised, such as that expressed by Linda Alcoff in her much-cited essay 'The Problem of Speaking for Others,' may broach the problem from the ethical perspective of an individual researcher. Alcoff argues that speaking about and for the oppressed from privileged locations places academics in danger of reproducing discursive violence and of distorting the subjectivities of the oppressed. While arguing that academics cannot in good faith simply retreat from discussing oppression, Alcoff suggests that ideally the academy needs to find ways of letting Others speak for themselves in the institutional context. Failing this seldom-explored option, however, she suggests that we adopt a greater self-reflexivity towards our own privileged speaking positions by examining our impulse to speak, by understanding that the location from which we speak is inextricably tied to the lives of others rather than autonomously detached, by accepting political and ethical responsibility for our connectedness to others, and by studying the possible effects of our speech on the oppressed themselves.

Writing on ethnocriticism, Arnold Krupat has also concluded that no matter how oppositional or self-reflexive the critical practice, we cannot escape from the violence implied when a privileged form of discourse theorizes about oppressed and muted subjects (6). Even though we cannot exonerate ourselves from the discursive violence implied by such privileged locations, Krupat suggests, we can at least produce *less violent* forms of knowledge by valorizing minority theories and by building a more detailed, contextual, and dialogic comprehension of minority groups and individuals (6, 26). None the less, even when oppressed subjects do manage to be heard in their own voices, Krupat warns against exaggerating the potential of oppositional discourse, reminding us to 'distinguish between speaking oppositionally and toppling the government' (11).

John Guillory cautions that the apparently liberatory shifts we are now seeing in boundaries around high culture and canons in North America may be changing the notion of what constitutes valuable cultural capital, but may obscure the fact that recruitment practices and the discourse of the humanities are still fundamentally élitist and rooted in power relations inside and outside the university. Against the popular myth that education is universal and egalitarian in North America, Guillory has argued convincingly in *Cultural Capital* that universities and especially humanities studies ultimately reproduce existing class stratification in the way knowledge is disseminated, cultural canons of taste and judgment are constructed, and members of élite groups are recruited. Guillory adapts to the North American cultural context Pierre Bourdieu's theory that universities in France function as sites of cultural reproduction where social inequities are actually reproduced more often than they are challenged. Both Bourdieu and

Guillory theorize the hegemonic role of universities in controlling access to knowledge through a tacit system based on the selective circulation of cultural capital.[3] The way knowledge is constructed and mystified within literary canons as accessible through 'good taste' more than learnable skills, Guillory argues, has historically served hegemonic interests by maintaining a sense of inherent distinction among social élites. The illusion of class distinction and the rationale for class dominance has rested in part on a rarefied ability to consume high culture and thus exercise 'good taste.'

The means of policing access to cultural capital in higher education may be as subtle as maintaining borders around a canon of bourgeois culture or assuming the human subject to have middle-class tastes, experiences, and subjectivities. Bourdieu suggests that university discourse itself maintains élite class groups by mystifying the language games and unspoken codes of good behaviour and good taste which form the basis of examinations and exchange between professors and students. Furthermore, Guillory cautions that the élitist function of academic discourse may remain essentially intact even when the object of study in the humanities shifts to the periphery and to ostensibly liberatory projects of study. Reading poverty narratives, for example, may only *seem* to democratize the subject of literary study if such shifts serve merely to generate yet another form of exclusive discourse that teaches privileged readers to consume popular culture in more and more complex ways – in short to aestheticize or to intellectualize marginal culture in such a way that its counter-cultural potential is effectively masked, neutralized, appropriated, or mastered. Guillory questions how liberatory the recent trend away from the literary canon is, given that it comes at a time when the humanities themselves are no longer as instrumental to the state as previously in maintaining social and cultural élites, and given the emergence of a technological society where the professional-managerial class do not require 'good taste' as much as other technological-managerial skills to serve the corporate élite. These theoretical insights into the fundamentally élitist, class

---

3 Since Bourdieu's and Guillory's discussions are specific to other national contexts (French and American respectively), they would need to be significantly adapted to inform a detailed discussion of the role of Canadian universities in the reproduction of class differences, unequal access to national culture, and a bourgeois national imaginary in Canada. Such detailed discussion is beyond the scope of the present study, but studies by Porter and Grayson in Canada were pioneers in the field.

nature of academic discourse in the humanities are relevant to the reading of poverty narratives because they warn us that greater representation of the poor within an essentially restricted discourse does not alone constitute significant cultural change in the lives of the poor.

Although Alcoff, Krupat, and Guillory caution against staging an idealized union between academics and oppressed groups, however, they also propose new positions for engaged critics who are actively trying to redefine intellectual labour in the context of more realistic forms of social connectedness. These are the types of self-reflexive intellectual spaces in which I talk about poverty and the poor in culture, in full awareness of the limited reach of academic discourse and of the viable possibilities for extending that reach.

Critical studies of poverty narratives can render symbolic violence against the poor more visible and coherent by depicting the impact of social boundaries on the subject. As poverty narratives attest, the psychic experience of being positioned on the outside as stigmatized Other is traumatic; it exacerbates the mental distress of being poor and becomes complexly intertwined with material hardship. A hypersensitivity to imaginary walls in poverty narratives calls attention to the symbolic and material borders that protect market privilege in our culture. Indeed, poor protagonists often accept rather than challenge the 'naturalness' of class borders and set about changing themselves in order to 'pass.' For example, protagonists intent on upward mobility in Ethel Wilson's *Lilly's Story*, Nellie McClung's *Painted Fires*, and John Marlyn's *Under the Ribs of Death* either subscribe doggedly to the work ethic or refashion their exterior self to fit middle-class and dominant ethnic standards. Conversely, other protagonists suffer severe emotional consequences in the form of self-doubt or fear of madness when they oppose class borders (such as the speaker in Cy-Thea Sand's 'A Question of Identity' and the hero of Adele Wiseman's *Crackpot*), while some break out of feelings of entrapment and paralysis by acting out in violent and psychotic ways the extremes of the outsider position (for example, by setting house fires, as in David Adams Richards's *Road to the Stilt House* and Sharon Riis's *The True Story of Ida Johnson*).

Schooling itself functions, in Louis Althusser's terms, as an institutional ideological apparatus which reproduces class boundaries. John Porter's controversial study, *The Vertical Mosaic: An Analysis of Social Class and Power in Canada* (1965), exposed Canada's failure as a nation to live up to its own democratic ideals of equal opportunity by not challenging barriers to educational opportunity that are multifaceted but clearly class-rooted. Porter observed that schools and universities maintain élites based on class and ethnicity through the level of recruitment and in the way knowledge is circulated and the image of Canada as a 'classless' nation is reproduced culturally by schools (165-98). Minority writing in Canada also testifies to the role schools play in asserting ethnic, racial, linguistic, and gender dominance; not surprisingly, then, numerous poverty narratives also testify dramatically that schools function as sites of cultural exclusion or acculturation of the poor. For example, schools and higher education are more often than not constructed paradoxically as holding out the promise of social mobility while enforcing social boundaries between classes in autobiographical and literary testimonies such as Cy-Thea Sand's 'A Question of Identity,' Maria Campbell's *Halfbreed*, Adele Wiseman's *Crackpot*, Alice Munro's 'The Beggar Maid,' Hugh Garner's *Cabbagetown*, and Margaret Laurence's 'Horses of the Night,' to name only a few.

On the whole, Canadian literary criticism has been relatively silent around the representational issues of poverty, class exploitation, and class struggle in the national literature – even with respect to the numerous literary works that have given sustained treatment to the subject of poverty (for example, David Adams Richards's *Road to the Stilt House*, Adele Wiseman's *Crackpot*, Irene Baird's *Waste Heritage*, Percy Janes's *House of Hate*, John Marlyn's *Under the Ribs of Death*, Marie-Claire Blais's *Une Saison dans la vie d'Emmanuel*, Laura Goodman Salverson's *Confessions of an Immigrant's Daughter*, Maria Campbell's *Halfbreed*, J.G. Sime's *Sister Woman*, Gabrielle Roy's *Windflower* [*La Rivière sans repos*], Norman Levine's *Canada Made Me*, Margaret Laurence's *The Diviners*, and Alice Munro's *Who Do You Think You Are?*) Clearly, poverty narratives have been available and circulating in the culture at large without ever having been perceived as an academic category of analysis relevant to the study of identity in the national literature. Class analyses of Canadian literature that have remained dispersed like so many seeds in the wind, these individual critical works have planted important ideas about the relation between images of class and lived class relations, with some mention of poverty, but have yet to be identified as a school or movement (for example, I am thinking in particular of analyses of social realism and power relations by Ben-Zion Shek, Patricia Smart, Anthony Purdy, and Kenneth Hughes; explorations of leftist nationalist themes by Robin Mathews and Paul Cappon and political radicalism by Dorothy Livesay, Frank Watt, and Robert McDougal; work poetry and fiction by Tom Wayman and Helen

Potrebenko; studies of poverty in Québécois literature by Michel Biron and Pierre Popovic and by Lucille Guilbert and colleagues; and analyses of oppositional trends in cultural studies by Rick Salutin). We need to ask if and how institutional practices have discouraged us from cultivating links among critics engaged in oppositional cultural projects based on class while nourishing those based on gender and race. Furthermore, we need to study the cultural implications of the silencing and exclusion of the poor and working class in the literary establishment from many angles – absences in the canon, curriculum, and critical history, but also in the student body and administrative and teaching positions. Can people from poor families afford the huge debts of postsecondary education and the sense of marginality if they do manage to make their way into the system? Are poor and working-class children as likely to consent to public and high school education as middle-class children are? Do poor children even aspire to higher education? Although these questions are beyond the goal of this study, which focuses on the politics of images as they occur in specific narrative contexts, I feel strongly that we should keep in mind, as a relevant frame for the analysis of images of poverty, the issue of institutional contexts and their role in the cultural muting of the poor. The institutional role is one which the narratives themselves often protest through testimonies about misrepresentation or lack of representation in schools, the publishing industry, higher education, and the mass media, not to mention government institutions charged with overseeing welfare, unemployment insurance, and child support. The latter group are often narrated as intrusive and controlling as the poor struggle to maintain dignity and the autonomy of their families (see works by Maria Campbell, David Adams Richards, Hugh Garner, and Sheila Baxter).

Terry Eagleton has argued that 'the extendibility of critical discourse' is 'theoretically limitless' and that, accordingly, we should ask of critical discourse 'not what the object is or how we should approach it but why we should want to engage with it in the first place' (203, 210). Certain critics, he notes, due to the self-consciously political nature of their inquiry, make both ideological and intellectual demands on their discourse. For example, the feminist critic does not engage in critical inquiry about gender merely for political ends, but also because she recognizes that since gender is central to many utterances, critical accounts which suppress such questions are 'seriously defective' (209). At the same time, Eagleton notes that neither the feminist nor the socialist critic will treat the analysis of class and gender as simply a matter of academic interest, of 'achieving a more satisfyingly complete account of literature,' without thought for how such inquiry might be transformative of a society which is deeply divided by class and gender. My reasons for approaching poverty narratives in this book are, likewise, both epistemological and political, aimed both at raising questions about poverty that will address a knowledge gap and at producing more radical knowledge about poverty that will help change the way we see and act on poverty in our everyday lives.

Conclusion: Taking a Position

Canadian achievement in every field depends mainly on the quality of the Canadian mind and spirit. This quality is determined by what Canadians think, and think about; by the books they read, the pictures they see and the programmes they hear. These things, whether we call them arts and letters or use other words to describe them, we believe to lie at the roots of our life as a nation.

Vincent Massey, The Massey Report 1951

Let the Old World, where rank's yet vital,
Part those who have and have not title.
Toronto has no social classes –
Only the Masseys and the masses.

B.K. Sandwell, 'On the Appointment of Governor-General Vincent Massey, 1952'

While the category of poverty narratives and the practices of cultural studies should not be idealized, the vision of culture we hold when we read poverty oppositionally looks ahead to cultural transformation. One such paradigm I have in mind when I read poverty oppositionally is that of a 'common culture' as the basis for a more inclusive notion of national culture (Williams [1958] 1989, Eagleton 1978). I would like to raise some final questions about re-imagining a more inclusive and pluralist paradigm of culture within which we see ourselves reading and teaching poverty narratives. Recently, scepticism has been growing about positing any homogeneous national subject – or as Massey put it: 'the Canadian mind and spirit' – as a basis for cultural or literary studies. Homogeneous constructions of the Canadian imagination contradict the recent emphasis on cultural pluralism both in academic study and in the official cultural paradigm of the Canadian mosaic (which itself conceals class differences as Porter so aptly revealed in *The Vertical Mosaic*). Unfortunately, however, whereas studies of multicultural writing in Canada have exposed the cultural hegemony of majority ethnic and racial groups and feminist studies have exposed the cultural hegemony of patriarchal traditions, the hegemony of the middle class cowed by a corporate élite has not been brought seriously into question as a class force that homogenizes national culture in the interests of economically privileged subjects – not, that is, by Canadian literary or cultural studies. In this day and age, reading poverty narratives as a meaningful part of national culture requires an act of the political will to know economically marginalized subjects, an act of self-reflexive questioning about the taken-for-granted paradigms of progress, bourgeois culture, and nation that have tacitly limited the scope of literary studies in Canada thus far.

A bourgeois national imaginary seldom calls attention to its own class nature. It effects its transcendence of class, its flight from class, by subtly excluding the voices of poor or working-class subjects who testify to class ruptures within the nation or by symbolically positioning them on the fringes of culture as the remnants of nation who deserve to be excluded. The study of national literatures as an institution is often complicit in reproducing a bourgeois national imaginary and a bourgeois global hegemony. Even though individual critics often hold differing, less classist visions of nation and global culture, we too often remain politely quiet about the exclusion of the cultures of the poor and the working class. It is not only the practices of high culture that reproduce classist notions of national culture; popular culture and the documented voices of the poor themselves may also be complicit in the rejection and distancing of class Others within the nation as they internalize blame and the dominant social myths of meritocracy and 'making it.' Consequently, I have tried to show that the ideology of images of poverty cannot be discerned merely from the class origins of the speaker, the level of cultural production, or the formal properties of genres. The ideology of images of poverty is made coherent ultimately in finding the relation between those images and the community, more specifically in the dominant beliefs about the poor and the everyday practices of symbolic and material power over the poor within that community. The construction of a psychosocial place of poverty may be specific to each narrative, but it is also tied to webs of meaning outside the text in culture as a whole. An oppositional reading project consciously places the fictions of poverty within a new, more radical paradigm of culture to shed light on how poverty is lived and represented in the shadows of a dominant imaginary.

As Terry Eagleton has put it in 'The Idea of a Common Culture,' 'belief in the possibility of a common culture is belief in the capacity of "high" culture, when shared and remade by a whole community, to be enriched rather than destroyed; it is also a belief that sharing at this level of cultural meaning can make sense only within the admission of the people as a whole to controlling participation in the making of culture as a whole way of life ...' (1978, 24). Eagleton's ideal of a common culture differs from certain idealist feminist and nationalist cultural paradigms – for example, Showalter's and Perry's somewhat idealized umbrella of a binding female culture and the concept of feminist audience, and Vincent Massey's of the 'quality of the Canadian mind and spirit' – in that it addresses the everyday reality of hegemonic control over cultural access and the differences and inequalities this entails. Eagleton's paradigm is thus an *ideal* for universal access and cultural redefinition rather than an *idealized* version of how culture actually functions.

In his earlier work by the same title, 'The Idea of a Common Culture,' Raymond Williams distinguished between an idealist politics that homogenizes cultural content and cultural access in order to posit a *culture in common* and an interventionist politics that tries to increase the participation of marginal groups while recognizing lived differences within a heterogeneous *common culture*. The former, Williams argued, idealizes cultural homogeneity while the latter recognizes differences in cultural access and production and wills these differences into view:

> There is some danger in conceiving of a common culture as a situation in which all people mean the same thing, value the same thing, or, in that usual abstraction of culture, have an equal possession of so much cultural property ... That kind of view of a common culture is perhaps better described by the phrase 'a culture in common,' but the argument is unreal. In any society towards which we are likely to move, there will, first of all, be such considerable complexity that nobody will in that sense 'possess cultural property' in the same way; people inevitably will have different aspects of the culture, will choose that rather than this, concentrate on this and neglect that. ([1958] 1989, 37)

Williams concludes that a community cannot realize itself when it suppresses the meanings and the values of whole groups, but neither can it realize itself by legislating homogeneity through a culture that claims to speak for all because that is an unrealistic goal. The ideal lies somewhere between these extremes, somewhere between conformity and consent, somewhere in the very process of creating culture together and participating in different ways in this process.

This is a radically inclusive view of culture very different from what we usually hear expressed in discussions about Canada's national identity resting on the shoulders of a select group of artists who create culture for us. The maintenance of walls between high culture and popular and mass culture, between artists and ordinary people, has tended to work against the democratization of the subject of national culture in Canada. Although in the colonial aftermath and in the shadow of the American cultural industry Canadians may have been hypervigilant about refinement of expression and excellence in their national literature in order to qualify against American and British models, this need no longer be the case. With international literary stars and thriving programs of study, we have the confidence and the energy to broaden our understanding of Canadian culture and include culture-from-below.

Leftist nationalists in Canada who have alluded to the need for an expanded notion of national culture over the generations have seen their work set adrift, 'orphaned' by the absence of any coherent or visible movement of class analysis in Canadian literary studies. These leftist visions of national culture are inclusive of working-class voices and conscious of the rifts that exist between classes within the nation, but they strive for a revisioning of nation that would draw these voices into a common culture. For example, Tom Wayman has challenged the dominance of bourgeois national culture by questioning its taken-for-granted representativeness: 'But if we consider in more detail that cultural possibility called "Canadian culture," to better understand what value it might have, the first problem surely is: which Canadians are we talking about? What is the range of experiences and ideas currently included in Canadian cultural artifacts? Whose Canada do we mean when we speak of Canadian culture?' (17). Robin Mathews based his left-nationalist analysis, *Canadian Literature: Surrender or Revolution*, on the assumption that the ideal of community in Canada is a value threatened by individualism and American cultural imperialism, but a value that is lived out in literature and everyday life whether or not it is acknowledged. Although both Wayman and Mathews prescribe cultural values, perhaps they would be less heavy-handed if they were not struggling against such strong winds of indifference to class issues in Canadian literary studies. Works by leftist nationalists need to be reclaimed as part of a tradition of counter-cultural criticism in Canada, one that has challenged academia to acknowledge class rifts within the nation and the power and possibility of alternative notions of community. We have a fascinating counter-cultural tradition in Canada which has included a wide range of political viewpoints in re-imagining the community of nation from sources as diverse as Margaret Laurence, John Ralston Saul, and Linda McQuaig. Granted, elsewhere in the world academics have had a more identifiable tradition of class criticism of their national literatures and cultural studies to build from. For instance, the paradigm of an inclusive, common culture that I have drawn on here has been discussed and theorized over generations by Williams and Eagleton in the context of a respected class critique of British culture.

Of course, what I am imagining here is not simply the celebration of counter-cultural statements regardless of their ideology or inclusiveness of spirit. Consider, for example, George Woodcock's anxiety that uneducated politicians and bureaucrats will confuse mass and popular culture with 'the arts' in Canada and thus subsidize the wrong kind of Canadian culture. Behind Woodcock's counter-cultural statement as an anarchist nationalist (as wary of joining groups or transforming society as he is of mass culture) is the liberal notion that a small group of individual artists can speak for the whole: 'They even talk of cultural industry, so that the arts become judged by the criteria of consumerism. The critic Herbert Read, in his anxiety to save the arts from the false values of the marketplace, once wrote a famous pamphlet which he called To Hell with Culture!, and in this book I shall adopt his title as my only slogan: To Hell with Talk of Culture, since in the modern age it submerges the arts in other activities that are in no way artistic, and so obscures the special role and the special claims of artists' (14). Woodcock, an authoritative voice in Canadian culture and one that is usually regarded as radical, lashes out at special interest groups and their claims to cultural representation and government funding and at the 'Philistines' (government bureaucrats) who cannot distinguish between the arts and mass culture (113). He agrees with Robertson Davies that the arts cannot be democratic because talent is not distributed equally, implicitly reducing the realizable ideal of common culture into the unrealistic one of a culture in common (115). Both of these counter-cultural statements are complicit in a rhetoric of excellence that builds walls around culture by designating a chosen few as the spokespeople for the nation. And consider Northrop Frye's whimsical cultural paradigm, which is attractive despite its overt exclusionary gesture: 'But when a mythology crystallises in the center of a culture, a *temenos* or magic circle is drawn around that culture, and a literature develops historically within a limited orbit of language, reference, allusion, belief, transmitted and shared tradition' (1971, 35). Perhaps Frye's paradigm excites us with the idea that the making and sharing of meaning is magical. But surely this is all the more reason for not denying this exchange to whole segments of the population. Surely it is even more magical to believe, like Eagleton and Williams, in the shared ideal of 'a common process of participation in the creation of meanings and values' (Williams 1968, 38).

As Canadian literary studies expands into cultural studies, we should be vigilant that the old exclusionary and élitist paradigms of bourgeois culture that underly reading practices are not being reactivated in more subtle ways. Similarly, as models of cultural studies from Britain, America, Australia, and New Zealand are being imported and adapted, we should be wary about how some reproduce a taken-for-granted distance between intellectuals and subaltern groups, thus mediating against the political project of re-imagining culture in a more inclusive way and putting that theory into practice. Many contemporary descriptions of the field of cultural studies render it commonplace to assume, for example, that the time for organic intellectuals, as Gramsci defined them, as the bridge between subalterns and cultural revolution, has passed. (For dissenting opinions that adapt Gramscian notions of organic intellectuals to current contexts, see works on the changing role of intellectuals by Pamela Fox, John Guillory, and Stanley Aronowitz.) Ironically, although Gramsci's conceptualization of hegemony and consent is regularly invoked to decode the symbolic power of cultural representations and the construction of identities, the part of his theory focused on praxis and close involvement between intellectuals and subalterns is, more often than not, shelved as impractical or irrelevant in a transnational age of corporate capitalism. Not only have we transcended class in questions of identity, these evolutionary histories of cultural studies imply, but we have also transcended nation and must focus, instead, on the relationship between commodities and individual identities on a global scale. But to focus on commodities and identity rather than on the corporate powers that control distribution and profits, or the complicit role of the middle class and the professional-managerial class, or the ways in which poor subjects are denied access to symbolic power in consumer capitalism, is to consent to the limits of hegemonic discourse under consumer capitalism. Similarly, to relinquish interest in the study of nation when turning to the study of commodities is to deny the potentially radical role of the nation-state (even in a transnational global economy) in regulating consumerism for health and environmental interests, or in regulating capital to ensure humane working conditions, or in uniting subjects under an inclusive concept of a local community empowered to protect its interests.

I noted earlier that the editors of *Relocating Cultural Studies*, Valda Blundell, John Shepherd, and Ian Taylor, have stated that although the early stages of cultural criticism in Britain involved self-criticism about intellectual inquiry into the working class (5–6), the exportation and adaptation of cultural studies to the less polarized and less class-marked societies of the United States, Australia, and Canada took the emphasis off class struggle and placed it in other areas, such as that of the struggles of aboriginal people against white domination. But what escapes me is how one can discuss the cultural domination of aboriginal people in any complex way without simultaneously focusing on material, lived reality, class relations, and poverty. Blundell and colleagues also argue, however, that the shift from national projects and internal struggles to the cultural front of global consumerism required a change of focus in cultural studies, in that values were no longer attached to concepts of nation but instead were linked to commodities themselves. This resulted, they maintain, in two significant shifts regarding the cultural intervention of intellectuals: first, an increased emphasis on questions of identity, and second, a less concretely political or interventionist strategy and a more textual and aesthetic approach to cultural struggle. Once again, something escapes me. How does a focus on questions of identity take cultural studies away from cultural intervention *with* those whose identities are emerging? If the role of cultural critics in Canada has become, as Blundell and colleagues suggest, largely one of posing questions of identity in relation to centres of power rather than a strategy of active alignment and engagement with the subjugated classes in order to take power eventually (9), why are questions of class and poverty still so taboo? Is there not an unspoken alliance between intellectuals and bourgeois/corporate hegemony when class issues are erased? Further, do we wish to describe marginal identities as the *object* of our discourse without engaging with their subjectivities and their causes? Is wresting power away from the centre necessarily a preoccupation only for radical, armed fringes or are we all involved in such a struggle, as Tony Bennett has suggested, each time we step outside literature to study culture from wider angles?

The version of Canadian cultural studies that portrays the move away from active engagement with subaltern groups as *natural* is actually an evolutionary version, not only of the role of intellectuals, but also of culture as a whole. Histories that situate political praxis in the past of cultural studies are a distanciation, not only from class politics, but from a variety of complex political goals that are community based. The danger of evolutionary histories of cultural studies is that they very subtly discourage current political projects within the new field by prematurely fixing a history and prescribing a future, and by reinscribing distance between intellectuals and ordinary people as a sign of progress. The possibility of a radical, bridging role for intellectuals is diminished by this version of culture and cultural studies because the method of study prescribed relies on textually based criticism and postmodernist shape-shifting in response to social realities while it dismisses other engaged forms of social connectedness as naive. For example, even Lawrence Grossberg's self-consciously complex and unstable history of the passage of cultural studies from Britain to the United States reinscribes distance between intellectuals and subalterns by unselfconsciously appropriating Gramscian terminology ('conjunctural' and 'war of position') that originally applied to detached bourgeois intellectuals speaking of revolution without the backing of ordinary people or knowledge of their subjectivities. He prescribes an amoeba-like subjectivity for intellectuals so that we can change shape to occupy various positions in a changing, postmodern world of complex identities and subjectivities. But I for one do not wish to be an amoeba. I would rather cultivate my complex subjectivity by studying the roots of my working-class past and of my current intellectual role in lived realities. If we see cultural studies as a new field of knowledge that has sprung naturally out of the old and evolved along the way as theoretically more sophisticated but politically detached, we may forget that cultural studies in Canada is what we choose to make it.

Through our choices of paradigms of culture, texts for the curriculum, models of academic discourse, versions of cultural history, and practices of reading, we as academics position ourselves daily in relation to hegemony. Refusing to see this does not make it less true. Traditional intellectuals, as Antonio Gramsci described them, function as deputies of the ruling powers but perceive themselves as autonomous and classless both because they are idealist in believing that philosophy and art transcend class issues and because they are so used to exercising privilege that it becomes invisible to them (4–9). Organic intellectuals, on the other hand, perceive themselves as tied to a particular class of people and work for the interests of those people. In other words, 'organic intellectuals' and subjugated people as historical agents work together to reach towards greater political awareness in order to free themselves from unconscious levels of oppression, for, according to Gramsci, subordinate people are subjugated not only physically but intellectually and imaginatively as well. The role of organic intellectuals to effect social critique and educate people is intimately tied to the ideal of a common culture and the concept that all people are capable of the high thoughts which may ultimately lead to cultural revolution (3, 324, 332).

The more fully we are aware of the silencing of poor and working-class voices in the study of Canadian culture, the more concerned we should become about the current trend 'away from the left' in the new fields of feminist criticism, postcolonial critique, and cultural studies. Evolutionary histories of Canadian cultural studies are placing organic intellectuals in the distant past and in another geographic location, as signposts passed by in the persons of Richard Hoggart, Raymond Williams, and E.P. Thompson. Notions of Foucault's specific intellectuals capable only of reduced resistance on a discursive level are being naturalized as the only possible positions for intellectuals these days. But if we study intellectuals in Canada in the detailed and historical way that Gramsci himself proposed, I am confident that we would uncover the fact that many of the people posing the most challenging and most informed questions of identity have in fact been doing so in an interventionist way as organic intellectuals and historical agents with strong organic links both inside and outside the university – people such as Tom Wayman, Makeda Silvera, Sheila Baxter, Helen Potrebenko, Arun Mukherjee, Dionne Brand, Antonine Maillet, Robin Mathews, David Fennario, Jeannette Armstrong, Elly Danica, George Elliott Clarke, and many more. If intellectuals can be organically tied to or at least informed by the subjectivities of communities based on ethnicity, gender, and sexual orientation, why can it not be so for the poor and the working class? My point is that although the questions which cultural studies asks about subaltern identity may have changed with geographical location, media advances, and global economic restructuring, for some time now many intellectuals have been formulating new cultural questions about identity out of a deeply felt concern for real people and lived power relations, rather than out of a concern primarily for textuality and aesthetics. Furthermore, despite theoretical concerns about the assumed autonomy of intellectuals to choose their positions independent of institutional and cultural contexts (Radhakrishnan), many theorists are still directly concerned with the ethical implications of the positions we occupy and to a certain extent choose. Linda Alcoff would have engaged intellectuals ask 'where the speech goes and what it does there' (26–7), a position that echoes Gramsci's hope that a new stratum of intellectuals would take positions rooted in everyday life rather than merely speak about them: 'The mode of being of the new intellectual can no longer consist in eloquence, which is an exterior and momentary mover of feelings and passions, but in active participation in practical life, as constructor, organiser, "permanent persuader" and not just a simple orator ...' (*The Prison Notebooks* 10).

Studying poverty narratives from an engaged position requires that we reflect not only on textual representations of poverty, but on how academics are involved in the making and sharing of meaning with poor and working-class people in this time and place. It means considering the possibilities for making intellectual labour count in these struggles.

This book was spurred by the belief in a common culture of inclusiveness rather than a culture homogenized through political dogma. I wanted to look specifically at how poor and once-poor women represented themselves and if and how these representations from the periphery were related to those at the centre and to lived practices of power over the poor. It was only in the course of this study that I realized fully the depth and complexity of class divisions in Canadian culture, the rigidity of social boundaries, the mass denial of class differences, the subtle reinforcement of those class differences through the exclusionary rhetoric of academic excellence and high culture, and the intimate relation between the category of national literature based on bourgeois nationalism and the exclusion of oppositional voices of the poor. I began to realize what it means that Canadian literary studies does not yet have an established body of knowledge upon which to build. We need oppositional cultural paradigms that would include the experiences and voices of the poor and the working class. We need surveys of working-class literature, studies of the reading habits of the poor and the working class, publishing histories of writing by poor and working-class people, anthologies, and sustained studies of poverty in Canadian literature.

In the absence of established research, however, there are always questions which would force into view the stories and voices cooling in the shadow of the dominant imaginary, not by idealizing coalition or essentializing difference, but by highlighting class interests and class tensions as significant aspects of identity. In chapter 1 of this study, I asked the following questions: 'Which fictions of poverty are most powerfully inscribed in our culture and why? How can we bring into view more of those versions which are the least powerful? What, if anything, does bringing these versions into view have to do with empowering the poor? What do various inscriptions of poverty mean in the context of the culturally muted experience of lived poverty? How can literary versions of poverty, which are usually valorized as aesthetic objects in high culture, be read side by side with testimonials by the poor – or, more to the point, why should they be?' While some answers to these questions were offered in the course of this book, many other questions did not come to light: questions about the relation between poverty and mothering, about the role of oral histories in the construction of the cultural memory of poverty, about the connection between poverty and the market in women's bodies, about the way poverty is discussed when literature is taught to children, and about the relation between the various genres and conventions of representing poverty: social realism, the grotesque, melodrama, postmodernism, and testimony. Rather than leave vital questions such as these languishing outside the magic circle around national culture, we must challenge the way these boundaries are drawn and how we as academics, our work, and poor people themselves are positioned in respect to them.

Appendix: Outlawing Boundaries

What kind of life can it be, I wonder, to produce this extraordinary fussiness, this extraordinary decision to call certain things culture and then separate them, as with a park wall, from ordinary people and ordinary work?
Raymond Williams, 'Culture Is Ordinary' 5

Some texts are born literary, some achieve literariness, and some have literariness thrust upon them. Breeding in this respect may count for a good deal more than birth. What matters may not be where you come from but how people treat you. If they decide that you are literature then it seems that you are, irrespective of what you thought you were.
Terry Eagleton, Literary Theory: An Introduction 8–9

The following discussion, rather than policing the boundaries of an exploratory category of poverty narratives by women, shows how tentative these limits are, while at the same time examining the pragmatic, strategic, and theoretical uses to which boundaries may be put in constructing a research project. After all, the idea of imagining a new category of narratives for political purposes is more about making old boundaries visible and about reading beyond and through their cultural implications than it is about erecting new and higher walls. When Williams regrets the 'fussiness' of classist walls between high culture and ordinary people, he is simultaneously questioning the rationale of setting up walls, rather than merely lamenting their positioning or whom they keep in or out. As I discussed in the conclusion, 'Taking a Position,' the ideal of a common culture advocated by Williams and Eagleton abhors the presence of cultural walls precisely because they block access to knowledge, cultural production, and cultural consumption in a very real way – for example, to the materially disadvantaged, subordinate, or counter-cultural. Thus, when a theorist works with a new category of narratives for the purpose of calling into question the taken-for-grantedness of old cultural boundaries around canons and genres, Williams's warning about fussiness is worth heeding in order that we not reinscribe exclusion in new forms or become so absorbed in methodology for its own sake that we forget that we are building towards a culture without walls, insofar as that is possible – a common culture.

Although I want to avoid such 'fussiness,' this discussion about the tentative boundaries of my working bibliography of poverty narratives is meant to illustrate that the category is not idealist but functional, not positivist but analytical and constructed, not comprehensive but selected. Looking back now, more than five years after I first compiled 'A Working Bibliography: Poverty Narratives by Canadian Women (1919–90s),' an author-title version of which appears at the end of this appendix, I am amazed at the defensiveness with which I constructed a survey that was really only a first step, a springboard to study. To understand this cautiousness, I have to remind myself how rigorously I needed to defend my own work at the time, how I had to leave one literature department quietly to be able to continue this doctoral research unimpeded in a comparative literature department across the country where an approach through class theory and cultural studies was not seen, at that time, as too sociological, too 'unCanadian,' or simply too risky. Furthermore, I have to remind myself of how I knew nothing of these fields of criticism and only a little more about Canadian literature, but was embarking on the journey of an autodidact determined to discover the underbelly of Canadian literature because I felt more akin to that underbelly than to highbrow culture. When I finally overcame the initial censure and began publishing in the field, I did receive warm encouragement from a number of prominent Canadianists; but even so, the very notion that poverty narratives might be relevant to the study of Canadian literature still earns reactionary sneers and dismissal from time to time.

As I discussed in chapter 1, the category's national character, its gender specificity, its focus on poverty as opposed to working-class experience, and its cross-class authorship are tied to the radical ideological and conceptual goals of 'fictioning a literature for political purposes,' namely to foreground issues of class and gender and to create a dialectic field in which hegemonic, marginal, and oppositional discourses on poverty can be juxtaposed. The epistemological and political boundaries of preliminary surveys matter fiercely to the way we imagine poverty and understand subjectivities of the poor. In the end, such choices also matter to broader issues, such as what is sayable, what is funded, what is published, what is listened to, and what graduate students are willing to bet their careers on. However, choices regarding the time span of the category (from 1919 to the 1990s) and the genre limitations are purely pragmatic. I will first explain the merely pragmatic choices and second discuss the more complex epistemological and political choices (for example, the cross-class nature of poverty narratives, the focus on poor versus working-class women, and the category's transgression of the canon) in order to draw out the constructedness of poverty narratives as a category of analysis. This means that poverty narratives are constructed as a result of thoughtful, yet tentative, choices made along the way, rather than being representative of an already existing body of texts that were discovered already out there or fully imagined as a coherent unit before the actual collection process began.

I began this research alone, with few ties to sympathetic researchers, and quite a bit of resistance or indifference from superiors in the academic community at that time. Exploratory reading strategies required vigorous theoretical defence, years of it, before poverty narratives were to be considered a viable academic or publishing project. Reading poverty narratives oppositionally is a ground-breaking task not only in Canadian criticism, but elsewhere, and therefore includes the practical exercises of the collection, selection, and recovery of texts from a hitherto unimagined literary and cultural space. Furthermore, the theoretical justification for doing so lies in a field of radical materialism and cultural opposition that has, overall, been devalued in Canadian literary criticism and cultural studies; hence the need to read widely in international theory to bring these skills home. With ongoing searches for theories to legitimate this exploratory work and for popular and non-literary narratives that could be read beside literary versions of poverty, I narrowed the range of study to non-dramatic prose, including autobiography and oral history along with novels, short stories, reportage, and letters. However, many important works of social protest in Canada have been in the form of poetry and drama (for example, contemporary works by Tom Wayman, Helen Potrebenko, Lillian Allen, David Fennario, Michel Tremblay, Dionne Brand, Rudy Wiebe, and earlier modern works by Raymond Souster, Dorothy Livesay,

Alden Nowlan, Milton Acorn, Miriam Waddington, and Ann Marriott). Likewise, the criticism of poetry and theatre in Canada may arguably have come much farther in examining the radical potential of documentary, ideology and form, and collective goals of protest shared by performers and audience than the criticism of prose literature has to this point in Canada. Yet genre limits were necessary to allow familiarity with a manageable body of texts; otherwise, the study would have spent its energy in a thinly presented survey or, even less desirable, in selecting representative works – an awkward approach given that premature notions of 'representativeness' are called into question through this study's oppositional reading practices.

Where pragmatic borders are concerned, we need to tolerate a certain amount of healthy disorder in the category. We need to allow ourselves to transgress our own working boundaries in pursuit of radical knowledge. Furthermore, we look into previously muted cultural areas for meaning and understanding of the disorderliness of everyday culture, not in pursuit of homogeneity or imposed orderliness. In pursuit of coherence and a common culture, one should push beyond the limits of working categories. In the body of this text, I have done so by inserting critiques of a nineteenth-century poem, Alexander McLachlan's 'We Live in a Rickety House,' and an excerpt from a contemporary poem, Sharon Stevenson's 'The Very Last Feminist Poem,' each of which said something too important to discount merely because of the original generic boundaries of the study. Since the goal of a category of poverty narratives is not generalization about this body of texts, since it is a means, not an end, one is free to read beyond initial, pragmatic boundaries in pursuit of relevant images and ideas.

In addition to outlawing rigid generic boundaries, I read outside of my own time limits in discussing McLachlan's nineteenth-century poem and Susanna Moodie's critical essay 'A Word for the Novel Writers,' because the attempt to understand poverty in twentieth-century culture requires knowledge of a genealogy of cultural values and discursive strategies which are historically rooted well before the turn of the century. Yet I did not begin my research with early Canadian narratives, not even by authors whose writing lives were marked and shaped by poverty, as, for example, Isabella Valancy Crawford's was (1850–87). There is no lack of references to poverty in settler and travel literature and popular, romantic fiction from the eighteenth and nineteenth centuries and earlier, but time limits had to be set for the initial survey stage. If one cannot begin from the beginning, a starting point must be designated. I gradually pushed back that date ten years or so to include Nellie McClung's *Painted Fires* (1925) and J.G. Sime's *Sister Woman* (1919). Originally, the Depression had seemed an important place to start because it is for many of us the most acceptable imaginative site for poverty in Canada. As I discussed in greater detail in the introduction and in chapter 6, 'Organized Forgetting,' Roger Bromley has suggested that this is also true of Britain, showing how contemporary poverty narratives can be questioned on their own narrative economy in respect to Depression-bound icons of poverty. Bromley concluded that contemporary culture displaces disruptive knowledge about poverty and history through processes of symbolic containment (as articulated through his own theory of representativeness) and organized forgetting or collective amnesia whereby contemporary claims of poverty pale in comparison to extreme, visual icons fixed in the Depression. In *The Hidden Injuries of Class*, Sennett and Cobb note another link between current-day imaginings of poverty and Depression memories; they suggest that the growing tendency to feel shame and indignity surrounding poverty and working-class status – in other words, to hold the individual responsible for his or her lack of social mobility within the New World economy as a land of opportunity – has supplanted the feeling of individual powerlessness and collective struggle that occurred during the Depression when poverty was recognized as an overwhelming fate, out of the hands of any one individual.

This tendency in Canadian culture to locate 'true' and 'deserving' poverty in the distant and discontinuous past while stigmatizing and blaming people who are currently poor is, as I mentioned briefly in the introduction and will discuss here in the section on transgressing the canon, reflected in the way Canadian culture is constructed for study. Until very recently, collections of a Depression genre of narrative have been the only sorts of literary anthologies of working-class voices available (for example, *Voices of Discord: Canadian Short Stories from the 1930s*, edited by Donna Phillips, and *The Depression in Canadian Literature*, edited by Alice Hale and Sheila Brooks), indicating a preference for constructing poverty and class issues in the context of a distant past. Two other types of anthologies have emerged more recently: collections of working-class women's writing by feminist little magazines such as *Fireweed* and *Room of One's Own*, and collections of work narratives and poetry (by Tom Wayman and Helen Potrebenko, for example). But these emergent types of anthologies of working-class narratives are also distanced from the hegemonic 'here and now' by marginal status as cultural capital that is devalued academically and aesthetically. The paucity of anthologies of works on poverty and working-class experience constitutes a meaningful form of forgetting and cultural muting in the mainstream, institutionalized study of Canadian literature, a blind spot which overlooks the production of revisionary and oppositional works by individual artists who have repeatedly represented social issues and by isolated critics who have struggled, largely alone, to map class analysis in Canadian literature. The process of exclusion is subtle, however, and largely unconscious. It is naturalized by the notion that Canada as a society is virtually classless, though few academics would openly endorse these popular assumptions.

i Useful Distinctions: Poor versus Working-Class Women

As I pointed out in the introduction, the categories of working-class women and poor women overlap but differ, largely in that the latter is cross-class, especially taking into account the phenomenon of the feminization of poverty. Consumption- rather than production-based, the category of poor women depends not on a definition of capital or labour or even family ties, but rather on the perception or experience of being poor for a short or an extended period of time.

A significant number of poverty narratives are by and about poor women who are not in the wage-labour market and are not working class but fall into the category of the lumpenproletariat in Marxist class theory. Welfare mothers, unemployed women, ill or handicapped women, and prostitutes, for example, are among the poor women who would fall under the (negative) rubric lumpenproletariat because of their 'parasitical' relation to the modes of production under Marxist theory. There are more fictional narratives about than by the lumpenproletariat, too few of whom can afford the room of their own and the annual salary that Virginia Woolf claimed was needed by women who would be writers. The absence of these voices in fiction is what makes the oral interviews with the homeless and the unemployed in Sheila Baxter's *No Way to Live: Poor Women Speak Out* so invaluable and the depiction of displaced poor women in Diana Collier's fictional rooming-house setting in *The Invisible Women of Washington* such an anomaly.

Another group of poor women who are not 'working class' are those middle-class women who, through the dissolution of the family, a major trend in the feminization of poverty, find themselves facing poverty and, sometimes, welfare. This would include women who choose to leave the home, knowingly facing reduced circumstances – for example, the protagonists in Constance Beresford Howe's *The Book of Eve* and in Ethel Wilson's *Swamp Angel*. (Of course, not all women who leave the home face poverty, for some leave a poor home to improve their lot: for example, Edna Jaques in her autobiography *Uphill All the Way* and Hagar in *The Stone Angel*.) Women's life-lines, personal choices, and care-giving functions under patriarchy result in various states of poverty: for example, temporary poverty, generational poverty, the welfare trap, or bohemian poverty.

Still other poor women not always considered 'working class' are those who work in white-collar clerical and service jobs as part of the petit-bourgeoisie, but who receive such low pay that they are among the working poor. This phenomenon of late capitalism which accompanied an increase in the number of women in the labour market is sometimes referred to as the 'proletarianization of clerical workers' or the 'pink ghetto,' and it is an important aspect of the feminization of poverty (Armstrong and Armstrong). Office workers and retail sales clerks who are among the working poor appear in the fiction of Nellie McClung, Dorothy Livesay, J.G. Sime, and Helen Potrebenko, for example, and writings by such ghettoized workers have been included in recent feminist collections of working-class women's writing where the operative class definition has been updated to reflect women's lived reality of the cross-class experience of poverty.

Thus the problem with focusing on 'working-class' writings by women as a category of analysis defined by traditional class theory is that it would segregate the writings of poor women working for a wage in particular types of manual labour or either born or married into working-class families from the writings of women who are poor because of other societal factors which are none the less systemic: poor office workers and sales clerks, poor divorced women and single mothers from different class backgrounds, and poor handicapped women, unemployed women, prostitutes, homeless women, and others from the lumpenproletariat.

ii Setting Up a Cross-Class Dialectic

The cross-class nature of the category of poverty narratives is intended to reflect the relational reality of poverty and the connectedness of the poor to the rest of the nation. The juxtaposition of texts from different levels of cultures and different subjective points of view does more than allow a smorgasbord of plurality; it helps reveal the dialectic and relational aspect of poverty so that counter-cultural and dominant images of poverty can be seen in interaction with each other. This is why I chose not to construct an idealist category of resistant poverty narratives, but to make reading strategies themselves resistant. Furthermore, read complexly as sites of struggle over different beliefs about poverty, a cross-class group of narratives reveals that meanings are negotiated and maintained out of particular interests rooted in lived power relations, but that these beliefs and meanings are not mechanically tied to the speaker's position in society. Some among the poor and the once-poor generate stories and cultural memory as a form of resistance and counter-culture; while others consent to negative constructions of identity and, in fact, reproduce them. Similarly the non-poor do not monolithically generate images of the poor that are exclusionary, for a number of the non-poor are activists or left-wing social critics who see the poor as systemically marginalized by market society and consumer capitalism in North America (for instance, Livesay and Wiseman). Understanding the struggle over meaning between the poor and the non-poor means challenging from the outset oversimplified notions that the ideology of poverty narratives can be directly discerned from the social status of the author or character. Resistant, subordinate, and dominant ideologies may surface in contradiction to the author's social identity or stated goals, and, remarkably, coexist in the same narrative. As poor subjects struggle with contradictory beliefs about what it means to be poor in a wealthy society, they will often adopt dominant images and points of view to blame themselves and others who are poor, but in the next breath summon a resistant spirit to protest such subordination.

There are, thus, three main reasons why a category of poverty narratives by women should be cross-class: first, in order to unsettle traditional nineteenth-century categories of class which did not adequately consider gender and the realities of women's private sphere – for example, the uneven distribution of wealth within the family unit, the domestic mode of production, or the complex, individual experiences of class devalued along with the status of private life (as we learn from works by Christine Delphy, Lise Vogel, Michèle Barrett, Lillian Robinson, and Carolyn Steedman). Second, a cross-class category can show how women move in and out of poverty, often in conjunction with their caregiving roles and reproductive functions. These narratives encourage us to bring into the spectrum of cultural studies recent sociological theories of the feminization of poverty in North America (such as those by Pearce, Goldberg et al., Gunderson et al., Torjman, the Armstrongs, Daly, and Gelpi and Hartsock et al.), even though these theories have been criticized as homogenizing and may be used most effectively in conjunction with more radical theories of class and gender such as those by Christine Delphy and Lise Vogel. The third reason for the juxtaposition of cross-class utterances has to do with the exploration of oppositional reading practices. A cross-class category allows one to bring together the subjective utterances of a wider range of women in order to discover subjectivities and discourses based on a variety of subject positions in respect to poverty, not all predictable or identifiable by objective class locations, not all oppositional, and not all constant in their construction of poverty as a psychosocial space. I believe that a cross-class category focusing on one aspect of a classist system – in this case, poverty – may be a less idealist and essentialist working category than those based on the class origins of the writers – although it is not meant to replace class-based categories of writing.

In practice, however, the cross-class nature of the category makes this study vulnerable to slippage between the terms, theories, and discourses of class and poverty, the more so because it is sometimes necessary to refer to a 'class' of poor women which is itself 'cross-class' in terms of Marxist theory (for example, including proletarianized clerical workers, single mothers on welfare and prostitutes or the lumpenproletariat, and divorced or elderly bourgeois women who live in poverty only at certain stages in their lives). Increasingly, I am trying to make these distinctions in my own writing, but many of the key sources of cultural theory and literary criticism which inform my own research frequently fail or refuse to make a clear distinction between poor women and working-class women. In particular, radical feminist critics who understand the unsuitability of nineteenth-century class theories to women's present lived realities (especially the feminization of poverty) seem purposely to allow slippage back and forth between terms as though in protest that there are no available terms to describe how women drift in and out of a special gendered class of the poor (as in the writings of Janet Zandy and bell hooks).

The category of 'poverty narratives by women' creates space for the consideration of works *about poor women* as well as works *by poor women* largely because most poverty narratives in Canada are usually written by once-poor women rather than poor women: for example, Nellie McClung's *Clearing in the West*, Edna Jaques's *Uphill All the Way*, Gabrielle Roy's *Bonheur d'occasion* and *Enchantment and Sorrow*, Laura Goodman Salverson's *Confessions of an Immigrant's Daughter*, Maria Campbell's *Halfbreed*, Adele Wiseman's *Crackpot*, and Sylvia Fraser's *Pandora*, to name just a few examples, are all retrospectives or fictional approximations of an experience of poverty which the authors had left behind by the time of writing.

For many, if not most, poor women, the resources, time, and motivation to write and access to public cultural production are out of reach, if not materially, then because of an interiorized sense of inferiority and alienation: such as that testified to by Cy-Thea Sand in 'A Question of Identity.' Tillie Olsen concluded about silences in literature that '[c]lass remains the greatest unexamined in the question of what discourages marginal writers from developing the creative potential universal to all' (169, 285). Olsen's own prototypical 'I Stand Here Ironing' fleshes out the issue of silencing by exposing the self-censorship internalized by working-class women who despair of the act of speaking out, not only because of material hardship but also because of self-perception. In general, the shorter the genre, the more accessible or the more comfortable it has been to poor women who narrate their stories from within the materially and spiritually harsh circumstances of poverty. Oral histories, personal essays, letters, and journals (also songs and protest poems, not included in this study, but see Paul Lauter's bibliography for the study of working-class women's voices in American culture) have been the genres most available to poor women as what we might refer to as a synchronous testimonial mode of narrating poverty while it is actually being experienced.

Because such synchronous utterances may not reach publication or be widely distributed, I assume that they exist in greater numbers than my own collection of titles shows at the end of this chapter. Among the few Canadian collections of women's utterances in this synchronous confessional mode are speeches and interviews such as those in Sheila Baxter's *No Way to Live: Poor Women Speak Out*, Makeda Silvera's *Silenced*, Prahba Khosla's 'Profiles of Working-class East Indian Women,' Marlene Webber's *Street Kids: The Tragedy of Canada's Runaways*, and Jennifer Horseman's *Something in My Mind besides the Everyday: Women and Literacy*; letters such as those to R.B. Bennett during the Depression collected in *The Wretched of Canada*; collective texts such as *Enough Is Enough: Native Women Speak Out*; and assorted short stories and essays in special issues of working-class women's writing, most notably by little feminist magazines such as *Fireweed* and *Room of One's Own* or other specialized journals such as *The Poor People's Press (The Voice)* published by the N.D.G. Anti-Poverty Group. Because traditional academic literary training leaves us almost totally unprepared to read these 'partial' utterances, we need to seek an oppositional reading practice which would draw them into our field of perception meaningfully. By 'meaningfully,' I am suggesting that we adapt our theoretical perceptions to the content and spirit of the narratives themselves or, at the very least, that we commit our theorizing to a greater acknowledgment of the material lives of poor subjects and the radical knowledge they may themselves produce.

Perhaps because professional writing has often been a way out of poverty for the once-poor writer, confessional retrospectives are in many cases writers' autobiographies (Jaques's *Uphill All the Way*); and the realist mode of fiction is often the *künstlerroman* (Fraser's *Pandora*, Laurence's *The Diviners*, and Munro's *Who Do You Think You Are?*). Most notable among the group of poverty narratives by Canadian women which are *künstlerromans*, however, are those by women who never actually experienced the harsh poverty they depicted: Blais's *Les Manuscrits de Pauline Archange* and Laurence's *The Diviners*. Another prominent genre among once-poor writers is the personal essay which speaks out directly on the subject of writing as it has been influenced by material and social conditions. Examples of personal essays about the writer's lived experience of poverty as formative of their experience of writing are Cy-Thea Sand's 'A Question of Identity,' Adele Wiseman's 'Memoirs of a Book-molesting Childhood' and Miriam Waddington's 'Mrs. Maza's Salon.'

A small but significant group of poverty narratives are by Canadian women who experienced a non-poor stratum of working-class reality or relatively hard times in the Depression but not the extreme degree of poverty related in their stories: for example, Margaret Laurence and Marie-Claire Blais have both depicted women and men living in extreme poverty although neither experienced such hardships directly (*The Diviners*, 'Horses of the Night,' *The Stone Angel*, 'The Loons,' *Une Saison dans la vie d'Emmanuel*, *Les Manuscrits de Pauline Archange*). An even smaller group of poverty narratives, but equally significant in terms of the canon of Canadian literature, are by women from economically privileged milieus: *Lilly's Story* by Ethel Wilson, Depression short stories and reportage in *Left Hand, Right Hand* by Dorothy Livesay, *The Double Hook* by Sheila Watson. These might be considered an extra-biographical mode of poverty narrative. Another type of extra-biographical poverty narrative occurs in cross-race writing about poverty: for example, Gabrielle Roy's *La Rivière sans repos* (*Windflower*) and Bridget Moran's *Stoney Creek Woman: The Story of Mary John*. It would be inaccurate to prejudge this extra-biographical mode as inauthentic simply because it is not testimony which issues from firsthand experience of poverty. Hypothetically, it is possible that an author who has not experienced poverty could create a convincing narrative through political insight, empathy, or close contact with others' experiences. Ethel Wilson admitted she had never known anyone like the poor single mother who is her protagonist in *Lilly's Story*; she merely 'imagined' what it would be like to be in that situation. And Adele Wiseman modelled Hoda, the fully sketched prostitute/protagonist of *Crackpot*, after a woman she had seen years before on a street corner and had heard rumours about. These are both convincing and culturally important poverty narratives born of empathy rather than firsthand experience. In addition to empathy, testimony has sometimes come from close contact with the poor: Bridget Moran and Dorothy Livesay worked as social workers in the communities they wrote about; Irene Baird posed as a nurse among male strikers; Gabrielle Roy taught in an Inuit community; and Emily Carr came to know poor Native people in her travels as a painter. Although extra-biographical narratives are not the same form of testimony as firsthand accounts, they may have enough truth value to function as literary testimony about poverty and, therefore, to serve a therapeutic social purpose. Beyond the issue of whether or not these extra-biographical testimonies have truth value, however, is the fact that they are part of a cultural stock of discourses on women's poverty which should be explored in its fullness. To exclude extra-biographical works from the category of poverty narratives on the grounds that they are somehow inauthentic utterances would be counter-productive because it would not allow the rereading of some of the best-known and most canonized of Canadian poverty narratives which have been culturally important producers of meaning around women's experiences of poverty.

iii Transgressing the National Canon

This new category emerges in the context of a national literature that has devalued class analysis in the past as a way both of imagining meaningful categories of texts and of decoding character and ideology within the narratives themselves. This does not mean that class analysis has been non-existent in Canadian literary studies, nor that class-conscious texts and other poverty narratives have been excluded from the canon. As discussed earlier, poverty narratives embrace the extremes: canonical works and ordinary utterances. Moreover, between these two extremes are a range of sites for narrating poverty: popular fiction, such as Nellie McClung's *In Times like These* and *Clearing in the West* and Sylvia Fraser's *Pandora* and *My Father's House*; devalued works by canonized authors, such as Adele Wiseman's *Crackpot*; and lesser-known works which have not been popularized or canonized, such as Irene Baird's *Waste Heritage*, Diana Collier's *The Invisible Women of Washington*, and Helen Potrebenko's *Hey Waitress*. It becomes clear from assessing the works according to their oppositional potential and canonic status that the national canon has not simply marginalized the most oppositional or 'authentic' voices in favour of more conventionally stylized versions of poverty, but that poverty narratives exist both inside and outside a canon that is itself shifting. This means that works such as *Crackpot*, *Cabbagetown*, and *Hey Waitress* may have been a little ahead of their time not so much due to public reception as to critical norms and categories within the study of a national literature. As we develop reading practices geared towards the interpretation of representations of poverty and class, the institution of Canadian literature will become more receptive to subversive, materialist themes.

Traditionally, class analysis in Canadian literary studies has maintained a conservative focus in respect to canon and methodology: it has studied mainly canonized works, the illumination of social and national vision in the text, the explication of configurations of class and economic relations, the analysis of social realism, and the historical mapping of a literary tradition of class-consciousness. These critical methods locate the discussion of class in the male sphere of public experience and openly prescribe what kind of class 'reality' should be represented textually. That is not to say that certain literary critics in Canada have not made isolated observations on the inscription of class and gender in applied readings of class-conscious texts – for example, in works by Ben-Zion Shek, Dorothy Livesay, Miriam Waddington, Kenneth Hughes, Frank Davey, Robin Endres, and Robin Mathews. But they have not questioned the fundamental issue of how gender intersects with class – even when the discussion has been about working-class women as writers and protagonists. Moreover, their focus, for the most part, has resulted in prescriptive aesthetics. A welcome departure from this trend has been Caren Irr's recent study, *The Suburb of Dissent*, an analysis of the cultural politics of dissenting American and Canadian literature in the 1930s. The isolated nature of class analyses in Canadian literature has been documented in sparse but fascinating left-wing bibliographies such as Rolf Knight's *Traces of Magma: An Annotated Bibliography of Left Literature* (1983) and Chris Bullock and David Peck's section on English-Canadian literature in *Guide to Marxist Literary Criticism* (1980). Lone voices have confronted the broader cultural and aesthetic implications of combined class, race, and gender bias in the institution of Canadian criticism: for example, Arun Mukherjee in *Towards an Aesthetics of Opposition*, Robin Mathews in *Canadian Literature: Surrender or Revolution* (1978), Robert McDougall in 'The Dodo and the Cruising Auk' (1963), and Himani Bannerjee in *Returning the Gaze*.

One of the earliest sustained analyses of social themes in English-Canadian literature was written in the late 1950s. F.W. Watt's doctoral dissertation, 'Radicalism in English Canadian Literature since Confederation,' in which he carefully traced the historical development of a radical socialist trend in poetry and prose, was never published, although a condensed and updated version of it appeared in 1965 in Klinck's *Literary History of Canada*. Watt did not directly challenge the existing canon because his method of analysis was mainly historical survey. But as he identified aspects of radicalism – such as Marxist utopic vision, social realism, anger and protest, anti-industrialism, and a spirit of collectivism – he unfolded, alongside his historical discussion and his statement of Marxist aesthetics, an implicit personal aesthetic favouring liberalism above dogma. The type of criticism which Watt engaged in was not radical itself, in today's sense of the word; it was, rather, a survey of radicalism. In a later volume of *The Literary History of Canada*, Barry Cameron's chapter on theory and criticism included an update on the trends in social criticism. Cameron makes the following observation about where the general tone and objectives of Canadian social criticism have been leading us: 'Those who hold such a representationist theory of language and literature – that is, a predominantly mimetic view of the relation between the text and a given preconstituted reality – tend to base their critical practice in the classic subject/object structure of knowledge, in the divorce between language and experience, central to empiricist epistemology' (120).

Among the problems which Cameron extrapolates from this tendency of Canadian social critics to assess representation according to 'authenticity' and to disregard more self-reflexive processes of critical discourse, has been the privileging of a certain consciousness, a certain concept of fixed or ideal reality, and therefore the corresponding prescription of aesthetic standards. Robin Mathews's *Canadian Literature: Surrender or Revolution* comes to mind because of its positing of an ideal community as a yardstick against which to measure literary worlds. Yet this would be a dismissive attitude to take towards the substantial contribution Mathews has made in terms of leftist nationalism in Canada. A more complete history of radicalism would be needed to decode the idealist and oppositional strains in his work. Misao Dean's paper on the relation between Mathews's 'vulgar' Marxism and present postmodernist positions in Canadian criticism, in *Canada: Critical Discourse / Discours critique* (1994), is a small but significant step in this direction.[1]

The only existing anthology of Marxist criticism of English-Canadian literature, *In Our Own House: Social Perspectives on Canadian Literature* (edited by Paul Cappon, 1978), was written mainly by sociologists considering the production and the institutionalization of Canadian culture. Flavouring the analyses throughout is the denunciation of the prevailing aesthetics of individualist modernism and the endorsement of collective movements and representations of community struggle, following Lukacsian arguments: 'Art and literature then should reflect contemporary historical conditions, and the changes that may occur through human effort' (12). (The collection shows, on the whole, a surprising lack of interest in questions of gender, considering it was published in the late seventies.) A special issue of *Canadian Literature* focused on class analysis in the mid-nineties but with little impact on the field as a whole. Another recent attempt at broadening social contexts, *New Contexts of Canadian Criticism* (edited by Ajay Heble and colleagues 1997), did not consider class important enough as a shaping

---

1 In a review of Mathews's *Treason of the Intellectuals* in *The Canadian Forum*, I touched on the marginalization of Mathews's work and his professional marginalization as testimony to the potency of his subversion of bourgeois nationalism. I still remember a session at the Learneds Conference when a Chinese student made the cultural *faux pas* of uttering Mathews's name beside Northrop Frye's and the room fell totally silent. No one would or perhaps could explain why the mere mention of the two names side by side was taboo, nor would anyone condescend to answer the question about social criticism. The blanket of silence was answer enough.

force on identity to include it alongside race, ethnicity, and gender in the late 1990s. In Blundell, Shepherd, and Taylor's *Relocating Cultural Studies*, even climate earns a more prominent spot than class among contemporary cultural issues affecting identity.

A sociology of class in the literary élite had a shaky beginning in two articles by Linda and Paul Grayson, 'The Canadian Literary Elite: A Socio-Historical Perspective' (1978) and 'Canadian Literary and Other Elites: The Historical and Institutional Bases of Shared Realities' (1980), but lacked the theoretical sophistication towards cultural analysis of John Porter's *The Vertical Mosaic: An Analysis of Social Class and Power in Canada* and Lucie Robert's *L'Institution du littéraire au Québec* (the latter is based on Jacques Dubois's theory of literature as a self-regulating institution).

Unfortunately, the schools of class criticism and feminist criticism have been largely divergent in Canada (as with cultural studies and class analysis), and that is why it has been necessary for me to go outside Canadian critical theory to discover ways of reading which illuminate both poverty and gender. The lack of class and materialist analysis in feminist criticism in Canada (compared for example with Britain and the United States) has not, to my knowledge, been documented or studied. The predominance of deconstruction and French feminist theory which occurred with the institutionalization of feminist criticism in Canadian universities may explain the lack of scholarly works in the domain of materialist feminist analysis and its relegation, instead, to the oppositional sphere of little feminist magazines.[2] It goes without saying that the more recent school(s) of feminist criticism have had a much greater impact on the development of theory in Canadian criticism than class criticism has (Cameron) and have produced a much greater body of writing (for example, see Barbara Godard's 'Bibliography of Feminist Criticism in Canada and Quebec' [1985]). Although materialist feminism as a school has made little impact on Canadian criticism in the last two decades, there have been exceptions – Clara Thomas, Elizabeth Waterston, Patricia Smart, Heather Murray, Carole Gerson, Dionne Brand, and Misao Dean – none of whom were self-consciously materialist in their method but who stressed history and social context to such an extent that their work on women writers often

---

2 See Theresa Ebert on the social logic of the eclipse of materialist feminism on the international front.

constitutes materialist analysis. In addition to the above-mentioned sources, certain left-wing periodicals, presses, and bookstores have made a constant, though perhaps undervalued, contribution to creating a sense of community among otherwise isolated materialist thinkers: for example, *The Canadian Forum, This Magazine, New Frontier*, Garamond Press, Hogtown Press, New Star Press, Fernwood Press, and Spartacus Bookstore, among others. A history of the resilience of these collectives outside the mainstream literary establishment, a few of which have attained mainstream status, would do much to construct a sense of the tradition of class analysis in Canada as a dispersed but ongoing movement.

Recently, a more self-consciously theoretical form of canon questioning has emerged to document, usually historically, the formation and institutionalization of Canadian literature and the devaluation or absence of certain minority writers and non-traditional genres. However, none of these recent works on canon-questioning (for example, *Canadian Canons: Essays on Literary Value*, edited by Robert Lecker [1991] and the ensuing debates by Frank Davey and others) have examined combined class and gender bias in the Canadian canon in any sustained way; the majority have reacted instead against realist bias, gender bias, and ethnocentricity. The nuances of bourgeois tastes and selection practices in the making of the Canadian canon have received some analysis, along with other historical determinants, by Carole Gerson in 'The Canon between the Wars: Fieldnotes of a Feminist Literary Archaeologist' in *Canadian Canons*, and in her full-length study *A Purer Taste: The Writing and Reading of Fiction in English in Nineteenth-Century Canada*. Critiques of the institutionalization of literary values are steadily emerging in respect to the reception of minority ethnic and Native writing, and some peripheral mention of class appears in these studies (for example, see *Literatures of a Lesser Diffusion: Les Littératures de moindre diffusion*, edited by Joseph Pivato and colleagues [Edmonton: University of Alberta Press, 1990] and Julia Emberley's *Thresholds of Difference: Feminist Critique, Native Women's Writings, Postcolonial Theory*). In particular, Enoch Padolsky, Sherry Simon, and Arun Mukherjee, among others, have been adamant that ethnicity cannot be isolated from class in studying minority ethnic writing because ethnic identity is so often mediated by class experience (see Padolsky's 'Canadian Minority Ethnic Writing in English,' Simon's *Fictions de l'identitaire au Québec*, and Mukherjee's *Oppositional Aesthetics: Readings from a Hyphenated Space*).

The conference that opened theoretically self-reflexive canonical discussion in Canada polled university teachers on their vision of the canon. However, as evidenced by the book of conference proceedings, *Taking Stock: The Calgary Conference on the Canadian Novel* (edited by Charles Steele, 1982) the cultural critique concentrated on biculturalism, multiculturalism, regionalism, and competing schools of criticism – passing over the poor, the working class, and women as groups with legitimate claims for representation. More recent texts emerging in cultural studies and the contexts of Canadian criticism promise to address earlier blind spots by giving at least a nod to the issue of class in the canon, but the subjectivities of poor people and the impact of class and poverty on individual and national identity have yet to appear at the centre of major literary studies in Canada.

Why retain the category of national literature if it has blocked counter-national critique or views of culture-from-below? Despite globalization and theories that the nation-states are dead, we still tend to know literatures via national categories even though we challenge the canons of these categories. For pragmatic and professional reasons, it is a strategic focus because universities still teach and examine students, hire experts, arrange conferences, and even publish papers according to fields of national literatures. More importantly, however, on a deeper discursive level, idealist constructions of nation often contribute significantly to the construction of poverty and the poor on the outside of civil society and, hence, on the outside of a category of national culture. For instance, Ruth L. Smith's analysis of the economy of a liberal humanist discourse whereby a seemingly 'natural' boundary places the poor and their needs on the outside of civil (market) society exposes the mechanisms whereby the subjectivities of the poor are denied by certain models of civil society functioning as exclusionary conceptual practices. It is important to see, as Carol Gerson has documented, that the cultivation of literary tastes and canon in Canada were shaped by a cultural project of nation building that was class-rooted, though not simplistically so. Much of the class-rooted nature of aesthetic assumptions about the national literature remains tacit, especially since the national literature has opened itself to canonic questioning by other interest groups such as feminists, Native people, multiculturalists, and gays and lesbians. While the idea of nation in Canada has often officially functioned as an idealist imagined community based on capitalist values from a largely bourgeois, nationalist perspective, other, more populist and democratic visions of nation have always coexisted with bourgeois or middle-class notions of nation, though none of these has been culturally dominant or has shaped the study of the national literature. In order to study the force of such ideological structures as New World / First World myths and meritocracy, we should, as Gramsci encouraged, glean an understanding first of their historical contexts, both local and national, and then of the superstructure within which these histories were shaped. It is enlightening to explore how the concept of nation and national culture may have historically shaped the construction of the poor as an internally colonized group or a nation-within-a-nation in order to decode present-day representations, but it is safe to assume that the ideology behind these images of the poor is elusive as it shifts and changes to incorporate potential difference and cultural resistance and transform that difference and resistance for hegemonic ends.

iv Poverty Narratives by Canadian Women (1919–1990s)

Alford, Edna. 'The Garden of Eloise Loon.' 1986.
Atwood, Margaret. *Alias Grace*. 1996.
Baird, Irene. 'Sidown, Brothers, Sidown.' 1976.
– *Waste Heritage*. 1939.
Baxter, Sheila. *No Way to Live: Poor Women Speak Out*. 1988.
– *Under the Viaduct: Homeless in Beautiful B.C.* 1991.
Beresford-Howe, Constance. *The Book of Eve*. 1973.
Blais, Marie-Claire. *Les Manuscrits de Pauline Archange*. 1968.
– *Une Saison dans la vie d'Emmanuel*. 1965.
Blondall, Patricia. *A Candle to Light the Sun*. 1960.
Brand, Dionne. *No Burden to Carry: Narratives of Black Working Women in Ontario 1920s–1950s*. 1991.
– *Sans Souci and Other Stories*. 1988.
Broadfoot, Barry. (As told to). *The Immigrant Years: From Europe to Canada 1945–1967*. 1986.
– *Ten Lost Years*. 1973.
Butala, Alice. 'A Day in Town.' 1939.
Cameron, Anne. *Aftermath*. 1999.
– *Kick the Can*. 1991.
– *The Whole Fam Damily*. 1995.
– 'The World Is Full of Magic.' 1989.
Campbell, Maria. *Halfbreed*. 1973.
Carr, Emily. *The House of All Sorts*. 1944.

– *Klee Wyck*. 1941.
Collier, Diana. *The Invisible Women of Washington*. 1987.
Culleton, Beatrice. *In Search of April Raintree*. 1983.
Dohaney, M.T. *The Corrigan Women*. 1988.
Endres, Robin Belitsky. 'Why I Left "The Left" to Write.' 1986.
Faessler, Shirley. 'A Basket of Apples.' 1969.
– *Everything in the Window*. 1979.
– 'Henye.' 1971.
Fireweed: A Feminist Quarterly. Class Is the Issue. 25 (Fall 1987).
Fireweed: A Feminist Quarterly. This Is Class Too. 26 (Winter/Spring 1988).
Flaherty, Martha. 'I Fought to Keep My Hair.' 1986
Fraser, Sylvia. *My Father's House: A Memoir of Incest and Healing*. 1987
– *Pandora*. 1972.
Gallant, Mavis. 'Jorinda and Jorindel.' 1956.
– 'Orphans' Progress.' 1956.
Gibson, Margaret. 'Ada.' 1976.
– 'Making It.' 1976.
Gillis, Tess. *Stories from the Woman from Away*. 1996.
Grayson, Linda, and Michael Bliss, eds. *The Wretched of Canada: Letters to R.B. Bennett*. 1971.
Hale, Alice K., and Sheila A. Brooks, eds. *The Depression in Canadian Literature*. 1976.
Henry, Ann. *Laugh, Baby, Laugh*. 1970.
Hewitt, Marsha, and Claire Mackay. *One Proud Summer*. 1982.
Holmes, Nancy. 'Bugs.' 1989.
Horseman, Jennifer. *Something in My Mind besides the Everyday: Women and Literacy*. 1990.
Hughes, Nym. 'Why I Can't Write about Class.' 1987.
Innis, Mary Quayle. 'Holiday.' 1932
– 'The Gift.' 1934.
– 'The Party.' 1931.
– 'Staver.' 1936.
Jaques, Edna. *Uphill All the Way: An Autobiography of Edna Jaques*. 1977.
Khosla, Prahba. Interviews and Trans. 'Profiles of Working-class East Indian Women.' 1986.
Knight, Phyllis, and Rolf Knight. *A Very Ordinary Life*. 1974.
Kogawa, Joy. *Obasan*. 1983.
Lambert, Betty. *Crossings*. 1979.
Lambert, Claudia. 'Lessons.' 1986.

Landsberg, Michele. *Women and Children First*. 1982.
Lau, Evelyn. *Runaway: Diary of a Street Kid*. 1989.
Laurence, Margaret. *The Diviners*. 1974.
– 'Horses of the Night.' 1967.
– 'The Loons.' 1966.
– *The Stone Angel*. 1964.
– *The Tomorrow-Tamer*. 1960.
Livesay, Dorothy. *Right Hand, Left Hand* 1977.
– 'The Waiting Room.' 1936.
Lysenko, Vera. *Men in Sheepskin Coats*. 1947.
– *Yellow Boots*. 1954.
McClung, Nellie. *Clearing in the West*. 1935.
– *Flowers for the Living: A Book of Short Stories*. 1931.
– *Painted Fires*. 1925.
MacDonald, Ann-Marie. *Fall On Your Knees*. 1996.
Maillet, Antonine. *Pélagie-la-charette*. 1979.
– *La Sagouine*. 1971.
Martens, Debra. 'The Holiness of Jazz and Art.' 1989.
– 'The Pip.' 1987.
Maynard, Fredelle Bruser. *Raisins and Almonds*. 1964.
Montero, Gloria. *Billy Higgins Rides the Freights*. 1982.
– *We Stood Together: First Hand Accounts of Dramatic Events in Canada's Labour Past*. 1979.
Moran, Bridget. *Stoney Creek Woman: The Story of Mary John*. 1989.
Morrissey, Donna. *Kit's Law*. 1999.
Mukherjee, Arun, ed. *Sharing Our Experience*. 1993.
Munro, Alice. *Dance of the Happy Shades*. 1968.
– *Who Do You Think You Are?* 1978.
Murphy, Barbara. *The Ugly Canadian: The Rise and Fall of a Caring Society*. 1999.
Ostenso, Martha. *Wild Geese*. 1925.
Phillips, Donna, ed. *Voices of Discord: Canadian Short Stories from the 1930s*. 1979.
Poor People's Press. (Oct. 1989–Summer 1991).
Potrebenko, Helen. *Hey Waitress and Other Stories*. 1989.
– 'My Mother, the Troublemaker.' 1988.
– *No Streets of Gold: A Social History of Ukrainians in Alberta*. 1977.
Riis, Sharon. *The True Story of Ida Johnson*. 1976
Ross, Veronica. *Fisher Woman*. 1984.
– 'God's Blessings.' 1984.

- 'Nels.' 1986.
Roy, Gabrielle. *Bonheur d'occasion*. 1945. Trans. *The Tin Flute*. 1947 and 1980.
- *La Détresse et l'enchantement*. 1970.
- *La Rivière sans repos*. 1970. Trans. *Windflower*. 1970.
Salverson, Laura Goodman. *Confessions of an Immigrant's Daughter*. 1939.
- *The Viking Heart*. 1945.
Sand, Cy-Thea. 'A Question of Identity.' 1987.
Sarsfield, Mairuth. *No Crystal Stair*. 1997.
Schram, Mary Lou Peters. 'Eviction.' 1992.
Silman, Janet. (As told to). *Enough Is Enough: Aboriginal Women Speak Out*. 1987.
Silvera, Makeda. 'And What If a Black Woman Decides ...?' 1984.
- 'Canada Sweet, Girl.' 1987.
- *Silenced: Talks with Working-class Caribbean Women about Their Lives and Struggles as Domestic Workers in Canada*. 2nd ed. 1989.
Sime, J.G. *Sister Woman*. 1919.
Smucker, Barbara Claassen. *Days of Terror*. 1981.
Sweatman, Margaret. *Fox*. 1991.
Sykes, Joy. 'Comments of a Working-class Crone.' 1987.
Szucsany, Desiré. 'The Suitcase.' 1989.
Tener, Anne E. 'Ruby's Education.' 1988.
Toronto Rape Crisis Centre – Working Class Caucus. 'Around the Kitchen Table.' 1988.
Tracey, Linda Lee. *On the Edge: A Journey to the Heart of Canada*. 1993.
Tynes, Maxine. 'Borrowed Beauty.' 1989.
- 'In Service.' 1988.
Waddington, Miriam. 'Mrs. Maza's Salon.' 1989.
Watson, Sheila. *The Double Hook*. 1959.
Webber, Marlene. *Street Kids: The Tragedy of Canada's Runaways*. 1991.
- *Food for Thought: How Our Dollar Democracy Drove 2 Million Canadians into Foodbanks to Collect Private Charity in Place of Public Justice*. 1992.
Weber, Lori. 'Trip with Brock.' 1989.
Weinzweig, Helen. *Basic Black with Pearls*. 1980.
- 'My Mother's Luck.' 1989.
Willis, Meredith Sue. 'Dreams of Deprivation.' 1988.
Wilson, Ethel. 'Lilly's Story.' 1952.
Wiseman, Adele. *Crackpot*. 1974.
- 'Memoirs of a Book-molesting Childhood.' 1986.

Bibliography

Abbott, Pamela, and Roger Sapsford. *Women and Social Class.* London and New York: Tavistock, 1987.

Adams, Ian. *The Poverty Wall.* Toronto and Montreal: McClelland & Stewart, 1970.

Adams, Ian, William Cameron, Brian Hill, and Peter Penz, eds. *The Real Poverty Report.* Edmonton: Hurtig, 1971.

Adorno, Theodor, and Max Horkheimer. 'The Cultural Industry: Enlightenment as Mass Deception.' *Dialectic of Enlightenment.* New York: Seabury Press, 1972. Rpt and trans. in During, ed. 29–43.

Ahmad, Aijaz. *In Theory: Class, Nations, Literatures.* London and New York: Verso, 1992.

Alcoff, Linda. 'The Problem of Speaking for Others.' *Cultural Critique* 16 (Winter 1991): 5–32.

Alcoff, Linda, and Elizabeth Potter, eds. *Feminist Epistemologies.* New York and London: Routledge, 1993.

Alford, Edna. 'The Garden of Eloise Loon.' *The Garden of Eloise Loon.* Lantzville, BC: Oolichan Books, 1986. 134–42.

Althusser, Louis. 'Ideology and State Ideological Apparatuses (Notes toward an Investigation).' *Lenin and Philosophy.* Trans. Ben Brewster. London: New Left Books, 1979. 136–70.

Anderson, Benedict. *Imagined Communities: Reflections on the Origin and Spread of Nationalism.* London: Verso and New Left Books, 1983.

Armstrong, Pat, and Hugh Armstrong. *The Double Ghetto: Canadian Women and Their Segregated Work.* Toronto: McClelland & Stewart, 1978.

– *Theorizing Women's Work.* Toronto: Garamond Press, 1990.

Aronowitz, Stanley. *The Jobless Future: Si-tech and the Dogma of Work.* Minneapolis and London: U of Minnesota P, 1994.

- *The Politics of Identity: Class, Culture, Social Movements*. New York and London: Routledge, 1992.
Atwood, Margaret. *Alias Grace*. Toronto: McClelland & Stewart, 1996.
Baird, Irene. 'Sidown, Brothers, Sidown.' *Revue de l'Université laurentienne / Laurentian University Review* 9.1 (Nov. 1976): 81–6.
- *Waste Heritage*. Toronto: Macmillan, 1939.
Balibar, Etienne. 'The Nation Form: History and Ideology.' In Balibar and Wallerstein, eds. 86–100.
Balibar, Etienne, and Immanuel Wallerstein, eds. *Race, Nation, and Class: Ambiguous Identities*. Trans. of *Race, nation, classe: les identités ambiguës*, Paris: Editions La Découverte, 1988. London and New York: Verso, 1991.
Bannerjee, Himani. *Returning the Gaze: Essays on Racism, Feminism, and Politics*. Toronto: Sister Vision, 1993.
- *Thinking Through: Essays on Feminism, Marxism, and Anti-racism*. Toronto: Women's Press, 1995. 17–40.
Barrett, Michèle. *Women's Oppression Today: The Marxist/Feminist Encounter*. Rev. ed. London and New York: Verso, 1988.
Baxter, Sheila. *No Way to Live: Poor Women Speak Out*. Vancouver: New Star Books, 1988.
- *Under the Viaduct: Homeless in Beautiful B.C.* Vancouver: New Star Books, 1991.
Belsey, Catherine. 'Constructing the Subject: Deconstructing the Text.' In Newton and Rosenfelt, eds. 45–64.
- 'Literature, History, Politics.' *Literature and History*. 1983. Rpt in *Modern Criticism and Theory: A Reader*. Ed. David Lodge. London and New York: Longman, 1988. 400–10.
Bennett, Tony. *Outside Literature*. London and New York: Routledge, 1990.
Beresford-Howe, Constance. *The Book of Eve*. Toronto: Macmillan, 1973.
Berger, P., and T. Luckmann. *The Social Construction of Reality. A Treatise on the Sociology of Knowledge*. 1966. Rpt Garden City, NY: Anchor Books, 1967.
Berger, Thomas. *Fragile Freedoms: Human Rights and Dissent in Canada*. Toronto and Vancouver: Clarke, Irwin, 1982.
Bessette, Gérard. *Une littérature en ébullition*. Montreal: Editions du jour, 1968.
Beverly, John. 'The Margin at the Center: On Testimonio (Testimonial Narrative).' *Modern Fiction Studies* 35.1 (Spring 1989): 11–28.
Bhabha, Homi, ed. *Nation and Narration*. London and New York: Routledge, 1990.
Biron, Michel, and Pierre Popovic, eds. *Ecrire la pauvreté: Actes du VIe Colloque international de sosiocritique, Université de Montréal, Sept. 1993*. Toronto: Editions du Gref, 1996.

Blais, Marie Claire. *Les Manuscrits de Pauline Archange*. Montreal: Editions du jour, 1968.
– *Une Saison dans la vie d'Emmanuel*. Montreal: Editions du jour, 1965.
Blondall, Patricia. *A Candle to Light the Sun*. Toronto: McClelland & Stewart, 1960.
Blundell, Valda, John Shepherd, and Ian Taylor, eds. *Relocating Cultural Studies: Developments in Theory and Research*. London and New York: Routledge, 1993.
Blyth, Jack A. *The Canadian Social Inheritance*. Toronto, Montreal, Vancouver: Copp Clark, 1972.
Boorstin, Daniel J. 'The Historian: A Wrestler with the Angel.' *New York Times Book Review*, 20 Sept. 1987.
Booth, Charles. *Life and Labour of the People of London*. 1892–7. 17 vols. London: Macmillan, 1902–3.
Bourdieu, Pierre. *Acts of Resistance: Against the Tyranny of the Market*. Trans. of *Contre-feux*. Trans. Richard Nice. Editions liber-raisons d'agir, France, 1998. New York: Polity Press, 1998.
– 'Cultural Reproduction and Social Reproduction.' *Knowledge, Education, and Cultural Change*. Ed. Richard Brown. London: Tavistock; 1973. 71–112. Rpt in *Power and Ideology in Education*. Ed. Jerome Karabel and A.H. Halsey. New York: Oxford UP, 1977. 487–511.
– *Distinction: A Social Critique of the Judgement of Taste*. Trans. of *La Distinction: Critique sociale du jugement*. 1979. Trans. Richard Nice. Cambridge, MA: Harvard UP, 1984.
Bramen, Carrie Tirado. 'The Picturesque and the Aesthetics of Poverty.' Paper read at the National Meeting of the Popular Culture Association, New Orleans, May 1993.
Brand, Dionne. *No Burden to Carry: Narratives of Black Women in Ontario 1920s–1950s*. Toronto: Women's Press, 1991.
– *Sans Souci and Other Stories*. Stratford, ON: Williams-Wallace, 1988.
Brantlinger, Patrick. *Crusoe's Footprints: Cultural Studies in Britain and America*. New York and London: Routledge, 1990.
Brennan, Timothy. 'The National Longing for Form.' In Bhabha, ed. 44–70.
Brenner, Johanna. 'Feminist Political Discourses: Radical versus Liberal Approaches to the Feminization of Poverty and Comparable Worth.' In Hansen and Philipson, eds. 491–507.
Broadfoot, Barry. *Ten Lost Years*. Toronto and New York: Doubleday, 1973.
– *The Immigrant Years: From Europe to Canada 1945–1967*. Vancouver and Toronto: Douglas & McIntyre, 1986.
Brodzki, Bella, and Celeste Schenck. 'Criticus Interruptus: Uncoupling Feminism and Deconstruction.' *Feminism and Institutions: Dialogues on Feminist*

Theory. Ed. Linda Kaufman. Cambridge and Oxford: Basil Blackwell, 1989. 194–208.
Bromley, Roger. *Lost Narratives: Popular Fictions, Politics and Recent History.* London and New York: Routledge, 1988.
Bullock, Chris, and David Peck, eds. *Guide to Marxist Literary Criticism.* Brighton, UK: Harvester Press, 1980.
Butala, Alice. 'A Day in Town.' *Canadian Forum* (May 1939). Rpt in Phillips, ed. 101–7.
Butler, Judith. *Gender Trouble.* New York and London: Routledge, 1990.
Cameron, Anne. *Aftermath.* Madeira Park, BC: Harbour, 1999.
– *Kick the Can.* Madeira Park, BC: Harbour, 1991.
– *The Whole Fam Damily.* Madeira Park, BC: Harbour, l995.
– 'The World Is Full of Magic.' *Earth Witch.* Vancouver: Harbour, nd. Rpt in Nemiroff, ed. 378–84.
Campbell, Maria. *Halfbreed.* Toronto: McClelland & Stewart, 1973.
Canada. *Women and Poverty Revisited.* Ottawa: National Council of Welfare, 1990.
Cappon, Paul, ed. *In Our Own House: Social Perspectives on Canadian Literature.* Toronto: McClelland & Stewart, 1978.
Carr, Emily. *The House of All Sorts.* 1944. Rpt Toronto: Clarke, Irwin, 1967.
– *Klee Wyck.* 1941. Rpt Toronto: Irwin Publishing, 1965.
Chatterjee, Partha. *Nationalist Thought and the Colonial World: A Derivative Discourse.* Tokyo and London: Third World Books, Zed Books, United Nations University, 1986.
Cherwinski, W.J.C., and Gregory S. Kealey. *Lectures in Canadian Labour and Working-class History.* St John's: Committee on Canadian Labour History and Hogtown Press, 1985.
Chomsky, Noam. *Class Warfare.* Interview by David Barsamian. Vancouver: New Star Books, 1997.
– *On Power and Ideology.* Montreal and New York: Black Rose Books, 1987.
Christian, Barbara. 'The Race for Theory.' In Hansen and Philipson, eds. 568–79.
Clifford, James. *The Predicament of Culture: Twentieth-Century Ethnography, Literature, and Art.* Cambridge, MA: Harvard UP, 1988.
Coldwell, Joan. 'Munro, Alice.' *The Oxford Companion to Canadian Literature.* Ed. William Toye. Toronto, Oxford, New York: Oxford UP, 1983.
Collier, Diana. *The Invisible Women of Washington.* Atlanta and Ottawa: Clarity Press, 1987.
Costello, Jeanne. 'Taking the "Woman" Out of Women's Autobiography: The Perils and Potentials of Theorizing Female Subjectivities.' *Diacritics* 21.2–3 (Summer-Fall 1991): 123–34.

Culleton, Beatrice. *In Search of April Raintree*. Winnipeg, MB: Pemmican Publications, 1983.
Daly, Mary. *Women and Poverty*. Dublin: Attic Press, 1989.
Davey, Frank. *Post-national Arguments: The Politics of the Anglophone-Canadian Novel since 1967*. Toronto: U of Toronto P, 1993.
de Certeau, Michel. 'Ecritures et histoires.' *Introduction de L'ecriture de l'histoire*. Paris: Gallimard, 1975. 7–23.
Delphy, Christine. *Close to Home: A Materialist Analysis of Women's Oppression*. Trans. and ed. Diana Leonard. Amherst: U of Massachusetts P, 1984.
de Man, Paul. 'The Resistance to Theory.' *Yale French Studies* 63 (1982). Rpt in *Modern Criticism and Theory: A Reader*. Ed. David Lodge. London and New York: Longman, 1988. 355–71.
Dentith, Simon, and Philip Dodd. 'The Uses of Autobiography.' *Literature and History* 14.1 (Spring 1988): 5–22.
Diamond, Sara. 'How Class Affects Women's Writing.' *In the Feminine: Women and Words / Les Femmes et les mots: Conference Proceedings 1983*. Ed. Ann Dybikowski et al. Edmonton: Longspoon, 1985. 32–6.
DiFazio, William. 'Why There Is No Movement of the Poor.' *Post-Work: The Wages of Cybernation*. Ed. Stanley Aronowitz and Jonathan Cutler. London and New York: Routledge, 1998. 141–66.
Dimock, Wai Chee, and Michael T. Gilmore, eds. *Rethinking Class: Literary Studies and Social Formations*. New York: Columbia UP, 1994.
Dodd, Philip. 'History or Fiction: Balancing Contemporary Autobiography's Claims.' *Mosaic* 20.4 (1987): 61–9.
Doheny, M.T. *The Corrigan Women*. Charlottetown, PEI: Ragweed Press, 1988.
Donovan, Josephine. *Feminist Theory: The Intellectual Traditions of American Feminism*. New York: Ungar, 1987.
Dubois, Jacques. *L'Institution de la littérature*. Brussels: Editions Labor / Fernand Nathan, 1983.
During, Simon, ed. *The Cultural Studies Reader*. London and New York: Routledge, 1993.
Eagleton, Terry. 'The Idea of a Common Culture.' *Literary Taste, Culture and Mass Communication: Vol. 1. Culture and Mass Culture*. Ed. Peter Davison et al. Cambridge and Teaneck, NJ: Chadwyck-Healey / Somerset House, 1978. 3–25.
– *Literary Theory: An Introduction*. Oxford: Basil Blackwell, 1983.
Easingwood, Peter, Konrad Gross, and Wolfgang Klooss, eds. *Probing Canadian Culture*. Augsburg: AV Verlag, 1991.
Easthope, Antony. *Literary into Cultural Studies*. London and New York: Routledge, 1991.

Ebert, Theresa. *Ludic Feminism and After: Postmodernism, Desire, and Labour in Late Capitalism.* Ann Arbor: U of Michigan P, 1996.

Ehrenreich, Barbara. *Fear of Falling: The Inner Life of the Middle Class.* New York: Harper Perennial, 1990.

Emberley, Julia V. *Thresholds of Difference: Feminist Critique, Native Women's Writings, Postcolonial Theory.* Toronto: U of Toronto P, 1993.

Endres, Robin Belitsky. 'Why I Left "The Left" to Write.' In Silvera, ed., *Fireworks*. 13–20.

Faessler, Shirley. 'A Basket of Apples.' *Atlantic Monthly* (1969). Rpt in *Women in Canadian Literature*. Ed. M.G. Hesse. Ottawa: Borealis Press, 1976. 137–47.

– *Everything in the Window*. Toronto: McClelland & Stewart, 1979.

– 'Henye.' *Tamarack Review* 56 (1971). Rpt in *The Narrative Voice: Short Stories and Reflections by Canadian Authors*. Ed. John Metcalf. Toronto, Montreal, New York, London: McGraw-Hill Ryerson, 1972. 28–47.

Fallis, George, and Alex Murray, eds. *Housing the Homeless and Poor: New Partnerships among the Private, Public, and Third Sectors.* Toronto: U of Toronto P, 1990.

Fanon, Franz. *The Wretched of the Earth.* Trans. of *Les damnées de la terre*. 1961. Trans. Constance Ferrington. New York: Grove Press, 1963.

Felman, Shoshana, and Dori Laub. *Testimony: Crises of Witnessing in Literature, Psychoanalysis, and History.* New York and London: Routledge, 1992.

Felski, Rita. *Beyond Feminist Aesthetics: Feminist Literature and Social Change.* Cambridge, MA: Harvard UP, 1989.

Fennario, David. *Blue Mondays.* Verdun, QC: Black Rock Creations, 1984.

Fetterly, Judith. *The Resisting Reader: A Feminist Approach to American Literature.* Bloomington: Indiana UP, 1978.

Fiske, John. 'Cultural Studies and the Culture of Everyday Life.' In Grossberg, Nelson, and Treichler, eds. 154–73.

– 'The Jeaning of America.' *Understanding Popular Culture*. 1989. Rpt New York and London: Routledge, 1991.

Flaherty, Martha. 'I Fought to Keep My Hair.' *Nunavut* 5.6 (June 1986): 4–6. Rpt in *Northern Voices: Inuit Writing in English*. Ed. Penny Petrone. Toronto, Buffalo, London: U of Toronto P, 1988. 274–8.

Foley, Barbara. *Radical Representations: Politics and Form in U.S. Proletarian Fiction 1929–1941.* Durham and London: Duke UP, 1993.

Fox, Pamela. *Class Fictions: Shame and Resistance in the British Working-class Novel, 1890–1945.* Durham and London: Duke UP, 1994.

– 'Recasting the "Politics of Truth": Thoughts on Class, Gender, and the Role of Intellectuals.' In Tokarczyk and Fay, eds. 219–38.

Fraser, Sylvia. *My Father's House: A Memoir of Incest and Healing*. Toronto: Doubleday, 1987. Rpt Toronto: Collins, 1988.
- *Pandora*. Toronto: McClelland & Stewart, 1972. Rpt Toronto: McClelland & Stewart, 1989.
Freire, Paulo. Foreword. In McLaren and Leonard, eds. ix–xii.
- *The Pedagogy of the Oppressed*. Trans. Myra Bergman Ramos. New York: Herder and Herder, 1970.
Freire, Paulo, and Henry A. Giroux. 'Pedagogy, Popular Culture, and Public Life: An Introduction.' *Popular Culture: Schooling and Everyday Life*. Ed. Henry A. Giroux and Roger Simon. New York, Westport, CT, and London: Bergin & Garvey, 1989. vii–xii.
Frye, Northrop. *The Critical Path: An Essay on the Social Context of Literary Criticism*. Bloomington and London: Indiana UP, 1971.
- 'Preface to an Uncollected Anthology.' *Studia Varia*. Ed. E.G. Murray. Toronto: U of Toronto P, 1957. Rpt in *Contexts of Canadian Criticism: A Collection of Critical Essays*. Ed. Eli Mandel. Chicago and London: U of Chicago P, 1971.
Gagnier, Regenia. *Subjectivities: A History of Self-Representation in Britain (1832–1920)*. New York and London: Oxford UP, 1989.
Galbraith, John Kenneth. *The Affluent Society*. 1958. 2nd ed, revised. New York and Toronto: New American Library, 1969.
Gallant, Mavis. *Home Truths: Selected Canadian Stories*. 1956. Rpt Toronto: Macmillan of Canada, 1981.
- 'Jorinda and Jorindel.' *Home Truths: Selected Canadian Stories*. 1956. Rpt Toronto: Macmillan of Canada, 1981. 17–28.
- 'Orphans' Progress.' *Home Truths: Selected Canadian Stories*. 1956. Rpt Toronto: Macmillan of Canada, 1981. 56–62.
Garner, Hugh. *Cabbagetown*. Toronto: Ryerson Press, 1968.
Geertz, Clifford. *The Interpretation of Cultures*. New York: Basic Books, 1973.
Gelpi, Barbara, and Nancy Hartsock, eds. *Women and Poverty*. Chicago and London: U of Chicago P, 1986.
Gerson, Carole. 'The Canon between the Wars: Fieldnotes of a Feminist Literary Archaeologist.' In Lecker, ed. 46–56.
- 'Mrs. Moodie's Beloved Partner.' *Canadian Literature* 107 (Winter 1985): 34–47.
- *A Purer Taste: The Writing and Reading of Fiction in English in Nineteenth-Century Canada*. Toronto, Buffalo, London: U of Toronto P, 1989.
- 'Sarah Binks and Edna Jaques: Parody, Gender, and the Construction of Literary Value.' *Canadian Literature* (1993): 62–73.
Gibson, Margaret. 'Ada.' *The Butterfly Ward*. Ottawa: Oberon, 1976. 5–27.

- 'Making It.' *The Butterfly Ward.* Ottawa: Oberon, 1976. 96–133.
Gillis, Tess. *Stories from the Woman from Away.* Wreck Cove, NS: Breton Books, 1996.
Gilman, Charlotte Perkins. 'The Yellow Wallpaper.' 1892. In *The Norton Anthology of Literature by Women: The Tradition in English.* Ed. Sandra M. Gilbert and Susan Gubar. 2nd ed. New York and London: W.W. Norton and Co., 1996. 1133–1144.
Giroux, Henry. *Border Crossings: Cultural Workers and the Politics of Education.* New York and London: Routledge, 1992.
Godard, Barbara. 'Bibliography of Feminist Criticism in Canada and Quebec.' In Godard, ed. 231–350.
- 'The Politics of Representation: Some Native Canadian Women Writers.' In New, ed. 183–228.
Godard, Barbara, ed. *Gynocritics / La Gynocritique: Feminist Approaches to Writing by Canadian and Québécoise Women.* Toronto: ECW Press, 1985.
Goldberg, Gertrude Schaffner, and Eleanor Kremen, eds. *The Feminization of Poverty: Only in America?* New York, Westport, CT, London: Praeger, 1990.
Goldie, Terry. *Fear and Temptation.* Montreal and Kingston: McGill-Queen's UP, 1990.
Gramsci, Antonio. *Selections from the Prison Notebooks.* Ed. and trans. Quintin Hoare and Geoffrey Nowell Smith. New York: International Publishers, 1971.
Grayson, Linda, and Michael Bliss, eds. *The Wretched of Canada: Letters to R.B. Bennett.* Toronto: U of Toronto P, 1971.
Grayson, Paul, and Linda Grayson. 'Canadian Literary and Other Elites: The Historical and Institutional Bases of Shared Realities.' *Canadian Review of Sociology and Anthropology* 17.4 (Nov. 1980): 338–56.
- 'The Canadian Literary Elite: A Socio-Historical Perspective.' *Canadian Journal of Sociology* 3.3 (Summer 1978): 291–308.
Green, Bryan. *Knowing the Poor: A Case Study in Textual Reality Construction.* London: Routledge and Kegan Paul, 1983.
Grossberg, Lawrence, Cary Nelson, and Paula Treichler, eds. *Cultural Studies.* New York and London: Routledge, 1992.
- 'The Formations of Cultural Studies: An American in Birmingham.' In Blundell, Shepherd, and Taylor, eds. 21–66.
Guilbert, Lucille, et al. *Pauvre et vagabond: Le quêteux et la société québécoise.* Laval, QC: Rapports et Mémoires de recherche du Célat no. 9 (nov. 1987).
Guillory, John. *Cultural Capital.* Chicago: U of Chicago P, 1993.
- 'Literary Critics as Intellectuals: Class Analysis and the Crisis of the Humanities.' In Dimock and Gilmore, eds. 107–46.

Gumbrecht, Hans Ulrich. '*Everyday*-World and *Life*-World as Philosophical Concepts: A Genealogical Approach.' *New Literary History* 24.4 (Autumn 1993): 745–61.

Gunderson, Morley, et al. *Women and Labour Market Poverty.* Ottawa: Canadian Advisory Council on the Status of Women, June 1990.

Gunnars, Kristjana. 'Laura Goodman Salverson's Confessions of a Divided Self.' *A Mazing Space*. Ed. Shirley Neuman. Edmonton: Longspoon Press, 1986. 148–53.

Hale, Alice K., and Sheila A. Brooks, eds. *The Depression in Canadian Literature*. Toronto: Macmillan, 1976.

Hall, John R., ed. *Reworking Class*. Ithaca, NY: Cornell UP, 1997.

Hall, Stuart. 'The Emergence of Cultural Studies and the Crisis of the Humanities.' *October* 53 (1990): 11–23.

Hall, Stuart, and Tony Jefferson, eds. *Resistance through Rituals: Youth Subcultures in Post-War Britain*. London: Hutchinson, 1975.

Hansen, Karen V., and Ilene J. Philipson, eds. *Women, Class, and the Feminist Imagination: A Socialist Feminist Reader*. Philadelphia: Temple UP, 1990.

Harding, Sandra. 'The Instability of the Analytical Categories of Feminist Theory.' In Malson et al., eds. 15–34.

Harrington, Michael. *The Other America: Poverty in the United States*. New York and London: Macmillan Co. and Collier-Macmillan, 1962.

Harvey, David, and Michael Reed. 'Paradigms of Poverty: A Critical Assessment of Contemporary Perspectives.' *International Journal of Politics, Culture, and Society* 6.2 (1992): 269–97.

Hawkesworth, Mary E. 'Knowers, Knowing, Known: Feminist Theory and Claims of Truth.' In Malson et al., eds. 327–51.

Hebdige, Dick. *Subculture: The Meaning of Style*. London: Methuen, 1979. Rpt London and New York: Routledge, 1988.

Heble, Ajay. 'New Contexts of Canadian Criticism: Democracy, Counterpoint, Responsibility.' In Heble et al., eds. 78–97.

– *The Tumble of Reason: Alice Munro's Discourse of Absence*. Toronto: U of Toronto P, 1994.

Heble, Ajay, Donna Palmateer Pence, and J.R. Struthers, eds. *New Contexts of Canadian Criticism*. Peterborough, ON: Broadview Press, 1997.

Helmes-Hayes, Rick, and James Curtis, eds. *The Vertical Mosaic Revisited*. Toronto: U of Toronto P, 1998.

Hennessy, Rosemary, and Chrys Ingraham, eds. *Materialist Feminism: A Reader in Class, Difference, and Women's Lives*. New York and London: Routledge, 1997.

Henry, Ann. *Laugh, Baby, Laugh*. Toronto: McClelland & Stewart, 1970.

Hewitt, Marsha, and Claire Mackay. *One Proud Summer*. Toronto: Women's Press, 1982.
Himmelfarb, Gertrude. *The Idea of Poverty*. New York: Alfred A. Knopf, 1984.
Hoggart, Richard. *The Uses of Literacy*. 1958. Rpt New York: Oxford UP, 1970.
Holmes, Nancy. 'Bugs.' In Nemiroff, ed. 192–7.
hooks, bell. *Feminist Theory: From Margin to Center*. Boston: South End Press, 1984.
– *Yearning: Race, Gender, and Cultural Politics*. Toronto: Between the Lines, 1990.
Horseman, Jennifer. *Something in My Mind besides the Everyday: Women and Literacy*. Toronto: Women's Press, 1990.
Hughes, Nym. 'Why I Can't Write about Class.' *Class Is the Issue: Fireweed* 25 (Fall 1987): 21–4.
Innis, Mary Quayle. 'Holiday.' *Canadian Forum* (Jan. 1932). Rpt in Hale and Brooks, eds. 3–8.
– 'The Gift.' *Canadian Forum* (June 1934). Rpt in Phillips, ed. 143–50.
– 'The Party.' *Canadian Forum* (June 1931). Rpt in Phillips, ed. 151–7.
– 'Staver.' *New Frontier* (Apr. 1936). Rpt in Phillips, ed. 173–81.
Irr, Caren. *The Suburb of Dissent: Cultural Politics in the United States and Canada during the 1930s*. Durham, NC, and London: Duke UP, 1998.
Irvine, M. Lorna. *Critical Spaces: Margaret Laurence and Janet Frame*. Columbia, SC: Camden House, 1995.
Itwaru, Arnold. 'Glorious and Free ... We Stand on Guard for Thee.' *Closed Entrances. Canadian Culture and Imperialism*. Ed. Arnold Itwaru and Natasha Konzek. Toronto: Tsar, 1994. 54–70.
Jaggar, Alison. 'Love and Knowledge: Emotion in Feminist Epistemology.' In Jaggar and Bordo, eds. 145–71.
Jaggar, Alison, and Susan Bordo, eds. *Gender/Body/Knowledge: Feminist Reconstructions of Being and Knowing*. New Brunswick, NJ, and London: Rutgers UP, 1989.
Jamieson, Nina Moore. *The Cattle in the Stall*. Toronto: S.B. Grundy, 1932.
Janes, Percy. *House of Hate*. Toronto: McClelland & Stewart, 1970.
Jaques, Edna. *Uphill All the Way*. Saskatoon: Western Producer Prairie Books, 1977.
Jenkins, Richard. *Pierre Bourdieu*. London and New York: Routledge, 1992.
John, Mary. *Stoney Creek Woman: The Story of Mary John*. Transcribed by Bridget Moran. Vancouver: Tillacum Library, 1989.
Johnson, Louise C. 'Socialist Feminisms.' *Feminist Knowledge: Critique and Construct*. Ed. Sneja Gunew. New York and London: Routledge, 1990. 304–31.
Kaplan, Caren. 'Resisting Autobiography: Outlaw Genres and Transnational Feminist Subjects.' In Smith and Watson, eds. 115–38.
Kaplan, Cora. 'Pandora's Box: Subjectivity, Class and Sexuality in Socialist-

Feminist Criticism.' *British Feminist Thought: A Reader.* Ed. Terry Lovell. London and Cambridge: Basil Blackwell, 1990. 345–66.

Kealey, Gregory S., and Peter Warrian, eds. *Essays in Canadian Working-class History.* Montreal and Toronto: McClelland & Stewart, 1976.

Keith, Michael, and Steve Pile, eds. *Place and the Politics of Identity.* London and New York: Routledge, 1993.

Khosla, Prahba, interviewer and trans. 'Profiles of Working-class East Indian Women.' In Silvera, ed., *Fireworks.* 154–60.

Klaus, Gustav. *The Literature of Labour.* New York: Harvester Press, 1989.

Knight, Phyllis, and Rolf Knight. *A Very Ordinary Life.* Vancouver: New Star Books, 1974.

Knight, Rolf. *Traces of Magma: An Annotated Bibliography of Left Literature.* Vancouver: Draegerman, 1983.

Kogawa, Joy. *Obasan.* Toronto: Lester & Orpen Dennys, 1981. Rpt Markham, ON, London and New York: Penguin, 1983.

Krupat, Arnold. *Ethnocriticism: Ethnography, History, Literature.* Berkeley, Los Angeles, Oxford: U of California P, 1992.

Kuester, Hildegard. *The Crafting of Chaos: Narrative Structure in Margaret Laurence's* The Stone Angel *and* The Diviners. Amsterdam and Atlanta, GA: Editions Rodopi BV, 1994.

Laclau, Ernesto, and Chantal Mouffe. *Hegemony and Socialist Strategy: Towards a Radical Democratic Politics.* London and New York: Verso, 1985.

Lambert, Betty. *Crossings.* 1979. Vancouver and Toronto: Douglas & McIntyre, 1989.

Lambert, Claudia. 'Lessons.' In Silvera, ed., *Fireworks.* 227–31.

Landsberg, Michele. *Women and Children First.* Toronto: Macmillan of Canada, 1982.

Lau, Evelyn. *Runaway: Diary of a Street Kid.* Toronto: HarperCollins, 1989.

Laurence, Margaret. *The Diviners.* Toronto: McClelland & Stewart, 1974.

– 'Horses of the Night.' *Chatelaine* 40.7 (July 1967). Rpt in Hale and Brooks, eds. 38–60.

– 'The Loons.' *Atlantic Advocate* (Mar. 1966). Rpt in Nemiroff, ed. 268–75.

– *The Stone Angel.* Toronto: McClelland & Stewart, 1964.

– *The Tomorrow-Tamer.* London: Macmillan, 1960.

Lauter, Paul. 'Working-class Women's Literature – An Introduction to Study.' *Radical Teacher* 15 (1979): 16–26.

Lecker, Robert, ed. *Canadian Canons: Essays in Literary Value.* Toronto: ECW Press, 1991.

Legaré, Anne. *Les Classes sociales au Québec.* Montreal: Les Presses de l'Université de Québec, 1977.

Leonard, Peter. *Postmodern Welfare: Reconstructing an Emancipatory Project.* London: Sage, 1997.

Lewis, Oscar. Introduction. *The Children of Sanchez: Autobiography of a Mexican Family.* New York: Random House, 1961. Rpt New York: Modern Library, 1969.

Lewis, Paula Gilbert. 'Female Spirals and Male Cages: The Urban Sphere in the Novels of Gabrielle Roy.' *Traditionalism, Nationalism, and Feminism: Women Writers of Québec.* Ed. Paula Gilbert Lewis. Westport, CT: Greenwood, 1985. 71–81.

Livesay, Dorothy. *Right Hand, Left Hand.* Erin, ON: Press Porcepic, 1977.

– 'The Waiting Room.' *New Frontier* (Dec. 1936). Rpt in Phillips, ed. 119–25.

Lysenko, Vera. *Men in Sheepskin Coats.* Toronto: Ryerson Press, 1947.

– *Yellow Boots.* Edmonton: NeWest Publishers, 1992. Rpt Toronto: Ryerson Press, 1954.

McClintock, Ann. *Imperial Leather: Race, Gender, and Sexuality in the Colonial Contest.* London and New York: Routledge, 1995.

McClung, Nellie. *Clearing in the West.* Toronto: T.H. Best, 1935.

– *Flowers for the Living: A Book of Short Stories.* Toronto: T.H. Best, 1931.

– *Painted Fires.* Toronto: Thomas Allen, 1925.

MacDaniel, Susan. 'The Changing Canadian Family: Women's Roles and the Importance of Feminism.' *Changing Patterns: Women in Canada.* Ed. Sandra Burt et al. Toronto: McClelland & Stewart, 1988. 103–28.

MacDonald, Ann-Marie. *Fall on Your Knees.* 1996. Rpt Toronto: Vintage Canada, 1997.

McDougall, Robert. 'The Dodo and the Cruising Auk.' *Canadian Literature* 18 (1963). Rpt in *Contexts of Canadian Criticism: A Collection of Critical Essays.* Ed. Eli Mandel. Chicago and London: U of Chicago P, 1971. 216–31.

McGuigan, Jim. *Cultural Populism.* London and New York: Routledge, 1992.

McLachlan, Alexander. 'We Live in a Rickety House.' *The New Oxford Book of Canadian Verse in English.* Ed. Margaret Atwood. Toronto and London: Oxford, 1982. 10.

McLaren, Peter, and Peter Leonard, eds. *Paulo Freire: A Critical Encounter.* London and New York: Routledge, 1993.

Maclean's. 1 Mar. 1993.

McQuaig, Linda. *The Cult of Impotence: Selling the Myth of Powerlessness in the Global Economy.* Toronto and London: Penguin, 1998.

McRobbie, Angela. 'Post-Marxism and Cultural Studies: A Post-script.' In Grossberg, Nelson, and Treichler, eds. 719–30.

Maillet, Antonine. *Pélagie-la-charette.* Montreal: Leméac, 1979.

– *La Sagouine.* Ottawa: Leméac, 1971.

Malson, Micheline, Jean F. O'Barr, Sara Westphal-Wihl, and Mary Wyer, eds. *Feminist Theory in Practice and Process*. Chicago and London: U of Chicago P, 1986.
Martens, Debra. 'The Holiness of Jazz and Art.' Unpublished manuscript. 1989.
– 'The Pip.' *Room of One's Own* 2 (1987): np.
Massey, Vincent. *Royal Commission on National Development in the Arts, Letters and Sciences* (The Massey Report). Ottawa: Government of Canada, 1951.
Mathews, Robin. *Canadian Literature: Surrender or Revolution*. Ed. Gail Dexter. Toronto: Steel Rail, 1978.
Mayhew, Henry. *London Labour and the London Poor*. 1849–52. Rpt London: W. Kimber, 1950.
Maynard, Fredelle Bruser. *Raisins and Almonds*. 1964. Rpt Toronto and New York: Doubleday, 1972.
Mettrick, Alan. *Last in Line: On the Road and Out of Work ... A Desperate Journey with Canada's Unemployed*. Toronto: Key Porter Books, 1985.
Mills, Sara. 'Authentic Realism.' *Feminist Readings / Feminists Reading*. Ed. Sara Mills, Lynne Pearce, Sue Spaull, and Elaine Millard. Charlottesville, VA: UP Virginia, 1989. 51–82.
Mishra, Ramesh. 'The Collapse of the Welfare Consensus? The Welfare State in the 1980s.' In Fallis and Murray, eds. 82–114.
Montero, Gloria. *Billy Higgins Rides the Freights*. Np: 1982.
– *We Stood Together: First Hand Accounts of Dramatic Events in Canada's Labour Past*. Toronto: Lorimer, 1979.
Moodie, Susanna. 'A Word for the Novel Writers.' *The Literary Garland* (Aug. 1851). Rpt in *Canadian Anthology*, rev. ed. Ed. Carl F. Klinck and Reginald E. Waters. Toronto: Gage, 1966. 58–63.
– *Roughing It in the Bush: Or Forest Life in Canada*. 1852. Rpt Toronto: McClelland & Stewart, 1987.
Moran, Bridget. (As told to). *Stoney Creek Woman: The Story of Mary John*. Vancouver: Tillacum Library, 1989.
Morrissey, Donna. *Kit's Law*. Toronto: Viking, 1999.
Moss, John. *A Reader's Guide to the Canadian Novel*. Toronto: McClelland & Stewart, 1981.
Mukherjee, Arun. *Oppositional Aesthetics: Readings from a Hyphenated Space*. Toronto: Tsar, 1994.
Mukherjee, Arun, ed. *Sharing Our Experience*. Ottawa: Canadian Advisory Council on the Status of Women, 1993.
Munro, Alice. 'The Beggar Maid,' 'Half a Grapefruit,' and 'Privilege.' *Who Do You Think You Are?* 1978. Rpt Toronto: Macmillan of Canada, 1989.

- 'The Shining Houses.' *Dance of the Happy Shades*. Toronto, Montreal, New York: McGraw-Hill Ryerson, 1968.
Murphy, Barbara. *The Ugly Canadian: The Rise and Fall of a Caring Society.* J. Gordon Shillingford, 1999.
Murray, Alex. ' Homelessness: The People.' In Fallis and Murray, eds. 16–48.
Nelson, Cary. 'Always Already Cultural Studies: Two Conferences and a Manifesto.' *Journal of the Midwest Modern Language Association* 24.1 (1991): 24–38.
Nelson, Sharon. *Women and Writing in Canada: A Report and Analysis of Research Findings*. Montreal: Metonymy Productions, 1982.
Nemiroff, Greta Hofmann, ed. *Celebrating Canadian Women*. Toronto: Fitzhenry and Whiteside, 1989.
New, W.H., ed. *Native Writers: Canadian Writing. Canadian Literature: Special Issue*. Vancouver, UBC Press, 1990.
Newton, Judith, and Deborah Rosenfelt, eds and intro. *Feminist Criticism and Social Change*. New York and London: Methuen, 1985.
Olsen, Tillie. 'I Stand Here Ironing.' *Tell Me a Riddle*. 1956. Rpt 1959. New York: Delacorte, 1961.
- *Silences*. New York: Dell, 1983.
O'Rourke, Rebecca. 'Were There No Women? British Working-class Writing in the Inter-war Period.' *Literature and History: Autobiography and Working-class Writing* 14.1 (Spring 1988): 48–63.
Orwell, George. *Down and Out in Paris and London*. London: Gollancz, 1933. Rpt London and New York: Penguin, 1989.
- *The Road to Wigan Pier*. London: Gollancz, 1937. Rpt London and New York: Penguin 1989.
Ostenso, Martha. *Wild Geese*. New York: Dodd Mead, 1925.
Ouellette-Michalska, Madeleine. 'La Critique littéraire ou l'écriture de la transparence.' In Godard, ed. 41–9.
Padolsky, Enoch. 'Cultural Diversity and Canadian Literature: A Pluralistic Approach to Majority Writing in Canada.' *International Journal of Canadian Studies* 3 (Spring 1991): 111–28.
Palmer, Howard. *The Settlement of the West*. Calgary: U of Calgary P, 1977.
Pearce, Diana. 'The Feminization of Poverty: Women, Work, and Welfare.' *Urban & Social Change Review* 11.1–2 (1978): 28–36.
- 'Toil and Trouble: Women Workers and Unemployment Compensation.' *Women and Poverty.* Ed. Barbara Gelpi, Nancy Hartsock, et al. Chicago and London: U of Chicago P, 1986. 141–61.
Perry, Donna. 'Procne's Song: The Task of Feminist Literary Criticism.' In Jaggar and Bordo, eds. 293–308.

Phillips, Donna, ed. *Voices of Discord: Canadian Short Stories from the 1930s.* Toronto: Hogtown Press, 1979.

Pivato, Joseph, S. Totosy, and M.V. Dimic, eds. *Literatures of a Lesser Diffusion: Les Littératures de moindre diffusion.* Edmonton: Research Institute for Comparative Literature, University of Alberta Press, 1990.

Poor People's Press. Nôtre-Dame de Grace, Montreal: N.D.G. Anti-poverty League (Oct. 1989–Summer 1991). 3 Mar. 1992 title changed to *The Voice.* (Circulation around 2000.)

Poovey, Mary. *The Proper Lady and the Woman Writer: Ideology as Style in the Works of Mary Wollstonecraft, Mary Shelley, and Jane Austen.* Chicago and London: U of Chicago P, 1984.

Porter, John. *The Vertical Mosaic: An Analysis of Social Class and Power in Canada.* Toronto: U of Toronto P, 1965.

Potrebenko, Helen. *Hey Waitress and Other Stories.* Vancouver: Lazara, 1989.

– 'My Mother, the Troublemaker.' *This Is Class Too: Fireweed* 26 (Winter/Spring 1988): 54–65.

– *No Streets of Gold: A Social History of Ukrainians in Alberta.* Vancouver: New Star Books, 1997.

Powell, Barbara. 'Laura Goodman Salverson: Her Father's "Own True Son."' *Canadian Literature* 133 (Summer 1992): 78–89.

Prentice, Alison, et al. *Canadian Women: A History.* Toronto: Harcourt Brace Jovanovitch, 1988.

Purdy, Anthony. 'On the Outside Looking In: The Political Economy of Everyday Life in Gabrielle Roy's *Bonheur d'occasion.*' *A Certain Difficulty of Being: Essays on the Quebec Novel.* Montreal and Kingston: McGill-Queen's UP, 1990.

Rabinowitz, Paula. 'The Great Mother: Female Working-class Subjectivity.' *Labour and Desire: Women's Revolutionary Fiction in Depression America.* Chapel Hill and London: North Carolina UP, 1991. 97–136.

– *Labour and Desire: Women's Revolutionary Fiction in Depression America.* Chapel Hill and London: North Carolina UP, 1991.

Radhakrishnan, R. 'Negotiating Subject Positions in an Uneven World.' *Feminism and Institutions: Dialogues on Feminist Theory.* Ed. Linda Kaufman. Cambridge and Oxford: Basil Blackwell, 1989. 276–91.

Rajan, Balachandra. 'Scholarship and Criticism.' *Literary History of Canada: Canadian Literature in English.* 2nd ed. Vol. 4. Ed. W.H. New. Toronto: U of Toronto P, 1990. 133–58.

Renan, Ernest. 'What Is a Nation?' Trans. of 'Qu'est-ce qu'une nation?' 1882. Trans Martin Thom. In Bhabha, ed. 8–22.

Ricard, François. *Gabrielle Roy: A Life.* Trans. of *Gabrielle Roy, une vie.* Montreal: Boréal, 1996. Trans. Patricia Claxton. Toronto: McClelland & Stewart, 1999.

Richards, David Adams. *Road to the Stilt House*. Toronto: HarperCollins, 1990.
Riis, Sharon. *The True Story of Ida Johnson*. 1976. Vancouver and Toronto: Douglas & McIntyre, 1989.
Rimstead, Roxanne. 'Mediated Lives: Oral Histories and Cultural Memory.' *Essays on Canadian Writing. Special Issue: Reading Canadian Autobiography* (Guest ed. Shirley Neuman) 60 (Winter 1996): 139–65.
– 'What Working-class Intellectuals Claim to Know.' *Race, Gender and Class: An Interdisciplinary Multicultural Journal*. Ed. Jean Belkhir. 4.1 (1996): 119–42.
Robert, Lucie. *L'Institution du littéraire au Québec*. Laval: Les Presses de l'Université Laval, 1989.
Robinson, Lillian S., ed. *Sex, Class, and Culture*. Bloomington: Indiana UP, 1978.
Robinson, Lillian S., and Lise Vogel. 'Feminist Criticism: How Do We Know When We've Won?' *Feminist Issues in Literary Scholarship*. Ed. Shari Benstock. Bloomington and Indianapolis: Indiana UP, 1987. 141–9.
– 'Modernism and History.' In Robinson, ed. 22–46.
– 'Working/Women/Writing.' In Robinson, ed. 223–53.
Roper, Gordon, et al. 'Writers of Fiction 1880–1920.' *The Literary History of Canada*. Ed. Carl F. Klinck. 2nd ed. Vol. 1. Toronto and Buffalo: U of Toronto P, 1976.
Ross, Veronica. *Fisher Woman*. Porters Lake, NS: Pottersfield Lake, 1984.
– 'Nels.' In *Moving Off the Map: From 'Story' to 'Fiction': An Anthology of Contemporary Canadian Short Fiction*. Ed. Geoff Hancock. Windsor, ON: Black Moss Press, 1986.
Roy, Gabrielle. *Bonheur d'occasion*. Montreal: Beauchemin, 1945.
– *La Détresse et l'enchantement*. Montreal: Boréal Express, 1984.
– 'Return to St. Henri: Reception Speech to the Royal Society of Canada.' 1947. Rpt in *The Fragile Lights of Earth: Articles and Memoirs. 1942–1970*. Toronto: McClelland & Stewart, 1982.
– *Windflower*. Trans. Joyce Marshall. 1970. Rpt Toronto: McClelland & Stewart, 1990. Trans. of *La Rivière sans repos*. Montreal: Beauchemin, 1970.
Rubin, Lillian Breslow. *Worlds of Pain: Life in the Working-class Family*. New York: Basic Books, 1976.
Salutin, Rick. *Living in a Dark Age*. Toronto: HarperCollins, 1991.
Salverson, Laura Goodman. *Confessions of an Immigrant's Daughter*. London: Faber & Faber, 1939. Rpt Toronto, Buffalo, London: U of Toronto P, 1981.
– *The Viking Heart*. 1945. Rpt Toronto: McClelland & Stewart, 1975.
Sand, Cy-Thea. 'A Question of Identity.' In *Class Is the Issue: Fireweed* 25 (Fall 1987): 5–62.
Sandwell, B.K. 'On the Appointment of Governor-General Vincent Massey,

1952.' *The Blasted Pine*. Ed. F.R. Scott and A.J.M. Smith. Toronto: Macmillan, 1957.
Sarsfield, Mairuth. *No Crystal Stair*. Norval, ON: Moulin, 1997.
Saul, John Ralston. *The Unconscious Civilization*. Toronto: Anansi, 1995.
Schram, Mary Lou Peters. 'Eviction.' *Room of One's Own* 15.1 (Mar. 1992): 20–34.
Scott, Joan Wallach. 'Experience.' *Feminists Theorize the Political*. Ed. Judith Butler and Joan W. Scott. New York and London: Routledge, 1992. 22–40.
– 'Gender: A Useful Category for Historical Analysis.' *Gender and the Politics of History*. New York: Columbia UP, 1988.
Sennett, Richard, and Jonathan Cobb. *The Hidden Injuries of Class*. New York: Alfred Knopf, 1973.
Shek, Ben-Zion. *Social Realism in the French-Canadian Novel*. Montreal: Harvest House, 1976.
Shotter, John. *Cultural Politics of Everyday Life*. Toronto and Buffalo: U of Toronto P, 1993.
Showalter, Elaine. 'Feminist Criticism in the Wilderness.' *Writing and Sexual Difference*. Ed. Elizabeth Abel. Chicago: U of Chicago P, 1982. 9–35.
Sicotte, Geneviève, and Pierre Popovic, eds. *Misères de la littérature*. Montreal: Département d'études françaises, Université de Montréal, 1995.
Sidel, Ruth. *Women and Children Last: The Plight of Poor Women in Affluent America*. New York and London: Penguin Books, 1986.
Silman, Janet. (As told to). *Enough Is Enough: Aboriginal Women Speak Out*. Toronto: Women's Press, 1987.
Silvera, Makeda. 'And What If a Black Woman Decides ...?' *Baker's Dozen: Stories by Women*. Ed. The Fictive Collection. Toronto: Women's Press, 1984. 91–6.
– 'Canada Sweet, Girl.' *Class Is the Issue: Fireweed* 25 (Fall 1987): 10–19.
Silvera, Makeda, ed. *Fireworks: The Best of Fireweed*. Toronto: Women's Press, 1986.
– *Silenced: Talks with Working-class Caribbean Women about Their Lives and Struggles as Domestic Workers in Canada*. 2nd ed. Toronto: Sister Vision, 1989.
Sime, J.G. *Sister Woman*. 1919. Rpt Ottawa: Tecumseh Press, 1992.
Simon, Sherry. *Fictions de l'identitaire au Québec*. Montreal: XYZ, 1991.
Sirois, Antoine. *Montréal dans le roman canadien*. Montreal, Paris, Brussels: Marcel Didier, 1968.
Smart, Patricia. *Writing in the Father's House: The Emergence of the Feminine in the Quebec Literary Tradition*. Trans. of *Ecrire dans la maison du père*, 1988. Trans. Patricia Smart. Toronto and Buffalo: U of Toronto P, 1991.
Smith, Dorothy E. *The Everyday World as Problematic: A Feminist Sociology*. Toronto: U of Toronto P, 1987.

Smith, Ruth L. 'Order and Disorder: The Naturalization of Poverty.' *Cultural Critique* 14 (Winter 1989–90): 209–29.

Smith, Sidonie. 'The Autobiographical Manifesto: Identities, Temporalities, Politics.' *Autobiography and Questions of Gender.* Ed. Shirley Neuman. London and Portland, OR: Frank Cass, 1991. 186–212.

Smith, Sidonie, and Julia Watson, eds. Introduction. *De/Colonizing the Subject: The Politics of Gender in Women's Autobiography.* Minneapolis: U of Minnesota P, 1992.

Smucker, Barbara Claassen. *Days of Terror.* Clarke, Irwin, 1979. Rpt Markham, ON / Middlesex, UK: Penguin/Puffin Books, 1981.

Sommer, Doris. 'Not Just a Personal Story: Women's Testimonies and the Plural Self.' *Life/Lines: Theorizing Women's Autobiography.* Ed. Bella Bodzki and Celeste Schenk. Ithaca, NY: Cornell UP, 1988. 107–30.

Special Senate Committee, Canada. *Poverty in Canada: Report of the Special Senate Committee on Poverty.* Ottawa: 1971.

Stanton, Domna C. 'Autogynography: Is the Subject Different?' *The Female Autograph: Theory and Practice of Autobiography from the Tenth to the Twentieth Century.* Ed. Domna Stanton. Chicago: U of Chicago P, 1987.

Steedman, Carolyn. *Landscape for a Good Woman: A Story of Two Lives.* London: Virago, 1986.

Steele, Charles, ed. *Taking Stock: The Calgary Conference on the Canadian Novel.* Toronto: ECW Press, 1982.

Stevenson, Sharon. *Gold Earrings: Selected Poetry.* Vancouver: Pulp Press, 1984.

Stich, K.P. Introduction. *Confessions of an Immigrant's Daughter.* By Laura Goodman Salverson. London: Faber & Faber, 1939. Rpt Toronto, Buffalo, London: U of Toronto P, 1981.

Strange, Kathleen. *With the West in Her Eyes.* Toronto: G.J. McCleod, 1937.

Stratford, Philip. *All the Polarities: Comparative Studies in French and English.* Toronto: ECW Press, 1986.

Straw, Will. 'Shifting Boundaries, Lines of Descent: Cultural Studies and Institutional Realignments.' In Blundell, Shepherd, and Taylor, eds. 86–102.

Strong-Boag, Veronica. Introduction. *In Times like These.* By Nellie McClung. 1915. Rpt with Introduction, Toronto and Buffalo: U of Toronto P, 1974.

Struthers, James. *The Limits of Affluence: Welfare in Ontario, 1920–1970.* Toronto: U of Toronto P, OHSS, 1994.

Sweatman, Margaret. *Fox.* Winnipeg, MB, and Minneapolis, MN: Turnstone, 1991.

Swindells, Judith. *Victorian Writing and Working Women: The Other Side of Silence.* Cambridge: Polity Press, 1985.

Sykes, Joy. 'Comments of a Working-class Crone.' *Class Is the Issue: Fireweed* 25 (Fall 1987): 82–5.

Szucsany, Desiré. 'The Suitcase.' In Nemiroff, ed. 355–8.

Tener, Anne E. 'Ruby's Education.' *Working for a Living: Room of One's Own* 12.2–3 (Aug. 1988): 47–52.

Thomas, Clara. 'The Strickland Sisters.' *The Clear Spirit*. Ed. Mary Quayle Innis. Toronto: U of Toronto P, 1966. 42–73.

Thompson, E.P. *The Poverty of Theory*. London: Merlin, 1978.

Thurston, John. 'Rewriting Roughing It.' *Future Indicative: Literary Theory and Canadian Literature*. Ed. John Moss. Ottawa: Ottawa UP, 1987. 195–204.

Tokarczyk, Michelle, and Elizabeth Fay, eds. *Working-class Women in the Academy: Labourers in the Knowledge Factory*. Amherst: U of Massachusetts P, 1993.

Torjman, Sherri. *The Reality Gap: Closing the Gap between Women's Needs and Available Programs and Services*. Ottawa: Canadian Advisory Council on the Status of Women, April 1988.

Toronto Rape Crisis Centre – Working-class Caucus. 'Around the Kitchen Table.' *This Is Class Too: Fireweed* 26 (Winter/Spring 1988): 69–81.

Tracey, Linda Lee. *On the Edge: A Journey into the Heart of Canada*. Vancouver: Douglas & McIntyre, 1993.

Tynes, Maxine. 'Borrowed Beauty.' In Nemiroff, ed.

– 'In Service.' *This Is Class Too: Fireweed* 26 (Winter/Spring 1988): 8–11.

Vallières, Pierre. *Les Nègres blancs de l'Amérique*. Montreal: Editions parti pris, 1968.

Veltmayer, Henry. *Canadian Class Structure*. Toronto: Garamond Press, 1986.

Vogel, Lise. *Marxism and the Oppression of Women: Toward a Unitary Theory*. New Brunswick, NJ, and London: Rutgers UP, 1983.

Waddington, Miriam. 'Mrs. Maza's Salon.' *Canadian Literature* 120 (Spring 1989): 83–90.

Watson, Sheila. *The Double Hook*. 1959. Rpt Toronto: McClelland & Stewart, 1966.

Watt, Frank. 'Radicalism in English Canadian Literature since Confederation.' PhD diss., University of Toronto, 1957.

Waxman, Chaim. *The Stigma of Poverty: A Critique of Poverty Theories and Policies*. 2nd ed. New York, Oxford, Toronto: Pergamon Press, 1983.

Wayman, Tom. *A Country Not Considered: Canada, Culture, Work*. Concord, ON: Anansi, 1993.

Webber, Marlene. *Food for Thought: How Our Dollar Democracy Drove 2 Million Canadians into Food Banks to Collect Private Charity in Place of Public Justice*. Toronto: Coach House Press, 1992.

- *Street Kids: The Tragedy of Canada's Runaways*. Toronto: U of Toronto P, 1991.
Weber, Lori. 'Trip with Brock.' In Nemiroff, ed. 234–42.
Weedon, Chris. *Feminist Practice and Poststructuralist Theory*. Oxford and New York: Basil Blackwell, 1987.
Weinzweig, Helen. *Basic Black with Pearls*. Toronto: Anansi Press, 1980.
- 'My Mother's Luck.' In Silvera, ed., *Fireworks*. 85–95.
Weir, Lorraine. 'The Discourse of "Civility": Strategies of Containment in Literary Histories of English Canadian Literature.' *Problems of Literary Reception / Problèmes de réception littéraire*. Ed. E.D. Blodgett and A.G. Purdy. Edmonton: Research Institute for Comparative Literature, University of Alberta Press, 1988. 24–39.
Williams, Raymond. *The Country and the City*. London: Hogarth Press, 1973.
- 'The Idea of a Common Culture.' 1968; and 'Culture Is Ordinary.' 1958. Rpt in *Resources of Hope: Culture, Democracy, Socialism*. Ed. R. Gable. London: Verso, 1989.
- *Marxism and Literature*. Oxford: Oxford UP, 1977.
Willis, Meredith Sue. 'Dreams of Deprivation.' *This Is Class Too: Fireweed* 26 (Winter/Spring 1988): 82–6.
Wilson, Ethel. 'Lilly's Story.' *The Equations of Love*. Toronto: Macmillan, 1952. 131–281.
Wiseman, Adele. *Crackpot*. Toronto: McClelland & Stewart, 1974.
- 'Memoirs of a Book-molesting Childhood.' *Canadian Forum* 67.758 (Apr. 1986): 18–28.
Woodcock, George. *Strange Bedfellows: The State and the Arts in Canada*. Vancouver and Toronto: Douglas & McIntyre, 1985.
Zandy, Janet, ed. and intro. *Calling Home: Working-class Women's Writing: An Anthology*. New Brunswick, NJ, and London: Rutgers UP, 1990.
- ed. *Liberating Memory: Our Work and Our Working-class Consciousness*. New Brunswick, NJ: Rutgers UP, 1995.
- ed. 'Working-class Studies.' *Women's Studies Quarterly*. 23. 1–2 (Spring/Summer 1995).

Index

Abbott, Pamela, and Roger Sapsford, 34
Adams, Ian, *The Poverty Wall*, 19; *The Real Poverty Report*, 162–3
aesthetics: aesthetic enthralment, 104, 110, 215; aestheticizing poverty, 14, 69, 110, 113, 192, 209–10, 219, 254, 270; and discourse, 122; and poverty, 20, 51–2, 73–4; erasure of disease, 101; the gaze, 104, 110, 216; low-brow and high-brow taste, 184; of anger, 206; of poverty narratives, 52; oppositional, 49, 51–2, 111–12; patriarchal aesthetics, 220; poverty narratives as a challenge to, 52
agency (*see also* resistance): and community leaders, 129; and dialogue, 160; feminist, 61; in materialist feminism, 135; lack of, 239; Marxist agency, 129
Ahmad, Aijaz, 200, 204, 231
Alcoff, Linda, 262, 268–9, 271, 279, 284–5
Althusser, Louis, 163, 271
Anderson, Benedict, 201
anti-poverty activism, 243–4; frontline, with the homeless, 244
anti-Theory, 122–42; description of, 123–5
Aronowitz, Stanley, 19, 23, 154, 175, 265, 280
authenticity, 298, 301; and social change, 124, 134
autobiography, 57–64, 143–73, 174–99; alternative reading strategies, 173; and class, 153; and collective memory, 174 (*see also* cultural memory); and counter-culture, 190–1, 196–9; and cultural amnesia, 17, 178 (*see also* cultural amnesia); and decolonization, 159, 169–73, 170; and hegemony, 158, 190–2, 196–9; and oppositional strategies, 172; and oral history, 244; and organized forgetting, 143–73, 166 (*see also* organized forgetting); and testimony, 57–64, 144, 249; and transformation, 124; and women, 199, 249; and working-class subjects, 172–3, 198; as history and/or literature, 199; ideology of, 171;

negative constructions of identity, 19, 143–72, 160, 192 (*see also* identity); popular working-class, 53; postmodern modes, 171–2

Baird, Irene, 35, 40, 51, 113, 191, 245, 265, 272, 298–9
Balibar, Etienne, and Immanuel Wallerstein, 9, 205, 210, 212
Baxter, Sheila, 21, 37, 44–5, 47, 52, 92, 133, 228, 242–5, 265, 273, 283, 292, 296; *No Way to Live*, 243; *Under the Viaduct*, 243–4
Belsey, Catherine, 30, 39, 48–9, 136–7, 181
Bennett, Tony, 122, 196, 296
Berger, Thomas, 157–8
Beverly, John, 57, 172, 198
Bhabha, Homi, 201
Blais, Marie-Claire, 46, 297
Blundell, Valda, John Shepherd, and Ian Taylor, 257, 281
Blyth, Jack A., 100–2, 188
Boorstin, Daniel J., 177
Bourdieu, Pierre, 21, 50, 62, 86, 88, 99, 104, 107, 112, 121, 150–1, 163, 205, 255, 269–70
bourgeoisie (*see also* class, middle class): and aesthetic enthralment, 215; and aestheticizing poverty, 254 (*see also* aesthetics); and class habitus, 99–100, 104, 106–11; and classlessness, 276; and feminism, 129; and the gaze, 104, 110, 216; and global hegemony, 276; and language, 99; and living space, 103; and national literature, 275–6; and nationalism, 200–1, 226, 235–6, 276 (*see also* Chatterjee, Partha; nation); and order, 107; and privilege, 266; and subjectivity, 126; and taste, 99, 105, 193–4, 218–20
Brand, Dionne, 154, 192, 258, 283, 289, 302
Brantlinger, Patrick, 127, 257
Brenner, Johanna, 131
Brenner, Timothy, 14, 225
Brodzki, Bella, and Celeste Schenck, 125
Bromley, Roger, 36–7, 53, 76, 166, 174–8, 180–1, 183, 185–6, 189, 193, 195–6, 228, 291; lost narratives, 177–8; organized forgetting, 174–7 (*see also* organized forgetting); popular culture, 196; poverty as landscape, 186
Bruser Maynard, Fredelle, 37, 174–5, 192–5, 197, 307
—, *Raisins and Almonds*, 192–5: and poverty as landscape, 192–3, 195; as mobility narrative, 192–5; aversion to working class, 193–4; bourgeois taste, 193–4; ethnicity and poverty, 193–5; memory, 195

Campbell, Maria, 19, 44, 64, 78, 144–5, 153–9, 165, 173–4, 192, 265, 272–3
—, *Halfbreed*, 144–5, 153–9; as testimony, 155; identity, 154; welfare, 156
Cappon, Paul, 272
charity, 96 (*see also* welfare); acts of, between women, 187–8; —, help-thy-neighbour doctrine, 188; —, international, 228, 230; Christian, Grey Nuns, 244; —, Salvation Army, 241; —, YMCA, 244; ideology of, 228, 230; secularization of, 101; soup kitchens, 241; Third World as object of charity, 231

Chatterjee, Partha, 9, 200, 204, 226–7, 230–1
Christian, Barbara, 63, 68, 127, 139, 140–1, 156, 262
class (*see also* the bourgeoisie; the middle class; mobility; the working class): acculturation, 106, 150, 217–18, 272; and cultural smuggling, 148; and education, 269–73; and gender, 130–7, 217–18, 219, 264, 292, 294–8 (*see also* the feminization of poverty; poor women); —, as reciprocal, 202–3; and nation, 213, 281; —, as reciprocal, 202–3; and poverty, 25–7, 264, 267, 292–7; and women's experience of poverty, 130–1; anger, 206, 216, 265; as taboo subject, 206, 258, 264, 266, 281, 301–2; categories of writing, 131; changing definitions of, 205; class analysis and gender, 6; class-conscious criticism, 78 (*see also* literature and literary criticism); class difference, 107; class distinction in Canada, 161; class habitus, 88, 99, 105, 107, 109; class psychology, 134; class travellers (*see* mobility); declassing as immigrant experience, 246, 248; distinction, 178, 237, 266, 269–70 (*see also* Bourdieu, Pierre); —, and literary canons, 270; —, and taste, 104–11, 217, 270; exploitation, 251, 264, 281; habitus, 221 (*see also* Bourdieu, Pierre); hegemony, 276 (*see also* Gramsci, Antonio); identity, 178–9 (*see also* identity); —, fear of crossing class borders, 271; —, fear of falling, 245 (*see* Ehrenreich, Barbara); —, in the private sphere, 197; —, lack of identification with the poor, 218–24, 264–7; —, solidarity, 265; in fiction, 135; in women's autobiographical writings, 15, 143–52, 174–82; lumpenproletariat, 49, 224, 292, 293, 295; privilege, 266; struggle, 7–77 (*see also* resistance); —, fear of, 264; theory of class, 178–9, 224, 263 (*see also* Marxist criticism)
cleaning: and self-definition, 69, 76, 117, 217; and upward mobility, 217–18; symbolic power of, for working-class women, 116; —, in *La Sagouine*, 116–17
Clifford, James, 59, 261, 263
clothing, 217; and mobility, 114–15, 217–18; masking poverty, 218; women's clothing, 217–18, 220
Collier, Diana, *The Invisible Women of Washington*, 40, 50–1, 245, 292, 299
colonization, 141 (*see also* Ahmad, Aijaz; Chatterjee, Partha; Fanon, Franz; Smith, Sidonie); and knowledge, 231–2; and language, 150; and nations, 180, 200; and postcolonial criticism, 200, 227; between First and Third World, 223–33; decolonizing the subject, 141, 159; neocolonialism, 228–31; of the poor, 19, 160–8, 225–30
common culture. *See* culture, paradigms of
community (*see also* nation; populism): alliances of witnesses, 58; alternative status-honour groups, 6, 153–9 (*see also* Waxman, Chaim); among the poor, 156–60, 214–16; and coalition politics, 133, 137, 265; and identity, 221; and nation, 221;

and opposition, 55, 60, 94, 98, 243; and social mobility, 63; and writers' role, 56; as settler colony, 100; creation of, 149; cultural recovery, 55; fictioning of, 55, 60; in populist criticism, 133; of the culturally excluded, 61

Costello, Jeanne, 35, 132–3, 199

criticism (*see* also cultural studies; feminism; intellectuals; knowledge; literature and literary criticism; reading strategies): and community, 140; and decolonization, 141; engaged, 53–6, 275–86; —, in Canada, 62, 275–85, 298–305; feminist, 123, 125; Marxist and feminist, 128; oppositional, 142; poverty and class, 62; socialist feminist, 135

cultural amnesia, 37 (*see also* cultural memory; organized forgetting); feminist theories of, 181–2; popular autobiographies, 53

cultural borrowing, 224. *See also* Sand, Cy-Thea

cultural capital, 56, 110, 148, 151, 153, 195, 207, 216, 217, 269–70, 292 (*see also* Bourdieu, Pierre; Guillory, John); and university, 151, 269–70

cultural exclusion, 151, 166, 225, 291–2 (*see also* marginalization; organized forgetting; the poor, invisibility of; the poor, misrepresentation of); and the working class, 50; cultural erasure, 223 (*see also* cultural muting); in representations of poverty, 51; narratives of, 50; social fictions, 52

cultural home (*see also* housing, homeplace): and working-class women, 138, 149; feminism and class-based coalition, 85

cultural invasion, 163, 259–60 (*see also* colonization; discourse; Freire, Paulo; the poor, invisibility of); by non-poor, 3

cultural memory (*see also* autobiography; Bromley, Roger; cultural amnesia; organized forgetting): and class, 179; and history, 176–7, 192; and nation, 176, 191–2, 221; and nostalgia, 187; and opposition, 221; and poverty, 187, 218, 221; collective memories, 192; individual memories, 222–3

cultural muting: and identity, 144; and poverty narratives, 292, 296; conditions for, 138

cultural recovery. *See* reading strategies, as recovery project

cultural reproduction, 238, 269, 371–2 (*see also* Bourdieu, Pierre); decolonizing the subject, 164; theorists, 163

cultural smuggling, 24, 145–53

cultural space. *See* housing, living space; poverty, as psychosocial space

cultural struggle: outside academic knowledge, 122

cultural studies, 253–60 (*see also* culture, paradigms of); and epistemology, 255–6, 262; and literary studies, 261, 270; and political engagement, 253–61, 280–2; failure to read poverty and class, 258–60, 280–5; in Canada, 257–9, 281–2; postmodernism and, 254–5, 281–2; schools of cultural studies, 255–7;

—, conjuncturalist, 256; —, culturalist, 255–7; —, structuralist, 255–7
culture: national, 15, 200–52, 275–86, 298–304; paradigms of (*see also* nation, developed nations: paradigm of development), common culture, 15, 49, 50, 207, 210, 219, 225, 250, 275, 277–9, 283–4, 287–8, 290; —, culture as webs of meaning, 253; —, feminist, 123, 276, 287–8; —, high culture, 269; —, inside/outside paradigm, 82; —, mass culture, 275, 278–9; —, popular culture, 278; popular and socialist culture, 74; reading, 86–7; women's culture, 132
culture-from-below, 25, 92, 205, 261, 278 (*see also* cultural studies; history-from-below; populism); aesthetics of, 216; as an academic approach, 270
culture of poverty. *See* Lewis, Oscar; poverty, theories of

Daly, Mary, 52, 161, 295
Davey, Frank, 14, 205, 207–10, 215, 299, 303
Delphy, Christine, 47, 80, 89, 134, 165, 182, 205, 294–5
Dentith, Simon, and Philip Dodd, 74, 171, 196, 198
discourse: academic, 20, 54–5, 61, 219–20, 225, 253–74; and difference, 140; and mobility, 114; and resistance, 119, 216–17, 220–1, 225, 260–1 (*see also* resistance); counter, 62; discursive dominance, 202, 269; discursive marginalization (*see also* marginalization); —, discovering the poor, 236; —, insults, 216; documentation, 44; exclusion, 67; idealist feminism, 132; liberal humanist, 65–7, 165; Marxist (*see* Marxist criticism); nationalist, 14, 200, 225, 277–8 (*see also* nation); poverty, 116; rationalist, 231; speaking for others, 268–9 (*see* discourse on poverty)
discourse on poverty, 21, 101, 227; academic, 267–73; authenticating claims of poverty, 228; euphemisms, 232, 250; inside/outside paradigm, 36, 65–7, 250; liberal humanist, 207; nation-within-a-nation (two-nations), 9, 204, 235–40, 304; New World, 250; self-help, 75; speaking for the poor, 268; symbolic containment of the poor, 226–38; testimonial, 268; three worlds (First World, Third World, etc.) 200, 227–8
Dodd, Philip, 74, 171, 196, 198–9
Donovan, Josephine, 129
During, Simon, 257

Eagleton, Terry, 15, 50, 142, 273, 275, 277, 279–80, 287; common culture, 210
Easthope, Anthony, 256
Ebert, Theresa, 126, 130, 209, 302
education, 5, 16 (*see also* Althusser, Louis; Bourdieu, Pierre; Freire, Paulo; Giroux, Henry); and cultural capital, 270; and cultural reproduction, 110, 118, 151, 163, 263, 271–2; —, class domination, 164; —, élitism, 5, 272; —, exclusion, 50, 63, 151, 272; —, schools as ideological state apparatus, 136, 263, 271; and repression, 64, 233;

Index 333

and social mobility, 269, 272; in poverty narratives, 81, 117, 150, 156, 187, 191, 195, 197, 217–18, 221–2, 224; radical pedagogy, 122, 267; residential schools, 233, 235; university, and class exclusions, 151; —, and cultural reproduction, 151; —, politics of, 268
Ehrenreich, Barbara, *Fear of Falling*, 11, 18, 23, 30, 114
élitism, 132, 269–70, 276, 278–80, 302
everyday, the, 77–85; and heterogeneity, 133; as site of knowledge, 123; in feminist literary criticism, 123; life stories, 77; power against poverty, 81–2

Fallis, George, and Alex Murray, *Housing the Homeless and the Poor*, 103–4. See also Murray, Alex
Fanon, Franz, 159, 176, 200
Felman, Shoshana, and Dori Laub, *Testimony*, 57–9, 77, 85, 118
Felski, Rita, 124, 125, 130, 137. See also feminism
feminism: and class as bourgeois, 129; and community, 276; and critiques of Marxism, 182–3; and deconstruction, 124–5; and history, 181–3; and literary criticism, 302; —, authentic realism, 124; —, neglect of realism, 124; and oppositional feminist magazines, 302; and oppositional reading strategies, 123, 125; and postmodern theory, 125; and space, private versus public, 183; ideological differences, 125; materialist feminism, 130, 183, 247, 302; populist feminism, 125; socialist feminism, 129;

theories of standpoint, 56; —, outlaw emotions, 61, 99; women and academic feminism, 123, 132
feminization of poverty, 6, 33, 69, 129, 131, 164, 292–3, 295. See also poor women; poverty
Fennario, David, 35, 152, 283, 289
Fiske, John, 50, 90
Fox, Pamela, 23, 26, 27, 89, 113, 143, 181, 209, 280
Fraser, Sylvia, 45–6, 296–7, 299
Freire, Paulo, 3, 48, 122, 160, 163–4, 259–60, 262, 267–8
Frye, Northrop, 65, 98–9, 185, 196, 280

Gagnier, Regenia, 35, 126–7, 174, 186, 189, 198, 228
Galbraith, John Kenneth, 5, 245
Gallant, Mavis, 10–11, 13
Garner, Hugh, 10–13, 35, 38, 64, 78, 113, 191, 264, 272
gaze, the, 111, 216
Geertz, Clifford, 59, 261–3; *post facto* theory, 262–3; 'thick description,' 262
Gelpi, Barbara, and Nancy Hartsock, 164, 295
Gerson, Carole, 68, 70, 72, 184–5, 302–4
Giroux, Henry, 267
Godard, Barbara, 141–2, 215, 268, 302
Goldberg, Gertrude Schaffner, and Eleanor Kremen, 164, 295
Gramsci, Antonio, 163–4, 177, 260, 262–3, 267, 280, 283–4, 305
Grayson, Paul, and Linda Grayson, 302
Green, Bryan, 3, 24, 43–4, 228
Grossberg, Lawrence, Cary Nelson, and Paula Treichler, 255–6, 282

Guilbert, Lucille, et al., 91, 101–2, 273
Guillory, John, 268–71, 280
Gunderson, Morley, et al., 17, 32, 164, 295

Hall, Stuart, 5, 74, 163, 196
Hansen, Karen V., and Ilene J. Philipson, 165
Harding, Sandra, 60
Harrington, Michael, *The Other America*, 11, 90, 161, 166–8, 204, 237–9, 266
Harvey, David, and Michael Reed, 25, 55, 168, 237, 266
Hebdige, Dick, 35, 90
Hennessy, Rosemary, and Chrys Ingraham, 126, 130
Himmelfarb, Gertrude, *The Idea of Poverty*, 9, 24, 90, 94–5, 97, 116, 228, 236, 237
history, 7, 9, 15, 20–1, 23–4, 26, 30, 32, 35, 37, 38–9, 52, 55–6, 58–60, 62, 75, 77, 85, 90–1, 95, 116, 126, 128–30, 135, 139, 141, 146–7, 150, 153, 155, 158–60, 166, 172, 175, 177, 179, 180–3, 186, 188, 190–2, 197–9, 201, 206, 210, 218, 224, 227, 230, 233–4, 238, 247, 249, 251, 255, 257, 261, 263–4, 267, 273, 282, 289, 291, 301–3
history-from-below, 24, 127, 263. *See also* culture-from-below; populism
Hoggart, Richard, 35, 63, 237, 256–7, 264, 267, 283
Holmes, Nancy: 'Bugs,' 117–21; —, homeplace, 117; —, resistance, 118–19
homeless, the (*see also* Fallis, George, and Alex Murray; homelessness; Murray, Alex; the poor); as a threat, 245 (*see also* Guilbert, Lucille); as national disgrace, 240; as nationless, 116; bag lady, 242; drifter, 240, 242; in Canada,103–4; in literary study, 91–2; interviews with, 240–4 (*see also* Baxter, Sheila; Mettrick, Alan; Webber, Marlene); media images of, 245; mobility, 17 (*see also* mobility); popular images, 17; street kids, 241–3
homelessness, 10, 17, 21, 38, 74, 85, 87–8, 91–4, 96, 103–4, 116, 159, 241–2, 244, 254 (*see also* housing); and gender, 242, 244, 293; and living space, 91; and squatting, 244–5; as crime, 11–13, 16 (*see also* poverty, misrepresentation of: criminalizing); —, Poor Laws, 97; in Canada, 10, 17, 38, 103–4, 241, 244; masking of, 90
hooks, bell, 63, 80, 88–9, 112, 116, 127, 140, 141, 295
housing, 86–121 (*see also* Fallis, George, and Alex Murray; the homeless; homelessness); and class habitus, 21, 88–9, 219–20, 238; and resistance, 89; and stigma, 119; as metaphor, 238; cultural identification, 90; genealogy of poor houses, 93–103; home (*see also* hooks, bell), as idea, 82; —, gender and class, 80–1; homeplace, 80–1, 82–3, 85, 88–9, 112, 117, 119, 177, 215; institutional intrusion, 93; living space, and bourgeois order, 88; —, boundaries of, 87; —, in literature, 104; —, in social theory, 91; —, materiality and subjectivity, 20; —, of the poor, 87–8; —, the politics of, 86–121; —, workhouses and confinement, 97; material entrap-

ment, 21, 89; middle-class houses, as blind, 86–7, 238; —, as orderly, 107; nineteenth-century attitudes, 97; poor houses, and identity construction, 223; —, and necessity, 88; —, and poor taste, 107–8, 222; —, and subjectivities, 90; —, as dens, 241; —, as dumps, 109, 219; —, as flophouses, 240; —, as public housing, 93, 97; —, as rooming houses, 292; —, as sites of resistance, 89 (*see* housing, homeplace); —, as sources of shame, 222; —, lack of privacy in, 108; —, rented spaces, 81, 88, 111–21, 120; —, social boundaries around, 21, 87; in poverty narratives, 86, 87, 90, 94–5, 103; —, reading houses, 87, 222–3; —, wall reading, 120–1

idealism: and feminism, 132; and populism, 277; and poverty narratives, 139, 276–7

identity: and acculturation, 107–9, 150 (*see also* class, acculturation; mobility); and alternative status-honour groups, 153–9 (*see also* Waxman, Chaim); and class barriers to education, 149; and class habitus, 88; and classed experience, 143–73, 183–91, 192–9, 301–2; and cultural boundaries, 152; and homeplace, 117 (*see also* housing, homeplace); and identification with the poor, 151–3; and lack of class identification, 177, 197, 218, 264; and language, 150, 157, 205–25; and poverty, 143–73, 154, 209, 212, 226–52, 264; and resistance (*see* resistance); and self-representation, 143–73, 174–99 (*see also* autobiography; testimony); and shame (*see* shame); and testimony, 153, 239–52; class identity (*see* class); constructions of, alternative constructions, 224–5, 264; —, negative constructions, 19, 143–73, 198, 294; family, 118; gender identity in Marxist criticism, 165, 294–5; group affliliation, 8, 154, 168–9, 200, 215, 225, 243, 249–50 (*see also* community; populism); identity politics, 133; marginal identity, 213–15; women's identity, 217–18; working-class (*see* the working class)

ideology: aesthetic gaze, 104; Alice Munro, 105; Althusserian, 48, 136; and deconstruction, 136; and reading practices, 48 (*see also* reading strategies); and representation, 76; liberalism, 77, 300; melodrama, 75; meritocracy (*see* meritocracy); of academic paradigms of poverty, 55; of author's position, 78, 276–7; of poverty narratives, 27, 107, 276–7, 294; of work, 73; patriarchal and bourgeois, 71; postmodernism, 282–4; Social Darwinism, 100; Social Gospel, 95, 97; taking a position, 275–85

intellectuals, 253–74, 257, 259–60, 282–4 (*see also* discourse, academic; education; knowledge); and élitism, 270–1, 280; hegemonic role of, 266–71, 282–3; oppositional role of, 257, 259–60, 266–8, 273–4, 283–4 (*see also* Freire, Paulo; Giroux, Henry; Gramsci, Antonio); organic intellectuals, 259–60, 280–4;

spokespeople for the poor, 268; staging solidarity, 271
Irr, Caren, 23, 26, 300
Itwaru, Arnold, 246

Jaggar, Alison, 60–1
Jamieson, Nina Moore, 187
Janes, Percy, 89, 264, 272
Jaques, Edna, 37, 174–5, 183–96, 293, 296–7; and class identification, 185, 189–90, 192; as a model for Sarah Binks, 184; as popular poet, 183–6
—, *Uphill All the Way*, 174–94; as poverty narrative, 189; class traveller in, 185, 189; individualism in, 190; memory in, 190–1, 196; mobility in, 190; nation in, 191–2; nostalgia in, 187, 189–90, 192; poverty as distant landscape, 185–6, 189
Jenkins, Richard, 151
John, Mary, 154, 192

Kaplan, Caren, 133
Kaplan, Cora, 69, 130, 135–6, 165, 174, 181, 202–3, 209
Klaus, Gustav, 57
Knight, Phyllis, and Rolf Knight, 35, 40, 78, 153
Knight, Rolf, 300
knowledge (*see also* discourse, academic; education; intellectuals); academic, 219, 253–74; alternative, 123, 203–5, 227; and cultural struggle, 122; and homeplace, 88–9; and social agency, 259–60; and subjectivity, 63, 136; as colonizing, 231; empirical, 263; —, and lived experience, 47, 59, 259–60, 262; —, knowledge claims, 268; epistemic authority, 60, 227, 268; exclusionary, 54; feminist criticism, 32; paradigms of poverty, 55, 65, 237, 266; post-structuralist claims, 124; radical, 4, 5, 224–7, 267–8, 273–7 (*see also* resistance); standpoint theory, 60, 261, 268; —, and the everyday, 60; —, outlaw emotions and subjectivity, 61, 99; struggle over meaning, 3, 6, 28–9; ways of knowing the poor (*see also* Green, Bryan; the poor), academic, 227, 253–74; —, as objects of knowledge, 225, 231, 254–5, 259; —, as subjects of knowledge, 224–5, 259–60; —, challenges to, 56; —, insider, 167, 169, 203–5, 243–4; —, radical, 224–6, 256, 259–60
Krupat, Arnold, 268–9, 271

Lau, Evelyn, 242
Laub, Dori. *See* Felman, Shoshana, and Dori Laub
Laurence, Margaret, 14, 35, 38, 64, 86, 108, 115, 203, 205–7, 211–12, 214–16, 218–19, 222, 224–5, 246, 264, 272, 279, 297
—, 'Horses of the Night,' 205
—, *The Diviners*, 205–26; as a mobility narrative, 205, 213–18; class differences, 108; class in, 205–26, 215, 217–24; community in, 210, 214–16; cultural memory in, 220–2; housing, 86–7; ideology of, 209–10, 216–17; individualism in, 209, 213; nation in, 203, 210, 212–13; poverty in, 213–15; reading class in, 205–6, 214–15; romantic nationalism, 209–10
Lauter, Paul, 130, 296
Lecker, Robert, 62, 303
Leonard, Peter, 8, 228

338 Index

Lewis, Oscar, 25, 166–8, 204, 238
Lewis, Paula Gilbert, 81
literature and literary criticism (*see also* poverty narratives; reading strategies): and community, 141; and cultural smuggling, 152; and élites, 267–75, 302; and the poor, 22, 24, 40, 72, 298–305; Canadian literature, 35, 37, 207, 258; —, class analysis in, 272–3, 278–9, 298–305; —, revisioning the national literature, 38, 275–86, 298–304, 305–8; canons, 269, 287–9; —, and cultural reproduction, 270; —, and popular literature, 184–6; —, and poverty and class, 219, 224–5, 258, 271–3, 287–9; —, Canadian canon, 184, 205, 207, 272, 278–80, 283, 298–305; 'fictioning' a literature, 39–64, 31, 39, 48, 261; image-of-poverty studies, 22–4; literary institutions, 142; national literature, 298–304.; —, more inclusive, 278 (*see also* literature and literary criticism: canons; common culture); —, national form, 210, 225; outside literature, 122, 261, 269, 273–4, 282; realism, 68–70, 125; —, authentic realism, 124, 298; —, in feminist criticism, 124–5; —, in nineteenth-century novel writing, 67–8; —, social realism, 83 (*see also* Shek, Ben-Zion)
living space. *See* housing

McClintock, Ann, 116
McClung, Nellie, 35, 65, 72–7, 185, 187, 264, 271, 291, 293, 296, 299; and class struggle, 75–6; and the poor, 75; *Clearing in the West*, 72–3; ideology, 73; in Canadian literature, 73; inside knowledge, 73; literature, 72
—, *Painted Fires*, 74–7; as mobility narrative, 74, 76; class traveller in, 76–7; populist aesthetics, 74
McDougall, Robert, 300
McGuigan, Jim, 49–50
McLachlan, Alexander, 21, 88, 94–6, 98–9, 101–2, 290
McQuaig, Linda, 8, 202, 245, 279
McRobbie, Angela, 35
madness. *See* poverty, and mental illness
Maillet, Antonine, 116–17, 283
Man, Paul de, 123
marginalization (*see also* cultural exclusion; discourse; the poor, misrepresentation of): by academic theories and practices, 141; cultural walls, 287–8; discursive strategies, 5, 18; margins as home, 82 (*see also* hooks, bell); of poor women, 32; of the poor, 67 (*see also* the poor, attitudes towards); symbolic violence, 6
market society, 4, 12–13, 16–18, 21, 33–4, 42, 47, 51, 55, 66–7, 77, 88, 93, 95–7, 102, 114, 117, 120, 134, 161, 165–7, 182, 191, 194, 200, 202, 217, 228, 231, 237–8, 245, 264–6, 271, 279, 285, 292–4, 304
Marxist criticism, 4, 24, 30, 48–9, 55, 88, 127, 129, 130, 132, 134, 153–4, 165, 178–9, 181–3, 196, 249, 254, 256–7, 261, 263–7, 292, 295, 300–1; Althusserian theory (*see* Althusser, Louis); and gender, 165; and the poor, 267; Gramscian theory (*see* Gramsci, Antonio); post-Marxism, 263

Massey, Vincent, 275, 277
Mathews, Robin, 258, 272, 278, 283, 299–301
Mayhew, Henry, 18, 236, 237
Maynard, Fredelle Bruser. *See* Bruser Maynard, Fredelle
memory. *See* cultural memory
meritocracy, 5, 19, 36, 76, 83, 114, 176, 189, 200, 213–14, 226, 231, 245, 265–6, 276, 305
Mettrick, Alan, *Last in Line: On the Road and Out of Work . . . A Desperate Journey with Canada's Unemployed*, 92, 95–6, 202, 240–2
middle class, the, 86–7, 107, 238, 276 (*see also* the bourgeoisie; class; market society); and 'fear of falling,' 18, 114 (*see also* Ehrenreich, Barbara; mobility); and poverty, 104; discontent with consumer capitalism, 18
Mills, Sara, 124
mobility (*see also* class): alienation, 218, 220; and cleanliness, 112–21; and clothing, 114–15, 217–18; and education, 218, 269–72; and nation, 74, 227; and speech, 115, 218; and taste, 104–11, 217; class travellers, 76–7, 174, 177, 185, 189, 193, 213, 222, 237, 239–42; downward, 243–4; —, declassing as immigrant experience, 70, 74, 246, 248; —, fear of falling, 18, 70, 72, 114, 245 (*see also* Ehrenreich, Barbara); in immigrant literature, 246; makeovers, 107–8, 111, 113–14, 215, 217–20; —, passing, 271; marrying up, 115, 150, 213; social, 76
mobility narratives (*see also* Bromley, Roger): and domestic work, 113, 115; in Canadian literature, 114–15; *Lilly's Story* (*see* Wilson, Ethel); *Painted Fires* (*see* McClung, Nellie); *Raisins and Almonds* (*see* Bruser Maynard, Fredelle); 'The Beggar Maid' (*see* Munro, Alice); *The Diviners* (*see* Laurence, Margaret); *Uphill All the Way* (*see* Jaques, Edna)
Moodie, Susanna, 35, 65, 67–72, 85, 187, 241, 290; and the poor, 67–72; bourgeois perspective, 69, 70–2; class and ethnicity, 70; declassing of, 70; double standard, 72; liberal humanism, 67–72; life-writing 70, 72; *Roughing It in the Bush*, 70–2; 'A Word for the Novel Writers,' 67–9, 72
Moran, Bridget, 154, 192, 298
Moss, John, 73
Mukherjee, Arun, 63, 141–2, 258, 268, 283, 300, 303
Munro, Alice, 21, 37–8, 88, 103–8, 115, 149, 152, 215–16, 218, 264, 272, 297
—, 'Shining Houses,' 105–6; bourgeois guilt, 106; ideology, 106
—, 'The Beggar Maid,' 88, 107–11, 215–16, 218; acculturation, 107–9; and bourgeois art, 105, 109; and 'social embarrassment,' 108; and taste, 104–11; as mobility narrative, 107–11, 215–16, 218; class habitus, 105, 107, 109; gaze, the, 111; gender and class subtext, 110
Murphy, Barbara, *The Ugly Canadian*, 38, 42, 96, 202, 245
Murray, Alex, 17, 92, 103, 242, 302 (*see also* Fallis, George, and Alex Murray)

nation: and community, 225; —, collective identity, 275; —, responsibility for citizens, 245; —, shared dreams, 168–9, 200, 215, 246, 249–50; —, shared past, 243; —, shared projects, 8, 243; and counter-culture, 204, 303; and discourse (*see* discourse, nationalist); and fragments, 8; —, disunity rationalized, 176, 235; —, exclusions, 226, 276; —, forgotten fragments, 174–7, 179; —, internal others, 227; —, lack of responsibility for the poor, 241; —, remnants, 3, 7–16, 22, 200–52; —, rifts and ruptures, 226, 250; and global hegemony, 8, 276, 280–8 (*see also* Ahmad, Aijaz); and narrative form, 225, 275; and nostalgia, 191; and poor women, 36–7, 177; and postnationalism, 8–9, 211, 280–1; and poverty, 7–15; —, as another country, 185–6, 189, 192–3, 195, 236–7, 240–1; —, as reciprocal, 7–15, 201–4, 305; —, the connectedness of the poor to nation, 7–15, 201–4, 294; —, two-nations paradigm, 9, 204, 235–40, 304; and the 'hollow state,' 9–10; and the poor, 200–1, 305; —, and their labour power, 245, 249; —, as internal other, 227, 236; —, as nationless, 8, 98, 245; and uncommunity (*see also* Chatterjee, Partha; nation, and fragments), as a rickety house, 98, 102; —, *The Ugly Canadian* (*see* Murphy, Barbara); as a site of resistance against global hegemony, 8, 10; Canada and the poor, 7–16, 200–52 (*see also* the poor, in Canada); counter-national sentiments, 211, 219, 239–47, 251–2, 279, 303; developed nations, affluence, 5–6, 103, 227–8, 240, 245, 265; —, classlessness, 235; —, First World as 'pacemakers,' 227, 244; —, New World, 100, 250–2; —, paradigm of development, three worlds, 231–2, 252; —, progress, 200, 226–8, 231, 243, 252; —, Third World, 8, 200, 226–7, 232; national imaginary, 65, 201, 212–13, 276; —, bourgeois nationalism, 9, 200–1, 226, 235–6, 276, 303; —, exclusion of the poor, 276; —, homogeneous national subject, 275; —, left nationalism, 202, 278–9, 302–3; —, myths, 103, 200, 226, 265 (*see also* class; meritocracy); —, national culture, 200–5, 298–301, 303–4; —, national dream, 168–9, 200, 215, 246, 249–50; —, nationalism, 191–2, 200–1; —, pluralism, 275–6; —, reimagining the nation, 7–15, 205–25, 225–7, 243, 245–6, 250, 275–80; 304; —, symbolic containment of the poor, 236, 226–38; national literature, 298–304 (*see also* literature and literary criticism); remnants of nation (*see* nation, and fragments)

need, 32, 48, 78 (*see also* Gunderson, Morley, et al.; Torjman, Sherri); necessity, 251; of the working poor, 251; public dialogue on, 268

Nelson, Cary, 255–6

New, W.H., 215

Newton, Judith, and Deborah Rosenfelt, 130

non-poor. *See* the bourgeoisie; the middle class; the poor, and the non-poor

Olsen, Tillie, 179, 296
organized forgetting, 37, 166, 174–9, 181, 183, 189, 195, 196, 199, 228, 291–2. *See also* Bromley, Roger; cultural amnesia; cultural memory
O'Rourke, Rebecca, 174, 179, 188–9, 197–8
Orwell, George, 78, 237, 241

Pearce, Diana, 33, 164, 295
politics (*see also* agency; community; populism; resistance): coalition, 48–52, 56, 85; engaged criticism, 53–6, 275–86; of erasure, 54, 56; of possibility, 56; politics of space, 214–15 (*see also* housing, living space); —, and academic paradigms, 90–1
poor, the (*see also* the homeless; poor women; poverty): academic study of, 20, 44, 54–5, 164–5, 267–74; and class warfare, 7, 77; and dirt, 116–17 (*see also* cleaning; mobility, and cleanliness); and disease and crime, 102; and idleness, 95, 116; and market society (*see* market society); and Marxist theory (*see* Marxist criticism); and opposition, 7, 54, 127, 160, 171, 198, 243, 248 (*see also* the poor, voices of; resistance); —, anger, 206, 265; —, talking back, 205–6; and popular myths, 16–21, 18, 41, 53, 161–2, 176, 178; and prostitution, 32, 113, 156, 159, 242, 358 (*see also* poor women, as prostitutes); and state intervention, 11–13, 16, 93, 97, 273 (*see also* welfare); and the 'hollow' nation, 8–9, 16; and the national imaginary, 7–15 (*see also* nation); and the non-poor, 5–6, 16, 162, 228–32 (*see also* the bourgeoisie; the middle-class); as a subculture, 25, 168; as bag ladies, 104, 242; as beggars, 5, 91–2; as colonized, 19, 160–8, 225–30 (*see also* colonization; identity, constructions of); as intrusive strangers, 102; as nationless, 8, 98, 245 (*see also* nation, and poverty); as objects of knowledge, 25, 130, 227 (*see also* Green, Bryan); as Other, 8, 102; as remnants of nation, 3, 7–16, 22, 200–52; —, nation-within-a-nation, 19; as social problem, 3, 24, 43–4, 95–8, 228; as subjects of knowledge, 7, 169–73, 224–5, 227, 241; attitudes towards, 11–14, 42, 44 (*see also* charity; knowledge, ways of knowing the poor; the poor, misrepresentation of; welfare); —, blaming, 96, 231; —, compared to non-poor, 228–32; —, deserving and undeserving poor, 54, 104, 162, 188; —, rice Christians, 95–6; —, social hysteria, 102, 228, 231; cultural representation versus political representation, 268, 270, 281; definition of, 26, 245, 292; —, heterogeneous and shifting membership, 16, 245; exclusion of, 3, 71, 213, 228, 276, 281, 292; —, outcast, 97; —, psychosocial space on the outside, 66; history of (*see also* Blyth, Jack; Guilbert, Lucille; Himmelfarb, Gertrude; Waxman, Chaim), in Britain, 236–7; —, in United States, 238–9, 265; identity of (*see* identity); images of (*see also* nation, and fragments; poverty,

images of; the poor, misrepresentation of; poverty narratives), dominant images, 6, 8, 40, 45, 235, 245, 276; —, image-of-poverty literary studies, 22–4; —, imported images, 102; —, in literary culture, 16, 23–4, 69; —, photographic images, 229–33, 254–5; —, social and textual construction, 6, 245; —, visual images, 41–2, 233; in Canada, 15, 20, 102, 115, 162, 226, 245, 252, 263; in New France, 101; in nineteenth-century culture, 94; in North America, 100, 166 (see also Ehrenreich, Barbara; Harrington, Michael); in Nova Scotia, 101; in Quebec, 91; in Upper Canada, 100; invisibility of, 5–6, 50–2, 292 (see also cultural exclusion; cultural muting; organized forgetting; the poor, misrepresentation of); —, blind spots, 23, 238, 258; —, ghettoization of, 238; —, projection onto Third World, 227–8; —, silencing of, 5–7, 218–19, 252–4, 281; misrepresentation of, 245 (see also identity, constructions of: negative constructions; poverty, misrepresentation of); —, as 'a race apart,' 9, 236, 241; —, as feminized, 69; —, as Other, 227, 235–6, 238–9; —, Duplessis Orphans, 102; —, media manipulation of, 50–1, 245; —, multiple stigmatizations, 6, 164; —, popular myths, 18, 162–3; pauperization of, 97 (see also the homeless, bag lady; the poor, as beggars); Poor Laws, 95, 97; rural poor, 187; treatment of, 96; voices of, 4, 51–2, 63, 144, 243–5, 252, 268, 284, 299; —, suppression of, 218–19, 261, 276–8; vulnerability and powerlessness of, 64, 120, 167, 245

poor women, 21, 23, 30, 32, 33, 34–7, 45, 50, 52, 61–2, 81–2, 85, 112, 115, 122, 127, 130, 131, 133–4, 143, 145, 160, 164–5, 175, 180, 188, 200, 204, 228, 243, 265, 267, 284, 292–3, 295, 296, 305, 334, 350 (see also the feminization of poverty; the homeless; the poor; working-class women); and academic discourse, 164–5; and disorder, 65–7, 69, 71, 77, 81–2, 85; and history, 179–80; and homeplace, 79–80, 81–3, 85, 88–9, 112, 117, 177 (see also hooks, bell); and self-help, 3; and the 'pink ghetto,' the proletarianization of clerical workers, 293; and welfare (see welfare); as bag ladies, 104, 242; as care-givers, 37, 187; as class-travellers (see mobility, class travellers); as homeless, 74, 85, 104, 242, 244, 293; as icons of nationhood, 36–7, 177; as marginalized, 32; as mothers, 81–2, 119–20, 249, 285; as prostitutes, 69, 113, 117, 178, 242–3, 285, 292–3, 295, 298; once-poor women, 296–7; proletarianization of clerical workers, 293; sexual violence against, 32; versus working-class women, 292–8

Poovey, Mary, 69

Popovic, Pierre, and Michel Biron, 62, 273

popular culture (see also Bromley, Roger; Hall, Stuart; Jaques, Edna): and hegemony, 196–7; popular autobiography, 181–3; popular poetry, 184–6 populism, 48–52 (*see also* McGuigan, Jim); and aesthetics, 216; and 'common culture,' 50 (*see also* culture, paradigm of); cultural populism, 49–50; cultural studies, 50; populist goals, 48–52, 139

Porter, John, 160, 180, 235, 258, 271, 272, 276, 302

postmodernism, 209, 211

Potrebenko, Helen, 153, 245, 265, 273, 283, 289, 291, 293, 299

poverty (*see also* the homeless; the poor; poor women): academic discourse on, 20, 44, 53–5, 164–5, 267–74; and bourgeois perspective, 92; and class, 41, 130, 178, 265, 292–3, 293–7 (*see also* class; Marxist criticism); and clothing, 90, 217, 218, 220 (*see also* clothing; mobility, and clothing); and colonization, 160–8, 226–8 (*see also* colonization); —, neocolonialism, 230; and contamination, 69, 101; and depressions, 240–1; and disease, 101; and disorder, 231; and education, 145–52, 151, 215–18, 220, 224–5, 267, 271–2 (*see also* education); and ethnicity and race, 111–21, 153–9, 228, 230, 232–5; and gender, 31–8, 130–6, 249, 292–3 (*see also* the feminization of poverty; poor women); and idleness, 95, 120; and industrialization, 95; and market society (*see* market society); and mental illness, 148, 151, 271; —, as strategy of self-defence, 242; —, resistance as madness, 120–1; and nation, 203–4, 237–8, 240, 275–6 (*see also* nation); —, as part of national culture, 275–8; and social hysteria, 102; and social mobility (*see* mobility); and the middle class, 104 (*see also* fear of falling; the middle class; mobility); and the working class, 18, 292–3 (*see also* the working class); as cultural home, 78, 85; as psycho-social space, 35, 68, 214–15, 271, 276, 295; as rickety house, 101; as social problem, 3, 24, 43–4, 96–8, 228; monetary solutions, 233; as stigma, 154, 169, 213, 215–17, 232–3 (*see also* shame; Waxman, Chaim, *The Stigma of Poverty*); 'conspiracy of silence,' 13 (*see also* cultural muting; organized forgetting; the poor, invisibility of; the poor, voices of); culture of (*see* poverty, theories of); definition of, 26, 245 (*see also* knowledge, ways of knowing the poor; poverty, theories of); —, consumption based, 34n8; —, measuring, 43–5; —, situational versus inherent, 245; —, social construction, 14, 67; —, subjective, 46–7; differences, 41; documentation, 43–4; identity construction (*see also* identity), collective identity, 264; —, individualism, 209; images of, 3–38, 40, 166 (*see also* the poor, images of); —, icons, 41, 45; —, ideology, 23; —, in literature, 23; —, popular images, 35, 40, 45; —, power of, 31, 60, 166; —, studies of, 24, 42–4; in an affluent society, 5, 38, 78, 103, 168–9, 227–8, 238, 240, 265; failure to consider redistributing wealth, 230, 232–3; in discourse (*see* discourse, on poverty); in literature (*see* literature and literary criticism); nine-

344 Index

teenth-century novels, 67–8; symbolic containment of the poor, 228–32, 236; theories of, academic theories compared, 237, 266; —, culture of poverty, 25, 166–8, 204, 236, 238–9, 266; —, development, 228, 238; —, feminization of (*see* the feminization of poverty); —, inside/outside of civil society, 65–7, 71, 77; —, Malthusian theory, 68, 95; —, new poverty, the, 238, 266; —, paradigms of, 55, 65, 237, 266; —, 'poverty of theory' about, 4, 263; —, subcultures of, 25, 168; —, 'toolkit of theory,' 253, 260–7; —, two-nations concept, 9, 204, 235–409

poverty: misrepresentation of, as another country, 185–6, 189, 192–3, 195, 236–7, 240–2 (*see also* nation, and poverty; two-nations paradigm); as distant landscape, 184–7, 189, 192–5, 218–19; criminalizing poverty, 11–13, 16, 68, 102, 235; dehistoricizing poverty, 235; distancing and concealing, 11, 236–7, 291–2; inauthenticating claims of, 174, 178, 228, 291; individualizing poverty, 75, 174–7, 179, 233, 242; naturalizing poverty, 165, 231, 271; pathologizing poverty, 232–3; projecting poverty, onto the Third World, 200, 203–4, 228, 235; psychologizing poverty, 204, 232–4; romanticized, 68–9, 72–3, 79

poverty narratives: aesthetics, 39–40, 52 (*see also* aesthetics); alternative reading practices, 29, 288–9 (*see also* reading strategies); and class, 22–30, 264, 294–5, 299 (*see also* class; Marxist criticism); and contamination, 114; and disorder, 290; and ethnicity, 111–21, 153–9, 192–9, 205–25, 292–3; and literature, 6, 9, 39–64, 112–13, 291–2 (*see also* literature and literary criticism); and nostalgia, 186–7; and representativeness, 290; and resistance, 21–2, 26, 28, 48–56, 154, 160, 171, 196, 210, 225, 243, 292, 295 (*see also* poverty narratives, genres related to poverty; resistance); —, anger, 31, 206; —, radical knowledge, 40, 57–64, 241, 287, 290, 297; —, sites of resistance, 22, 27, 28, 31, 77, 152, 170, 172, 299; —, songs, 206; —, struggle for meaning and power, 28, 63, 144, 254, 284, 287, 294, 299; therapeutic power, 53–6, 57–64, 66, 138; and retrospection by once-poor women, 295–6; and silence, 31, 51, 160, 292, 299; and social mobility, 114 (*see also* mobility, mobility narratives); and the American/Canadian Dream, 18; as an analytical category, 4, 22–30, 260–2, 272, 287–308; as constructed, 22–31, 39–64, 288–9; —, cross-class nature, 27–8, 292–8; —, gender specific, 34–5; —, generic limits, 28, 290–2; —, national limits, 304–5; —, reading beyond limits, 290; —, time limits, 288–92; —, versus survey, 287–90; canonical and non-canonical, 22–3, 37–8, 39–64, 72, 272, 298–305; counter-cultural knowledge, 44, 45, 55–6 (*see also* knowledge); cultural exclusion, 21, 25, 31, 50–2, 138, 144, 175, 223, 234, 254, 273, 287–92, 299; discourse and ideology, 36 (*see also* discourse); everyday lives, 13, 29–30, 31, 42, 66, 77–8, 290 (*see also* the everyday); gender specific, 34–5; genres related to poverty, 40, 285; —, autobiography, 242 (*see also* autobiography); —, Depression stories, 291–2, 296; —, documentarism, 239–42; —, forms of poverty narratives, 22–30, 40, 287–308; —, oral history, 243–5; —, proletarian fiction, 209; —, protest literature, 290–1, 296; —, realism, 67, 72, 83, 124; —, reportage, 239–42; —, testimony, 45, 57–64, 58, 239–52, 296, 298 (*see also* testimony); human narratives, 122; in Canadian literature, 38, 113–15, 282, 298–304; of black domestics, 115–16; reading oppositionally (*see* reading strategies, oppositional); reception of, 205–6, 246, 248–9, 258, 276, 299; role of criticism and teaching, 53–6, 267–74; women's, 31–8, 33, 287–92, 305–8; —, and the disorderly body, 65–84, 114

Prentice, Alison, et al., 76–7, 115

Purdy, Anthony, 62, 78, 84

Rabinowitz, Paula, 137

Radhakrishnan, R., 123, 125, 133, 172, 268, 284

reading strategies, 3, 29, 61, 89, 92, 99, 138; and cultural memory, 199; and cultural power, 55, 270; and students, 142; and subjective knowledge, 62, 99, 105, 211 (*see also* knowledge); as recovery project, 39–64, 40, 138, 210, 260–1, 270, 273, 276, 289; as social therapy, 53–6, 57–64, 66, 138; class knowledge and solidarity, 139; filtering cultural differences, 40, 142; oppositional, 3, 4, 7, 10, 23–30, 32, 35, 40, 43–4, 48, 50, 53, 93–4, 104, 135–6, 142, 189, 199, 202, 204, 249, 254, 261, 275, 289–90, 295, 297 (*see also* aesthetics, oppositional); —, criticism, 20, 39–64, 142, 151, 253, 269, 273, 301; —, 'from the inside out,' 138; —, 'the resistant reader,' 105; —, and alternative cultural values, 26, 224–6, 260–1; —, and the notion of a 'common culture,' 27, 210, 297 (*see also* culture, paradigms of); —, with 'a toolkit of theory,' 253, 260–7; positions from which to read, 210, 269–71, 275–86

Renan, Ernest, 176, 201

resistance, 22–30, 39–64, 77–85, 111–21, 137–42, 143–73, 239–52, 253–9, 298–304 (*see also* aesthetics, oppositional; agency; anti-poverty activism; class, struggle; Fox, Pamela; Freire, Paulo; Gramsci, Antonio; hooks, bell; knowledge, radical; Marxist criticism; poverty narratives, and resistance; reading strategies, oppositional); and madness, 120–1; autobiography as, 158–9, 169–73 (*see also* testimony); cleaning as, 119; counter-national imagining, 211, 226, 239–52 (*see also* nation); domestic and emotional, 113, 120; homeplace as (*see* housing, homeplace); leaving home as, 113, 215, 293; outlaw emotions (*see* feminism; knowledge, standpoint theory); political activism, 159, 243–4; public dialogue, 268; radical pedagogy, 267; reappropriation,

120; sharing as, 226; squatting as, 24, 244–5; struggle over meaning (*see* knowledge; poverty narratives, and resistance); talking back, 216–17; to bourgeois aesthetics, 121

Richards, David Adams, 3, 35, 38, 64, 89, 208n3, 271, 273

Robert, Lucie, 62, 302

Robinson, Lillian S., and Lise Vogel, 130, 150, 165, 294

Roy, Gabrielle, 21, 35, 37, 38, 65, 77–81, 82–5, 112–13, 117, 154, 272, 296, 298

—, *Bonheur d'occasion*: capitalism, 78; homecoming, 80–3; home and the body, 80–1; poverty, 77–85; social realism, 80, 84–5

—, *La Détresse et l'enchantement*, 78–80; autobiographical position, 78; poverty, 79–80; poverty as home, 83; social realism, 82

Salverson, Laura Goodman, 34, 64, 78, 154, 187, 190, 246–51, 265, 272, 296

—, *Confessions of an Immigrant's Daughter*, 246–52; challenges to the national dream, 246, 249–50; gendered experiences of poverty, 246, 249; reception of, 246, 248–9; reimagining nation, 250; social critique, 250–2; testimony to class and poverty, 246–52; women divided by class, 247–9

Sand, Cy-Thea, 19, 44, 143–54, 159, 165, 173–4, 265, 271–2, 296–7

—, 'A Question of Identity,' 145–52; class and gender, 147–8; cultural exclusion, 147; cultural smuggling, 148, 152, 153–4

Scott, Joan Wallach, 35, 181–2

shame, 143–68, 215, 253 (*see also* identity; the poor, attitudes towards; Waxman, Chaim); and alternative status-honour groups, 153–9, 174, 212, 265; and blame, 156–7, 294; and resistance, 26–7, 144; and self-representation, 143; and social embarrassment, 105, 223, 243

Shek, Ben-Zion, 62, 84, 258, 272, 299

Showalter, Elaine, 132, 138, 277

Sidel, Ruth, 67, 164

Silman, Janet, 40, 159

Silvera, Makeda, 34, 37, 52, 115–16, 258, 283, 296

Sime, J.G., 34, 272, 291, 293

Smart, Patricia, 78, 81, 272, 302

Smith, Ruth L., 36, 55, 66–7, 71, 77, 90, 101, 116, 165, 231, 304

Smith, Sidonie, 159, 171, 198; and Julie Watson, 19, 170–1

Sommer, Doris, 172, 198

space. *See* housing, living space; poverty, as psychosocial space.

Steedman, Carolyn, 27, 63, 89, 113, 134, 141, 169, 172–4, 181–3, 197–8, 205, 209, 249, 262, 294

Steele, Charles, 304

Stevenson, Sharon, 128, 290

Strange, Kathleen, 187

Stratford, Philip, 83–5

Straw, Will, 258

Strong-Boag, Veronica, 75

Struthers, James, *The Limits of Affluence: Welfare in Ontario, 1920–1970*, 188n2

subject, the, 66, 125, 142; class and gender, 135, 130–6; colonized, 150, 160–8, 170 (*see also* colonization); decolonized, 159, 169–73; definitions of, 126–7; limited positions, 142; positions of women, 130–6, 148; subject positions, 57, 66, 125, 142, 198, 295; —, the poor as subjects of knowledge, 224–5, 259–60, 295

subjectivity, 126–9, 130–6, 137–42, 295; and Althusserian ideology, 136; and deconstruction, 136, 169–73; and marginalization, 128; and materialist feminism, 134, 136–7; as knowledge, 136, 137; hierarchy of subjectivities, 140–1; in fiction, 135, 289, 295; in literary discourse, 137; in Marxism and feminism, 129; in materialist feminism, 134

testimony, 57–64, 239–45, 246–52 (*see also* Beverly, John; Felman, Shoshana, and Dori Laub; Sommer, Doris); and alternative knowledge, 57–64; —, lived experience, 47, 59; and audience, 118; and class difference, 153; and community, 58–9; and empowerment, 45, 52, 120; —, bearing witness, 58–9, 64, 118; —, socially therapeutic power, 56–8; —, subversive discourse, 46; and literature, 40–7, 52, 57, 77; and nation, 243–4, 252; and populist feminist criticism, 127–8; and self, 243; and the unspeakable, 58; and trauma, 58; —, the 'unadressable Other,' 118; collaboration, 56; —, researcher's role, 52; disempowered subject position, 57; Holocaust, 57; images of the poor in, 77 (*see also* the poor, images of; poverty, images of); identification, 85; inside knowledge, 47, 59; post-representation, 57, 298; —, referentiality, 57; —, representation, 59; —, truth claims, 56, 251; standpoint, 56; theories of, 56, 59, 251

theory (*see also* cultural studies; gender; knowledge; nation; poverty); a 'toolkit of theory,' 260–7; and anti-Theory, 122–6, 141; and emotions, 61; and experience, 124; and human narratives, 122; and the everyday, 122; as disorderly, 262–3; as exclusionary, 139–40; cultural studies, 253–75; feminist, 131–2; limitations of, 227, 253, 259–61, 263–4; —, 'the poverty of theory,' 4, 123–6, 256, 263, 283; marginal standpoint, 56; materialist feminism, 137; minority theories, 269; of class habitus, 88, 99; of poverty (*see* poverty, theories of); of representation, 124; of stigmatized identity, 162, 168; outlaw emotions, 61; *post facto*, 262 (*see also* Geertz, Clifford); race for, the, 140; self-reflexive, 262, 269, 271, 275; standpoint, 60–1; strategies by African Americans, 140

Thomas, Clara, 70, 72, 302
Thompson, E.P., 256, 263, 283
Thurston, James, 70
Tokarczyk, Michelle, and Elizabeth Fay, 150
Torjman, Sherri, 32, 48, 268, 295
Tracey, Linda Lee, 25, 239–41
Tynes, Maxine, 34, 116, 154

Vogel, Lise, 150, 165, 294–5

Watt, Frank, 272, 300
Waxman, Chaim, *The Stigma of*

Poverty, 6, 19–20, 90, 116, 154, 162, 164, 167–9, 212, 232, 265; —, alternative status-honour groups, 153–9, 174, 212, 265

Wayman, Tom, 180, 258, 272, 278, 283, 289, 291

Webber, Marlene, 241–2, 296

Weedon, Chris, 124, 137

welfare (*see also* Blyth, Jack; Leonard, Peter; Murphy, Barbara; Struthers, James); and public relief, 97, 100; and social control, 156, 188n2; and women, 188, 244, 292–3; —, single mothers, 188, 292–3; as a moral discourse, 188n2; history of, 188; in Canada, 100; late capitalism, 67

Williams, Raymond, 15, 21, 50, 63, 95, 163–4, 177, 181, 204, 219, 239, 256–7, 267, 275, 277, 279–80, 283, 287–8; common culture, 210 (*see also* culture, paradigms of); residual forms, 204

Wilson, Ethel, *Lilly's Story*, 114–15. *See also* poor women; working-class women

women: academic, 61; and history, 180; and home, 116; and literature, 220; and poverty, 81–2 (*see also* the feminization of poverty; poverty, and gender); domestic walls, 120–1; domestic work, 116; in class and gender analysis, 132; living with class and gender, 135; without homeplace, 115–16; working-class, 81–2

Woodcock, George, 279

working class, the, 18, 34–5, 55, 65, 70, 105, 138, 143, 151, 153, 165–6, 178, 180, 182, 193, 198, 208, 221, 223, 225, 265, 267, 273, 276, 281, 282, 284–5, 304 (*see also* Aronowitz, Stanley; Marxist criticism); and home, 116; and university, 107–9, 149–51, 213–16, 220, 224 (*see also* education); complicity of the working class, 151–2, 163, 179; envy of the rich, 197; identity, 134; in Canada, 239–41; in North America, 249, 265; inside knowledge of, 82, 138; labour, 249–51; literature, 209; working-class history, erasure of, 179; —, feminist critique of, 180–3; —, fragmented, 176–7, 179, 263; —, Marxist version of, 181–3, 263; —, working-class subjects, 13, 189, 263, 276; —, writing, 26

working-class women, 26, 33–4, 50, 53, 56, 60–1, 71, 76–7, 81–2, 89, 106, 111–13, 115–16, 129–31, 134–5, 137, 138–9, 143–6, 148, 153–4, 161, 165–6, 172–3, 177, 179–83, 185, 189–90, 196, 247, 249, 267, 289, 291–3, 295–6, 297, 300; and cultural home, 138; and mothering, 77–85, 111–21, 249; and university, 150–1

writing: and class slippage, 131; and decolonization, 160; and personal recovery, 147; as cultural intervention, 160; as smuggling cultural capital, 153; as witnessing, 160; strategies, 198; surviving poverty, 82; women's, 31

Zandy, Janet, 23, 55–6, 82, 116, 127, 130, 134, 137–9, 141, 144, 146, 160, 262, 295